"Thomas methodically examines the nexus of money and power in Virginia and produces a well-documented indictment of 'the Virginia way.' This should be required reading for anyone interested in modern Virginia politics."
—Dwayne Yancey, editorial page editor at the *Roanoke Times* and author of *When Hell Froze Over: The Untold Story of Doug Wilder*

"Practitioners of recent politics and governance in Virginia have given author Jeff Thomas rich materials to work with, across a spectrum of issues, in this no-holds-barred recounting of 'the Virginia way.' Until this book makes a considerable difference in politics as usual, they will no doubt continue to do so."
—Peter Wallenstein, Virginia Tech, author of *Cradle of America: A History of Virginia*

"In *Virginia Politics and Government in a New Century: The Price of Power*, Jeff Thomas demolishes the state's conceits that it operates by the honorable principles of gentlemanly cavaliers. As his richly reported work reveals, the state is run entirely opposite to the Jeffersonian values it pretends to embrace."
—Peter Galuszka, reporter at *Style Weekly* and author of *Thunder on the Mountain: Death at Massey and the Dirty Secrets Behind Big Coal*

"A mosaic of recent political maneuvers in Virginia, this book coalesces into a sharp indictment of what now passes for governance by our elected representatives. Readable, well-paced, optimistic at base—a fine antidote to the self-dealing complacency of the so-called 'Virginia Way.' We can do better than 'Virginia Pay-to-Play,' and we deserve better, as Thomas's work makes plain. It's enough to wrinkle the nose on the marble statue of Washington over there in the Capitol rotunda."
—Stephen Nash, University of Richmond, author of *Virginia Climate Fever: How Global Warming Will Transform Our Cities, Shorelines, and Forests*

VIRGINIA POLITICS
& GOVERNMENT
IN
A NEW CENTURY
THE PRICE OF POWER

JEFF THOMAS

To Steve —
With great regard for your scholarship,
activism, and friendship —

[signature]
11-12-16

H
THE
History
PRESS

Published by The History Press
Charleston, SC
www.historypress.net

First published 2016

Manufactured in the United States

ISBN 978.1.46713.740.9

Library of Congress Control Number: 2016941439

For Mom

Whenever the people are well informed,
they can be trusted with their own government.
—Thomas Jefferson, inscription at entrance to the Virginia Capitol

But now,
with a most inhuman cruelty,
they who have put out the people's eyes,
reproach them of their blindness.
—John Milton, *Apology for Smectymnuus*

CONTENTS

Introduction: The Virginia Way and the Governor   11

1. Legislature: Elections and Entitlements   25
2. Corporate Politics: Power and Ethics   55
3. Policymaking: Health Care Reality and Ideology   79
4. Local Government: Education and Economic Development   111
5. Higher Ed: Manufacturing Crises at the University of Virginia   133

Conclusion: The Commodification of Government   167
Methodology and Literature Review   175
Acknowledgements   181
Notes   183
Bibliography   257
Index   263
About the Author   271

THE VIRGINIA WAY
AND THE GOVERNOR

There's nothing that has been done here that violated the law.
I know that in my heart and in my soul.
—*former governor Bob McDonnell, eight months after his eleven felony convictions*[1]

The "Virginia Way" is a political philosophy describing how our government does business inseparably from politics. The first corollary is that politicians should be trusted; the second, trustworthiness. John Chichester, who served thirty years as a Virginia state senator, defines the Virginia Way as the following:

> *In large part, the "Virginia [W]ay" is rooted in the deep sense of responsibility that goes with occupying the space of our founding fathers—those who shaped this great nation with a bold vision that continues to inspire the world. Virginia's citizens intuitively feel the weight of that responsibility and honor our extraordinary past by taking a studied and deliberative approach to our future.*[2]

In light of recent history, this book suggests another definition: the Virginia Way is a euphemism for corruption.

As Robert Caro argued in his masterful study of political power:

> *Although the cliché says that power always corrupts, what is seldom said, but what is equally true, is that power always reveals. When a man*

is climbing, trying to persuade others to give him power, concealment is necessary: to hide traits that might make others reluctant to give him power, to hide also what he wants to do with that power; if men recognized the traits or realized the aims, they might refuse to give him what he wants. But as a man obtains more power, camouflage is less necessary. The curtain begins to rise. The revealing begins.[3]

The purpose of this book is to describe how power works in Virginia state government in the second decade of the twenty-first century.

VIRGINIA POLITICS AFFECTED THE NATION

From 2012 to 2016, Virginia punched above its weight politically, and what happened in Virginia mattered greatly to the nation and the world. Virginia had become one of the quintessential swing states in which presidential elections were won or lost. Republican strategist Karl Rove wrote that Virginia was the second-most important state in the 2016 elections, after Florida, while former Republican National Committee chairman Ed Gillespie declared that "Republicans won't win in 2016 without Virginia."[4] Other states might swing, but if so, they would swing only in a landslide after victory had already been achieved via the swing states. Virginia's thirteen electoral votes were vital to victory, and it was imperative that pundits and national politicians comprehended the state's political essence.

Virginia was also emblematic of the New South and larger changes in American politics. Demographic shifts and migration patterns had caused a breach in the Solid South.[5] Virginia voted for Obama in 2008 and 2012 by 7 percent and 4 percent margins, respectively, breaking a Republican winning streak dating to Lyndon Johnson's 1964 landslide.[6] Democrats swept the 2013 statewide elections, and a Democratic attorney general, lieutenant governor and governor replaced the three Republicans elected in 2009.[7] In "the closest statewide election in Virginia's history," both attorney general candidates received a rounded 49.89 percent of the vote, and Mark Herring won with a minuscule 165-vote margin after a recount of more than 2.2 million votes cast.[8] The two other statewide offices, Virginia's Senate seats, were held by Democrats and had been since 2009, while both were held by Republicans in 2007.[9] It had yet to be determined whether Virginians would consistently vote Democratic, but the trend was clear: Virginia had become a bipartisan state.

Presidential strategists had thus used Virginia as a proving ground for future tactics. Hillary Clinton's 2016 presidential campaign lifted personnel, strategy and technology directly from Governor McAuliffe's 2013 bid.[10] McAuliffe managed her 2008 campaign, and his 2013 manager, Robby Mook, was promoted to Clinton's 2016 campaign chief, to be joined by more than a dozen other top McAuliffe campaign aides. Mook parried attacks on McAuliffe's controversial past by rising above the fray, a strategy that he would attempt to emulate for Clinton. McAuliffe trumpeted liberal values on policies such as race, gun control and gay rights, and his support was found to increase Democratic voter turnout, a lesson that Clinton seemed to be practicing in mid-2016.[11] McAuliffe's and Clinton's policy shifts were watershed moments in the Democratic Party's social issues tactics that conventional wisdom had long dictated would backfire in Virginia and the South.[12] Clinton's campaign operation emerged within a new paradigm of data-driven early voter organization, and *Time* opined that "the victorious McAuliffe campaign has become an ex post facto lab experiment for Clinton's current bid for the White House."[13]

The Supreme Court's 2010 *Citizens United* decision upended decades of bipartisan campaign finance law and prior Supreme Court decisions via the rationale that corporate campaign money was speech, corporations were legally persons, and therefore, unlimited corporate campaign contributions were protected by the First Amendment's guarantee of freedom of speech.[14] As the 2016 presidential election neared, commentators argued that the floodgates had opened for a relative handful of wealthy people to attempt to finance elections or self-fund campaigns and ostensibly dictate the terms of those campaigns.[15] A large academic study of political power showed that fundraisers' influence extended beyond campaigns to policy implementation, which generally reflected the will of the influence-peddlers rather than the citizenry.[16] Virginians were getting into the game. Virginia contained the most generous top donors of any swing state except for Florida and was visited by seemingly every major candidate who tossed his or her hat into the ring.[17] Former governor Jeb Bush of Florida, for example, hosted a fundraiser at Richmond's five-star Jefferson Hotel with a minimum ticket price of $5,000, at which former Virginia attorney general Richard Cullen told reporters that Bush's message was: "He thinks that our party shouldn't be viewed as the party of the wealthy."[18]

Aside from its swing state and donor status, Virginia had enormous political power due to its proximity to Washington, D.C. National political figures—like former Republican National Committee (RNC) chair Ed Gillespie, former Democratic National Committee (DNC) chair Terry McAuliffe and former U.S. Navy secretaries Jim Webb and John Warner—ran for gubernatorial or U.S. Senate seats in Virginia. Conversely, Virginia politicians were frequently selected to lead the party: former governor Jim Gilmore and Senator Tim Kaine had chaired the RNC and DNC, respectively, while Senator Mark Warner had chaired the National Governors Association and gave the keynote address at the 2008 Democratic National Convention. Governor Bob McDonnell had chaired the Republican Governors Association and gave the party's response to President Obama's inaugural State of the Union address. In mid-2016, Kaine and Warner were both being mentioned among a handful of vice presidential candidates, as was McDonnell, before his convictions.[19] Kaine was ultimately selected.

THE VIRGINIA WAY

The preeminent story in state politics in 2016 was the reconstruction of ideology in the wake of Governor McDonnell's corruption convictions. To map this reconstruction, one must separate political rhetoric from reality. To give an example, in his State of the State speech in January 2015, Governor McAuliffe called for the legislature to pass pay equity for women, Medicaid expansion, gay marriage, campaign finance reform, ethics reform and several gun control laws. None of those was passed, although a weak ethics law came together at the last minute.[20] Instead, the most substantial piece of legislation that came from the legislature was a bill to deregulate the electric monopoly Dominion Power and cancel refunds customers were owed due to overbilling.[21] State Senator Donald McEachin, chairman of the Senate Democratic caucus, said after the session, "I think the commonwealth can celebrate that we have a governor that has been able to find common ground with the people across the aisle. Obviously, there are places where we differ with Republicans, whether it's gay rights or gun safety or Medicaid expansion, and we'll have ample time to drive those points home."[22] Democrats and Republicans clashed passionately over rhetoric, while in the end, the economic policies they supported were mostly uniform. This was the reality of the political-economic nexus called the Virginia Way.

OUTLINE

"In republican government, the legislative authority necessarily predominates," James Madison wrote, and the founders conceived the legislature as the branch closest to the people, who ideally meted out summary judgments and voted out legislative curmudgeons.[23] Consequently, the legislature has by far the most power of the three branches, particularly in states, where the executive powers of governors pale in comparison to those of the commander-in-chief. "Unlike Congress, which, however broad its power, must in theory at least trace those powers to specific grants in the federal Constitution, a state legislature is held to have all legislative powers not forbidden it," wrote A.E. Dick Howard, the principal author of Virginia's current constitution.[24] This book focuses on the state legislature because it is the most formidable branch of state government, where laws and appropriations originate, vetoes may be overruled and officials can be impeached and removed in a systemically broken body that is, in theory, accountable to voters—and to readers.[25] An informed citizenry can affect the legislature more than it can the judiciary or the executive bureaucracy.

Chapter one describes how unpopular politicians won elections and reviews the privileges legislators bestowed on themselves. Virginia politicians ensured against electoral accountability by rigging elections, and myriad electoral shackles kept Virginians at bay: selection of candidates, gerrymandering, financial and logistical barriers, electoral timing, purges and permanent disenfranchisement. There was no constitutional remedy against a runaway gerrymandered legislature: it could steamroll courts and even break governors. Legislators were supposed to be closest to the people and the ballot box, but how many Virginians supported the Virginia Way?

The undemocratic politics of Virginia government were manifested in its undemocratic policies. Chapter two summarizes deregulation and ethics reform, the two dominant themes of the 2015 legislative session, while chapter three reviews the health consequences of government corruption and the 2014 legislative imbroglio over Medicaid expansion.

The triumph of cronyism over public education had tragic effects on all levels of Virginia citizenry. Chapter four contrasts several lavishly funded economic development deals with the dilapidated K-12 infrastructure in the capital.

The political machinations of selling the reins of government to the highest bidder were evident in the decades-long defunding of the state's flagship university, the University of Virginia, as explained in chapter five.

The book concludes with final thoughts, methodology, literature review, notes and bibliography.

The remainder of this introduction discusses Bob McDonnell's corruption scandal.

THE VIRGINIA WAY LEADS TO FELONY CONVICTIONS

Bob McDonnell was one of the most talented politicians in Virginia history. He was popular, legislatively deft, charismatic and telegenic. The governor was elected in a 2009 landslide and maintained a "positively herculean" 60 percent approval rating, enough to spur 2012 vice presidential speculation.[26] He was also the only Virginia governor to be indicted, tried or convicted for crimes he committed in office.[27]

In 2014, the Virginia Way reached a boiling point. Prosecutors and media encircled Governor Bob McDonnell and the first lady with gumshoes, subpoenas and a trial. At issue were tens of thousands of dollars in bribes buttressed by a never-ending cascade of self-justifications that collapsed ignominiously and absolutely. This section is a backdrop for documenting how other, interconnected gears of the Virginia Way operate; while the McDonnells were convicted in the most public manner, the corrupt system quietly churned onward, so this book discusses the McDonnell trial only briefly.[28]

The Irradiated Tobacco Salesman

Jonnie Williams was a salesman who accumulated a $100 million fortune over a thirty-year career that trailed a wake of bankruptcies, victims, investigations and other flotsam.[29] Williams's company, Star Tobacco, began as a tobacco company, and when Williams microwaved tobacco, he claimed he invented a safer cigarette.[30] He patented the process, sued the Reynolds tobacco giant for infringement and settled for $5 million. He got his company, renamed Star Scientific, out of the cigarette business and tried to convince people that a neurological panacea could be made by, miraculously, irradiating tobacco leaves.[31] This last grift was summarized by a *Bloomberg News* reporter: "Williams cooked tobacco in microwaves from Wal-Mart, packaged it in candy-like lozenges and tried to turn Virginia's oldest cash crop into an elixir for old age." How did

McDonnell enter the picture? "If you're a Virginia company, you want to make sure you have access to these people," Williams later testified. "He's a politician, I'm a businessman."[32]

Quid Pro Quo[33]

The indictment detailed the inseparability of the Williams-McDonnell relationship from ingratiating bribes. Before they even met, Williams had granted Bob use of his private jet for gubernatorial campaigning. Though they were later briefly introduced, only at a political fundraiser at New York City's Four Seasons Hotel after Bob's election did they get the chance to speak. First Lady Maureen McDonnell incongruously asked Williams for help in procuring a dress for the upcoming inauguration, and Williams agreed to buy her one from the high-end designer Oscar de la Renta, a purchase that was forestalled by one of the governor's senior policy advisors. Later that month, the first lady e-mailed the advisor:

> I need to talk to you about Inaugural clothing budget. I need answers and Bob is screaming about the thousands I'm charging up in credit card debt. We are broke, have an unconscionable amount in credit card debt already, and this Inaugural is killing us!! I need answers and I need help, and I need to get this done.

The following October, Williams provided Bob with a private round-trip flight to California. Williams joined the governor on the return flight to pitch Anatabloc, his microwaved tobacco panacea. McDonnell initiated a meeting between Williams and Virginia's secretary of health, who rejected Williams's Anatabloc entreaties. In February 2011, the McDonnells attended a Star Scientific dinner of health professionals at Richmond's Jefferson Hotel at which Bob enthused about Anatabloc.

The McDonnells traveled to New York City in April, and Maureen beseeched Williams to take her shopping, which he did, spending $10,999 at Oscar de la Renta, $5,685 at Louis Vuitton and $2,604 at Bergdorf Goodman. In return, she ensured that Williams sat next to Bob at a political dinner that night.

Then, the dam broke. A few weeks later, the McDonnells had a private dinner with Williams and his wife at the governor's mansion ("the mansion"), followed days later by a dinner between Maureen and Williams in which she told him about the first couple's financial problems. She asked for a $50,000 loan in exchange for advancing Williams's business interests. After speaking with Bob, Williams agreed to a loan without any paperwork. She also asked for $15,000 to defray the cost of their daughter's upcoming wedding, and Williams made out checks to Maureen for $50,000 and $15,000. At the end of May, Bob and his sons played golf at the tony Kinloch Golf Club; though Williams was not there, he picked up roughly $270 for food and drinks, $400 at the course shop and $1,700 for golfing.

Flush with Williams's cash, Maureen had a spending spree on June 1, 2011. She began by opening a stock market account and made just one order, for more than $30,000 in Star Scientific stock. Later, she took her chief of staff to Florida on Williams's private jet, where she touted his company to investors and announced that the mansion would host Anatabloc's official launch party.

At the end of July, the McDonnells enjoyed an all-expenses-paid vacation at Williams's multimillion-dollar lake house, complete with recreational use of a boat and a Ferrari, which the McDonnells drove back to Richmond. The night they returned, Bob e-mailed his secretary of health to schedule a meeting between Williams, Maureen and a senior health advisor the next morning at the mansion. Here, Williams offered his proposal for securing state funding for his company and suggested that the government should test his tobacco-radiation pills on state employees. After the meeting, Maureen asked Williams to purchase a Rolex watch engraved with "71st Governor of Virginia" that she could give to her husband for Christmas. Williams did. The next day, Maureen purchased $2,500 more Star Scientific stock. The month of August saw the Anatabloc launch in the mansion, as well as the McDonnells racking up thousands more dollars of charges for golfing on Williams's account. Maureen continued speaking publicly about Anatabloc throughout the fall.

At a health leaders' conference held at the mansion on February 29, 2012, Maureen arranged for Williams and dozens of Star Scientific employees and affiliates to attend. Afterward, the McDonnells, Williams and a scientist ate a $1,423 dinner in Richmond on Williams's tab.

The next week, Williams and Bob plotted to transfer money to Bob while shirking reporting requirements. They nixed the idea of transferring fifty thousand shares of Star Scientific (about a quarter-million dollars worth) and settled on a no-paperwork loan of $50,000 to a tiny real estate corporation owned by Bob and his sister. Williams asked a personal assistant to write the check and hide the identity of the recipients; when the assistant wrote "Maureen McDonnell" in the memo line, he told the assistant to void the check and write one with no name. Bob asked for and received another $20,000 for the company in May.

On March 21, 2012, Bob had a meeting with Virginia's secretary of administration, supposedly about lowering state health care costs. He theatrically took a bottle of Anatabloc from his pocket and brandished it, claimed he had taken it and it benefited him personally, then he instructed the secretary to schedule a meeting with Williams's company.

That month, the mansion's chef resigned over petty theft allegations, a story that the Associated Press broke on March 23.[34] The chef had been interviewed by the FBI on March 8 and told investigators that he had information about the McDonnells' improprieties.[35]

Cover-Up

Washington Post reporters Rosalind Helderman and Laura Vozzella published the first story on the McDonnell-Williams scandal on March 30, 2013.[36] The gift-graft pendulum modulated over the next year. The McDonnells took another lavish vacation, received free and reduced cost yard and maintenance work from Williams's brother and obtained private jet flights for their daughters, all on Williams's dime. For whatever reason, they took no other action for him. They then ostentatiously returned all of the tangible gifts and money and attempted a cover-up, unwittingly adding to their indictment.[37]

The easiest were spokespersons' lies to the media: Williams was a family friend they had known for five years, he and the McDonnells' daughter paid for her wedding and they were trying to help his company, just as they would any other business.[38] All were fabrications.

Disclosure laws were harder to get around. There was the matter of the $120,000 in paperless and uncollateralized "loans" that might not look like loans to observers. Bob omitted most on his financial disclosure forms by stating obtusely that he owed $10,000 to $50,000 to a creditor in "Medical Services" in 2011 and "Health Care" in 2012. Maureen similarly sold her Star Scientific shares at the end of December 2011 and 2012 and repurchased them after Bob's annual disclosure forms were filed in January so that Bob's conflicts disclosures listed that he and Maureen owned no stocks at all. In a fitting salute to posterity, as of April 1, 2016, the disclosure forms were still incorrect.[39]

Bank loan applications cannot be so easily manipulated, and when Bob applied for a loan without listing these liabilities, he was ultimately charged with making feloniously false statements to a bank.

Maureen also did not comport herself well when the FBI came calling in February 2013. She erected a shaky house of cards about the whole imbroglio. She asked for invoices for the previously free yard work and returned the designer dresses with a doleful letter pretending that they were on loan to her from good friends for a future charitable auction. For the letter, she would garner her own charge of obstruction of an official proceeding.

Plea Deal Rejected

Prosecutors offered a plea deal to the McDonnells, under which Bob would plead guilty to one felony count of making false loan statements to a bank and Maureen would be charged with nothing.[40]

On the one hand, the McDonnells faced unsympathetic facts and Jonnie Williams's testimony, for which he had been granted full immunity.[41] On the other hand, they had a popular governor and talented communicator in a conservative court on his political doorstep who had to convince just one juror to doubt the federal government. The McDonnells and their attorneys must have felt the dice were loaded when they rolled them.

Charges

The main facts of the case were publicly known even in the initial article, though more revelations percolated throughout the summer and fall of 2013. By December, a federal grand jury was ready to return indictments, but they were delayed by unnamed senior officials in the Justice Department until after McDonnell left office due to term limits.[42] Ten days after they left the mansion, Bob and Maureen McDonnell were indicted on January 21, 2014.[43] They were both charged with the following felonies:

Conspiracy to commit honest-services wire fraud (1 count);
Honest-services wire fraud (3 counts);
Conspiracy to obtain property under color of official right (1 count);
Obtaining property under color of official right (6 counts); and
Making false statements (1 count).

Additionally, Bob was charged with making false bank statements and Maureen with obstruction of an official proceeding. They both faced a maximum of thirty years in prison.[44]

The Defense Rests

One of Bob's attorneys lashed out in a statement: "The federal government's decision to use these deceitful tactics in order to prosecute a popular and successful Republican Governor immediately upon his leaving office is disgraceful, violates basic principles of justice, and is contemptuous of the citizens of Virginia who elected him."[45] Strangely, between the time of this statement and the trial, a similar defense of government overreach, which perhaps would appeal to more than one in twelve Virginians on jury duty, was cast aside for a preposterous defense theory. The McDonnells would hinge their cases on the defense that their marriage was so broken that they were incommunicative, and it would therefore have been impossible for them to conspire together.

At the trial, the McDonnells demonstrated resolve in not even glancing in each other's direction for hours, despite the fact that they sat one seat apart around an L-shaped table. A man slouched between them at the angle of the "L" and, unlike the other defense attorneys, sat mute. The defendants would, from time to time, jot a note on a scrap of paper and slide it in front of the silent lawyer. After a few minutes, he would lean forward and push the paper to the other defendant. This was how the spouses interacted during the trial.[46]

Unfortunately for the McDonnells, the estranged marriage theory proved impossible to believe. They had lived together, for one. FBI agents testified that they had spent 90 percent of nights with each other in the mansion.[47] During the time of the conspiracy, they took eighteen vacations together over a twenty-two-month period.[48] As if in a bad movie, the two showed up together in late May 2014 for pre-trial hearings with new, matching blond-turned-gray dye jobs.[49] The prosecution even showed newspaper photographs of the two walking into court, hand-in-hand.[50] Their tactlessness may have insulted the intelligence of the jurors, who were supposed to believe Bob's tearful testimony of a marriage so broken it prohibited communication.

The jury had little trouble in convicting the McDonnells of all the corruption charges against them. (The judge later threw out Maureen's obstruction charge.[51]) In a silver lining possibly indicating Americans' greater dislike for banks than politicians, they were acquitted of making false statements on loan documents.[52] One by one, peers unanimously convicted Bob of selling his office to a cartoonish businessman who claimed irradiated tobacco could help cure "Alzheimer's, schizophrenia, Parkinson's disease, and multiple sclerosis, among others."[53] They were found guilty of a combined nineteen felonies, including graft, conspiracy and wire fraud. Though the sentencing guidelines called for ten to twelve years, the Reagan-appointed judge sentenced Bob to two years in federal prison and Maureen to one.[54] "I don't know how it could be any better for you," an appeals court judge later said.[55] Promising vindication at every turn, the McDonnells were wrong about everything.

Crisis of Faith

Other Virginia Way participants faced an existential moment: reassessment or retrenchment? Immediately after the verdicts, Virginia Way advocates commenced its reconstruction. A bipartisan who's who of state and federal senators, attorneys general, CEOs, representatives, councilmen, mayors, donors and hangers-on—more than four hundred in total—united to vouch for the convicted governor's morals and ask for leniency. Pens and mouths that seemed never to address the interests of ordinary citizens were borne in defense of one of their own.[56]

Distinguished columnist George Will wrote that the case represented the "criminalization of normal political interactions. …The Supreme Court has held that 'ingratiation and access…are not corruption,' and that the government may not target for proscription 'the general gratitude a candidate may feel toward those who support him or his allies, or the political access such support may afford.'"[57] In the 2014 *McCutcheon v. FEC* decision Will quoted, the next paragraph defined the difference. "Any regulation must target instead what we have called '*quid pro quo*' corruption or its appearance," the conservative justices wrote in the majority opinion. "That Latin phrase captures the notion of a direct exchange of an official act for money. …'The hallmark of corruption is the financial *quid pro quo*: dollars for political favors,'" they wrote, citing precedent.[58] *Quid pro quo* corruption was precisely what McDonnell was convicted of, not "ingratiation and access."

Unbelievably, dozens of legislators publicly claimed they were unable to delineate between *quid pro quo* graft and everyday politics. They signed an amicus brief maintaining that the verdict "puts at risk of federal criminal prosecution every public official who accepts a gift and performs any action that may impart some benefit to the donor. If this new construction of the federal anti-corruption statutes is approved by this Court, Virginia's legislators may be forced to scale back constituent services and other socially beneficial efforts." Furthermore, they contended that federal bribery law did not supersede Virginia's looser definitions, a baffling abandonment of the U.S. Constitution's Supremacy Clause, which stated that federal law preempts state law.[59]

As one of McDonnell's character witnesses, former governor and Democratic presidential candidate Doug Wilder asked the court for leniency and argued that "without question, had [McDonnell] not run into the difficulty, he would have been ranked as one of the best governors that Virginia has ever had." But because McDonnell was stigmatized and could no longer be vice president or president, "he has been punished, been punished indelibly, forever. …If [he] were to be given fifty years, it wouldn't be any more punishment in terms of how he has suffered."[60]

On April 1, 2015, the executive director of the state Republican Party, Shaun Kenney, opined that "in Virginia's rather poisonous political environment, you can go to jail for vitamin pills."[61] On that same day, a sitting United States Senator, Democrat Robert Menendez of New Jersey, was indicted for strikingly similar bribery allegations vis-à-vis directing health care staffers to meet with a gift-giving businessman seeking government money. The principal distinction was that unlike the McDonnell case, the Justice Department did not delay the indictments until after the senator had left office; the same allegedly politicized Justice Department was more lenient on the Republican McDonnell than the Democratic senator. Unmentioned also was the fact that Kenney himself had earlier called on McDonnell to resign—and not for "vitamin pills." "When you see these sort of things and you see $50,000 trips to New York City, when you see $70,000 loans, $6,500 Rolexes, I think that crosses the ethical plane," he said in 2013.[62]

A reporter asked former Democratic Virginia attorney general Anthony Troy if Bob did anything wrong.

> What the governor did was "not a crime," Troy said.
> But did he do anything wrong?
> "No. Not at all," Troy replied.
> Not even ethically?
> "Not even ethically…On the quid side there was not a single violation of Virginia's conflict of interest laws. You may criticize the laws, but there was not a single violation of Virginia law."[63]

The state did not pursue charges against the McDonnells. They were convicted of breaking federal laws.[64]

Six former Virginia attorneys general—two Republicans and four Democrats—wrote to the Fourth Circuit Court of Appeals in January 2015 arguing that

> *the expansive interpretation of federal law on which his conviction is based is erroneous. It is completely alien to any legal advice that any of us would have given to any governor of Virginia. Moreover, that expansive interpretation, if allowed to stand, would wreak havoc upon the public life of Virginia by casting a shadow of federal prosecution and imprisonment across normal participation in the democratic process.*[65]

This was written after the governor's trial and unanimous conviction of multiple corruption felonies. This astonishing public support of graft may have been unprecedented in the history of American politics.

Ordinary citizens felt no such urge. In fact, more than two-thirds of Virginians saw corruption in the governor and justice in his fall.[66] The unanimity of the jury found its mirror image opposite in practitioners of the Virginia Way. One month after their last court appearance and free during appeal, the McDonnells, supposedly too estranged to speak, were seen together at a comedy show, sitting next to each other, chatting and laughing.[67] In June 2016, the Supreme Court vacated all of McDonnell's convictions.

LEGISLATURE

ELECTIONS AND ENTITLEMENTS

Patterns of domination are so entrenched within them that this renunciation would become a threat to their own identities.
—Paulo Freire[68]

In theory, the legislature was supposed to be the branch of government closest to the people, but there are myriad ways that legislators distanced themselves from the will of their voters.

On August 23, 2011, six Republicans faced off for nomination to the Virginia House of Delegates' Fifty-Sixth District, west of Richmond:

Dr. Dave Brat, an economist and political activist who would later become famous for defeating U.S. House Majority Leader Eric Cantor in 2014;

Graven Craig, an attorney;

Dr. Surya Dhakar, a dentist;

Peter Farrell, a twenty-eight-year-old "amateur thespian";

Dr. Jack Manzari, a physician and businessman; and

Steve Thomas, the chairman of the Spotsylvania County Republican Committee.[69]

A four-person Republican panel was empowered to decide the nominee. Smart money may have been on the photogenic Brat, or perhaps the political chairman or a longtime local doctor. But one crucial biographical tidbit was omitted, which alone demonstrated the Virginia Way. Peter Farrell was the son of Dominion Resources CEO Thomas Farrell, the nephew and godson of McGuireWoods chairman and former attorney general Richard Cullen and the maternal great-nephew of Elmon Gray, one of the "powerful politicians who dominated the state Senate," as Elmon's father, the lumber heir Garland Gray, had before him.[70] With that, the outcome was predetermined.

They nominated Farrell, and in the majority Republican district, these four votes guaranteed election to a seat representing ninety thousand people in "the smallest turnout in human history."[71] Farrell did not even live in the district; he had to move there after he was selected.[72]

From August 11 to August 31 of that year, Farrell's father gave him $10,000, and twenty-three of the twenty-eight others who donated to him worked for his uncle's law firm.[73] Disclosure forms for the five fiscal years from 2010 to 2014 showed that he owed his father the highest reportable level of debt: "more than $50,000."[74] When Steve Thomas was asked if Thomas Farrell's $500,000 in political donations could account for the nomination of the candidate who by any measure was least qualified, he replied, "That [money] played a factor. Any honest person would say so."[75]

In his first legislative session, Farrell "was presenting a bill before the Courts of Justice Committee that clarified language in the state's bonding regulations governing property. He seemed somewhat uncomfortable with the dense subject matter" and was called out by several colleagues. No matter—the bill passed anyway.[76]

In Virginia, most legislators were elected based on gerrymandering, or primogeniture or money—seemingly everything save for qualifications. This chapter will discuss Virginia legislators' tactics of gerrymandering, redistricting, off-year elections, voter suppression, official entitlements, FOIA exemptions and secret votes that kept them in power.

LEGISLATIVE ENTITLEMENTS

Dave Ress summarized the scope of lawmakers' entitlements in an outstanding eight-part series, "The Virginia Way: Politics, Power, and Profit."[77] The goodies piled up quickly:[78]

- Senators earned $18,000 per year and delegates $17,640, an average amount for lawmakers (twenty-eighth out of fifty states). Yet this was for part-time work, as legislative sessions were only forty-five or sixty days long each year, depending on whether it was an even or odd year. The Speaker's salary was $36,321.

- Lawmakers received a $15,000 district office allowance per year, with no reporting requirements. This was in addition to General Assembly offices and staff, which were fully paid for. "I think what it was, was a back-door salary increase," said Senator David Marsden. House Majority Leader Kirkland Cox admitted that for tax purposes, he just counted the office allowance as personal income.

- Virginia was one of six states that permitted unlimited campaign contributions. These could be used for personal expenses, and almost all campaigns were uncompetitive.

- Lawmakers were the only part-time state employees that received full-time health insurance benefits—in their case, "the state's extremely generous health insurance plan."

- They were also the only part-time state employees to receive pensions.

- They received a $180 per diem when the legislature was in session. (To give an idea of comparable living expenses, in mid-2016, a very comfortable apartment was available at the Edison, one block from the Virginia Capitol, for $949 per month, or about $31 per day.)

- They received $200 per day for attending a committee or state commission meeting.

- They received travel reimbursement "for a weekly round-trip home during the session. Three quarters of Virginia legislators received more than $1,000 for that last year."

At the lowest salary level, assuming no committee meetings, campaign contributions or mileage reimbursements, a legislator would receive $44,520 per year plus state health insurance and pension.[79] In 2016, the legislature passed a budget that increased their $200 per diem to $300—a 50 percent increase—while teachers' salaries were raised just 2 percent.[80]

Unlimited Personal Use of Campaign Funds

Lawmakers granted themselves unlimited latitude in using campaign funds for personal use.[81] Did they want to go to dinner, pay rent or send their children to private school? Campaign funds were fair game.[82] A ban on using campaign funds for personal use applied solely when politicians closed their campaign accounts, and accounts could be left open indefinitely.[83] "It's really the wild, wild West out there," said former delegate Joe May. "I've seen things that really would be truly questionable."[84] For example, one delegate "reportedly spent nearly $30,000 on travel, food, and cellphone expenses in an 18-month period."[85] One lawmaker who had not faced a challenger in over a decade spent "$300,000 from his campaign account on numerous luxuries: a membership in a private business club, meals at Ruth's Chris steakhouses around the country, and more than $2,000 at high-end Richmond restaurants during legislative sessions" from 2011 to 2015, while another spent nights at the palatial Jefferson Hotel in Richmond in order, he claimed, to promote tourism.[86] "Virginia is the only state where lawmakers can raise unlimited campaign donations from anyone, including corporations and unions, and spend the money on themselves," wrote Alan Suderman of the Associated Press.[87]

In 2014, Delegate Marcus Simon introduced a bill that banned the personal use of campaign contributions and still permitted reasonable uses entailed in campaigning. It was tabled by an unrecorded voice vote and ultimately died.[88] A similar bill was defeated in 2016. "These are not government funds; these are private funds. Why should the government step into what is basically a private transaction?" asked Delegate Mark Cole, who headed the committee on election law.[89] In 2015, Senator Chap Petersen introduced a bill to repeal the personal income tax credit for campaign contributions. It passed the Senate almost unanimously but died by unrecorded voice vote in the House.[90]

When lawmakers were elected, the flow of business lobbyist money was turned on and helped provide a tenfold or more advantage in fundraising to incumbents over opponents.[91] Those running unopposed could expect tens or even hundreds of thousands of dollars. "It makes a mockery of the electoral process," said Norfolk State University professor Olusoji Akomolafe. "They're buying influence."[92] Senate Majority Leader Tommy Norment, for example, raised more than $1 million in cash for his 2015 reelection when he faced no primary or general election challengers.[93] Republican House Appropriations chair Chris Jones had not faced a Democratic challenger in the past eight elections. During that time, he raised almost $2 million.[94] Federal candidates faced a $2,700 individual and $5,000 PAC donation ceiling.[95]

The messy financial conflict of donor and politician was put into relief by Dan Casey of the *Roanoke Times*. Former attorney general and gubernatorial nominee Ken Cuccinelli had successfully sued a shell operation that used his name to raise $2.2 million while giving his campaign only $10,000. Casey contrasted Cuccinelli's behavior in this case with a nationwide veterans' fundraising scam helmed by Cuccinelli donor and confidence man John Donald Cody that cheated Americans out of $100 million. Cody's grift could not operate in Virginia because, as a transparent con, it could not pass regulatory muster. Remarkably, a novice with no knowledge of Virginia politics perceived exactly what to do. Cody was Cuccinelli's second-largest donor and gave $55,000 to his attorney general campaign. Cody spread an additional $11,500 to the leaders of the legislature, and his bill to exempt veterans' charities from minimal reporting requirements passed unanimously. He then preyed on Virginians and stole $2 million from them.

When the scandal broke in May 2010, Cuccinelli defended his benefactor. Five months later, after all the other politicians had given their illicit funds to legitimate veterans' organizations, Cuccinelli followed. Unlike the other shell company, he never used his substantial powers as attorney general to file charges against Cody, who was sentenced to twenty-eight years in prison—in Ohio.[96]

Lobbyists Wrote Laws and Legislators Got Free Vacations

Nothing stood for the cynicism and corruption that pervaded American politics better than the American Legislative Exchange Council (ALEC). It was quite literally a charity where corporate lawyers drafted legislation with state lawmakers for a fee, while lawmakers received free travel.[97] As of 2012, "at least 115 current or former members of the Virginia General Assembly have ties to ALEC, either by sponsoring bills, attending conferences or paying membership dues, according to the ProgressVA study. The state has spent $232,000 during the past decade to send legislators, primarily members of the Republican-controlled House of Delegates, to ALEC conferences and meetings."[98] Over fifty ALEC-penned bills had been introduced in the legislature.[99]

At the time this book went to press, Speaker Howell had been a member of the ALEC board of directors since 2003, including a stint as national chairman in 2009, and was a major proponent of its supposed benefits to Virginians.[100] When ALEC was publicly excoriated for incubating "stand your ground" laws implicated in the shooting death of an unarmed seventeen-year-old, Howell responded that "it's discouraging, disappointing to see this intimidation, this extortion that's going on against ALEC right now."[101]

Disclosure Free-for-All

The self-policing that lubricated the Virginia Way machine was a cesspool of abuse. As reported by the commissioner of the Virginia Department of Elections, "omitting a donation that should have been reported subjects the campaign committee—not the candidate—to a $500 penalty." The clerks of the House and Senate reviewed politicians' disclosure forms, which were then sent to a four-member panel of the Rules Committee. Over a period of half an hour to an hour, members supposedly looked through fifty reports. In her twenty-four years as Senate clerk, Susan Schaar said that no member had ever faced penalties for disclosure failures. In his tenure as House clerk, G. Paul Nardo had also never seen any disciplinary action over disclosure.[102] The legislature did not make this information available online: disclosure forms were available for physical inspection at the Board of Elections office in Richmond. A yeoman's citizen organization, the nonprofit Virginia Public Access Project, had posted disclosures online beginning in 1997.[103]

Gifts from "personal friends" did not have to be disclosed: the McDonnells did not face state disclosure penalties for Jonnie Williams's freebies, citing the elastic "personal friend" exemption.[104] They relied on the same when they neglected to report a $23,000 vacation from William Goodwin, a friend about whom Bob McDonnell could not recall under oath either the number of his children or a single one of their names. A half dozen members of McDonnell's staff revised their disclosures after his scandal broke. Delegate David Ramadan was questioned by investigators before the McDonnell trial for giving undisclosed jewelry to the McDonnells and retained Senator William Stanley as his attorney.[105] Goodwin, Ramadan and the staffers were never charged.[106]

Government Revolving Door

Part-time Virginia politicians did well for themselves financially, but their salaries could be raised even further at the tail end of their careers. The 2013 elections were followed by a flurry of resignations: three delegates and two senators, with all five seeking lucrative state employment.

Senator Henry Marsh, eighty, became a part-time board member of the Alcoholic Beverage Commission for $122,000 per year.

Senator Phil Puckett, sixty-seven, was slated for appointment to the Tobacco Commission, and his daughter was slated for a judgeship. These offers fell through amid a bribery probe.

Delegate Bob Brink, sixty-six, became deputy commissioner of aging for $110,000 per year.

Delegate Algie Howell, seventy-six, secured a job with the parole board at $112,455 per year.

Delegate Onzlee Ware, fifty-nine, became a juvenile court judge for $142,000 a year.[107]

Why give up an important job after reelection? The salary boost substantially raised these former lawmakers' pensions, which were based off the three highest-paid years of government service.[108]

The legislative-to-executive revolving door spun frequently. In 2011, Senator William Wampler, fifty, resigned to become executive director of the public New College Institute for $170,000 a year, while Delegate Glenn Oder, fifty-three, resigned to become executive director of the Fort Monroe Authority for "$160,000 a year and a free house."[109] He himself had voted to create the Fort Monroe Authority.[110] Nine additional legislators had followed this promotion path since 2005.

Corporate Revolving Door

Former officials were tapped for their Rolodexes by the triumvirate of Richmond legal powerhouses: Williams Mullen, Hunton and Williams and McGuireWoods. McGuireWoods, for example, had on its payroll former delegates Richard Hobson and Preston Bryant and the former director of the Virginia Democratic House Caucus, Heather Martin.[111] From the executive branch, in early 2016 it employed, to pick just ten at random:

Frank Atkinson, former policy director for Governor George Allen;[112]

Tyler Bishop, former co-chair of Governor Terry McAuliffe's higher education transition team;[113]

Mark Bowles, former finance co-chair for McAuliffe's inauguration;[114]

Richard Cullen, former attorney general of Virginia;[115]

James Dyke, former secretary of education for Governor Doug Wilder;[116]

Stephen Horton, former deputy chief of staff for Governor Jim Gilmore;[117]

Generra Peck, former deputy director of legislative affairs for McDonnell;[118]

Michael Reynold, former deputy director of policy for McDonnell;[119]
Andrew Smith, former finance director for McAuliffe;[120]
Michael Thomas, former chief of staff for Allen.[121]

McGuireWoods also employed Tucker Obenshain, daughter of senator and former Republican attorney general nominee Mark Obenshain. McAuliffe's chief of staff, Paul Reagan, worked there before moving to government.[122]

Sometimes the revolving door became an open gate, as legislators wrote laws and simultaneously cashed in with lobbying firms. Senator Jill Vogel and Delegate Eileen Filler-Corn both worked for lobbying firms. When Delegate Tim Hugo was elected in 2003, his firm, the Tim Hugo Group, reported less than $50,000 in lobbying income. Four years later, it was making over $250,000 annually. "Working as a legislator has had a negative impact on my business," Hugo claimed.[123]

Electing Judges and Getting Paid to Bring Cases Before Them

Legislators elected judges in only two states: South Carolina and Virginia.[124] Furthermore, judges did not receive life tenure in Virginia, and even Supreme Court judges were subject to periodic twelve-year reappointments by the legislature. Experts pointed out that this was an overt separation of powers conflict in which the judiciary depended on the legislature and was therefore less likely to antagonize its employer.[125] Furthermore, "Virginia sets no limits on legislators representing clients before state agencies. No state has a blanket ban, but 19 set some limits. Virginia is not one. Nor is it one of the 15 states that requires legislators to name businesses they represent."

Not only did lawmakers fail to recuse themselves when their day jobs included practicing law, but clients also actively sought out powerful lawmakers to represent their interests before the judges they elected. Delegate Jennifer McClellan was an attorney for Verizon, on whose behalf she argued in front of the State Corporation Commission. "I guess people at the commission know I am a delegate, but it never comes up," McClellan said. "When I go there, I am wearing my lawyer's hat not my legislator's."[126]

Self-Dealing

McDonnell had an ambiguous view of public media money. He used his line item veto in 2011 to reduce funding for public educational television and radio by $424,000.[127] The *Washington Post* noted the harm that would be caused by this veto, which was McDonnell's sole alteration of a $78 billion budget: "The money was cut from a portion of public broadcasting funding that is for public school teacher development and television programming used directly in schools." Senator Dick Saslaw said, "It penalizes a lot of the children's programming that, particularly in rural areas, that is [*sic*] a part of the educational system."[128] In the same budget, film grants and tax credits were substantially increased, with discretionary grants raised from $200,000 to $2 million per year in 2011 and tax credits from nothing to $1.25 million in 2011 and $2.5 million in 2013.[129] "In today's free market, with hundreds of radio and television programs, government should not be subsidizing one particular group of stations," McDonnell proclaimed. "We must get serious about government spending. That means funding our core functions well, and eliminating spending on programs and services that should be left to the private sector."

Did film incentives create jobs? Experts said that they were a waste of money, and a producer of Steven Spielberg's *Lincoln*, which received $3.5 million from the state, confirmed that the film chose Virginia for its authentic setting.[130]

In a balanced budget environment such as Virginia, every penny spent was necessarily taken from somewhere else. "To finance the film subsidies, the state has to rob Peter to pay Paul," said economist Bob Tannenwald. "It has to take cops off the street, teachers out of the classroom and shutter firehouses to get the cash to pay the subsidy."[131]

Delegate Peter Farrell seemed to take a page out of Barack Obama's senatorial playbook by attempting to never take a stand that might come to haunt him in later elections.[132] He was 1 of just 2 out of 140 state lawmakers who had a 100 percent rating in 2013 from the Virginia Tea Party Patriots Federation.[133] One rarely found his name in the news, except in one instance.

A *Washington Post* profile quoted Peter Farrell's self-described biography:

> *"I majored in political science, but I took every single friggin' acting course I could." After graduation, the redheaded Farrell moved to New York to try to act professionally, but came home after only five months. "I wanted to be the next Tom Hanks; clearly that has not worked out. I wish I at least*

*could have tried at least a little more than I did, even if I had completely
fallen on my face—at least I would have known.*[134]

Farrell was able to pursue acting, in a sense. In 2014, his father wrote, and
father and son co-produced and acted in, *Field of Lost Shoes*, a Civil War
movie. This movie was somewhat unusual for observers in that it removed
the decision-making of two public figures from the exigencies of gatekeepers
and external pressures; thus, it shed the most direct light on their characters
and modi operandi. The elder Farrell

> *studied the business of movies, its revenue streams and cost structures. They
> also started casting about for a director, producers and actors, all with an
> eye toward holding down costs. Farrell viewed moviemaking through the
> same business lens of running a utility. "I don't know how to run a nuclear
> power plant. My job is to make sure we have the right people in place to run
> a nuclear plant. I don't know how to make a movie. My job was to hire the
> right people to make it happen."*[135]

At a meeting of potential investors at the five-star Jefferson Hotel, "he made
salad the main course to send a message to investors that he was a cost-
conscious filmmaker."[136] A crowdfunding campaign reflecting public interest
in the film raised $550 out of a $700,000 goal.[137]

Associated Press reporter Alan Suderman looked into the movie and
found a hotbed of graft and conflicts of interest.[138] Despite not being able to
generate a public commitment to fund even one-tenth of 1 percent of the
film, the lawmaker and his father received $200,000 in grants and $800,000
in tax credits for the movie from Virginia. He claimed that he was not
enriching himself via his and his father's movie and changed his financial
disclosure forms when a reporter began asking questions:

> *Farrell also initially listed income of more than $10,000 from the film
> on his 2013 annual financial disclosure form. But after receiving inquiries
> from The Associated Press earlier this month, Farrell said that listing was
> in error and amended his form Monday to show that he was paid between
> $10,000 and $50,000 by a separate production company owned by his
> father called Tredegar Filmworks.*

(Tredegar Ironworks was a Confederate factory one passed on the drive to
Dominion headquarters.)[139]

> *Farrell said he was paid by his father's production company for work on "Film [sic] of Lost Shoes" as well as other projects. He said none of his producing work counted toward the $800,000 tax credit the film received from the state. Farrell said his duties as co-producer involved "grunt work" like helping to pay bills and locating office space...On its application to the state film office, "Field of Lost Shoes" staff indicated the tax credits and grants were "the primary reason" the movie choose [sic] to shoot in Virginia instead of Georgia or Canada, which also have film incentive programs.*[140]

Viewers of the film may have been skeptical of the claim of Canadian or Georgian competition, as it was filmed onsite at unique Virginia locations such as the governor's mansion and Virginia Military Institute.

Usually when a politician gets caught with a hand in the cookie jar, he gives the money back, but here, the verbal tongue-twisting became comical. In regards to the nearly $2,000 he received for his role in the film, Farrell played an awkwardly punning victim: "Some may be bothered that I might be paid as an actor. But I would hope that they would understand that the union made us do it."[141] The elder Farrell did not return the reporter's requests for comment.

The premiere attracted a veritable who's who of Richmond's power elite, including the lieutenant governor and Speaker of the House.[142] Governor McAuliffe praised the movie in a ceremony on the steps of the Capitol, and a busy part of downtown Richmond was shut down as "about 250 VMI cadets in full uniform marched along Grace Street with their band from the theater to the state Capitol" and back, a use of public university and other resources of unknown scale.[143]

A reviewer wrote:

> *Strained Southern accents and fake facial hair are the primary ingredients of Sean McNamara's low-budget Civil War drama dramatizing the events leading up to and including 1864's Battle of New Market. Displaying what can charitably be described as revisionist history and failing to match the impact of such similarly styled historical dramas as* Gettysburg *and* Gods and Generals, Field of Lost Shoes *feels strictly like small-screen fodder.*[144]

For the $6 million projection, Thomas Farrell cast himself as an advisor to Abraham Lincoln (whereas in real life he had advised Bob McDonnell), Peter Farrell played a Union officer and several other family members were employed as background actors.[145]

Political commentator James Bacon wrote:

> *This is one more instance of Virginia's political class picking the pockets of taxpayers and redistributing it to the wealthy and politically connected. Republicans, who increased this particular subsidy under the McDonnell administration, are blocking the expansion of Medicaid on the grounds that we can't afford it (which we can't). But they're OK with subsidizing a millionaire's personal artistic passion? Shame! Shame!*[146]

The *Richmond Times-Dispatch*'s editorial board also blasted the legislator: "Farrell doesn't vote on the tax credit when it comes up, but he still thinks it's a useful economic development tool. No word on whether he also believes in unicorns."[147] It cautioned that state film incentives were a rip-off and called for their repeal.

"I'm pretty sure that when we adopted that legislation we weren't thinking about movies that were going to be financed and produced by legislators," deadpanned Delegate Scott Surovell.[148] The *Field of Lost Shoes* government subsidies would have paid for two years of cuts in rural education media and still refunded some money to taxpayers.

In another egregious instance of self-dealing, a lawmaker wrote a bill directly affecting herself, her family and her employer. The dimensions of oyster packaging containers might seem esoteric and inconsequential. Not so for Delegate Margaret Ransone, an employee of her parents' oyster company. When she sponsored a bill to lower the minimum container size, it passed the House and became law with little notice. "I would, of course, recuse myself from any votes that disproportionally impacted or were perceived as disproportionally impacting the company I work for," she said.[149]

Archaic Page Labor

During legislative sessions, legislators utilized a labor force alien to 2016 or even 1916, consisting entirely of thirteen- and fourteen-year-olds.[150] These children fetched papers and coffee for lawmakers for $145 per week in salary and $125 per week in expenses—for full-time work—for a total cost of half a million dollars per session.[151]

The Virginia legislature was an outlier compared to similar government programs. The U.S. House of Representatives ended its page program in 2011.[152] The U.S. Senate had a page program open to sixteen- and seventeen-year-old students.[153] Virginia's Governor's Fellows Program was open to all Virginia students who were rising college seniors or older.[154] And Virginia court clerkships were de facto restricted to law school students or graduates.

Working in Opulent Buildings and Gardens

Legislators and their staffs had the privilege of working on sculpted grounds in the historic Capitol. The legislative chambers were as plush as a museum, with a courteous and professional staff and their own dedicated Capitol Police force.[155] Notwithstanding this opulence, in 2014, they added a $300 million rider to the state budget to build themselves a new legislative office building. According to Travis Fain of the *Daily Press*:

> *Legislators have been back and forth for years about what to do with the current General Assembly Building, which is actually several buildings of various ages, all connected together. It has plumbing issues, air quality issues and asbestos in the walls and ceilings. It needs a new fire suppression system, and that means ripping out the asbestos, House Appropriations Chairman S. Chris Jones said. Repair costs would mount quickly.[156]*

Democratic Senate leader Dick Saslaw remarked that "the best thing that can happen to this building is 100 sticks of dynamite."[157]

> *"It's a life-safety issue that's driving this," said House Appropriations Chair Chris Jones. "It's not us wanting to have a new building." The plan had been to borrow up to $300 million in bonds to tear the building down, construct a new one, renovate another building nearby and build a new parking deck for Capitol Square. The state would repay the money over 20 years and, with interest included, the cost would hit about $430 million.[158]*

Their building looked nice, in my opinion, and nothing like the deplorable school conditions found within two miles of the state legislature.[159] Miserly politicians seemed to become men of largesse and hyperbole when their own fates were concerned.

Governor McAuliffe blocked this $300 million item.[160] "I hope those legislators will recognize the message their actions send to 400,000 Virginians who need access to health care, not a new building for 140 state legislators," he said.[161] In perhaps the most egregious self-dealing yet chronicled, when a $2.1 billion omnibus bond issue for desperately needed investments in colleges, hospitals, museums, parks, the Virginia War Memorial and other projects came up in 2016, the legislature prohibited expenditure of those funds without the governor's approval of the $300 million for the legislature's new office building. This bill passed almost unanimously, and McAuliffe funded it.[162]

HIDING VOTES

Government was subject to laws regarding public hearings, notices, transparency and information. Yet the following bills were voted down in 2015 in Virginia, without constituents knowing who voted, how or why:

- A bill that prohibited personal use of campaign contributions. Died by unrecorded voice vote.[163]
- A bill that created a nonpartisan redistricting commission. Died by unrecorded voice vote.[164]
- A bill that prohibited discrimination based on sex. Died by unrecorded voice vote.[165]
- A bill that repealed the personal income tax deduction for campaign contributions. Passed the Senate almost unanimously and died by unrecorded voice vote in the House.[166]
- A bill that taxed electronic cigarettes and used the funds for kindergarten and pre-K. Died by unrecorded voice vote.[167]
- A bill that allowed seniors seventy-five years or older to go to the front of voting lines, if they chose. Died by unrecorded voice vote.[168]
- A bill that created an animal cruelty offender list for felons convicted of animal cruelty. Died by unrecorded voice vote.[169]
- A bill that prohibited health providers from trying to change the sexual orientation of minors. Died by unrecorded voice vote.[170]
- A bill that required training in reporting child abuse for those lawfully obligated to report child abuse. Died by unrecorded voice vote.[171]
- A bill that made it felonious for someone with a suspended license to recklessly drive and kill someone. Died without any vote.[172]

This is just a small sampling of bills that were killed without lawmakers ever taking a public vote. The total number of votes killed in this way numbered more than six hundred; the ghosts of sixty bills lay behind every bill listed here in that session alone. In a particularly ironic twist, a 2016 "bill to require recorded votes died without a recorded vote."[173]

Transparency Virginia, a nonpartisan group of citizen volunteers, attended the 2015 legislative session and reported on its findings.[174] It observed the proceedings of 79 percent of House committees and 64 percent of Senate committees.

> *In the House, 825 of the 1,892 bills (44%) died in sub/committee [sic].*
> *Of those 825, 104 died with a recorded vote, while 513 died without a recorded voice vote and 117 died without any vote at all. All told, the House defeated 76% of its bills without going on record. Only 24% of bills killed were done so with each member accountable for his/her own vote. ...*
>
> *A different picture emerged in the Senate, where rules state that votes must be recorded. A smaller percentage of bills died in Senate sub/committees: 388 of 1,652 (23%), and of those, just 7% of bills died without a recorded vote or any vote at all.*

Transparency Virginia created the following table on the 2015 session:[175]

TABLE 1. 2015 HOUSE BILLS*

2015 Bills and Committees	Total Considered	Stricken from Docket or Incorporated into Other Bills	Died	Died by Recorded Vote	Died by Unrecorded Voice Vote	Died Without Any Vote	% Died Without Recorded Vote or Any Vote
Agriculture	100	6	31	4	21	0	68%
Appropriations	186	7	105	5	72	21	89%
Commerce and Labor	140	3	71	5	55	8	89%
Counties, Cities and Towns	62	5	13	5	1	2	23%

---

* Transparency Virginia, "The Virginia General Assembly: The Case for Improved Transparency," April 14, 2015. https://transparencyvirginia.files.wordpress.com/2015/04/transparencyvareportreleased.pdf, p. 18. Adapted from original and used with permission of Transparency Virginia.

2015 Bills and Committees	Total Considered	Stricken from Docket or Incorporated into Other Bills	Died	Died by Recorded Vote	Died by Unrecorded Voice Vote	Died Without Any Vote	% Died Without Recorded Vote or Any Vote
Courts of Justice	313	19	138	9	97	13	80%
Education	177	7	73	7	49	10	81%
Finance	119	6	52	7	36	3	75%
General Laws	164	11	53	3	36	3	74%
Health, Welfare and Institutions	146	7	45	6	25	7	71%
Militia, Police and Public Safety	80	3	41	2	33	3	88%
Privileges and Elections	131	5	83	9	29	40	83%
Rules	128	2	63	1	56	4	95%
Science and Technology	13	0	5	3	2	0	40%
Transportation	133	10	52	38	1	3	8%
Total	1,892	91	825	104	513	117	76%

Delegate Mark Cole, chair of the Privileges and Elections Committee, said that "the vast majority of those votes are recorded, or have the ability to be recorded if a member requests it. There's nothing done in secret."[176] Approximately 83 percent of bills in his committee were killed by unrecorded voice votes.[177]

The next year, things got even worse: while in 2015, 50 percent of all bills in the House and Senate had not received a recorded vote, in 2016, 68 percent did not.[178]

FOIA EXEMPTIONS

Certain Freedom of Information Act (FOIA) exemptions made sense, such as undercover police work and state bank account numbers. However, the legislature carved out broad exemptions for itself and the other branches of government, meaning that much of government decision-making was done in the dark. There were over 170 exemptions in law.[179] These exemptions in case after case frustrated the media, good government groups and citizens who relied on both.[180]

In the redistricting lawsuit below, lawmakers invoked FOIA exemptions based on attorney-client privilege and working documents exemptions.[181] The sweeping working papers exemptions were of unlimited duration and covered hundreds of officials and staff working for legislators, the governor, the lieutenant governor, the attorney general and mayors, making this the broadest working papers exemption in America.[182]

Investigations of lawmakers' financial disclosure improprieties were exempt from FOIA.[183] Peter Farrell sponsored a bill in the same month the McDonnells were indicted to expand FOIA exemptions to prevent details of investigations of waste, fraud and abuse from being made public, but the bill was defeated.[184]

The Virginia Supreme Court had wide latitude, not only in FOIA exemptions, but also in the conflicted process of policing itself. When the *Daily Press* sought to investigate sentencing trends in Virginia's criminal justice system, employees of the Supreme Court denied their requests and continued to do so even after Virginia's FOIA Advisory Council released an opinion supporting the newspaper.[185] A Supreme Court administrator claimed that fulfilling this request "would violate the principle of separation of powers."[186] The Supreme Court also ruled in favor of the FOIA exemption for aspects of the methods of execution in death penalty cases.[187]

Wide-ranging exemptions touched on seemingly every facet of the public's business. Attorney-client privilege was cited in blocking the release of documents relating to the abrupt termination of Richmond's former chief administrative officer, Byron Marshall.[188] Papers of public university presidents were granted their own generous FOIA exemption, the only such one in the United States.[189] In the firing of the University of Virginia president Teresa Sullivan, officials refused to release key e-mails under an ill-defined "personnel" exemption.[190] Economic development documents were shielded from the public.[191] Lastly, Virginia Beach police withheld information from the family of a young suicide victim concerning the investigation into his death.[192]

"GERRYMANDERING, A SIN AGAINST DEMOCRACY"

Virginia had become one of the archetypal swing states in American presidential campaigns.[193] Enter "gerrymandering, a sin against democracy committed with equal zeal by Republicans and Democrats," as the *Richmond Times-Dispatch* editorialized.[194] Among the sequelae were "(a) reduction in two-party competition, (b) protection of incumbents, (c) partisan bias, (d) less competitive elections, (e) reduced voter turnout, (f) voter apathy, (g) polarization, (h) gridlock and (i) lack of accountability in government."[195] In a state evenly split between parties, gerrymandering provided Republicans with a supermajority of seats in both the federal House of Representatives and the state House of Delegates.

TABLE 2. VIRGINIA'S CONGRESSIONAL DISTRICTS, EXPECTED PERCENT
DIFFERENCE BETWEEN DEMOCRAT AND REPUBLICAN VOTE SHARES, 2013*

District	Representative (Party)	Partisan Leaning
9	Morgan Griffith (R)	R + 15
6	Bob Goodlatte (R)	R + 12
7	Eric Cantor** (R)	R + 10
1	Rob Wittman (R)	R + 6
5	Robert Hurt (R)	R + 5
4	Randy Forbes (R)	R + 4
10	Frank Wolf (R)†	R + 2
2	Scott Rigell (R)	R + 2
11	Gerry Connolly (D)	D + 10

* Cook Political Report, "Partisan Voting Index: Districts of the 113th Congress," http://cookpolitical.com/file/2013-04-49.pdf; David Wasserman, "Introducing the 2014 Cook Political Report Partisan Voting Index," Cook Political Report, http://cookpolitical.com/house/pvi. The Cook Partisan Voter Index estimated what percentage above the national presidential election average would vote for a given party. For example, if a Democratic and Republican presidential candidate each won 50 percent in Virginia, it would be expected that the Republican candidate would win 65 percent of the vote in the Ninth District and 34 percent in the Eleventh. Of seats with a +3 or more advantage, only 10 out of the House of Representatives' entire 435 seats were held by the opposite party. Thus, it is fair to conclude that a +3 advantage is a "safe" seat.
** Eric Cantor's seat was held by Republican Dave Brat beginning in 2014. GovTrack, "Members of Congress: Virginia," *https://www.govtrack.us/congress/members/VA.*
† Frank Wolf's seat was held by Republican Barbara Comstock beginning in 2015. GovTrack, "Members of Congress: Virginia." *https://www.govtrack.us/congress/members/VA.*

District	Representative (Party)	Partisan Leaning
8	Jim Moran (D)‡	D + 16
3	Bobby Scott (D)	D + 27
VA	Statewide	Toss-Up

The partisan leanings of each of Virginia's congressional districts illustrated the artificially drawn wedges that the state legislature imposed. In the House of Representatives, eight of Virginia's eleven seats were held by Republicans; if the seats were representative, five or six would be Republican.[196] As it stood, "just one seat is truly competitive—only as a result of the retirement of GOP Rep. Frank Wolf" in the Tenth District, which was won by Barbara Comstock in 2014.[197]

As strategist Karl Rove wrote, "He who controls redistricting can control Congress."[198] Federal district lines were drawn by state legislatures or their designees, such as commissions, every ten years after the United States

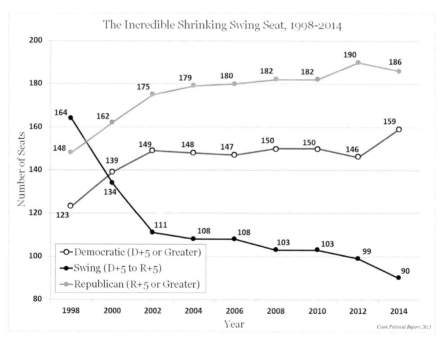

Competitive House Districts, United States, 1998–2014. *David Wasserman, "Introducing the 2014 Cook Political Report Partisan Voting Index," Cook Political Report, http://cookpolitical.com/house/pvi.*

census.[199] Before the 2010 census and realignment, national Republicans orchestrated REDMAP, a politically ingenious plan to win control of state legislatures and press for partisan redistricting advantage, thereby affecting the makeup of Congress.[200] Parochial politicians were targeted with salvos of television ads paid for with corporate and multimillionaire cash.[201] In one ad channeling Willie Horton, a former prosecutor and death penalty supporter was accused of being soft on an African American convict who had raped and killed an eleven-year-old child. In the "hooker ad," a moderate was compared to a money-clutching prostitute. In another, a sombrero was superimposed on the image of a dark-haired Caucasian Democrat with the tagline: "Mucho Taxo! Adios, Señor!" These ads worked, and their targets lost elections.[202] The leader of REDMAP, operative Ed Gillespie, went on to claim Virginia's Republican Senate nomination and narrowly lose to Mark Warner in 2014.[203]

Americans could see this playing out across the country.[204] In 2012, President Obama won the White House by about 5.0 million votes, and Democratic House candidates beat Republican candidates by about 1.4 million votes, while Republicans garnered a thirty-two-seat majority in the House of Representatives.[205] When Democrats won the White House in 2008, they had increased their majorities in the Senate and House. The difference was that Republican state legislatures had gerrymandered their way into a majority following the 2010 census and elections, and Republicans swept into power in statehouses nationwide.

Chris Jankowski, Republican Senate Leadership Committee president, said, "You can spend hundreds of millions of dollars fighting over a couple dozen congressional districts over 10 years, or you can spend significantly less and impact the shape of those congressional elections over 10 years via state legislative elections. It was a cost-effective analysis that truly bore out in reality."[206] According to Republican U.S. Senator Tom Coburn, this was an "incumbent protection system," designed by politicians, not citizens.[207]

UNCONSTITUTIONAL GERRYMANDERING

Gerrymandering was intentional, and its illegal lines could persist without redress through the span of many elections. From the 1960s through the 2010s, "not a single decade passed without a Virginia congressional or state legislative

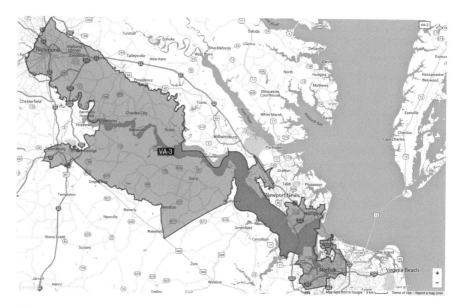

Virginia's Third Congressional District, 2010–16. *Google Earth screenshot.*

redistricting plan being invalidated, whether in federal or state court, and whether based on the federal equal protection clause or Voting Rights Act or the state constitution."[208]

In its most recent iteration, African American representation was hotly debated in Virginia's 2010–12 redistricting. The Democratic Senate offered a plan to decrease the Third Congressional District's percentage of African Americans from 56 to 45 percent and increase the Fourth District's from 34 to 53 percent.[209] In the plan that passed, the Third District's percentage of African Americans remained at 56.[210] In 2014, a panel of three federal judges, all appointed by Republican presidents, declared that the boundaries of Virginia's Third District were an unconstitutional gerrymander.[211] They ruled that the district, which resembled the constellation Orion, packed African American voters in so tightly that it violated the Fourteenth Amendment's guarantee of equal protection under the law.[212]

The lines of unconstitutional districts, the Third and several adjacent to it, were in place for the 2012 and 2014 federal elections, and the officials who drew the map faced no sanction for illegally disenfranchising tens of thousands of Virginians. As if to show how crucial gerrymandering was even to famous politicians' electoral prospects, after Virginia's lines were reconfigured by court order in 2016, Representative Randy Forbes,

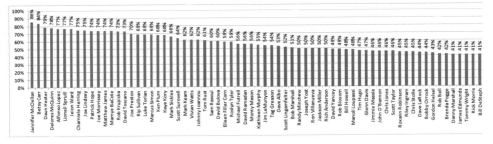

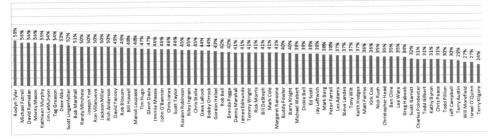

Virginia House District Partisanship, 2013. The heading "Herring % in 2013" refers to the percent of the vote received by Democratic Attorney General Mark Herring against Republican nominee Mark Obenshain. Both candidates received 49.89 percent of the vote. The graphs thus indicate the partisan makeup of Virginia's House districts. Note that this graph was unevenly split into two graphs because it is so wide (one hundred delegates). *Lowell Feld, http://www.bluevirginia.us/diary/12974/how-many-seats-could-virginia-dems-gain-in-the-house-of-delegates-in-2015.*

who had represented Virginia's Fourth District in Congress for more than fifteen years, announced he was running for election in the Second District, where he did not even live.[213]

GERRYMANDERING IN THE VIRGINIA HOUSE AND SENATE

Incumbents prohibited party competition in both the Senate and House during the 2010–12 reapportionment. Lieutenant Governor Bill Bolling could have broken a 20–20 tie to pass the Republican Senate plan but refused. Republicans gained a momentary 20–19 advantage in the Senate on Martin Luther King Day in 2013, when civil rights icon and Senator Henry Marsh was attending President Obama's second inauguration. They used this opportunity to ram through their chosen map, which would have severely gerrymandered the Senate, just like the House.[214] This was too much for Speaker of the House William Howell, who scuttled the plan.[215]

In the plan that eventually passed, lawmakers maintained the status quo: an evenly split Senate and a Republican-dominated House.[216] Journalists were left to perform an odd Rorschach test to describe the end results: one district resembled "an upside-down automobile transmission"; another, "a partially eaten cookie"; and a third, "Italy's bootlike outline, without the heel." As one columnist wrote, "Districts that resemble snakes say a lot about the legislators who draw them."[217] Putting legislators in charge of drawing their own districts was a gross conflict of interest, other commentators noted.[218] Only a handful of Virginia's Senate and House seats were competitive. Political author and activist Lowell Feld graphed the partisanship of Virginia's legislative districts.[219]

Note the large numbers of House Republicans with slight partisan edges in their districts compared with Democrats, most of whom won in landslides. The Senate, which was not gerrymandered, was evenly split, reflecting the purple nature of the state. Even then, less than a handful of forty Senate seats were even competitive.

Following the ruling that the Third Congressional District was unconstitutional, voters filed a lawsuit in federal court claiming similarly unconstitutional gerrymandering in twelve House of Delegates districts.[220] When lawmakers sought to block the release of state e-mails as evidence under the lawsuit, *Daily Press* reporter Travis Fain authored a rare kind of article explaining that he had to retract a quote because of the audacity of its lies. In an earlier article, Fain had written:

> *"What do they have to hide?" House Democratic Leader David Toscano asked Thursday. If the maps were drawn fairly, and Republicans discussed it, "let's see what they've been saying to each other," Toscano said.*
>
> *Then I noticed Toscano's name on a list of 29 legislators asked in the case to waive their privilege and release documents, and he wasn't one of the four who waived. Suddenly, his concerns for openess did not seem so quoteable* [sic].[221]

A bipartisan group of six senators—including Democratic leader Dick Saslaw—was found in contempt of court for refusing to release documents even after a judge ordered them to do so.[222] The suit was tied up in court through yet another round of elections.

Another suit was filed claiming that legislators violated the Virginia Constitution's requirement that districts be "composed of contiguous and compact territory."[223] In court filings, lawyers nonchalantly admitted that their redistricting was driven by political spite, which was perfectly legal, as opposed to racial bias, which was not.[224] Delegate Chris Jones testified that "he tried to accommodate requests from 75 to 80 delegates in the 100-member body who sought to tweak lines, sometimes to draw out precincts where they had historically performed poorly. Sometimes delegates wanted the boundaries changed to draw out a potential primary challenger, he said."[225]

It is important to note the unprecedented aggressiveness of extreme gerrymandering: in 2015, for the first time in the history of Virginia, every single incumbent who sought reelection in the general elections won: a perfect 122 out of 122.[226]

PRIMARY WINS AND LOSSES

Senate leader Norment stated his views on the will of voters succinctly: "Never in the remainder of our chronological life [*sic*] is the House of Delegates going Democratic."[227] Beyond narrow partisan cutoffs, two-party elections did not function in Virginia: elections were decided by party machines, which submitted them to a self-selected electorate that would inconsequentially ratify the party's will. As the *Richmond Times-Dispatch* editorial board put it, "Elections are still six months away, but we can already predict who the loser will be: you."[228] In six hundred House of Delegate elections spanning six elections from 2003 to 2013, only nineteen incumbents lost.[229] In what the *Roanoke Times* called "Soviet-style elections" in 2015, nobody even bothered to oppose 23 out of 40 senators and 66 out of 100 delegates.[230] Only 18 of 140 legislative seats even faced a primary challenger in 2015.[231]

Well over 70 percent of registered Virginians voted in every presidential contest since recordkeeping began in 1976 through 2012, save a low of 68.5 percent in 2000.[232] In contrast, the 2015 state primary turnouts ranged from 2.8 percent to 15.6 percent with an average of just 7.7 percent.[233] All state legislative primaries from 2007 to 2015 drew from a low of 1.4 percent to a high of 16.4 percent of registered voters.[234] This meant that most meaningful votes took place only in textbooks.

INCUMBENT PROTECTION ACT

Notwithstanding this incumbent advantage, politicians rigged the system even more. Virginia was the only state where politicians could choose the method of their party nomination: caucus, convention, primary or something else—in what was labeled the "incumbent protection act."[235] In one shameful example, Senator Ralph Smith announced his retirement in 2015 a mere thirty-six hours before the upcoming election filing deadline. He neglected to tell anyone save his thirty-year-old assistant David Suetterlein, whom he promptly endorsed. As if that wasn't enough, Smith also used his prerogative as incumbent to choose a canvass rather than primary election for the Republican nomination.[236] When the filing deadline came, only Suetterlein had collected the requisite 250 signatures, which in practice was impossible to do in a day and a half.[237] He ran unopposed for the Republican nomination.[238] He was guaranteed election in a district that leaned Republican by almost thirty percentage points.[239] After Suetterlein was elected, he introduced a bill to repeal the very law that he had so recently taken advantage of, but it was voted down in a Senate committee.[240]

KEEPING VOTERS AWAY FROM THE POLLS

As Iowa held a unique place in American politics, Virginia's "off-off-year" elections took center stage in the year after presidential elections.[241] Choosing governors in 2013, 2017 and so on, depressed turnout and disengaged the electorate as compared with presidential election years.

If presidential elections were "on-years," midterms were "off-years" and the years Virginia governors were elected were "off-off-years," then Virginia state senators were elected every four years in almost comical "off-off-off-years": 2011, 2015, et cetera.[242] Here, Virginians followed political news less closely, turnout was lower and, for many citizens, there was little justification in voting if one's district was gerrymandered, as almost all were. Concomitantly, there was little reason for politicians to encourage voting since elections were basically charades.[243] One might think politicians zeroed in on cutting waste would combine elections to save time and money, but a constitutional amendment to align federal and state elections beginning in the year 2030 failed without receiving a vote in the 2015 legislative session, just as a similar bill had in 2007.[244] Political reporter Dave Ress estimated the Republican partisan advantage from off-off-year elections at 5 to 12 percentage points.[245] A close look at the Virginia House percentages in the earlier graphs demonstrated a remarkable Republican advantage: even in districts with 54 percent voting for a Democratic attorney general, and one with a high of 61 percent, Republicans pulled off victories.

ELIMINATING VOTING RIGHTS

Virginia politicians were caught up in the national movement to impose rearguard voting rights restrictions. In both 2012 and 2014, legislators curtailed the forms of acceptable ID that voters could show at polls, eventually requiring in-state photo IDs.[246] Numerous studies and reports found that the voter fraud this was purportedly designed to address was all but mythical.[247] For example, a large review uncovered thirty-one documented fraudulent votes out of one billion cast (0.0000031 percent).[248] In a lawsuit challenging these laws, Virginia's top election official testified "that he was not aware of any case of voter impersonation in Virginia over the past 20 years."[249] On the other hand, the state board of elections estimated that 200,000 Virginia voters, most poor or elderly, lacked driver's licenses that could be used to vote.[250]

Incarceration was another method of disenfranchisement. America's prison population skyrocketed after the War on Drugs began in the 1970s.[251] The Virginia Beach police chief summarized the sentiments of a statewide task force of local and state officials as: "We had a war on drugs. We've lost miserably."[252] America imprisoned more people than any other nation in the world and had the second-highest incarceration rate in the world, behind the tiny island nation of Seychelles.[253] Officials said that Virginia "currently houses 30,369 inmates at a cost of $27,462 per year per inmate and a total of $833 million annually."[254]

In thirty-nine states, rights were automatically restored after probation was completed or earlier.[255] It conceivably made sense that prisoners who completed their sentences and paid their debts to society should be able to vote, make amends and rebuild their lives, but not in Virginia. Here, felons needed to go through a lengthy and bureaucratic process in order to restore their voting rights, even if they had already been released from prison.[256]

A report from the Sentencing Project showed that Virginia was extreme with regards to its voting policies. More than 450,000 Virginians, or more than 7 percent of Virginia voters, had lost the right to vote—the fourth-highest percentage in the nation.[257] Virginia also had the third-highest percentage of African American voters who had lost their voting rights, more than 20 percent in total. About 243,000 African American Virginians could not vote.[258] To put it in perspective, two states, Maine and Vermont, did not disenfranchise prisoners at all, while less than one-half of 1 percent of people in Massachusetts, New Hampshire, North Dakota and Utah were disenfranchised.[259]

As the issue of ex-felon voting rights gained national prominence, Virginia's government responded. Republicans, including McDonnell, when he was both a delegate and governor, pressed the issue and restored voting rights to several thousand nonviolent offenders.[260] McDonnell also supported a constitutional amendment to automatically restore voting rights that passed the Senate but was defeated in the House in 2013.[261]

Governor McAuliffe made "major changes to the restoration of rights application process for offenders of more serious crimes, including shortening the application from 13 pages to just one page and removing burdensome requirements such as notarization and letters to the governor." In the first year and a half of his administration, McAuliffe restored more voter rights than any governor had over their entire four years.[262] In April 2015, McAuliffe issued an executive order that "banned the box" on state employment forms and prevented initial job screenings from asking about criminal history.[263] The executive order maintained criminal history questions for financial or police positions and allowed background checks for every job if the applicant moved past an initial screening.[264] That summer, he sought further reforms to restore parole, which had been abolished in a law-and-order frenzy in the 1990s, and to prohibit fees from preventing former prisoners from regaining voting rights.[265] In 2016, he made national headlines when he issued an executive order to do what McDonnell had failed to accomplish: restore the voting rights of all felons who had served their sentences. More than 200,000 people regained their voting rights, and as this book was going to press, state Republican officials, including the leaders of the House and Senate, sued McAuliffe to try to reverse the order.[266]

PEOPLE VERSUS THE VIRGINIA WAY

The organizing tactics used by Tea Party and progressive activists in Virginia produced victories that overcame some of the inertia imposed by the legislature and in doing so helped to remake the national political landscape.

Netroots Took Down Senator George Allen

The Democratic grassroots takedown of Senator George Allen in 2006 mirrored the Tea Party's later Cantor triumph. Allen was the popular son of a former Washington Redskins coach and had cultivated a Reaganesque blend of telegenic folksiness with populist conservatism.[267] He drew national attention for being the lone Republican to topple an incumbent Democratic senator in 2000, when he beat Chuck Robb, President Lyndon Johnson's son-in-law.[268] In 2005, he led the field in *National Journal*'s polling of 2008 presidential prospects, and *Congressional Quarterly*, *National Review*, *New Republic* and *American Spectator* featured him on their covers.[269] Perceptive activists saw weaknesses in Allen's armor: Virginia and the nation were trending Democratic, Robb had been tarnished by a sex scandal, Allen faced more intense coverage as a presumptive presidential nominee and Internet-based politics had come to the fore.[270]

When blogger Lowell Feld read that Jim Webb, one of Reagan's former secretaries of the navy, was contemplating running for Senate, Feld began contacting supporters and urging them to write to Webb to share their thoughts on his candidacy. After meeting with Webb—and comparing him with state Democrats' putative choice, technology executive Harris Miller—Feld was convinced of Webb's merits. He launched a "Draft Jim Webb" movement and conducted with just a half a dozen activists the first sampling of support and strategy for Webb to consider. This movement would form the core of volunteer and fundraising support necessary for Webb to launch his campaign. "I don't think Jim would have gotten in without the draft," said Webb's deputy campaign manager Adrienne Christian.[271] When Webb beat Miller in a close primary, sources across Virginia politics credited the netroots.[272] It was a Webb intern, not a Miller intern, who caught Allen on tape using a racial slur.[273] This moment seems to have ended Allen's career in elective office and was repeatedly cited as a leading factor in both Webb's 2006 win and Tim Kaine's 2012 Senate victory over Allen.[274]

Grassroots and Majority Leader Eric Cantor

Economics professor Dave Brat wanted to serve in the state legislature before Peter Farrell, but "the political machine in the area under [Congressman Eric Cantor] came down into play, and I don't think people got a fair voice in that election. That really prompted me to get more energized at how to get the people a true voice at the table."[275]

Eric Cantor was an entrenched politician who had parlayed his comfortable suburban district into a $16 million personal fortune as House majority leader.[276] As a protégé of Speaker John Boehner, Cantor was next in line to attain the speakership.[277] Poll after poll showed Cantor achieving crushing, landslide victories over Brat.[278] The only poll nationwide to show otherwise was a local straw poll hosted by the Virginia Tea Party website The Bull Elephant (TBE) that Brat won by forty points.[279] Winning would be nearly impossible, one journalist wrote, and "one of the greatest political upsets of modern times."[280]

Where others saw an immovable object, Brat sensed vulnerabilities. He galvanized conservative media like Mark Levin, Breitbart.com and especially radio host Laura Ingraham, who linked Cantor with unpopular immigration "amnesty."[281]

Nobody in national or Virginia politics publicly anticipated the defeat except TBE blogger Alexis Rose Bank and Virginia Right! blogger Tom White.[282] Cantor did not even bother to come to his district on election day, showing up later only to watch returns and eventually concede.[283] In many absences over a period of years, he failed to understand that voters disliked him.[284] Tea Party activist Jamie Radtke wrote, "I still remember the private meeting I had with his consultant, Ray Allen, five years ago when he told me, 'Eric Cantor will never hold a town hall meeting. Over my dead body! You hear me?'"[285]

In the aftermath of the defeat, political journalists found that Cantor's riches were spent in ways that harmed his campaign. Brat was outspent by 25:1.[286] Cantor spent more at steakhouses than Brat did for his entire campaign.[287] When Cantor began to purchase and run television ads slandering Brat as "a liberal college professor," said Christopher Newport University professor Quentin Kidd, "his negative turn played into this narrative that Cantor couldn't be trusted...that he was out of touch with the conservative principles of the district, and was using Washington-style campaign tactics to beat his opponent down."[288] Steve Albertson wrote, "The counties where Cantor won happen[ed] to be the three counties outside the Richmond media market, meaning that the less they saw Cantor's TV spots or heard his radio ads, the more likely people were to vote for Cantor."[289]

With all these factors in play, none would have mattered if individual citizens had not banded together and voted. In the end, it was not close.

Primary turnout was up an astonishing one-third over 2012 levels, and Brat triumphed by eleven points.[290]

These local elections had monumental ramifications for the nation. When Peter Farrell's dad bought his underqualified son an election, a losing candidate, Dave Brat, was incensed enough to mount a successful primary challenge to House Majority Leader and Speaker-in-Waiting Eric Cantor in Virginia's Seventh Congressional District. Lacking a successor to Speaker John Boehner, the House of Representatives was thrown into disarray when Boehner declared he would resign in 2015, damaging Congress's ability to govern going into the 2016 presidential election.[291]

Many politicians were insulated from reality, but some who abused the public trust eventually understood that though the consequences may have been unforeseen for them, they were just as real for citizens.

2
CORPORATE POLITICS

POWER AND ETHICS

Politics is not a spectator sport. Our employees and our company participate in
[it] just like every other industry, business, nonprofit and organization out there.
That's how democracy works.
—David Botkins, Dominion spokesperson[292]

No one utility or no one company has any more clout or influence on a member
than a citizen.
—Senator Kenny Alexander[293]

Virginia's 2015 legislative session began with a preemptive September 2014 article by Speaker of the House William Howell and Senate Majority Leader Tommy Norment promising ethics reform.[294] In "Rebuilding Trust, Our Pledge to Virginians," they struck every note right and forcefully.

"Virginia's reputation has been tainted," they wrote. "The events of the past 18 months have been a painful ordeal for all who care about Virginia." Citizens' pain was "unacceptable" to them, who took "an oath," "a solemn vow that transcends party labels and ideologies," "to honesty and integrity."

"Public trust and the integrity of elected leaders are essential to the success of representative democracy," they wrote. "When the public loses confidence in those processes and those entrusted with significant responsibility and power, the system can crumble."

The milquetoast reforms of the 2014 session were "no longer sufficient in meeting the expectations of the people of Virginia. A higher standard having been set, we must meet it…We pledge today to the people of Virginia to take the additional steps necessary to rebuild the trust and confidence we ask of you."

"We will re-examine every aspect of our ethics, transparency and disclosure laws," they pledged. "We will build on the steps taken during this year's session and seek to enact reforms that are stronger and more stringent. Where questions arise, we will provide answers. Where mistakes are identified, we will provide fixes. Where loopholes exist, we will close them. Simply put, where action is needed, we will act." Urgent action would require a suspension of politics as usual. "We are committed to working across the aisle and hope that the significance of this issue will inhibit the all-too-common partisan nature of our political debates. There is simply too much at stake for demagoguery and partisanship. Together, we are committed to giving Virginians the government they deserve."

The Uses of Power

Dominion Power was a state-regulated electric monopoly. When millions of citizens and businesses turned on the lights or ran factories in Virginia, they paid Dominion, the scale of which was determined by the state government. By the dawn of the 2015 session, Dominion had made a practice of overcharging customers by tens or even hundreds of millions of dollars every year. After a 2007 biennial refund law was enacted, ending a failed "10-year period aimed at creating competition in the electric industry," $726 million was refunded to Virginians in 2010, and in 2012, $78.3 million.[295] The State Corporation Commission, tasked with regulating state monopolies and power rates, had never once found that Dominion had undercharged.

On January 19, 2015, Senator Frank Wagner introduced a bill he admitted Dominion wrote that would cancel future refunds.[296] Attorney General Herring pointed out these refunds were estimated at $280 million for 2015 alone, and it would seem the audits and refunds were working for consumers. At this suggestion, Wagner became incensed. "I'll be damned if people who haven't done a thing to protect the consumers of Virginia are going to sit there and say I'm the one not protecting the consumers of Virginia," he said.

Wagner had received $43,100 in campaign contributions from Dominion since 1997, or less than $2,500 per year.[297] As we have seen, campaign contributions are effectively unregulated and can be used for personal expenses. According to financial disclosures, he owned between $5,000 and $50,000 in Dominion stock.[298] Wagner was not alone. Many legislators' disclosures revealed their financial stakes in a state monopoly that they regulated.

TABLE 3. LEGISLATORS OWNING DOMINION STOCK, 2015*

Legislator	Value of Dominion Stock
Bill DeSteph	More than $250,000
Peter Farrell**	$5,001 to $50,000
Keith Hodges	$5,001 to $50,000
Chris Jones	$50,001–$250,000
Barry Knight	More than $250,000
Manoli Loupassi	$50,001–$250,000
Randy Minchew	$5,001 to $50,000
Tommy Norment	$50,001–$250,000
Ralph Northam	$5,001 to $50,000
Walter Stosch	$50,001–$250,000
Frank Wagner	$5,001 to $50,000

"It's little wonder Virginia's General Assembly sometimes resembles less a citizen legislature than a landed aristocracy," wrote the *Richmond Times-Dispatch* editorial board.[299] Wagner had other large financial stakes in the myriad companies he regulated, including the cigarette giant Altria, headquartered in Richmond.[300] Presidents and presidential candidates typically put their assets in blind trusts, but not Virginia politicians.[301] Forty-four out of 140 legislators owned more than $5,000 of stock in companies that directly lobbied the legislature.[302] In a rare response to charges of self-dealing, Wagner sold his Dominion shares on February 3.[303]

---

* Virginia Public Access Project, "Candidates Who Own Stock in Dominion: 2014," http://www.vpap.org/seis/stockholders/120206-dominion/?sei_period=16.
** Peter Farrell is the son of Dominion CEO Tom Farrell.

THE SPECTER OF ETHICS

Along with Dominion, the specter of ethics haunted the session. While Senate leader Norment wrote in September 2014 of Virginia's "tainted" reputation through "18 months" of "a painful ordeal for all who care about Virginia," in February 2015, he said in the Senate, "You know why we are doing this? Because the media is on our backs."[304] He had once written of valiant politicians surmounting pettiness to close loopholes, answer questions and fix problems. The ethics bill was a "bastardized piece of legislation," he later said on the Senate floor.[305] "You can't legislate people's behavior"; therefore, one shouldn't, the legislator claimed, an assertion echoed by many lawmakers that would, if accurate, deem any criminal laws, as well as lawmakers, irrelevant.[306]

The Senate minority leader perhaps could have benefitted from the miasma of venality and dysfunction that voters saw swirling around the GOP-controlled Capitol, but like Republican voters, Democratic voters would witness more of the same. "They need to quit calling this thing an ethics bill, because you can't legislate ethics," Dick Saslaw insisted. "You can legislate reporting guidelines, but you can't legislate ethics, and that's where the confusion comes. This law does not certify us as 100 percent pure people."[307]

The House minority leader had even more to gain by opposing Republicans' ethics charade, as his party represented just one in three seats in the lower chamber and could hardly be less influential. Yet his views showed total accord with the Speaker and Senate leaders. "While you cannot legislate ethical behavior, we can establish certain bright line standards for what is permissible and what is not," David Toscano said. "That is what we have done with this bill."[308]

Senator John Watkins, for one, believed that free gifts were a part of his salary. "The press isn't going to be satisfied until [gifts are] zero. Maybe that's the way we should be going, but if we do, everybody in here deserves a pay raise, commensurate with what directors of a company with a budget as big [sic]."[309] Watkins's financial disclosures revealed that he was a multimillionaire with diversified interests in land, stocks, mutual funds and closely held corporations, yet he was incredulous that a law might crimp the $2,160 in lobbyist gifts he received in 2014.[310]

Wherever reporters turned, lawmakers' self-pity and sense of persecution were common, seemingly universal. "To Sen. Tom Garrett, it's an 'exercise in self-flagellation.' To Sen. Bryce Reeves, it's a 'bureaucratic nightmare' that lawmakers are being forced to approve."[311]

On the first day of the 2016 legislative session, Norment solved what he saw as the problem by barring the media from the Senate floor for the first time in anyone's living memory. "Someone should point out to him that he is a public official, and offer to explain what the 'public' part of that term means," wrote the *Richmond Times-Dispatch* editorial board.[312] "You'll get used to this refrain during the session," he said of carrying out the people's business: "I have no comment."[313] The press regained its longtime seat three weeks later, after much of the session work had been completed, but its tables were replaced by schoolchildren's desks.[314]

Was it the media's fault? A poll of Virginia voters found that "distrust of political leaders crossed party lines, gender and race: 68 percent of Democrats, 63 percent of Republicans, 64 percent of males, 69 percent of females, 65 percent of whites, and 76 percent of African Americans said they agreed" that politicians "are less ethical than they used to be."[315] Politicians grasping for rationalizations were insulated from the real world.

PUBLIC LIES FOR PRIVATE GAINS

Dominion rationalized its rate hike bill that Wagner sponsored by stating that the Environmental Protection Agency's (EPA) pollution rules would lead to rate spikes for consumers, and Dominion needed this refund money to pay for rules implementation.[316]

Dominion's 2010 official corporate history listed twenty-four power plants that the company had closed, from coal to oil to nuclear to dams, nineteen of them built before 1945 and all built in 1970 or earlier.[317] The book favorably described Dominion's future investments in carbon emissions reduction, such as the 2008 groundbreaking of a "clean-coal" plant, research on emission reductions and investments in wind, hydropower and biomass.[318] It further noted the consistent year-over-year declines in sulfur dioxide, mercury and nitrogen oxide emissions Dominion had achieved from 1998 to 2010 and was projected to achieve through 2015.[319] These decisions long predated Barack Obama's administration. Did Dominion express anger at lowering its pollution then? On the contrary, it was proud.

Peter Galuszka, who had served as Moscow bureau chief for *BusinessWeek* and wrote a book on the energy industry, examined the basis of Dominion's assertions. Dominion had announced in 2011 that two power plants built in the 1950s would be shut down due to obsolescence and unprofitability, and

CEO Tom Farrell said that closing these plants was "the most cost-effective course to meet expected environmental regulations and maintain reliability for our customers."[320]

When an environmental group released a 2013 report criticizing Dominion for operating the dirtiest power plant in Virginia in Chesterfield County, a populous county abutting Richmond, spokesperson Dan Genest claimed that the group "conveniently ignores several publicly announced steps that we are taking to further reduce our carbon footprint, including retiring more than 900 megawatts of coal generation in 2015."[321] Dominion's website proclaimed the plant was "the largest fossil-fueled power station in Virginia." The plants were ancient, with the six units beginning operations in 1992, 1990, 1969, 1964, 1960 and, unbelievably, 1952.[322] The plants would be closed, in decisions long predating the EPA rules that Dominion scapegoated, because they were outmoded.

In a 2014 news conference supporting a 550-mile natural gas pipeline through the heart of Virginia, Governor McAuliffe said that "this will allow Dominion, who has coal plants that are 50, 60 years old, which they plan on shutting down—this is a lot less emissions [*sic*]."[323]

Claiming that hiking rates would protect consumers from rate hikes seemed an audacious fallacy even by the standards of corporate politics. The Clean Air Act said power plants should pollute less; therefore, customer refunds should be cancelled, Dominion would have the public believe. Dominion was already mothballing antiquated power plants, a common practice it had been undergoing for decades that was nevertheless laid at the feet of 2014 Clean Air Act rules to justify hiking rates.

The money would not help keep electric bills low, as Dominion claimed, but would come from increasing people's bills. The lies seemed invented for public consumption, as Dominion evidenced no such concerns for lowering bills even when less expensive options presented themselves. Later that year, Dominion would submit a plan for a new nuclear reactor between Richmond and Washington that would be more expensive than equivalent generation from natural gas or solar and would increase customers' electric bills by 25 percent, according to Dominion's own analysis.[324]

More bizarrely, there was no Clean Air Act rule, as the EPA had merely proposed one that had not gone into effect or even been finalized. The proposed date for the standards to begin to take effect was the summer of 2020 at the earliest.[325] Beyond that, the plan was further expected to be tied up in court challenges for an uncertain period spanning many years.[326] When similar rules had been proposed for cars, trucks and planes, those companies did not rush to the Virginia legislature asking for handouts.[327]

The public benefit of past anti-pollution laws far outweighed the costs to industry. Bloomberg reported that "according to the EPA, the [similar 2010] proposed rule would yield more than $120 to $290 billion in annual health and welfare benefits in 2014, including the value of avoiding 14,000 to 36,000 premature deaths. The healthcare [*sic*] costs alone far outweigh the estimated annual compliance costs of $2.8 billion."[328] A larger 2010 review estimated that the benefits of the 1990 Clean Air Amendments were $2 trillion over thirty years and would save 230,000 lives, at a cost to industry of $65 billion, or a cost-benefit ratio of 1:30.[329] Members of the American Lung Association and other asthma and allergy groups noted that the enforcement of the proposed regulation "would prevent hundreds of premature deaths and thousands of asthma attacks in Virginia alone."[330]

The facts had not changed: Dominion morphed what had been a point of corporate pride in 2010, a voluntary business decision in 2011, a rebuttal to environmentalists in 2013 and a selling point for a business-minded governor in 2014 into an oppressive government mandate in 2015 in order to sell gullible politicians on rate hikes.

The *Richmond Times-Dispatch*'s Jeff Schapiro dug up another rationale and put it front and center in his influential column:

> *As momentum built for Virginia's latest accommodation of the utilities, the investment adviser UBS—in an alert to the markets—labeled Dominion the "king of the hill." Citing the company's spin to stock pickers at a private meeting in Manhattan last week, UBS said the latest legislation "removes one of the largest single risks" to higher earnings: That the SCC [State Corporation Commission], if only temporarily, would be blocked from determining whether Dominion makes too much money.[331]*

During this time of universal public and media denunciation, legislators passed a resolution by unrecorded vote lauding Dominion:

> *...WHEREAS, countless Virginians remain grateful for Dominion's outstanding service; now, therefore, be it*
> *RESOLVED by the Senate, the House of Delegates concurring, That the General Assembly hereby commend Dominion Resources, Inc., for winning* Electric Light & Power *magazine's prestigious Utility of the Year designation for 2014; and, be it*

> *RESOLVED FURTHER, That the Clerk of the Senate prepare a copy of this resolution for presentation to Thomas F. Farrell II, chair, president, and chief executive officer of Dominion Resources, Inc., as an expression of the General Assembly's gratitude and admiration for the company's commitment to service.*[332]

A *Virginian-Pilot* columnist suggested that perhaps politicians "should serve all their constituents. Lawmakers aren't supposed to be servile minions to industrial bigwigs, fawning over every request."[333] He was ignored, of course.

2015 POWER BILL

This was hardly happening behind closed doors. The Dominion bill, along with ethics, were the top two issues of the session, and the media covered them clearly in dozens of articles. In testimony before a Senate committee, representatives from local charities who received small sums from Dominion testified about the good the bill would do.[334] It came out later that millions of dollars in charitable donations, including to organizations that testified on Dominion's behalf and even employed lawmakers, had been added to customers' electric bills.[335] Businesses whose bottom lines were at stake were under no illusions: "They have been seeking to avoid a base rate reduction in 2013. And in 2014, they were seeking to avoid a base rate reduction. And in 2015, they are seeking to avoid a base rate reduction," said a representative of Virginia businesses that would be harmed by the rate increases.[336]

Even if the bill passed, it still had to survive the veto pen of Governor McAuliffe, who had a short window to flex his political muscle before he became a lame duck. He had refused to take corporate or PAC money from Dominion in his unsuccessful gubernatorial campaign in 2009, though he accepted money from its executives and employees.[337] His tune had changed by 2013, when he took $75,000 from the company.[338] McAuliffe negotiated the final bill personally with Farrell in meetings not attended by Attorney General Herring, who had been the most outspoken opponent of the bill and whose purview included protecting consumers.[339] They agreed to a modest $85 million lowering of rates for 2015, "declare[d] it is in the public interest to expand use of renewable energy, and require[d] a company-financed assistance program for low-income, disabled and elderly customers."[340]

The rate hike bill soared to landslide passage, 72–24, in the House and an astonishing 32–6 in the Senate.[341]

The bill did not require the building of any solar facilities; however, Dominion's announcement of an extant $700 million solar power investment was moved up a few days as a public relations stunt.[342] This conflated the deregulatory bill with the solar plan in the minds of the Sierra Club and the Southern Environmental Law Center, and their employees praised the announcement.[343]

A member of the State Corporation Commission noted that it was unconstitutional for the legislature to set electric rates, as this was explicitly reserved for the commission in the Virginia Constitution.[344] Apparently, even that was no impediment.

2015 ETHICS BILL

The legislature passed a bill when Dominion wanted it. What about the public?

The public had no say in the ethics bill but learned what happened later from the *Washington Post*.[345] Different ethics bills had passed the House and Senate by February 10, and lawmakers were operating under an accelerated timeframe to pass all bills by February 27 so they could go home a day early. From February 10 until February 26, lawmakers did little to negotiate. The night before the artificial deadline, they met for just two hours and again from 8:00 a.m. to 10:00 a.m. the next day. One of the obstacles in negotiation, said Delegate C. Todd Gilbert, was the querulous fear: "Are we creating traps that people are going to unwittingly fall into?" By eight o'clock that night, the pressure had mounted, and the Speaker threatened to adjourn, thus leaving the Senate to explain the failure to pass any ethics bill whatsoever. With the Speaker's threat hanging like Damocles's sword, leadership finished a forty-nine-page bill, and "with the latest plan for reforming ethics in Virginia still hot off the photocopier, senators had less than half an hour to page through and decide whether to take it or leave it." They took it.

Lawmakers who did not want to pay for their own dinners and vacations must not have read the bill. Instead of ending legislative entitlements, or even moderating them, the 2015 bill eliminated a cap on gifts that had been enacted in 2014. To reiterate: the 2015 bill *weakened* Virginia's ethics laws. The bill had these provisions:[346]

- Eliminated the $250 annual cap on gifts to lawmakers. Individual gifts were to be less than $100, and total gifts were unlimited. (Governor McAuliffe was later able to make a minor change: annual gifts from a given lobbyist were capped at $100 per year, yet gifts worth less than $20 did not count toward this limit.[347])
- Exempted gifts from "personal friends" from any limits.
- Lawmakers could choose not to report free meals received in performing "official duties," a definition encompassing conceivably anything politicians did outside their homes.
- Refused to put any limits on the use of campaign funds, "which some lawmakers use routinely to pay for their meals, groceries, gas and other personal expenses."
- Created an ethics "advisory council" that could not issue subpoenas or fines but could exempt particular events and trips from limits. One of the first members to be appointed was Norment himself.[348] "The problem with this council to begin with is that it only exists to provide cover," said Delegate Marcus Simon.[349] After the panel was filled, one of its first official actions was to sign off on Commerce Secretary Maurice Jones's acceptance of free luxury box tickets from the Washington Redskins while they were trying to do business with the state.[350]

At this turn of events, Delegate Manoli Loupassi channeled Nixon: "I hate this system. It makes us look like crooks and we're not. I make a good living, but guys who aren't as lucky, it turns 'em into beggars...They're looking around every night for someone to take them out to eat."[351] Legislators all received generous per diems, as mentioned earlier.

The media reached a point of incredulousness. "Virginia desperately needs substantive ethics rules to curb abuse by elected officials," ran a May 2015 headline in the *Daily Press* over a picture of Bob McDonnell at the courthouse. "Half-measures won't cut it. The expectation that disclosure is sufficient to keep lawmakers in line no longer holds true. And the longer we go without real, substantive reform, the deeper will grow the contempt of voters for elected officials and the greater the disconnection of citizens from their government."[352]

"If you're looking for culprits in the sleazy orgy that seemed to engulf so much of Richmond in recent years," wrote a *Virginian-Pilot* columnist, "blame the avaricious legislators who got to the General Assembly and acted like entitled brats on Christmas morning."[353]

HOW MUCH FOR YOUR VOTE?

A reporter asked Delegate Scott Surovell, "Would Dominion be this influential without campaign contributions?"

"Nah," he said. "I think it would be very unlikely they could pull it off without contributing. There are few industries that get any bills through that don't contribute. That's the way the majority operates."[354]

The operating truism of Virginia politics was that the Virginia Way is pay to play; people elected politicians, and politicians like Frank Wagner worked for their donors. As the state's largest donor, it logically followed that Dominion must have been able to steamroll political opposition, as the health insurance lobby had in the past to stop national health care reform, for example.[355] Millions of dollars in television ads were "still the nuclear weapon" in campaigns, said Obama campaign strategist David Axelrod—and no one can dodge a nuclear bomb.[356] To put it bluntly, politicians might have felt compelled to surrender to opposition that could send them home, and they arguably might have been justified in doing so.

Yet Dominion leeched off the ultimate irony in Virginia politics: there was no nuclear threat to subdue independent politicians; they were bought not for millions but for only thousands of dollars a piece in campaign contributions. In 2014, Dominion's $649,540 in campaign donations, plus $19,939 in gifts, bought 104 votes (72 House, 32 Senate) in 2015.[357] The going price for a vote in the Virginia legislature was $6,437.30 ($669,479 divided by 104).

Federal contractors were barred from making federal campaign contributions, a protection against corruption that was extended to Virginia's government-guaranteed monopoly on liquor sales but not the one for electricity.[358] If campaign contributions really had no effect on legislators, as spokesperson David Botkins averred, then why give one cent?[359] Why does Dominion specifically take legislators, of all people, out for fancy dinners and not ordinary citizens? Dominion could have instantaneously exempted itself from charges of influence peddling by ceasing its political gifting altogether, but it chose to take the heat.

"Dominion's lawmaker education efforts about energy policy are built on relationships over many years," said Dominion spokesman David Botkins.[360] This money seemed to buy obedience and indoctrination: legislators may have been the only Virginians who believed lobbyists started taking them to steakhouses after they were elected out of the goodness of their hearts. The "gifts" that legislators strove to protect were petty, mostly less than a few hundred dollars, and thirty-one legislators received them in 2014.[361]

Dominion didn't "carry any clout," said Senator Kenny Alexander, who had received tickets to Washington Redskins football games from Dominion and voted for the rate hike bill. "No one utility or no one company has any more clout or influence on a member than a citizen."[362]

"Dominion power [*sic*] has been great to Virginia," said Delegate Lionell Spruill.[363]

Dominion's money metronomically bought the public's money. For $669,479, Dominion received an estimated $280 million in 2015 alone. Assuming that held for the decade-long life of the bill, Dominion received $2.8 billion in rate hikes for less than $0.001 billion in graft. In other words, a $6,437.30 investment in each legislator yielded $26,923,076.92 in rate hikes on the Virginia public—and Dominion had 104 such investments in the bank. Imagine a slot machine where you put in $1, got $4,180 and never lost: that was Dominion's stranglehold on the government. No wonder Wall Street was excited.

ETHICAL DENOUEMENT

As if to typify the sordid hypocrisy of Virginia politics, Senate Majority Leader Norment managed to get himself in a sex scandal at the end of the 2015 "solemn vow" legislative session. In telling innuendo, Norment conceded to the *Virginian-Pilot* that "exceedingly poor judgment as it was, I was interested in exploring other relationships…I am pleased to say that later in 2011, [he and his wife] were able to work through our issues including me having to share with her some of my misbehaving which was painful but necessary for a reconciliation."[364] Reporters pointed out that adultery was still a misdemeanor in Virginia.[365]

Norment's affair was with a lobbyist, and her firm had lobbied on 126 bills from 2011 to 2014. Norment abstained from none of the 63 that reached the Senate floor.[366] Within a few weeks, reporters sought information about Norment sponsoring two of her bills. As he lawyered up with former Virginia attorney general Richard Cullen, Norment's ostensible contrition disappeared. "This is a nonissue you are desperately attempting to make into an issue on legislation that never became law," he told the media. "Senate Bill 653 was not even brought to me by the lobbyist whose character and good name you are assassinating, nor did the lobbyist promote the measure to me."[367] The FBI interviewed Norment several times but closed the case without pursuing charges.[368]

In contrast, another former Virginia lawmaker who dated and married a lobbyist "generally abstained" on her bills and sought a formal opinion from the attorney general before they got married.[369] Norment and Speaker Howell had promised to "re-examine every aspect of our ethics, transparency and disclosure laws."[370] They had lied, publicly and outrageously, and had gotten away with it.

WORKING IN THE LEGISLATURE AND SLEEPING IN THE JAIL

Not to be outdone, Delegate Joe Morrissey entangled himself in one of the most unseemly spectacles in American politics. In June 2014, the fifty-five-year-old Morrissey was indicted on counts of taking indecent liberties with a minor and child pornography for allegedly having sex with his seventeen-year-old receptionist, taking pictures and sending them to a friend.[371] Purported evidence was persuasive, such as "nearly simultaneous text messages to their friends about what had happened."

Morrissey claimed, however, that incriminating text messages were planted on his and the girl's phone by her spurned lover. At a live press conference, he asserted that "our experts have uncovered the hacking device, the serial number and the texts." He then incongruously read aloud a text message from his former employee and alleged lover saying, "OMG, I just [expletived] my boss."[372] "We do want to apologize for the foul language from a state delegate," a CBS anchor improvised as the live feed was cut.

One week before his scheduled December trial, Morrissey and prosecutors reached an Alford agreement, an arcane tactic in which a defendant acknowledges there is enough evidence to convict but does not admit guilt.[373] Evidently, the multiple-hacked-cellphone defense was not airtight. The girl's sister gave another explanation for the plea. "I uncovered everything from the first text from the first encounter," she said. "I followed them home. I witnessed things he knew I was going to testify to. Mr. Morrissey has made my life a living hell since it started. He has had people follow me, harass me, harass people I haven't spoken to in 10 years."[374] He was sentenced to twelve months in jail with six suspended, to begin immediately, and could leave jail only to go to work.[375] The girl was now eighteen years old, pregnant and engaged to Morrissey.

The usual din of politicians calling on others to resign when they are in the headlights crescendoed. There was resolute talk in the legislature of expelling Morrissey, which required a two-thirds vote, and Morrissey had no allies left.[376] He would reportedly be the second member expelled in Virginia history and the first since 1876.[377] Corruption and illicit sex were routine enough, but by an unclear delineation, lawmakers felt this was beyond the pale.

The next week, he resigned from his office and simultaneously announced he was running for his former seat as an independent in the upcoming special election, before the 2015 legislature was seated.[378] With three weeks for the opposition to campaign, voters in his Democratic district reelected him over the Democrats' nominee, an unknown alpaca farmer.[379]

At that point, Virginia had achieved a moment likely unprecedented in the history of the republic: a sex offender spent his nights in jail and his days writing laws in the state legislature.[380] His legislative record that session was nonexistent, as any bill he sponsored was killed. He received little acknowledgement except when he drew scorn for voting against a bill banning pornography in prisons.[381]

In the first week of the session, he was indicted on new felony charges for allegedly committing perjury and forging documents that helped him gain leniency in his original plea.[382] The charges were dismissed because his wide-ranging plea deal granted him immunity from any charges stemming from the case.[383]

If Morrissey was expelled, his seat would be open, and in a special election, he would again run as an independent and win.[384] In 2016, he announced his candidacy for mayor of Richmond.[385] It was, for Morrissey, a masterstroke.[386]

PRICE OF MONOPOLY

Dominion was not a private business; it socialized losses and privatized gains. One can imagine the structural problems inherent in a quasi-governmental organization that operated to maximize its own bank account.

In an arrangement usually found with too-big-to-fail banks, Dominion insulated itself from competition and was not subject to the market's invisible hand. The State Corporation Commission (SCC) guaranteed Dominion a minimum rate of return on equity (ROE).[387] This bears repeating: Dominion was guaranteed by the government a minimum of 10.0 percent return. The SCC, in lowering the minimum return from 10.4 to 10.0 percent in 2013, noted that this "is 'fair and reasonable to the company, permits the attraction of capital on reasonable terms, fairly compensates investors for the risks assumed, enables the company to maintain its financial integrity'… and is in line with other peer group investor-owned electric utilities."[388] Even with this high ROE, "an expert witness for [Attorney General] Herring told the SCC that Dominion's rates are currently too high by about $630,000 a day, while SCC staff said the figure was about $860,000 a day."[389] If deregulating Dominion was supposed to lead to gains in efficiency, then perhaps government should not have stepped in to eliminate investor risks.

In May 2015, a Credit Suisse analyst asked Farrell about Virginia's new legislation. He became tongue twisted and platitudinous, as he usually did when he dissembled.

> *Analyst: Are there any major things you guys need to change operationally to be able to manage earning your ROE for such a long period without the review process or something we should be watching change strategy-wise out of the business?*
>
> *Farrell: Well, there will be—just to make sure there is not a big deal, but there is nuance in this. There is a[n] ROE reset in 2018. There is not in this biannual. And that will apply to the riders going forward. There is no earnings test. But there is a ROE review. We are just—Dan, I would just say that we will focus very carefully on how we manage the business. And we expect to be able to balance the needs of our customers and our other constituency—constituents—as we go through the next five years.*[390]

This private talk of "balance" for "our other constituency" had been absent from the public debate, where supposedly Virginians were getting lower electricity rates. The contradictory dual mandate to ratepayers and Wall Street banks like Credit Suisse was entirely absent internally. In Dominion's official history, Thomas Hamlin, vice president of investor relations, said that investors "are the ultimate owners of the company; we are caretakers of their capital. Our job is to take care of them the best way we can—by investing their money in the business so that it produces good returns."[391]

A Dominion spokesperson noted Farrell's compensation "was based on performance toward meeting goals set by the company's board, including earnings, safety, diversity, return on invested capital, stock performance and strategic business plans."[392] There was no mention of keeping rates low or protecting public health. Farrell received a 59 percent increase in pay for fiscal year 2014, to $17.3 million, more than the CEOs of Aetna, Citigroup,

DuPont, General Motors, McDonald's and many other larger companies with global household names.[393] It is difficult to put this number in perspective, but even assuming no holidays or weekends off—ever—Farrell made twice as much in one day as the average American did all year.[394] During that year, Dominion's net income fell by 23 percent, its revenue fell 5 percent and its operating earnings increased 5 percent.[395] He was thus handsomely rewarded for subpar earnings performance. "There is no basis for believing that if companies don't pay $84 million they won't attract top talent," said economist Dean Baker as an example. "You go back 40 years and they had smart, hard-working people too. They were well-paid, but not like they are today."[396] If someone invented something that changed the world, she should be rewarded, but should a Dominion CEO, who is, in practice, a quasi-government official guaranteed to make money off of taxpayers, be paid one hundred times more than the governor's generous $175,000 annual salary?[397]

From 2012 to 2015, Dominion stock underperformed; the Dow Jones Industrial Average outperformed Dominion by about half, while the S&P 500 almost doubled and NASDAQ almost tripled.[398] Leading universities and investment funds, including Oxford, Georgetown and the Rockefeller Brothers Fund, divested themselves from coal or even all fossil fuel companies.[399] In 2016, Mary Washington became the first public university in Virginia to divest itself from large fossil fuel companies.[400] Judged on its merits, Dominion was a bad investment.

Incentives were misaligned with performance and innovation, and a Dominion board and legislature that should have aligned those incentives seemed to act like a rubber stamp to the detriment of shareholders, employees, customers and the state. As we saw, Farrell's main contribution to Virginia in 2015 was to ask a paid-for legislature to claw back customer refunds. If one excoriates welfare recipients while exalting government subsidies to big business, we must ask, at what level does welfare became laudatory? Ten thousand dollars? Ten million?

As a fitting coda to Dominion's safety record, in July 2015, three transformer explosions rocked the heart of downtown Richmond shortly before the midday lunch hour, in one case reportedly shooting a fireball twenty feet into the air at Main Street and Sixth. Similar explosions occurred in 2014, 2010 and 2007, knocking out power to traffic lights and whole city blocks, closing Richmond's busiest streets and, in the 2015 case, shutting down the court system statewide because its servers ran through the affected area. One Dominion worker suffered smoke inhalation, and by some miracle, there were no other injuries.[401] No calls for investigation were forthcoming from any public official. It seemed Richmonders must simply endure random manhole detonations from time to time.

DOMINION LAGGED BEHIND PEERS

Judged by objective standards, Dominion's record as a utility company was poor. Virginia ranked thirty-fifth in the nation in energy efficiency.[402] An independent watchdog ranked Dominion dead last in clean energy.[403] Even tiny Delaware installed more solar panels than Virginia in 2014, the most recent year figures were available.[404]

TABLE 4. WORST U.S. INVESTOR-OWNED ELECTRIC UTILITIES FOR CLEAN ENERGY*

Rank	Renewable Energy Sales	Annual Energy Efficiency, Cumulative	Annual Energy Efficiency, Incremental
1	SCANA	Entergy	Dominion
2	Southern Co.	Dominion	PSEG
3	Dominion	Pepco Holdings	Entergy
4	AES	SCANA	FPL
5	Entergy	PSEG	Southern Co.

Farrell, in his foreword to the corporate hagiography *Dominion's First Century*, wrote that Dominion boasted "reliability unrivaled by any energy company in the land."[405] Did it? U.S. Department of Energy figures showed Dominion customers suffered a total of forty-three federally reportable blackouts from 2000 to 2015, which affected a cumulative 8.66 million people, more than the population of the entire state.[406] New Jersey's Public Service Enterprise Group won the industry's regional award for most reliable utility in the mid-Atlantic for fourteen straight years.[407] (Other companies won in the nation's five other regions in the most recent available year.[408]) JD Power measured another indicator of reliability—customer satisfaction—and found that Dominion ranked seventh out of thirteen for large electric companies in its

---

* CERES, "First-of-Its-Kind Report Ranks U.S. Electric Utility Companies' Renewable Energy Efficiency Performance," July 24, 2014, http://www.ceres.org/press/press-releases/first-of-its-kind-report-ranks-u.s.-electric-utility-companies2019-renewable-energy-energy-efficiency-performance. Adapted from original.

region alone, not to mention nationwide.[409] What Farrell wrote was simply untrue, according to independent experts.

Senator Wagner and Dominion maintained during debate over their rate hike bill that "Dominion's rates are already among the lowest in the nation."[410] Dominion spokespeople noted that "the average Dominion bill of $109 is about $25 lower than the national average," ignoring the seminal role of Virginia's mild climate.[411] In reality, Virginia's electricity costs were easily findable and precisely average, the twenty-sixth highest in the nation of all states and Washington, D.C.[412] The cheapest power in the country was in Washington State, which was widely served by public utilities (adding competition) and also the country's leader in hydropower.[413]

PRIVATE USE OF OTHERS' PROPERTY

Few things were more American than the right to private property. It thus came as quite a shock when placid farms were encroached on by surveying crews and hundreds of rural mailboxes were stuffed with threatening legal letters.[414] The shock became an earthquake as an entire region discovered Virginia code 56-49.01, a 2004 law that permitted natural gas companies to enter, survey and test drill people's land even without their express permission.[415]

Other states utilized ballot measures to check recalcitrant legislators. Virginia did not allow its citizens to amend its laws, and only after they had been twice through the legislature did constitutional amendments pass to the people, which led to wily politicians shoehorning sensible-sounding legalese into the Virginia Constitution. Consider the text of the following from 2012:

> *Shall Section 11 of Article I (Bill of Rights) of the Constitution of Virginia be amended (i) to require that eminent domain only be exercised where the property taken or damaged is for public use and, except for utilities or the elimination of a public nuisance, not where the primary use is for private gain, private benefit, private enterprise, increasing jobs, increasing tax revenue, or economic development; (ii) to define what is included in just compensation for such taking or damaging of property; and (iii) to prohibit the taking or damaging of more private property than is necessary for the public use?*[416]

Does it sound good when you read it? It did to the 74 percent of Virginians who voted for it. Lawyers, particularly Attorney General Ken Cuccinelli, drafted the law in order to reinforce state powers. Localities were hamstrung in their eminent domain ability, a right granted within reason by the Takings Clause of the Fifth Amendment to the U.S. Constitution.[417] Furthermore, a constitutional right of way was cut for utilities—including private power, rail and phone monopolies—to do as they pleased.[418] In effect, the 2004 eminent domain law had received a broad exemption for utilities under a 2012 constitutional amendment ostensibly protecting private property from seizure for private gain.[419]

Commentator A. Barton Hinkle put the shoe on the other foot:

> *Thought experiment: What are the odds of the Virginia General Assembly passing a law that allowed private individuals to enter the headquarters of Dominion Resources over the company's objections—so long as the individuals had a good reason to, and gave the company advance notice?*[420]

The surveyors who trampled across western Virginia worked for a Dominion contractor in anticipation of cutting a 550-mile tract from the mountains of West Virginia to Norfolk for a pipeline for natural gas obtained from hydraulic fracturing, or fracking.[421] Another 300-mile pipeline was set to run from West Virginia to Chatham, where it would hook up with a line going to North Carolina. The two would cross each other near Clarksburg, West Virginia.[422] Pipeline construction would require a 125-foot-wide path and a 75-foot permanent easement.[423] The suggestion to run these pipelines along existing highway and utility right of ways was ignored.[424] Unlike the ethics and rate hike bills, in which McAuliffe negotiated for marginal improvements, he capitulated on the pipeline battle before it even began and supported it in an announcement with Farrell.[425]

Even before the pipeline was laid, harm had been done.[426] Contractors working for Dominion filed lawsuits against 116 landowners who prohibited survey teams from entering their land.[427] Fears over the pipeline negatively affected property values, according to local real estate agents.[428] Representatives for the Wintergreen ski resort questioned whether their $40 million hotel project would be able to proceed, while another developer plainly stated, "I will not be building this [planned $35 million] resort project if Dominion's pipeline goes through my property," as it would under the proposal.[429] It was estimated that an explosion from one of the pipelines would have an impact range of more than one-fifth of a mile (1,115 feet) in all directions, and dozens of homes were set to lie within just 100 feet of the pipeline.[430] Pipeline accidents accounted for forty-six deaths nationwide from 1996 through 2015, and it was far from clear that the pipelines would be stable in the event of a natural disaster.[431] Dominion tried to assuage its critics by saying that cheaper gas would be available locally, but its price to hook up to the line was $5 to $8 million.[432] Furthermore, the pipeline's long path to the port city of Norfolk, as opposed to refineries nearer the source, seemed like evidence that Dominion planned to export the gas overseas, as it planned to do beginning in 2017 from a $3 billion Maryland facility on the Chesapeake Bay.[433]

The conflict continued to bubble as this book went to press. Surveyors were arrested for trespassing in Craig County, Virginia.[434] A pipeline opposition fundraising campaign was halfway to its $1 million goal, and lawyers offered their services for free to landowners who wished to protect their property from encroachment.[435] The legislature responded to the public uproar by voting unanimously in a Senate committee not to repeal the 2004 law permitting gas companies private surveys of others' lands without their permission.[436]

CAPITALISM MINUS COMPETITION

The state government did not have an energy policy; it was simply written by Dominion lawyers. For all intents and purposes, a monopolistic corporation controlled the government like a marionette. As Dominion vice president Thomas Wohlfarth said, "The General Assembly sets the policy, and they do a very good job at it."[437] Even Dominion spokesman David Botkins "could not name a piece of legislation in the past five years in which Dominion did not get what it wanted from the General Assembly."[438] Could one even say that the legislature existed? If one believed in representative government, there had been, in effect, a coup.

Was one coup enough? In the 2015 bill, "Dominion would retain the ability to ask for special permission to raise rates."[439] A UBS investment report foretold that "while [Dominion] has earnings certainty for the investment horizon, it could look to cement even more."[440]

In April 2015, Dominion held a press conference denouncing the rules it had once claimed to fix. Chief environmental officer Pam Faggert said, without irony, that "the rate for Virginia is not justifiable; it's unfair."[441] In July 2015, a few months after the legislature gave him everything he wanted, Farrell co-wrote a rhetorical paean to the free market that in practice called for more government giveaways to state businesses.[442]

When the proposed emission targets for Virginia were revised in August 2015 to permit more pollution, and even when the Supreme Court issued a stay of the rules pending a future decision by that same body, Dominion and the legislature did not give back the implementation money logically saved.[443] In fact, the company sought an additional $129.5 million in rate hikes for planned solar farms in October 2015, while that same week Amazon announced of its own volition a commitment to build a solar farm that would quadruple Virginia's solar capacity within two years without any such state incentives.[444] Dominion received clearance for yet another rate hike—this one for $40 million—in early 2016.[445] Nevertheless, its lobbyists continued to attack the clean energy rules, just a year after they had very publicly received the rate hikes supposedly necessary to pay for them.[446]

McDonnell's former secretary of natural resources wrote in February 2016:

> *The EPA is mandating that the commonwealth reduce its carbon dioxide emissions by 36 percent. This government policy will raise the cost of electricity annually by 14 percent, impacting every household (rich or poor), business, day care, church, firehouse, police station, school and government building…At the end of my term as secretary of natural resources we announced that, between 2010–2014, Virginia reduced emissions of sulfur dioxide 66 percent, nitrogen dioxide 43 percent and carbon dioxide 27 percent. This was largely due to the efforts of the professionals at the Department of Environmental Quality and the actions of Virginia's corporate citizens. …[W]ith this EPA rule, we see the impacts on Virginia's coal communities. Coal mines are being shut down, miners are losing their jobs, the dreams of coal families are being shattered, coal companies are filing for bankruptcy and whole towns in Southwest Virginia are being threatened.[447]*

It is hard to find the rational argument in this, but let us stick to the facts: Dominion had already hiked rates and therefore harmed the people and organizations he mentioned, ostensibly to pay for this very pollution rule; the emissions reduction targets promulgated by the EPA represented rates of decline in emissions that were less significant than the ones he himself had achieved and boasted of; and the EPA rules that he blamed for past coal miner unemployment had not gone into effect and would not go into effect for at least another four years. As noted earlier, Dominion had announced closures of sixty-year-old power plants for decades before these EPA rules were even proposed.[448]

Dominion told a completely different story in a filing in federal court in which the company supported the new Clean Air Act Rule. "Petitioners suggest that the impacts of the Rule will result in 'higher rates and less reliable electricity' for consumers," Dominion's lawyers wrote.

> *Because of the key compliance flexibilities highlighted above, Dominion does not agree that the Rule will necessarily result in such disruptive effects to the power sector and its consumers. Assuming that the key compliance flexibilities in the Rule remain available and that states implement the Rule's requirements in a reasonable and cost-effective manner, Dominion believes that compliance with the Rule is challenging but feasible and can be managed through a diverse generation fleet.[449]*

This court filing was directly contrary to its public relations position over many years.

If the future heralded more venality, so had the past:

> *In the 1970s, Dominion's antecedent, the Virginia Electric and Power Company, was teetering on bankruptcy because of its expensive push into nuclear energy. The SCC, over the objections of consumers and populist firebrand Henry Howell Jr., approved multiple rate increases to save the company…*
>
> *In the 1990s, the utilities were deregulated by the state and federal governments. Electric customers were free to choose their providers. Competition would cut prices. It didn't work out. Instead, it generated enormous windfalls for the companies and their executives. Consumers were boiling mad.*
>
> *In 2007, because the best defense is a good offense, Dominion proposed reregulation—but only if SCC oversight was not too onerous. Dominion got what it wanted: a short leash for the SCC.[450]*

Dominion managed, on more than $2 billion profit in 2011, to not only pay no effective federal taxes but also to get a federal tax refund of $13 million—a negative 0.6 percent tax rate. In 2012, it made $392 million in profit and received a $125 million refund, for a negative 32 percent effective federal tax rate.[451]

"We went through a period of deregulation in Virginia for about ten years," said Farrell. "We've gone into reregulation in Virginia. But over all these years, we've worked as hard as we can to have a good relationship with the regulators and the political infrastructure of the state, because it's important for them and important for us."[452] The same strings had been pulled in 2014, when Dominion was again the legislature's top priority. In that session, $400 million had been shaved off a refund by allowing Dominion to write off "development costs of a nuclear power plant the company may not eventually build."[453] "I'm not sure that we are being prudent. We have taken the discretion away from the [State Corporation Commission] and given it to the company," said Senator Watkins, who became outraged at gift legislation the next year.[454] The final votes were 74–

21 in the House and 32–6 in the Senate, almost identical to 2015, with Watkins reversing his earlier votes for the bill.[455] Dominion also got taxpayer money to bury power lines in 95–1 and 40–0 votes.[456]

The EPA had not yet proposed the preliminary Clean Air Act rule that would become a target of opportunity in 2015. In 2015 and 2014, and going back decades earlier, the public rationales differed, but the private impetus and legislative results were identical.

A summary of the legislative session by the Associated Press showed the Dominion bill was by far the most substantial thing that got done in 2014. The other five listed outcomes were: extending the time to find a mentally ill person a bed from six to twelve hours; lowering the number of standardized tests students take from twenty-two to seventeen; an even less effective ethics bill; permitting hunting on Sundays; and mandating that "new textbooks purchased for Virginia public school students will have to note that the Sea of Japan is also considered the East Sea."[457]

FREE MARKET THEORY

The private sector was supposed to be the fount of creativity and risk-taking, but instead of innovating, it can be argued that companies like Dominion leaned on the welfare state. If one believed businesses took priority over people, then artificially inflating electricity rates hurt all businesses in Dominion's service area, as well as hospitals, charities, schools and everyone else who flipped a switch or worked for a business that did. By late spring 2015, the Richmond public school system was already factoring an additional $561,000 into its budget for higher utility costs.[458] It was remarkable to see Dominion steamroll all comers, even employers with tens of thousands of employees like navy contractor Newport News Shipbuilding, whenever it was pointed out that Dominion's legislative priorities were clumsy bait-and-switches.[459]

There was a tension between coddling Dominion and minimizing electricity rates. The Dominion monopoly made money via raising electric rates in the same way that the government did via tax hikes. Every cent spent on hiked electric bills was taken out of consumers' pockets and businesses' investments, and this regulatory capture harmed Virginia's economy and decreased Virginians' standards of living. Legislators who would seemingly go to the grave before voting for a tax increase simultaneously raised electricity rates by billions of dollars.

Nobel Prize–winning economist Joseph Stiglitz contended that the best of both worlds was when business and government worked together for citizens, as in World War II, and the worst was when business and government conspired against people, as in the 2008–9 financial crisis.[460] Political theorist Sheldon Wolin called the worst of both worlds, perhaps stridently, "inverted totalitarianism," wherein the liberating potential of competitive markets and the ballot have been co-opted by an oligarchy of unaccountable corporate monopolies beyond disciplining by consumers or voters.[461] Whatever Dominion was, it was not capitalist, for it had none of the benefits of capitalism and all of the drawbacks of socialism.

STEWARDSHIP AND FREE WILL

It did not have to be this way. The director of public utilities in Richmond, which provided another necessary public utility—water—at cost, made $139,740 per year without manipulating the legislature or the government guaranteeing a return on investment for Wall Street speculators.[462]

In the biblical sense, "dominion" meant not exploitation but stewardship, as Pope Francis exhorted in his encyclical.[463] Alone in all creation, humankind had free will to spend its fleeting time helping others or maximizing its own wealth. Take the 2015 legislative session, which gridlocked over ethics reform policies supported by the majority of Virginians, while the same partisan legislators united and kowtowed to not just the needs but also every wish of Dominion Power.[464]

Some Virginians tried to lobby against Dominion in 2015. A professor at Randolph-Macon College went to the Capitol and shared her realization:

> I watched as a group of high-school students was brought into one senator's office—a senator who didn't have time to meet with us—to explain its cause. The students spent less than 10 minutes, but came out all smiles, eager as pups. Someone had listened to them.
>
> What should I feel at the sight? Should I be buoyed by their enthusiasm? Charmed by their naïveté? Embittered by the thought that they were merely being duped? Saddened that someday they'd learn how things really worked?[465]

3

POLICYMAKING

HEALTH CARE REALITY AND IDEOLOGY

You have to take the axe and swing it all the way back.
It hurts my arms and right here.
—*"Jackie," seven-year-old child tobacco laborer, pointing to her shoulders*[466]

W hen the Asthma and Allergy Foundation of America published its yearly "Asthma Capitals" in 2015, ranking the worst American cities for asthma sufferers, it held marginally good news for some children: Virginia Beach slipped from the thirty-sixth-worst American city to fifty-seventh.[467] Members of the Virginia legislature, largely concerned with giving corporate welfare to benefactors, probably missed the good news for Richmonders. Richmond was ranked the second-worst city for asthma sufferers in the United States, down from the top rank it had attained in 2014, 2013, 2011 and 2010.[468] Coming in behind Richmond were Philadelphia and Detroit, cities not exactly renowned for quality of life.[469] According to the doctors at the Asthma and Allergy Foundation, Richmond was the asthma capital of America.

On the day after Christmas 2013, Delegate Bob Marshall published a remarkable article. "In 2008," he wrote, "Oregon expanded Medicaid for low-income adults. Two years later, 6,387 adults covered under the expansion were contrasted to 5,842 Medicaid-eligible adults not included in the expansion. The *New England Journal of Medicine* reported that 'Medicaid coverage generated no significant improvements in measured physical health outcomes in the first 2 years, but it did increase use of health care services.'"[470] It would be a significant finding if Medicaid insurance did not make people healthier, since boondoggles should logically be repealed.

The actual text of the *New England Journal of Medicine* article revealed a discrepancy. In the conclusion to the abstract, the doctors wrote that "Medicaid coverage generated no significant improvements in measured physical health outcomes in the first 2 years, but it did increase use of health care services, raise rates of diabetes detection and management, lower rates of depression, and reduce financial strain."[471] Marshall had cut off the rest of the sentence in order to mislead the public about the doctors' findings.[472] There was no debate among medical experts that Medicaid coverage improved people's health, as in the Harvard School of Public Health press release, "Expanding Medicaid to Low-Income Adults Leads to Improved Health, Fewer Deaths."[473]

MEDICAID EXPANSION

If blocking ethics reform was the focus of the 2015 legislative session, stopping Medicaid expansion was the focus in 2014. Expanding Medicaid was part of the Affordable Care Act ("Obamacare") when, in 2012, the United States Supreme Court upheld the heart of the law while declaring that provisions expanding Medicaid were optional for states.[474] Expanding Medicaid covered all citizens under 138 percent of the federal poverty level. The federal government paid 100 percent of all costs between 2014 and 2016 and would phase down to 90 percent of costs by 2020, the level at which it would remain.[475] Virginia's rural hospitals were in dire straits, and with an estimated half of them running operating deficits, their association supported Medicaid expansion to shore up their losses in compulsory emergency and other uncompensated care.[476] An estimated 210,000 to 400,000 Virginians would gain health insurance if Medicaid were expanded.[477] A Christopher Newport University poll found that Virginians supported Medicaid expansion by two to one (61 percent to 31 percent).[478]

HEALTH CARE DOUBLETHINK

George Orwell defined doublethink as "the power of holding two contradictory beliefs in one's mind simultaneously, and accepting both of them. …To tell deliberate lies while genuinely believing in them, to forget any fact that has become inconvenient, and then, when it becomes necessary again, to draw it back from oblivion for just so long as it is needed, to deny the existence of objective reality and all the while to take account of the reality which one denies."[479]

Virginia had one of the most parsimonious Medicaid programs in the country: an upper-income limit of a $5,000 per year for a family of three meant Virginia ranked forty-eighth in per capita Medicaid spending.[480] Governor McDonnell and Democrats had reached a deal on a regressive transportation tax increase in 2013 in exchange for fair and open debate on Medicaid expansion in 2014.[481] As Speaker Howell tended to do when he got in a bind, he wrote an article in the *Richmond Times-Dispatch*, this time with Delegate Kirk Cox.[482] They stated three justifications for blocking Medicaid expansion:

- "First, Obamacare is a disaster. The website barely works, premiums have skyrocketed and perfectly good health care plans have been canceled. Virginia cannot irresponsibly entangle itself in Washington's health care mess."

The HealthCare.gov website seemed to be working well. I used it find my parents the same Anthem coverage for $400 per month for which they had been paying $2,400 per month. All in all, it took thirty minutes. By early 2014, more than 7.3 million people were estimated to have done the same.[483] All of this had nothing to do with Medicaid.

- "Second, Medicaid needs reforms. Medicaid costs are out of control, patients are not receiving the quality care they deserve and the program is plagued by waste, fraud and abuse."

The rate of cost growth of Virginia Medicaid had decelerated from 9.5 percent in 1990–99 to 3.3 percent in 2010–14.[484] Medicaid costs were coming in below projections, and studies showed that Medicaid recipients had better health outcomes than the uninsured, as mentioned above.[485] The nonpartisan Government Accountability Office estimated the level of Medicaid waste, fraud and abuse at 5 percent.[486] On the other hand, the Dominion bill that the Speaker shepherded through the House wasted billions, and he had no apparent qualms about passing a budget that spent $300 million on a new building for legislators and their staffs.[487] Nor did he appear to have any problems with less-publicized ACA spending. A Reuters investigation showed that Virginia had availed itself of tens of millions of dollars in "Obamacare" grant money, as had every populous state in America.[488]

- "Finally, and perhaps most importantly, Obamacare's Medicaid expansion would have significant, long-term ramifications on Virginia's budget process. We're skeptical of any promises on the future costs of Medicaid expansion. We do not think the federal government will be able to keep its promise to pay the bill and we do not think long-term projections of 'savings' will pan out."

Virginia politicians' supposed aversion to federal spending came off as curious, to say the least, as Virginia was the second-largest recipient of federal money per capita nationwide. A 2014 report for the Speaker's House noted that Virginians paid $64 billion in federal taxes and received $136 billion in federal spending; a staggering 20 percent of the state economy was based on federal largesse.[489] The recession-proof taxes that flowed to Virginia's treasury came largely from Northern Virginia, home to federal headquarters as diverse as the Pentagon, National Science Foundation, FDIC and CIA, among many others, while eastern Virginia's economy was dependent on military bases and defense contracts. The existing, non-expanded Medicaid program in Virginia received a much less generous 50 percent match from the federal government.[490] If a 90 to 100 percent match to expand Medicaid was so immoral, then logically the Speaker should have refused not just Medicaid but also all federal funding, much of which was in relatively less remunerative 50 percent matching funds.

Other Republicans claimed that the federal government could not afford it. Attorney general and gubernatorial nominee Ken Cuccinelli made this the cornerstone of his campaign. Former vice presidential nominee Paul Ryan joined a Cuccinelli conference call to note:

> *This is like budget pixie dust claiming that this money is all of a sudden going to come raining in from Washington and pay for all the things you want to do in state government. It's just not so. It's misleading. …It's basically gambling with other people's money that isn't going to arrive.*[491]

While Cuccinelli and the Speaker started publicly citing Ryan's claims, independent analysts said they had no merit. Politifact found that the funds that would have gone to Virginia for Medicaid expansion amounted to 0.3 percent of the federal deficit and thus would not make a difference in the remote chance of a federal debt-driven panic.[492] Another analysis by the Commonwealth

Institute, a Virginia think tank, found that Medicaid expansion in Virginia would save $1.64 billion over the first nine years (2014–22) and create twenty-three thousand permanent jobs.[493]

Most state legislatures had expanded Medicaid by 2015, creating a two-tiered health insurance system in the United States. States that expanded Medicaid were seeing drastic declines in the percent of uninsured citizens, while those that did not expand Medicaid were seeing lesser improvements and an uninsurance rate more than twice as high.[494]

The federal government had kept up its end of the bargain. While political opportunists unendingly anticipated falling skies, the rest of America had seen "the largest drop in the uninsured rate in four decades."[495] The same people who claimed that tax cuts magically paid for themselves also maintained that a more than 9:1 federal-state infusion of health care dollars would bankrupt Virginia.[496] To reiterate, legislators seemed to have no problem with appropriating $300 million in state funds to build themselves a new office building: just 4 out of 140 voted against doing so.[497]

Figure 1. Trends in Uninsurance for Adults Ages 18 to 64 from Quarter 1 2013 to Quarter 3 2015

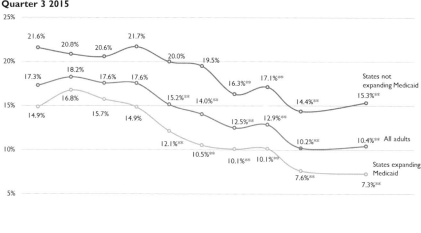

Source: Health Reform Monitoring Survey, quarter 1 2013 through quarter 3 2015.

Notes: Estimates are regression adjusted. States expanding Medicaid before September 2015 are AZ, AR, CA, CO, CT, DE, DC, HI, IL, IN, IA, KY, MD, MA, MI, MN, NH, NV, NJ, NM, NY, ND, OH, OR, PA, RI, VT, WA, and WV. Estimates are not available for quarter 2 2015 because the Health Reform Monitoring Survey shifted from a quarterly fielding schedule to a semiannual schedule in March 2015.

*/** Estimate differs significantly from quarter 3 2013 at the .05/.01 levels, using two-tailed tests. Statistical significance is only reported for estimates after quarter 3 2013.

Effect of Medicaid Expansion on Rates of Adults Without Health Insurance. *Urban Institute,* *"Trends in Uninsurance for Nonelderly Adults from Q1 2013 to Q3 2015," http://hrms.urban.org/ quicktakes/Gains-in-Health-Insurance-Coverage-under-the-ACA-Continue-as-of-September-2015-but-Many-Remain-Uninsured.html.*

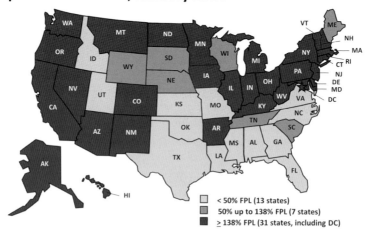

Figure 7

Medicaid Income Eligibility Levels for Parents of Dependent Children, January 2016

< 50% FPL (13 states)
50% up to 138% FPL (7 states)
≥ 138% FPL (31 states, including DC)

NOTE: Eligibility levels are based on 2015 federal poverty levels (FPLs) for a family of three. The FPL for a family of three in 2015 was $20,090. Thresholds include the standard five percentage point of the FPL disregard.
SOURCE: Based on results from a national survey conducted by the Kaiser Commission on Medicaid and the Uninsured and the Georgetown University Center for Children and Families, 2016.

Medicaid Eligibility Levels by State, 2016. *Kaiser Family Foundation, "Medicaid Income Eligibility Levels for Parents of Dependent Children, January 2016," http://kff.org/medicaid/slide/medicaid-income-eligibility-levels-for-parents.*

When Virginia hospitals later offered to pick up the state's share, alleviating the alleged fiscal pressures on the state budget, that, too, was rejected.[498] The deal to consider Medicaid in exchange for pro-business tax cuts turned out to be a bait and switch, and opponents began offering altogether different justifications.[499] For example, Delegate Steven Landes claimed on Christmas Eve 2015 that Medicaid expansion could cost Virginia "over $1 billion" per year in 2022. Politifact ruled this claim false and estimated that expansion would save Virginia $34 million by 2020 and cost just $3 million in 2022. Landes's numbers were off by a factor of more than three hundred.[500] Facts and years of results had not borne out Howell's and Landes's assertions, but their hostility to health care that objective observers and years of experience in other states indicated would save money and provide care to hundreds of thousands of Virginians continued as Medicaid expansion was voted down again in 2016.[501]

INVISIBLE PEOPLE

The economics were clear, but more important were the human costs of lack of health care. Desperate people in Wise County made them evident to the nation.

The Remote Area Medical team had delivered charity care in Haiti, India, sub-Saharan Africa—and Virginia. After the Virginia-Kentucky District Fair and Horse Show concluded each year, volunteers cleaned the animal stalls to make way for human patients, like modern-day Mary and Josephs, who began lining up at 3:00 a.m. for a chance at needed medical care. When a reporter visited in 2007, 2,500 were seen over the clinic's three days, and hundreds more were turned away.[502]

A team from *60 Minutes* found a husband, wife and child asleep in a car in below-freezing temperatures after they had driven two hundred miles to the clinic. "Why did you come?" they were asked. "I've been in some very excruciating pain," the man replied. "Who are the people who come here?" the team asked a University of Virginia volunteer doctor. "It's the working poor, middle of their lives, most with families, most not substance abusers and employed without adequate insurance."[503]

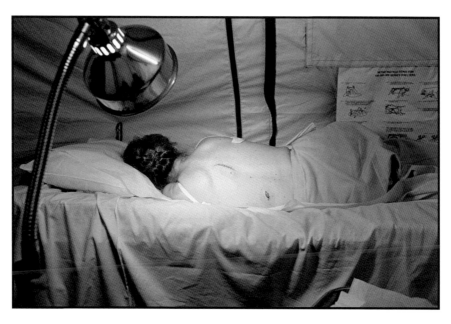

A patient in an animal stall at the Remote Area Medical clinic, Wise County, Virginia. *Larry Towell/Magnum Photos. Sara Corbett, "Patients Without Borders,"* New York Times Magazine, *November 18, 2007.*

A Harvard study found that forty-five thousand Americans died each year from lack of health insurance, while in every other developed country, health care was as universal and uncontroversial as public school.[504] For the suffering, this was their course of life. For Americans unaccustomed to ordinary poverty, Virginia was on national television: "The difference was visibility. This time, we had to watch."[505]

Governor McAuliffe did what he could in the face of the legislature's intransigence in 2014 and

> *issued what his office called "emergency regulatory actions" to cover 20,000 people with severe mental illness and 5,000 children of low-income state workers. The initiatives are to be paid for with $40 million left over in the current budget. Continuing them beyond the fiscal year ending next July will require the General Assembly's approval. Mr. McAuliffe also announced outreach efforts to get 160,000 unenrolled adults who are eligible for health insurance through the federal marketplace to sign up, as well as 35,000 unenrolled children eligible for Medicaid.[506]*

"I Could Now See Clearly..."

Witnessing this destitution in the world's wealthiest country could have profound consequences. For two decades, Wendell Potter was one of the leaders of the insurance industry's fight against health care reform. In 2007, he traveled to Wise County to put CIGNA's public relations spin on the fairgrounds clinic. He recounted his epiphany:

> *The scene inside was surreal. I felt as if I'd stepped into a movie set or a war zone. Hundreds of people, many of them soaking wet from the rain that had been falling all morning, were waiting in lines that stretched out of view. As I walked around, I noticed that some of those lines led to barns and cinder block buildings with row after row of animal stalls, where doctors and nurses were treating patients. Other people were being treated by dentists under open-sided tents. Many were lying on gurneys on rain-soaked pavement. Except for curtains serving as makeshift doors on the animal stalls, there was little privacy. And unlike health fairs I had seen in shopping centers and malls, this was a real clinic. Dentists were pulling teeth and filling cavities, optometrists were examining eyes for glaucoma and*

cataracts, doctors and nurses were doing Pap smears and mammograms, surgeons were cutting out skin cancers, and gastroenterologists were conducting sigmoidoscopies.[507]

The power of my experience in Wise County really hit home a couple of weeks later as I was boarding one of the two private jets CIGNA uses to fly executives around the country. I flew on those jets several times a year. With conference tables, video screens, leather seats, and deep carpet, they make first class on a commercial airliner look shabby. As usual, on this flight, which was taking me to a meeting in Connecticut, a uniformed attendant brought me lunch on a gold-rimmed plate and handed me gold-plated flatware with which to eat it. My thoughts turned immediately to the people I had seen being treated in animal stalls just days earlier. A few months later, I saw an article in Architectural Digest *with a headline reading, "Romancing the Stone: In the Hills of Eastern Pennsylvania Rises a Prototypical French Farmhouse." Amid a sequence of elegant photos, it described a twenty-four-room mansion inspired by "ancient stones of* la France profunde*" and featuring "an impossibly French" kitchen.*[508]

The house was owned by the former CEO of CIGNA. "I could now see clearly, those people in Wise County would not have had to stand in line in the rain for hours to get care in animal stalls if so much of the money Americans spend for health care didn't wind up in the pockets of insurance company executives and their Wall Street masters."[509]

Potter read *Profiles in Courage* and the Bible, focusing on "where the Apostle Paul advises Christians to 'cast all their anxiety' on God," and then resigned his position to become a whistleblower.[510]

How did ordinary Virginians get so sick?

Big Cigarettes

The tobacco conglomerate Altria, headquartered in Richmond and formerly known as Philip Morris, employed about 3,900 people in the Richmond area and 9,000 people globally, while controlling half of the American cigarette market.[511] Tobacco was responsible for an estimated 9,200 premature deaths in Virginia alone every year.[512] It may sound harsh, but it was an inescapable fact that Altria killed more Virginians each year than it employed. The imbalance was starker nationally, where cigarettes killed nearly half a million people annually, on average taking ten years from each life.[513]

Health care costs from tobacco in Virginia were estimated at $1.92 billion in 2009, or about 0.5 percent of GDP and $300 billion nationally, with profits at $4.5 billion worldwide.[514] Since Altria was responsible for half this toll, the nation was subsidizing Altria to the tune of nearly $150 billion per year. If cigarette companies merely paid for the damage they caused, it seems they would be bankrupted, so it was intrinsic to their business model to avoid moral and financial responsibility. Americans lived under a two-tiered system of justice, where the rich were by and large above the rule of law, according to Pulitzer Prize–winning reporter Glenn Greenwald.[515] For example, despite cigarette companies' much higher body counts, dealers of illicit drugs were being sentenced to decades in prison.[516]

Tobacco's Child Labor

In the long litany of abuses carried out by cigarette companies in Virginia, it seemed difficult to think of one more disturbing than the child labor and nicotine poisoning documented by Human Rights Watch in its report, "Tobacco's Hidden Children."[517] It was hard to find words to describe the suffering uncovered in the 137-page child tobacco labor report.[518] Investigators interviewed more than 140 child laborers; the median age was thirteen, and the youngest interviewee was seven years old.[519]

The majority of child laborers interviewed were in poverty and stated that they worked to buy basic supplies of living. For example, "Raul" said, "I work so that I have money to buy clothes for school and school supplies, you know, like crayons and stuff. I've already bought my backpack for next year."[520]

Thirteen-year-old "Elena" said that in the tobacco fields, "I felt very tired…I would barely eat anything because I wouldn't get hungry. …We would get our lunch break and I would barely eat, I would just drink. … Sometimes I felt like I needed to throw up. I never did. It had come up my throat, but it went back down."

"Gabriella" described the living nightmare of watching her daughter Elena suffer: "Sometimes I saw that she couldn't bear it. She was going to faint. She had headaches, nausea. Watching her was so hard."[521]

Amid the dehumanizing poverty, health and safety laws were ignored:

> *Nearly three-quarters of children interviewed by Human Rights Watch in North Carolina, Kentucky, Tennessee, and Virginia, 97 out of 133, reported feeling sick—with nausea, vomiting, loss of appetite, headaches, dizziness, skin rashes, difficulty breathing, and irritation to their eyes and mouths—while working in fields with tobacco plants and in barns with dried tobacco leaves and tobacco dust. Many reported being exposed to pesticides and to extreme temperatures and unrelenting heat while working in tobacco fields. Some stated that they used sharp tools and cut themselves, or operated heavy machinery and climbed to significant heights, risking serious injury.[522]*

These symptoms, described by many other children in the report, were consistent with green nicotine sickness, which people suffered when a toxic amount of nicotine was absorbed through the skin.[523] "Children," the researchers wrote, "are particularly vulnerable to nicotine poisoning because of their size, and because they are less likely than adults to have developed a tolerance to nicotine.[524] …According to the US Surgeon General's most recent report, 'The evidence is suggestive that nicotine exposure during adolescence, a critical window for brain development, may have lasting adverse consequences for brain development.'"[525]

"Exposure to large doses of pesticides can have severe health effects including spontaneous abortion and birth deformities, loss of consciousness, coma, and death," the researchers wrote, citing medical experts.

> *Long-term and chronic health effects of pesticide exposure include respiratory problems, cancer, depression, neurologic deficits, and reproductive health problems. Children are uniquely vulnerable to the adverse effects of toxic exposures as their brains and bodies are still developing, and they consume more water and food, and breathe more air, pound for pound, than adults.[526]*
>
> *Just over half of the children interviewed by Human Rights Watch—63 out of 120—reported that they saw tractors spraying pesticides in the fields in which they were working or in fields adjacent to the ones in which they were working. These children often reported being able to smell or feel the chemical spray as it drifted towards them. A few children stated that they applied pesticides to tobacco plants with a handheld sprayer and backpack, or operated tractors that were spraying pesticides on tobacco fields. Children also reported experiencing a range of symptoms after coming into contact*

with pesticides while working in tobacco farming, including burning eyes, burning nose, itchy skin, nausea, vomiting, dizziness, shortness of breath, redness and swelling of the mouth, and headaches.[527]

According to ten-year-old "Marta," "They were like spraying it to make it grow bigger the time we went. It was in the same field as us. It was on the other side of the field. The smell was very nasty. I felt nauseous after that."[528] For fourteen-year-old "Marissa," "The spray affects my asthma. When I smell it, it makes me nauseous, short of breath, even if I'm not really doing anything."[529]

Tobacco harvesters utilized sharp knives and tools unsuitable for children. Ten-year-old "Lucio" said, "I got hurt once when I got the axe, and I got cut somewhere on my feet. I was swinging at the plant and I missed and hit my leg."[530] Fourteen-year-old "Adriana" recalled, "Last year, I was in the field, and I was trying to cut, and I picked up the plant and it was wet. And I slid because it was raining and it was wet, and the spike went into my hand. My dad put a bandage on it to stop the blood and keep out the infection."[531] "Andrea," a sixteen-year-old child laborer who had worked in tobacco fields for ten years, said, "When I was using the hoe, I cut myself on my leg with the blade of the hoe. I didn't need to go to the hospital. I just kept working. I was bleeding, but I was in the middle of the field and I couldn't do anything."[532] Children younger than eighteen could not even buy cigarettes or vote in the United States because society did not deem them cognitively able to make those important decisions.

Seventeen-year-old "Isaac" cut off two of his fingers on an elevated riding mower used to trim seedlings on an assembly line. After his fingers were surgically reattached, the employer gave him $100 in compensation. "I don't work comfortably. In my hand, I don't have strength. Only in [the lower] half of the hand I have strength."[533]

"Gregory" and "Jackie" described the pain they felt harvesting tobacco. "Cutting [tobacco plants] is the hardest because there's a big, giant row and you have to go all the way down the row, and come all the way back," said Gregory. Gregory was Jackie's nine-year-old brother; Jackie was seven years old.

"You have to take the axe and swing it all the way back. It hurts my arms and right here," Jackie remembered as she pointed to her shoulders, apparently too young to known the word for them.[534]

PROTECTING CHILD LABOR

Like all of the issues discussed in this book, the facts were hardly hidden from view. Human Rights Watch was a respected global charity whose child tobacco labor report was covered in hundreds of articles, including in the *Wall Street Journal*, *Washington Post*, *New York Times*, Associated Press, *Time* and *CNN*.[535] The lead investigator published an op-ed in the *Richmond Times-Dispatch*:

> *"Theo," a 16-year-old Virginia boy, told me how he felt while cutting down tobacco plants during the harvest: "I got sick to my stomach and a little dizzy, and I felt like I was going to throw up." Fourteen-year-old "Jacob" also worked on tobacco farms in Virginia. "I get a little bit queasy, and I get lightheaded and dizzy," he said. "Sometimes I feel like I might pass out. It just feels like I want to fall over."[536]*

In response, Delegate Alfonso Lopez introduced a one-page bill to ban child labor in tobacco fields, with exemptions if the child or guardian gives consent or if children worked at farms owned by a family member. In addition, the bill funded one child labor inspector for the state.[537] Altria and R.J. Reynolds had ostensibly banned child labor in their supply chains for those under sixteen and pledged to increase worker safety protections for sixteen- and seventeen-year-old minors in response to the report.[538]

The bill's hearing drew emotional testimony from children's advocates and former laborers.

"One of the refrains we hear from kids who do this kind of work is, when they get the tobacco sickness, they say, 'I felt like I was going to die,'" said Reid Maki of the Child Labor Coalition.[539]

There was a bipartisan consensus on what to do. Democratic Delegate Johnny Joannou abruptly asked one witness, "Are you saying my parents were stupid?" A reporter covering the hearing approached Joannou after the hearing, and he admitted that he did not work on a farm when he was young; rather, he washed dishes in his family's restaurant.[540] Republican Delegate Daniel Marshall stated, "My grandmother raised tobacco. I grew up in a tobacco family...Only thing they made were accusations, didn't hear any facts. The other issue that I worried about is it [*sic*] tobacco this year, what's next year?"[541] The bill was tabled by an unrecorded voice vote, where it died without any other action.[542]

It bears mentioning that these politicians did not have an aversion to passing major regulations that raised taxes on virtually all Virginians, as in

Dominion's $2.8 billion refund-killing scheme. Their positions on child labor could not fairly be attributed to anti-government principles. They worked for the government and were enriched by it, after all. It was not easy to comprehend how the political response to a conflict between child laborers and cigarette companies benefited cigarette companies, yet that was exactly what happened.

CIGARETTE POLITICS

The tobacco industry came under enhanced scrutiny in the 1990s after internal documents revealed a half-century-long campaign of propaganda, ingratiation, corruption and conspiracy. Food and Drug Administration commissioner David Kessler, who served under Presidents George H.W. Bush and Bill Clinton, wrote in his memoir about whistleblowers who came forward with documents that proved tobacco corporations not only buried the incontrovertible evidence tying cigarettes to lung cancer but also intentionally manipulated the nicotine content of cigarettes in order to create generations of customer addicts.[543] His team's work led to the landmark 1998 Master Settlement Agreement (MSA), which resolved lawsuits from forty-six state attorneys general in exchange for hundreds of billions of dollars over twenty-five years and marketing restrictions to mitigate childhood smoking.[544]

After the MSA, Altria changed its business practices, but not in the way one might have expected. First, it adopted the name Altria in an attempt to shed the tarnished Philip Morris brand name. The American public, in general, despised the tobacco industry, with roughly four out of five believing that it deceived the public in order to sell harmful and addictive products.[545] Second, it stepped up marketing efforts, focusing on youth. Third, it increased promotion of smokeless tobacco products unaffected by the MSA. Lastly, it exported the century-long American campaign of lies and addiction across the developing world, where most of its users and profits originated in the next century.[546] Instead of forming smaller, issue-specific front groups, these global expansion efforts have used the U.S. Chamber of Commerce to push their agenda.[547]

Was the coddling of Altria due to economic impact? By 2015, tobacco was the tenth-largest agricultural commodity in Virginia, behind chickens, cattle, milk, soybeans, turkeys, greenhouses/nurseries, corn, hay and

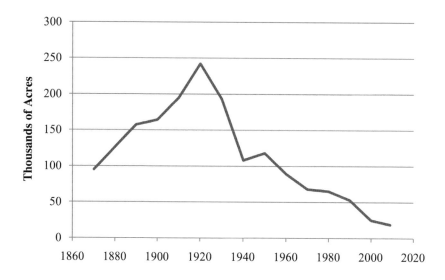

Virginia Tobacco Acreage, 1870–2009. *Center for Tobacco Control Research and Education at the University of California, "The High Cost of Compromise: Tobacco Industry Political Influence and Tobacco Control Policy in Virginia, 1977–2009," 2010, p. 15.*

wheat.[548] The decline of tobacco had nothing to do with partisan politics but was part of a trend dating to the 1920s.[549] Virginia produced 7 percent of American tobacco, and in 2007, the last year for which statistics were available, 895 Virginia farms produced tobacco, compared to 8,113 tobacco farms in Kentucky.[550]

Despite tobacco's low value compared to crops such as hay, Virginia politicians seemed to reflexively protect the cigarette industry. Virginia's thirty-cent tax per cigarette pack was the second-lowest in the nation, behind Missouri.[551] Jonnie Williams's Star Scientific was a tobacco company that sought to test its snake oil on state employees. And Virginia's loose tobacco laws were one of the reasons Richmond was ranked as the worst city for asthma sufferers in the United States in 2010, 2011, 2013 and 2014.[552]

It looked like Altria bought legislative loyalty with cold, hard cash. Besides Dominion, Altria was the most generous corporate donor to state candidates.[553] On a scale of 0 to 10 (total opposition to total support of cigarette regulations), researchers found that "for every $1,000 in campaign contributions [from tobacco interests] received in 2007, legislators were -0.6 points more pro-tobacco industry and for every $1,000 in total contributions [from all sources] they were on average -0.1 points more pro-tobacco."[554] Altria's campaign contributions totaled more than $5 million over the past twenty years; only nineteen legislators in the period from 1999 to 2007 did not receive money from tobacco companies.[555] A number of legislators had financial stakes in cigarettes. Senator Walter Stosch, who served from 1990 to 2016, was appointed to the board of Universal Corporation in 2000.[556] Disclosures revealed that Delegate Delores McQuinn made "more than $10,000," the highest disclosure bracket, working for Altria each year from 2009 to 2012.[557] Former lieutenant governor John Hager was a tobacco executive.[558] Many legislators were heavily invested in the cigarette company they regulated.

TABLE 5. LEGISLATORS OWNING ALTRIA STOCK, 2014*

Legislator	Value of Altria Stock
Peter Farrell	$50,001 to $250,000
Lynwood Lewis	$5,001 to $50,000
Manoli Loupassi	$5,001 to $50,000
Delores McQuinn	More than $250,000
Randy Minchew	$5,001 to $50,000
Frank Wagner	$5,001 to $50,000

People in the highest strata of power typically had overlapping corporate and philanthropic board memberships.[559] Dominion and Altria, Richmond's corporate-political behemoths, possessed concentric spheres of influence in 2016.

TABLE 6. OVERLAP BETWEEN ALTRIA, DOMINION AND UVA BOARDS OF DIRECTORS

Altria Board**	Title	Dominion Board†	Title
Martin Barrington	CEO, Altria	Tom Farrell	CEO, Dominion; UVA Rector (ret.)

* Virginia Public Access Project, "Altria: Candidates Who Own Stock in Altria, 2014," http://vpap.org/seis/stockholders/110931-altria.
** Altria Group, Inc., "Board of Directors," http://www.altria.com/About-Altria/Board-of-Directors-and-Committees/Board-of-Directors/Pages/default.aspx.
† Dominion Resources, Inc., "Board of Directors," https://www.dom.com/corporate/investors/governance/board-of-directors.

Altria Board	Title	Dominion Board	Title
Tom Farrell	CEO, Dominion	Michael Szymanczyk	CEO, Altria (ret.)
Gerald Baliles	VA Governor (ret.)	Helen Dragas	UVA Rector (ret.)
John Casteen	UVA President (ret.)	Mark Kington	UVA Vice Rector (resigned)
7 Others		6 Others	

As we saw with the nonsensical Dominion refund bill, which effectively raised taxes on Virginians and businesses, it was hard to reconcile these corporations' political power with their economic contributions, which in Altria's case was decidedly negative.

Co-opting Virginia Commonwealth University

Even after the MSA, Altria stuck by its model of funding outside research. In 2008, it struck up an unusually strict bargain with Virginia Commonwealth University under which VCU scientists worked essentially as paid contractors using university facilities. Their work was classified as proprietary information for Altria, which reserved the right to veto any publication of their findings. The contract broke university rules governing intellectual property and went against the widespread movement of medical schools and health organizations refusing cigarette money.[560] A director of the Virginia chapter of the American Lung Association said, "VCU is a public institution to serve the public good; tobacco has harmed public health more than any other product in history."[561]

The courtship was not one-sided. That year, Jerome Strauss, the dean of VCU Medical School, approached Altria with a proposal to test the effects of nicotine patches on pregnant women and their unborn children. A Duke University researcher drily summarized his own Altria-funded research on the topic: "Basically we found that nicotine during development is not a good thing."[562] Altria turned down the idea, and Strauss continued to serve as dean in 2016.[563]

Cigarette Slush Fund

The payments made to Virginia under the MSA were split: 10 percent to prevent childhood smoking and obesity, 40 percent to health care and 50 percent to the Tobacco Indemnification and Community Revitalization Commission, an economic development fund for historically tobacco-producing counties.[564] About half the total money had been paid out to Virginia, or $2 billion out of $4 billion total, as of 2014.[565] The commission was a prism reflecting every facet of the Virginia Way.

Shortly after the commission was founded in 1999, member and state secretary of finance John Forbes presented it with a proposal to grant $5 million to the Literary Foundation of Virginia (LFV), which received two installments of $2.5 million. LFV was a paper foundation headed by his wife and, after his 2002 retirement, Forbes himself for annual salaries of $130,000. Forbes constructed two other shell entities to pass wire transfers from LFV as payment for services that never occurred. He would subsequently use the bank account of the final shell entity as a personal account. Of the $5 million, Forbes stole $4 million for himself and his wife.[566] He then attempted to conceal his fraud from FBI investigators.[567] He pleaded guilty in federal court in 2010 and received ten years' imprisonment.[568]

While there appeared to be no interest in oversight of external grants, the commission chairman, Delegate Terry Kilgore, maneuvered millions of dollars in grants close to home. His father, John Kilgore Sr., was head of the Scott County Telephone Cooperative board, which was awarded more than $7 million from the commission. The board paid the elder Kilgore "about $20,000 in 2012 for working an average of one hour a week." The Scott County Economic Development Authority, headed by Terry's brother John Jr., received more than $14 million from the commission. In the sixteen-year history of the commission, Terry had been vice-chairman for ten and chairman for four and had not recused himself from voting for family members' projects.[569]

Jonnie Williams testified that he sought money from the commission to study his irradiated tobacco pills.[570] Terry Kilgore's twin brother, former attorney general and gubernatorial nominee Jerry Kilgore, testified that he worked as a lobbyist for Williams and suggested that Williams ask the commission for money.[571] Unbelievably, Jerry was also Williams's lawyer during the McDonnell trial.[572]

Economic development was something of a misnomer throughout the commission's history. When Dominion needed a pipeline built to a new power plant, the commission calculated that a grant of $6.5 million would aid construction. Then, the commission voted to give Dominion's pipeline partner $30 million. It was reported that the grant money was inflated due to pressure from McDonnell's office. "I think we ought to be able to ask questions and find out what's happening," said Delegate Tommy Wright. "Having said that, I still support the project."[573]

Much of the money did not aid economic development. For those inheriting archaic federal allotments of four-acre tobacco farms, the commission was a windfall. Journalist Peter Galuszka discovered that "many holders didn't even live in Virginia. In Brunswick County, about 28 percent didn't live in Virginia but in cities such as Philadelphia, Baltimore and Las Vegas. On Halifax County's list, one holder lived on the Gold Coast of downtown Chicago."[574]

An in-depth investigation of six Danville grant recipients by the *Danville Register & Bee* discovered a pattern of broken promises:

- North American Mold Technology received $520,000 for pledging to hire 120 employees. The most recent figures showed it had 64 employees on the payroll with one more year left to meet its obligations. This was the most "successful" of the companies examined.
- Norhurt received $625,000 for pledging a $2.2 million investment and had invested only $1.1 million.
- U.S. Green Energy received $1.6 million for pledging to create 372 jobs. Instead, it had "anywhere from three to 30 part-time workers on the floor above a $15 an hour pay level."
- Hybrid Vehicles received $420,000 for pledging to create 150 jobs. The most recent filings stated the company had nine employees.
- Allergease received $1.25 million for pledging to hire 150 employees. The company later reported having 4 employees.
- River District Development received $250,000 from the commission and $600,000 from the governor's economic development fund for pledging to hire forty employees and keep an additional sixty on the payroll. The reporter found that the company had zero employees.

Finally, the commission was at the center of backroom dealings that helped scuttle the prospects for Medicaid expansion. In January 2014, Democrats regained Senate control with Lieutenant Governor Ralph Northam's ability to cast a tiebreaking 21–20 vote.[575] In their budgets, Democrats included Medicaid expansion, Governor McAuliffe's top campaign promise; House Republicans did not, and a July 1 government shutdown loomed if neither side blinked.[576] That June, Senator Phil Puckett resigned his seat, throwing control of the Senate to Republicans.[577] It was found that Puckett had abdicated in exchange for employment on the commission and a state judgeship for his daughter.[578] McAuliffe's chief of staff and U.S. Senator Mark Warner called Puckett and Puckett's son to try to prevent his resignation, and Warner allegedly dangled a federal judgeship for Puckett's daughter.[579] Senate Republicans passed a new budget stripped of the language in the Democratic budget that would have permitted a backdoor Medicaid expansion, and McAuliffe was left to either sign a budget or shut down the government in the face of a united legislature. He signed.[580] The FBI, U.S. Attorney's Office and a federal grand jury investigated the scandal and declined to indict.[581] In January 2015, the legislature elected Puckett's daughter, Martha Puckett Ketron, to a judgeship.[582]

A 2011 audit suggested reforms and "said the tobacco commission is too large, does not meet frequently enough and fails to scrutinize projects."[583] Only nine of the twenty-six recommended reforms had been even partly implemented three years later.[584] In 2015, Terry Kilgore sponsored a successful bill to modestly reform the commission, including changing the name, posting grant awards online and requiring that at least thirteen of the twenty-eight members "have experience in business, economic development, investment banking, finance, or education"—seemingly quite broad criteria.[585]

Tobacco commission money was supposed to mitigate the consequences of deindustrialization, yet in one columnist's mind, it functioned as "a slush fund to help the politically connected," whose failure kept many in Virginia's poorest counties mired in desperation and pain.[586]

TRAFFICKING VERSUS TAXES

Thirty-one-year-old Maher Mustafa was confident in his cigarette smuggling prowess. From 2014 to 2015, he allegedly made more than 350 cash withdrawals over the federal reporting requirement level of $10,000 and neglected to report any of them. He left behind a note in a safe deposit box found by investigators: "Dear Agent…Good luck. Try to be faster and smarter next time. Have a good day."[587]

With the second-lowest cigarette taxes in the nation, experts noted that Virginia's $0.30-per-pack tax was a magnet for cigarette traffickers in New York City, where taxes of $5.85 a pack ensured enormous profits on the black market.[588] An estimated 20 percent of cigarettes, or 100 million per year, bought in Virginia were smuggled out of the state.[589] Cigarette smuggling brought with it a series of crimes, "among them burglary, credit card fraud, identity theft, money laundering—and possibly murder."[590] Virginia lost revenue from smuggling: wholesale buyers at places like Sam's Club avoided the Virginia tax, which was collected at the retail level.[591] Two responses were given when a reporter pointed out that the problem would be mitigated if cigarette taxes were raised. Many described the power of tobacco companies' campaign contributions in determining public policy. Others, including physician and delegate John O'Bannon, as well as an Altria spokesperson, blamed New York.[592]

POWER PLANT POLLUTION

Cigarettes were not Virginians' only source of illness. Coal country dominated the list of the worst American cities for mortality from power plant pollution. Out of the 359 largest cities in the country, Virginia's Roanoke, Danville, Winchester, Lynchburg, Bristol and Harrisonburg were all in the top twenty.[593] Virginia as a whole was the seventh-worst state for death rates from power plant pollution and the only state with a coastline in the top ten. An estimated 358 Virginians died every year from power plant emissions.[594]

Dominion had a long history of pollution and violations. In 2003, it agreed to pay $1.2 billion, the largest settlement for Clean Air Act violations in the nation's history.[595] Its official corporate history took a creative view of this:

> *Today, Dominion's environmental focus is sharper than ever. Not only does the company strive to comply with all environmental rules and regulations set forth by the EPA and state agencies, it also takes proactive steps to help shape the law in ways that benefit the company and its customers. Perhaps the most notable example is the company's historic 2003 settlement with the EPA governing air emissions.*[596]

Why exactly the settlement was "historic" was not mentioned, but the company's laser-like focus on environmental protection seemed not to have lasted. Almost exactly ten years later, Dominion entered a consent decree with the EPA to pay more than $13 million for polluting states in the Midwest and Northeast.[597] In 2015, the Nuclear Regulatory Commission (NRC) said that three infractions, one of which was a "willful violation" of safety reporting guidelines, were uncovered at a Dominion nuclear plant in Connecticut.[598] "The three apparent violations, which follow three mid-level safety violations at Millstone [nuclear plant] in 2014 and a fourth last month, also have prompted Connecticut officials to request a special meeting with the NRC," a reporter noted.[599]

Two of the largest coal companies in the United States also paid large fines as part of consent agreements for polluting Virginia. In 2011, Arch Coal agreed to pay $4 million for alleged violations of the Clean Water Act in Virginia, West Virginia and Kentucky.[600] Three years later, Bristol-headquartered Alpha Natural Resources agreed to pay more than $200 million for over six thousand violations of the Clean Water Act related to coal mining in Appalachia.[601] A quarter of Virginia's "river and stream miles and about 80 percent of the surface areas of our lakes and streams (including the Bay) are now 'impaired' by bacterial or chemical pollution," wrote Virginia's top environmental journalist.[602] As of 2012, Virginia was the fifth-worst state in the country for toxic waste dumping in freshwater sources, according to the Environment America Research and Policy Center.[603]

Richmond used to be the headquarters of Massey Energy, which operated politically much like Altria and Dominion. After a 2010 explosion at Upper Big Branch mine killed twenty-nine miners and revealed systemic violations of health and safety laws, the company was bought by Alpha Natural Resources, which subsumed it under its headquarters in Bristol.[604] It seemed to maintain Massey's influence peddling and donated more than $3 million to Virginia politicians from 2003 to 2016.[605]

Burning coal produced tons of toxic coal ash, and at a time when government incompetence in Flint, Michigan, was making national headlines for poisoning that city's water supply, two state governments' reactions to its dumping in state rivers illustrate important contrasts.[606] Dominion greeted the new year in 2016 by securing a permit to dump 255 million gallons of its coal waste, including more than three times the safe limit for the known carcinogen hexavalent chromium made infamous in the film *Eric Brockovich*, into the James River upstream from where Richmond drew its drinking water.[607] Not to worry, a Dominion spokesperson assured Richmonders, the president of Dominion "has paddled on the James since he was a child and has been known to kayak or canoe to work." Dominion will test its own toxic waste, "and we will post the results of the water testing on our website to make sure the process is transparent." Therefore, its safety will be ensured.[608]

The company's assurances of safety were the same even when it had not followed its touted cleanup methods, or any cleanup methods at all. Reporters at *InsideNoVA* got Dominion to admit one year after the fact that it had dumped thirty-three million gallons of untreated coal ash wastewater into a tributary of the Potomac River, which divided parts of Virginia from Maryland. An aerial tour by an environmental watchdog showed "a pumping mechanism, lighting and piping" going from the coal ash pond directly into the creek, which "suggested the pond water was drained at night." Dominion then promised to treat the waste before dumping it.[609] It was later revealed that Virginia's top environmental official, tasked with approving these dumping permits, had attended the 2013 Masters Golf Tournament on Dominion's dime.[610] Maryland's Republican governor, Larry Hogan, who was not co-opted by Dominion's campaign contributions, sued Virginia and Democrat Terry McAuliffe's administration for permitting the discharge.[611]

"The ash pond closure project now taking place at Possum Point is a positive environmental development," said spokesperson David Botkins. "We are following sound, established practices as well as the letter of state and federal law. We are being pro-active, safe and working with a sense of urgency." Dominion dumped toxic waste at night, denied doing so for a year, reversed itself once caught and told the public it was a "safe" and "positive environmental development."[612] It also expected the public to believe it would objectively test the effluent it was dumping into Richmond's water supply because the president of Dominion "has been known to kayak or canoe to work."[613]

CAMPUS COAL PLANT SICKENED STUDENTS

A small power plant sat across Old Turner Street from Virginia Tech dormitory Thomas Hall. Every week or so, trucks dumped piles of coal on the ground, where it lay until it was burned.[614] Students had protested the health consequences of the plant, which provided 7 percent of campus electricity, for over a decade.[615] In the case of Haley Fuller, "I had never really been sick in my life. I go to Thomas Hall and I first break out with a virus that gave me hives all over my body. But most notably was the sinus infection that I had that continued for about a month."[616]

For Ann Bruce:

> *At the beginning of the year we were encouraged to put filters in our windows, but my roommate and I decided not to just because we didn't think much of it at the time. But, at the end of the year during move out day, I remember touching the inside of the window frame, and I had black coal ash all over my hand. I was shocked because I realized I had been breathing that all year, which may have explained why I had two cases of bronchitis and a lung infection that year.*[617]

Another student had the following experience:

> *While living in Thomas, Catlett suffered severe health problems including tonsillitis and pharyngitis, and she was told by doctors at Schiffert Health Center that the problems were caused by exposure to coal dust from the plant.*

"I lived there my first semester and got sick six or seven times. I got to the point where they put me on antibiotics for the whole semester," Catlett said. "I missed most of my classes, because I was up all night because I couldn't breathe." Catlett moved to Main Eggleston Hall during the second semester of her freshman year and has not had respiratory problems since.

Virginia Tech spokesman Mark Owczarski said in 2006, "I do know that there are discussions looking into ways to improve upon and exceed the federal standards. When that money is available and when it is possible to do so, I'm sure the university will move in that direction."[618] At a 2011 protest calling for shutting down the power plant, students pointed out that their university had enough funds for a $94 million arts center.[619] Virginia Tech's total budget was $1.28 billion in 2013–14.[620] In 2012, Thomas Hall became the residence of Corps of Cadets (military education) students, who had less institutional freedom to speak out, a campus reporter wrote.[621] Energy expert Peter Galuszka noted, "As the usual way of doing business prevails, the cycle of injustice endures."[622]

In a similar case in Alexandria, Virginia, citizens painstakingly proved that a layer of fine ash coating their neighborhoods originated from a nearby power plant. They discovered "fine particulates, which can easily spread many miles downwind and have been found to be a public health hazard, triggering respiratory disease. They are also an important risk factor for cardiopulmonary and lung cancer."[623] Once that was demonstrated, it was only a matter of time until the plant shut down.[624] This initial finding was not in doubt in the case of Virginia Tech, which in 2016 was still exposing its students to carcinogens and itself to lawsuits.

Despite the known health and environmental consequences, Virginia continued to subsidize coal. A 2011 state audit concluded that the $31 million annual coal tax credit did not have any effect on coal industry employment and economic activity.[625] Four years later, Dominion lobbyists arrested the legislative momentum behind reducing the coal tax credits, and Governor McAuliffe vetoed their extension. The legislature reauthorized the wasteful coal tax credits for another five years in 2016, and McAuliffe again vetoed their extension in 2016.[626]

CURRENT AND FUTURE CLIMATE CHANGE

The Virginia Constitution was perhaps unique in the world in explicitly recognizing the importance of oyster life, in Article XI, Section 3: "The natural oyster beds, rocks, and shoals in the waters of the Commonwealth shall not be leased, rented, or sold but shall be held in trust for the benefit of the people of the Commonwealth."[627] In 2014, the Chesapeake Bay was 30 percent more acidic than it was before the industrial revolution, driving a 98 percent decrease in the oyster population.[628]

Evidence indicated that Virginia's climate was changing. If trends continued, "then Virginia will be as hot as South Carolina sometime around 2050, and as hot as northern Florida by about the year 2100."[629] Duke University scientist James Clark had been running experiments on the effect of higher carbon dioxide on forest growth, and he found that, unfortunately, plants in mid-Atlantic latitudes did not seem to grow more or alter their growing seasons in higher carbon dioxide environments.[630]

The worst-case scenario for sea level rise was seven and a half feet by 2100. Virginia's largest city, Virginia Beach, along with New Orleans, was at or near the top of many experts' lists for American cities most susceptible to sea level rise.[631] If the ocean rose by just one-fifth that much, one and a half feet, large swaths of Virginia Beach, Hampton Roads, Norfolk, Chesapeake, Suffolk, Newport News, James City County, Charles City County, New Kent County, Henrico County, Richmond County and the Eastern Shore would be inundated, with larger sections flooded during storm surges.[632] Hampton Roads, which witnessed more than a foot of sea level rise in the last century, was, at the same time,

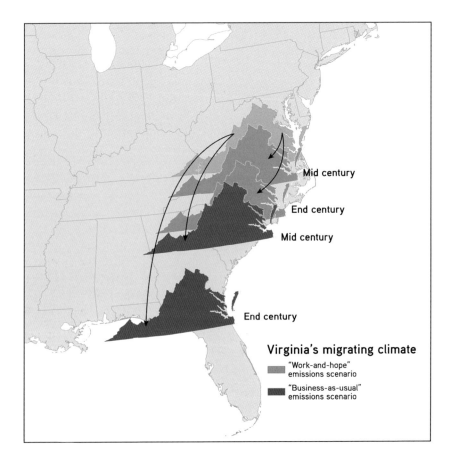

Projected changes to Virginia climate this century. *Steve Nash*, Virginia Climate Fever.

sinking and was accordingly "experiencing the highest sea level rise [of any locale] along the Atlantic Coast."[633]

How did Virginia's government prepare for this? The Office of Climatology had a single employee.[634] Governor Kaine, who served from 2006 to 2010, convened a climate panel that included one climate scientist.[635] McDonnell shelved its recommendations, and McAuliffe asked that they be reexamined in another report.[636] "The Virginia Department of Environmental Quality does not have the expertise to study climate change issues," wrote a spokesperson. There was no agricultural research on climate change at Virginia's land grant colleges, and there were no guidelines from engineers at the Department of Transportation.[637] The Virginia legislature remained reactionary and "opposed using the term 'climate change,'" while Dillon's rule compounded the problems by hamstringing local government responses.[638]

The most notorious story of Virginia and climate change was former attorney general Ken Cuccinelli's internationally lampooned "witch hunt" against a former University of Virginia climate professor, five years after a similar stunt from a Texas politician had come up empty.[639] Scientists were committing civil disobedience to attempt to stop climate change, but for Virginia politicians, it seemed that, as author Clive Hamilton put it, "things whose existence is not morally possible cannot exist."[640]

SMITHFIELD'S ABUSES

For decades, Smithfield Foods was a Virginia-based pig monopoly that bought legislatures and bankrupted small farms by vertically integrating American agriculture and remaking farm communities into contract labor fiefdoms. To do so, Smithfield carved a path out of the state's environment and well-being, according to agriculture reporter Christopher Leonard.[641]

Not to be outdone by Dominion's record-breaking Clean Air Act settlement, in 1997 Smithfield recorded the largest Clean Water Act fine in American history for its 6,982 violations. The company had been dumping pools of untreated pig effluent into the Pagan River in violation of a 1991 consent agreement requiring it to treat its animals' waste.[642] Scientists noted that "industrial pig waste contains a host of pernicious substances: ammonia, hydrogen sulfide, cyanide, phosphates, nitrates, and heavy metals. The waste also nurses more than 100 microbial pathogens that cause illness in humans, including salmonella, cryptosporidia, streptococci, and giardia."[643] At the time, the Pagan River downstream from the dumping site had been off limits to shellfishing for the last "27 years because of high levels of fecal bacteria and is considered unhealthy for swimming."[644] At the trial, plant supervisor Terry Rettig was sentenced to thirty months in jail for falsifying safety documents and destroying evidence.[645]

Smithfield harmed humans and animals. An undercover investigation of Smithfield's factory farm in Waverly, Virginia, by the Humane Society of the United States documented:

> *A lame pig was shot in the forehead with a stun gun and thrown into a trash bin while still alive. A video shows the large pig with "kill" spray-painted*

on its back being dragged by its snout, shot in the head and thrown into a large trash bin while trying to wiggle free, then breathing heavily as it lay dying, surrounded by dead pigs.

Employees jabbed pigs with gate rods to get them to move.

Pigs biting their crates—what the organization called a sign of frustration—so hard they bled.

Pigs with open sores because they couldn't move in the crates.

An employee cut a basketball-sized abscess from a pig's neck with an unsterilized razor.[646]

Three workers were fired after evidence of this abuse was reported.[647]

In 2013, Smithfield was sold to Chinese meat company Shuanghui International Holdings.[648] Spokespeople said that Smithfield would operate much the same, though the new company's top priority would be making more meat for Asia.[649]

Virginia and the nation were facing an epidemic of obesity and associated health problems, which, like cigarettes, were being exported across the globe, even though the connections between disease and meat eating were well known.[650] A large study concluded that there was a "roughly 40% reduction in mortality from cancer in vegetarians and fish eaters compared with meat eaters."[651] The American Heart Association stated that "many studies have shown that vegetarians seem to have a lower risk of obesity, coronary heart disease (which causes heart attack), high blood pressure, diabetes mellitus and some forms of cancer."[652] Specifically, red meat consumption was correlated with higher rates of colorectal, esophageal, liver and lung cancers.[653] Consequently, the American Heart Association advocated replacing red with lean meats, while limiting processed meat (bacon, hot dogs, sausage, et cetera), while the American Institute for Cancer Research recommended that individuals limit their consumption of red meats to less than three ounces per day and avoid processed red meats entirely.[654] Researchers at the Johns Hopkins Bloomberg School of Public Health wrote:

A strong body of scientific evidence links excess meat consumption, particularly of red and processed meat, with heart disease, stroke, type 2 diabetes, obesity, certain cancers, and earlier death. Diets high in vegetables, fruits, whole grains and beans can help prevent these diseases and promote health in a variety of ways. Why does meat increase health risks? Studies give several reasons: high saturated fat and cholesterol content, high energy density, carcinogenic compounds found in processed meat and formed during high-temperature cooking, a compound called L-carnitine in red meat that may promote plaque build-up in the arteries, and the lack of health-protective plant foods in high-meat diets.[655]

The chairman of Harvard's nutrition department stated, "If you step back and look at the data, the optimum amount of red meat you eat should be zero."[656]

With this evidence, it was striking that meats from companies like Smithfield remained at the center of American plates. Scientists and nutritionists had known since at least the 1970s that eating meat and animal products like cheese, except for small quantities of lean meats, had severe health consequences, but food policy expert Marion Nestle noted that this message was scuttled by the meat industry co-opting Congress for decades, just as cigarette companies had.[657] Leonard contended that despite scientific guidance, the global paradox of starvation and obesity was largely driven by a continued Depression-era policy of subsidizing American grain crops to the tune of billions of dollars per year.[658]

RICHMOND'S TRAGEDY AND BEACON

We have seen the effects of corporate politics on rural Virginians, but what about cities? Life expectancy was sixty-three years in Haiti, Sudan and Richmond's Gilpin Court.[659] VCU researchers mapped the extreme health disparity in Virginia's capital, where concentrated pockets of poverty coexisted with ostentatious wealth.

Gilpin Court was the oldest public housing project in Richmond, a part of North Jackson Ward formed as pieces of Richmond's tapestry were torn asunder by the 1950s construction of Interstates 95 and 64, which merged to run through the former epicenter of Richmond's African American culture and civic life.[660] A snapshot revealed that the disparities within Richmond were more severe than in the surrounding counties.[661] Story after story depicted a cycle of violence and deprivation. To pick one month at random, as Richmond's police chief was leading a walking tour through Gilpin Court in April 2015, a youth was shot on the street two blocks away.[662] One week later, four people were shot in broad daylight on a Sunday afternoon.[663] A few days after that, two hundred residents in the eleven-story senior living tower suffered a forty-eight-hour blackout.[664] Residents endured five days without hot water later that spring.[665]

Twenty-four-year-old Shanika Williams was not surprised by these statistics because she had "experienced a homicide in these areas plenty of times of someone close to me, compared to a neighborhood that's not in the projects."[666] Across town in Westover Hills, life expectancy was the highest in the city at eighty-three years.

Richmonders did not have to search for emergency care like those in Wise County. All comers were served by the physicians and health staff at VCU's Medical Center, one block north of Capitol Square. Abutting Interstate 95, the Medical Center stood "as an architectural gateway, a symbol of our city," I wrote in an op-ed supporting a children's hospital there.[667] Patrons represented a melting pot of central Virginia—everyone gets sick at one time or another, after all. The child who was shot during the police chief's tour was taken there, as was Governor McAuliffe when he broke seven ribs after being bucked from a horse.[668] An in-depth profile noted that miracles took place every day in the emergency room, one of five Level I trauma centers in the state.[669]

The VCU hospitals were excellent, but they were not out of the ordinary. Much of their physical plant, like the Critical Care tower, was new, but some was antiquated. If the state legislature paid as much attention to all corners of Virginia as it did to itself, perhaps all citizens would have had access to a good hospital. Political stonewalling was arguably the only roadblock stopping all Virginians from enjoying the health care birthright of citizens in England, Israel, Japan and all other developed countries.[670] One economist calculated that if the United States spent as much per person and cut out inefficient insurance and government bureaucracies—as those nations that covered everybody did—our country would be running surpluses instead of deficits far into the future.[671]

HOPE AND ASHES: "I GUESS THAT SOUNDS CONTRADICTORY"

"Are you unaware," Rousseau asked, "that vast numbers of your fellow men suffer or perish from need of the things that you have to excess?"[672]

Six years after its first report on southwest Virginia, the *60 Minutes* team returned to visit Virginians waiting on care dispensed from a clunky Winnebago.[673] They interviewed Glenda Moore, a McDonald's biscuit maker and smoker who could not afford health insurance. She would qualify for Medicaid if it was expanded in Virginia.

"They did a CAT Scan and an X-ray and found the blood clot had went [*sic*] to my lung," Moore said. "But they also saw another mass on my lung. And then transported me to a bigger hospital. They found the lesions in my brain, so I was diagnosed with stage IV lung cancer and brain cancer."

"What are the doctors telling you?" asked the newsman.

"I start my treatment on Monday, the brain radiation, and he seemed very, I mean, he seemed optimistic."

"Are you hopeful?"

"I am. I have been. I don't know, I just feel very hopeful."

It was pointed out during Virginia's Medicaid debate that legislators gave themselves full-time government-sponsored health insurance for part-time work.

> *"I'm a big proponent of having a part-time legislature," said Speaker of the House William J. Howell, R-Stafford. The benefit is legislators whose lives at work and in the community give them a better insight into the state's real needs, he said. But he also believes it's appropriate that legislators are the only part-timers entitled to enroll in the state's unusually generous health insurance plan, and to get a state pension when they retire.*
>
> *"I guess that sounds contradictory."*[674]

That settled, Speaker Howell continued blocking Medicaid. Three months after her interview, Glenda Moore was dead.

4

LOCAL GOVERNMENT

EDUCATION AND ECONOMIC DEVELOPMENT

The strong do what they can and the weak suffer what they must.
—Thucydides[675]

What caused Richmond to be America's asthma poster child?[676] As reported in *Style Weekly*:

> *In a 2000 study, the Joint Commission on Health Care told Gov. Jim Gilmore and the Virginia General Assembly that the level of asthma preparedness in state schools was inadequate. Asthma attacks were becoming a chief cause for school absences and the commission recommended developing an action plan. Yet in 2008, the Richmond Public Schools discontinued an in-school asthma awareness program created by Bon Secours and the Medical College of Virginia, called CARMA—Controlling Asthma in the Richmond Metro Area. Principals had decided to devote more time to standardized test preparation.*[677]

Another *Style Weekly* cover story investigated the sort of problems that caused Richmond's disease distinction.[678]

At a tour of Carver Elementary School, less than two miles from city hall and the Capitol, there were

> *three classrooms that everyone in the Richmond Public Schools and City Hall administration should be required to see: art, music and the gym.*

"The Moore Street School, built in the 19th century, is an attached annex of Carver Elementary. No longer in use, it's become a rodent-infested, dilapidated arm of the school, separated from students by plywood and drywall." *Tom Nash, "Caving In," Style Weekly, April 8, 2014, http://www.styleweekly.com/richmond/caving-in/Content?oid=2055218. Scott Elmquist.*

Each is worse than the last. In the art room, fabric replaces missing cabinet doors. There's little sunlight allowed through the gauzy haze of what passes for windows. The music room has a concave floor, no direct sunlight and two small space heaters. Then there's the gym, which is a set of hula hoops and a concrete floor, painted black.

Two years after these and other problems had been so prominently exposed, a sixteen-inch-long, five-pound piece of tile fell from the seventy-year-old building and hit an elementary student on the head while he was waiting in line.[679]

The reporter and school board vice-chair Kristin Larson toured Thompson Middle School, where

the smell of the tar water mixed with lemon-scented Lysol assaults the nostrils and doesn't let go…A school administrator tells Larson it's been getting worse. More leaks, more of the 504 students complaining of headaches. One teacher has called in sick. A student circulated a petition protesting the conditions. (She didn't have a hall pass and was reprimanded.)

The problem stems from a hasty patch job on the roof last spring. It was a stopgap measure whose time came and went.

Black water oozed from the roof and almost fell on Larson. "I wanted to leave the room and throw up," she said. The cost to fix the oozing Thompson roof was $90,000.

Next on the tour was Armstrong High School:

Never mind dead rodents—Armstrong fights live ones. It got so bad, she says, that snakes became a problem as well. Led around by an administrator who also doesn't want to be named, Gray looks at the locker rooms. The girls' is dominated by peeling paint, rust and a white residue that looks like it should wash off, but doesn't. The boys' is faring a little better since the last time she saw it. Shower floors are covered in cigarette butts, but the hardware is newer.

In the fall of 2015, the school left 975 students and their parents in limbo when it had to shut down for days in order to repair a broken cooling system.[680] That spring, school board officials said that if requested emergency funding was not forthcoming, they would have to close Armstrong, four elementary schools and two specialty schools in order to save a total of $3 million.[681]

Richmond superintendent Dana Bedden, who came to the job from Washington, D.C., said that Richmond's buildings were the worst he had ever seen. The previous year's school facilities report called for $26 million in immediate repairs—but Larson and school board member Kim Gray looked and discovered similar dire reports from 2002 and 2007, none of them acted on.[682]

THE MAYOR TOOK ACTION

Richmond government found itself with a small surplus in 2014 as the economy emerged from a long recession. Mayor Dwight Jones proposed cutting real estate taxes from 1.20 percent to 1.19 percent per year at a total cost of $2 million citywide, so owners of a $400,000 home, for example, would save $40 in taxes per year.

The mayor dismissed the need for school repairs by saying, "The reality is that only about 11 percent of our population is being served by" public schools.[683] His spokesperson added, "We seem to talk as though every household is sending kids to schools. I think about 11 percent of our population is representing the kids who need to be served in schools. When you start speaking…like it's the entire city's responsibility, maybe all the residents, maybe all the taxpayers, maybe don't feel that way if they're not using the public schools."[684] To clarify, 11 percent of Richmonders were students, notwithstanding families and businesses who depended on public schools. Paul Goldman and Norman Leahy noted that Mayor Jones's gaffe was nearly identical to the damaging contention by 2012 Republican presidential nominee Mitt Romney that "there are 47 percent who are with [President Obama], who are dependent upon government, who believe that they are victims, who believe the government has a responsibility to care for them, who believe that they are entitled to health care, to food, to housing, to you-name-it." This view was so extreme that it may have scuttled his presidential prospects.[685] Virginia's Democratic establishment, on the other hand, was silent in the face of Jones's "11 percent" comments.[686]

REDSKINS REDISTRIBUTION

The reticence to spend money in order to clean up Richmond's toxic schools appeared to vanish when the Washington Redskins headed south seeking handouts. The team was hardly pressed for cash; the Redskins were the ninth-wealthiest sports franchise in the world, ahead of all NBA franchises, and college teams of any sport.[687] Its players enjoyed similar status. Its defense alone ran up a $22,159 dinner at one Washington steakhouse.[688] Yet for them, fiscal scolding about "11 percent" was suspended in favor of a public trough that runneth over.

Richmond contracted with the Redskins to bring their seventeen-day training camp to town in exchange for constructing a $10 million training facility on city land, among other goodies. Mayor Jones promised that the city would see an additional $8.5 million in economic activity each year as a result and was ridiculed by experts. Sports economist Rob Baade noted that money spent on recreation was typically constant; in other words, camp attendees would simply spend less money elsewhere, for no net economic gain.[689] Regardless, the deal was inked. The city donated a seventeen-acre parcel, including a recycling center, community garden, wooded area and parking lot, on prime land adjacent to the Science Museum of Virginia and Children's Museum of Richmond, and razed it.[690] Then, the city built artificial turf fields and a sports medicine facility.[691] Bon Secours, a health care nonprofit, put up $6.4 million for leasing one floor of the facility and the naming rights to the Bon Secours Washington Redskins Training Center.[692] A second-floor lessee and additional sponsors would bring in about $4 million, supporters said.[693]

In addition to economic revitalization, the camp was supposed to provide community benefits. It would be an "amenity-rich urban green space" and "year-round asset to the community," according to the mayor's spokesperson.[694] Richmond's press secretary said the location would be a "great fan viewing area during camp, but that doesn't suggest that it doesn't work for residents for the other 49 weeks of the year. It was precisely designed with the community in mind."[695]

During construction, which ran $1 million over budget, old-growth trees that were to be preserved for a park were bulldozed.[696] "This was tragic," said a local resident. "It was a beautiful park. These trees were probably 70 to 80 years old." Mayor Jones said that "we're going to find out exactly how it happened. Exactly why it happened." The next day, he released a statement saying the site was flattened deliberately. "Everyone knows we cannot put the trees back and this is not reversible," he stated. "I want to close by saying that I don't want this problem to deter us from completing this project."[697]

After the first Redskins training camp in 2013, businesses were incensed that the forecast windfall never materialized, "with only a nearby McDonald's, bar and diner reporting a significant increase in customers."[698] "I was very disappointed last year," said a local proprietor who set up outside the gates. "I did not feel any trickle down effect from this boon that was supposed to happen."[699] Local food trucks were barred from entering the gates in favor of national chains.[700] The year after, food truck spaces outside the camp cost $2,500, a fee that only five local restaurants paid. A hot dog vendor stated that he sold about fifteen hot dogs per day, 10 to 15 percent of his normal volume. Business was so bad that just two remained by the last day of camp.[701]

The Redskins solicited volunteer "ambassadors" to assist with crowd control, parking, information and other services. The team paid the city $65,000 for three hundred volunteers in 2014. For their labor, "the Redskins provide team pins to volunteers who work five seven-hour shifts. Those who work 10 shifts get to attend an autograph session. And those who work 13 shifts earn a trip to a game at FedEx field." The notion that citizens technically volunteered for the city was part of a convenient ruse, since "if

Mayor Jones is greeted by supporters at the Redskins Training Camp. *Tina Griego, "2013 Richmonder of the Year: Mayor Dwight C. Jones," Style Weekly, December 31, 2013, http://www. styleweekly.com/imager/mayor-dwight-c-jones-revels-in-the-grand/b/original/2011882/fad2/cover_feature1-1.jpg. Scott Elmquist.*

the Redskins had created the ambassadors program to recruit free help in the stadium on game days, there is little doubt it would violate federal wage and hour law," said University of Virginia law professor J.H. Verkerke.[702]

In his 2014 State of the City address, Mayor Jones maintained that "the plan generated $40 million in new private investment in the city."[703] His previously touted $8.5 million figure had inexplicably quadrupled. Politifact rated the statement "Half True," judging that the actual economic development figure was the money that the city itself had spent.[704] The facility's second-floor tenant never materialized, perhaps because it would be required to vacate the building each year for the entirety of the camp, and $1.1 million in anticipated sponsorship fees came to zero.[705] City officials abandoned the tenant search entirely in 2016.[706] If this was part of Jones's stated strategy of expanding the tax base in order to funnel revenue to poverty mitigation, it failed at step one.[707]

The Redskins' charitable foundation donated $100,000 to a high school football field, less than 1 percent of the public subsidy to their camp, to be paid only if matched with local contributions.[708] A poignant story illustrated the city's predicament:

A Richmond City Council resolution aimed at giving city high schools more use of the Bon Secours Washington Redskins Training Center has been scrapped by its patrons. The resolution…would have urged the Richmond Economic Development Authority to work with the Richmond School Board to allow six high school football games to be played at the facility each year. The resolution was withdrawn Thursday. The proposal failed to gain traction after school officials said they probably could not afford the costs involved, such as renting bleachers and lights.[709]

The fields sat unused for about 350 days per year.

Even this was not enough for the Redskins. When the NFL changed its rules on goalpost heights, Richmond footed the $4,353 bill for replacements.[710] Governor McDonnell gave $4 million toward the Redskins corporate offices in Northern Virginia, while Loudon County put up $2 million and Richmond another $400,000. The facilities receiving tax dollars were already located in Loudon.[711]

BALANCING THE LEDGER

To secure the camp deal, Bon Secours leased a former school building valued at $7.6 million for $5,000 per year for sixty years and agreed to pay $100,000 to Richmond Public Schools annually for ten years.[712] Bon Secours' initial $100,000 payment was not made until a former school board member inquired about its nonpayment six weeks after the money was due.[713]

Richmond Public Schools released the most extensive report on school facilities' needs in the city's history in 2015.[714] Its depths were almost unfathomable. In just eight of fifty-seven schools were no repairs necessary. One third of the city's schools were more than seventy years old, and another third were between fifty and seventy years old.[715] The report assessed most as in need of significant renovations and a dozen, including seven elementary schools, as so unsalvageable that they should be completely gutted or torn down. The estimated cost was $645 million over ten years just to get buildings up to date;[716] $645 million was a lot of money—less than three years of Dominion refunds under its 2015 rate hike bill or approximately the amount Virginia spent on economic development subsidies from 2010 to 2015.[717]

TABLE 7. RICHMOND PUBLIC SCHOOLS
COMPREHENSIVE FACILITIES NEEDS, 2015*

School Renovations	Complete/ Replace	Major	Moderate	Minor	Additions	No Work Necessary
Elementary	7	5	4	4	12	5
Middle	3	2	0	1	2	2
High	0	3	1	0	0	1
Specialty	2	1	1	2	0	0

"In consecutive years, a city school—Elkhardt Middle this year and Fairfield Court Elementary last year—had to be closed midyear because of health and safety issues," wrote a local sports columnist. "A city with school problems can't be asked to spend millions to placate a private enterprise."[718] In the upcoming school year, it was estimated that Richmond schools would have to spend $1.2 million on trailer rentals to serve seven overcrowded schools and $2.3 million the year after that. To alleviate the problems, Mayor Jones suggested consolidating and closing schools.[719] City councilwoman Kathy Graziano compared public schools to luxury goods, claiming that "it's like [school funding advocates are] saying 'I want to have a Gucci bag, but I don't have the money for a Gucci bag.'"[720] Their generous professional sports sponsorships devolved to wary penny-pinching when confronted with Richmond's public schools.[721]

BIG BUSINESS' SOLUTION

The plight of Richmond students cropped up on business radars from time to time. In 2007, twenty-six of the most powerful corporate leaders in Richmond released an open letter outlining their remedies for Richmond's public schools.[722]

We are convinced that the city is at a tipping point unlike any it has seen in over 150 years. One area continues to be of tremendous concern to us,

---

* Facilities Task Force, "Richmond Public Schools Facilities Needs Report for the Period of FY 2016—FY 2025," Richmond School Board, April 13, 2015, http://www.croppermap. com/documents/SBPresentationApril132015v3.pdf, 20.

however, and if it is not addressed now, will prevent the city from becoming a world-class place to live and work. This challenge is the performance of our city's public schools system, which continues to be one of the most expensive and least effective in Virginia—if not the nation…The educational statistics are alarming and constitute, in our view, an emergency situation that must be dealt with immediately and with bold action. A few facts stand out (based on 2004 figures from the SchoolMatters, a service of Standard & Poor's):

Richmond spends more than $10,500 a year for each student in its system, yet less than 57 percent of those funds actually go toward instruction rather than administration…

And Richmond Public Schools now spends more than $12,000 of its operating budget per student. So while Richmond spends the most among its peer localities, its students see the lowest percentage of resource in the classroom. These figures do not take into account the enormous amount of unused space in underutilized school buildings…

[Under our proposed reforms, a]*n elected School Board would be abolished…*

Richmond's schools are not producing the type of employees we need for the future in sufficient numbers…Together, we need to send a signal to the people of Richmond that its next generation of citizens will be successful, productive, and healthy, and that we will fight hard to make that promise come true. We stand ready to help.

It took journalists little time to reveal the authors' lack of basic familiarity with the problems of Richmond's public schools. *Style Weekly* reporter Chris Dovi interviewed the people one might expect to know and care about the problems (e.g., education leaders).[723]

Tichi Pinkney-Eppes, president of the Richmond Council of PTAs:
"It's almost a slap in the face. [Is it] saying the person who comes to the table with the most money should be the one in charge?…You don't include us. You think you know everything that's right for our children."
"None of the 26 signers contacted the PTA, Pinkney-Eppes says. Pinkney-Eppes says she's excited that leaders of some of the region's largest companies might lend their muscle to improving Richmond schools. While she says she'd like to cooperate with them, she wants parents to be invited to the table early—and she doesn't want citizens to lose the right to elect their School Board members."

Carol Wolf, school board representative:
"The citizens of the city need to remind Mayor Wilder and his pals that before Wilder ever received his 80 percent mandate, the elected School Board was approved by more than 80 percent…How many of these people who are bearding [sic] this proposal live in the city, have ever sent their kids to city schools, have spent any time in a city school…[or] employ children from Richmond or their parents?"

Greg Muzik, principal of Mary Munford Elementary School:
"As a principal with more than 30 years' experience in the Richmond public school system, I have received a good deal of feedback from parents and teachers about the recent letter from 26 business leaders proposing a governance change as a solution to our urban school challenges. No one thinks this is a good idea. But I am less concerned about the proposal for an appointed board than the potential damage this kind of public criticism does to the system. These business leaders have publicized misleading and outdated data to show that our schools are in some sort of crisis."[724]

One prominent blogger concurred that "a new school board is not what Richmond Public Schools needs. What it needs is caring business leaders who put their money and their time where their mouth is [sic],"[725] while another labeled the letter "a blatant and rather heavy-handed power grab… nothing but public education as prescribed by Ukrop's Super Markets, Dominion Resources and Philip Morris tobacco."[726]

By this point, the media had taken to calling the signatories "The Gang of 26." Signers realized they had misfired. John Adams, chairman of the Martin Agency, said that they weren't "attempting to shanghai anybody." Dominion said that letter originator and first signatory Thomas Farrell was out of the country and unavailable for comment (presumably, in a country without telephones).[727]

The letter exposed what for some may have been astonishing ineptitude, and the plan was aborted. What price did they pay? The next year, Farrell "had the last laugh, heading the search committee for Richmond's next school superintendent."[728]

Funding Schools Helps Students

The claim that school funding did not help children was brought out time and again by people like those who signed the 2007 Richmond Public Schools letter or by Congressman Dave Brat, previously a professor at Randolph-Macon College, who said, "My hero Socrates trained in [*sic*] Plato on a rock. How much did that cost? So the greatest minds in history became the greatest minds in history without spending a lot of money."[729]

The wisdom of this was not exactly borne out by the evidence. A study considering sixty years of data from 146 countries concluded that "each year of additional average schooling translates into at least a 2 percent increase in economic output."[730] Furthermore, throughout school, "a 10 percent increase in per-pupil spending each year for all twelve years of public school leads to 0.27 more completed years of education, 7.25 percent higher wages, and a 3.67 percentage-point reduction in the annual incidence of adult poverty."[731]

The most extensive study of the effects of early childhood education began in Michigan in 1961, when a group of poor youngsters attended a high-quality preschool and were compared with those who were the same in all respects, except for preschool. The results over decades were astounding: the preschool group had substantially better educational achievement, employment, family and financial situations and were less likely to commit crimes or be on public assistance. These futures were not predetermined by birth, circumstance or IQ but could be changed if given a chance in the few years before kindergarten. The program cost an inflation-adjusted $13,000 per year per student.[732]

Virginia government could teach children effectively. Its magnet Thomas Jefferson High School for Science and Technology routinely topped the rankings of best high schools in America. Students were not taught on rubble piles but received additional state funding to procure state-of-the-art technology and equipment, which were marshalled for autodidactic research projects.[733] In recent years, the school had even started "to build facilities for neuroscience and oceanography."[734] At higher levels, Jefferson Scholars, the top students at the University of Virginia, received six-figure scholarships and additional opportunities, not fewer.[735] From a moral perspective, many, if not most, of the signatories of the corporate school takeover letter sent their offspring to private Collegiate School, where tuition exceeded $20,000 annually.[736] These elite schools and other top universities provided students and educators with more money, not less.

Poorer districts had structural reasons for increased government spending compared with wealthier districts: more students with mental and physical disabilities, more students whose first language was other than English and more spending on nutrition.[737] This differential spending arose from childhood poverty, not from laboratory purchases or some mythical black hole of waste, fraud and abuse.

"Despite being the 11th wealthiest state, Virginia is 41st in state funding per pupil," wrote two school leaders. "That's closer to the bottom of the barrel than the top tier. Per-pupil state spending is down 16 percent, when adjusted for inflation, since 2009."[738] As James Ryan, dean of the Harvard Graduate School of Education, argued, if money truly did not matter, then certainly corporate titans would have no objection to equalizing school expenditures with their own salaries.[739] Or, one superintendent said, "if money doesn't make any difference, how come the rich spend so much on their schools?"[740]

MILLIONS TO MOVE HEADQUARTERS ONE BLOCK

Any navel-gazing engendered by the corporate leaders' public belly-flop was repressed in short order as the ostensible lovers of the free market again felt compelled to sack the public coffers. The McGuireWoods law firm, Virginia politics' revolving door and sinecure, wanted a new headquarters. Its current location was one of the most eye-catching buildings in Richmond, a luxurious collage of marble, glass, green space and a larger-than-life bronze tableau of naked men hoisting sails.[741] The location was so good, they felt they might as well keep it.[742] With the current headquarters taking up the block between Canal, Cary, Ninth and Tenth, the new headquarters would be at Canal, Cary, Ninth and Eighth.[743] The new site, a parking lot, was purchased for $6.2 million from its owner, Dominion, while the city gave away the $1.6 million road bisecting the lot for free.[744] In addition, the law firm received from the city an additional $3.0 million grant and $11.25 million bond issue, to be supposedly repaid by parking fees and taxes on the building itself.[745] CCA Industries elected to follow McGuireWoods and flip its one leased floor to the other side of Ninth Street.[746] The CEOs who benefited from taxpayers' largesse—Richard Cullen of McGuireWoods, William Goodwin of CCA Industries and Thomas Farrell of Dominion—each signed the letter decrying the lack of adequate public schools.

A partner at Clayco construction company said the law firm was considering moving to the suburbs and the subsidies kept them in the city.[747] Not so, according to Cullen, who "said he is pleased that Clayco decided to build the office tower because it allows the law firm to remain in downtown Richmond."[748] This was reiterated at the groundbreaking by managing partner George Keith Martin, who would go on to become rector of the University of Virginia Board of Visitors: "This is probably the last prime site in the central business district. This allows us to stay in the same vicinity, and we also think it's very important for the city, because by building on this site, one could argue we're going to help stabilize Cary street [sic]."[749]

Were those subsidies necessary to attract business? In 2016, another office building was contracted to be built two blocks away for a similarly short relocation of SunTrust yet without the public funds the other hundred-yard relocation received.[750] McGuireWoods surely stayed in the city for the same reason that it was already located there, as Richmond's two other legal powerhouses, Williams Mullen and Hunton and Williams, were, too: it was the nexus of Virginia business, finance and politics, and two blocks from the Capitol, governor's mansion, Supreme Court, federal court of appeals and Federal Reserve.

Mayor Jones praised the deal. "Economic studies show that this project will generate 812 construction jobs with more than $50.7 million in wages; another 1,653 jobs, including retaining more than 630 at McGuireWoods; and new cumulative tax revenues for the City are estimated to be more than $117 million over the next 30 years," he said.[751] His development official enthused that "this is a solid deal. Our part is being financed by taxes that are new…It's not money out of our existing budget."[752] "It is not a subsidy," said the mayor's spokesperson.[753]

Owners of the new building, estimated to cost $124 million, would pay about $1.5 million in taxes each year in the very optimistic scenario that the building was accurately assessed and did not depreciate.[754] It is hard to reconcile that with the mayor's $117 million talking point. Even under these inflated projections, over the thirty years it would take just to repay the city, more than a generation of children would be educated in Richmond's run-down schools.

If the headquarters deal created a problem where none had been—namely, a vacant former headquarters—everyone involved seemed to sweep it under the rug. Within a few months, a real estate analysis issued a warning of default for the imminently vacant James Center building, and the loan went into default and then foreclosure in early 2016.[755]

McGuireWoods Headquarters, new and old. *Google Earth screenshot.*

The new headquarters abutted Kanawha Plaza, a public park that also served as the city's largest homeless encampment.[756] In approving the law firm's public subsidies, one city council member expressed hope that the new development would help improve the park.[757] Instead, Richmonders desperate for aid and shelter, including those suffering from mental illness, would live in the shadow of a reflective building constructed with public funds.[758] Even that was not enough. "In an act of urban vandalism" in the summer of 2015, unnamed corporate backers bulldozed the plaza and then withdrew promised funds for its reconstruction.[759]

On the morning of January 3, 2016, Irving "Peanut" Ward, nicknamed after the character Snoopy, was found frozen to death on the steps of a local daytime homeless service provider. Though the exact reason for his fate may never be known, homeless people and advocates suspected he was either turned away from a nearby shelter or did not even attempt to check into it because of its shoddy and insecure conditions.[760] In mid-2016, the plaza remained closed and lifeless, and Dominion announced its own plans to gut or demolish its office tower at Canal, Cary, Eighth and Seventh and erect a new one at Canal, Cary, Seventh and Sixth.[761]

Later Jones, who had long claimed to keep a firewall between his roles as mayor and pastor of First Baptist Church, attracted the attention of public corruption investigators for allegedly conflating city and church duties. The story was still developing as of press time, but it was undisputed that he filled 10 percent of his senior governmental positions with members from his church and that some of them conducted church business from public accounts during work hours, seemingly with Jones's knowledge. As his lawyer, he hired Cullen, who told the *Richmond Times-Dispatch* that if an FBI investigation "is the biggest blemish on soon-to-be eight years in office, I think [Jones] can hold his head up high."[762]

STATE PRIORITIES

The problems were hardly unique to Richmond: local charity groups forlornly tried to plug the flood of human misery across the state. "What are the problems that poor children face?" a Bristol principal was asked.

> *"Couch-surfing homeless," she says of one child, referring to the practice of sleeping on couches in different homes. "Vision- and hearing-disabled. Grandmother raising them. Trauma in the home. Homeless, doubled-up. Gifted. Two parents. Single mother. Daddy home from Afghanistan—PTSD," she says...Kindergarten cubbies were donated by the local Home Depot, which helped restore part of the school's aging playground. O'Reilly Auto Parts donated $800 to fund snacks for the after-school program. The local Kiwanis Club does free vision screening for students and for the past two years has donated 100 pairs of shoes to children in need. "We have a lot of toes popping out," [she] said.[763]*

On the same day, the same newspaper reported that the state would spend an exorbitant $1.3 million on a different problem: refurbishing the Capitol's statue of George Washington riding a horse.[764] I saw the statue countless times; there was nothing wrong with it, so far as I could see.

PUBLIC-PRIVATE PARTNERSHIP

A map of the existing, untolled Route 460 and the planned, tolled Route 460 made one wonder who would choose to pay the toll. They run parallel to each other from Petersburg to Suffolk.[765]

This question may not have been asked in a rush to sign a public-private partnership contract and score a victory for McDonnell's "number 1 transportation priority." The executive branch had wide berth to land such contracts without legislative approval, and McDonnell sprinted to complete one before the 2013 legislative session. Federal and state transportation officials, as well as private corporate partners, expressed skepticism over the feasibility of the project but were shunted aside by Transportation Secretary Sean Connaughton's brusque e-mail, later revealed, exhorting officials to "Close the deal!" When the ink was dry, environmental permits had not been issued, and money started to flow without work having substantively begun. When the McAuliffe administration took office, it did not cancel the contract for more than a year, during which time $256 million went to U.S. 460 Mobility Partners—a combination of private Spanish and Pennsylvania firms—without a solitary inch of road being laid.[766]

The $1.4 billion project called for $1.1 billion in public money and $300 million of private bonds issued through an independent state entity called Route 460 Funding Corporation. They were near junk status and received concomitantly higher interest rates, unlike bonds issued under the state's AAA rating. In the fine print of the contract, investors would be paid by the state if tolls were not built on the road. Since there was no road, there were no tolls, and the McAuliffe administration announced in 2015 that bondholders on the hook for the boondoggle would be bailed out by the state, even though Virginia's credit was not at stake. They must be bailed out, House Appropriations chairman Chris Jones opined, because it "would put a bad taste in the minds of investors as relates to Virginia" if they were not.[767] The state negotiated a total payout of $260 million and received absolutely nothing in return for a sum that would have paid for much of Richmond's needed school construction.[768]

A GOOD ECONOMIC DEVELOPMENT DEAL

One deal seemed to illustrate that economic development did not have to be a misnomer. In 2014, a few miles downriver from Richmond, Chesterfield County secured the largest capital investment from a Chinese company in the history of the United States. Two billion dollars from Shandong Tranlin Paper was projected to create two thousand jobs by 2020 at an average annual pay of $45,663, which would itself increase Chesterfield's tax base by 1 percent, or $3 million per year. The plant was planned for one of the poorest areas in the county on idle fields formerly used for tobacco crops and would manufacture brown paper for American consumers in a method billed as much more environmentally friendly than that used to make white paper. The brown paper would come from straw and farm waste rather than trees, and its byproducts could be used as fertilizer. To secure the deal over North Carolina, Virginia and local governments offered conditional incentives that could reach up to $31 million. As of press time, the deal was proceeding as scheduled, though oversight and healthy skepticism should continue until the above targets are met.[769]

Mayor Jones gave $11 million to the Redskins and $14 million to McGuireWoods, Dominion and CCA Industries for a relative song; Virginia gave $260 million to U.S. 460 Mobility Partners for nothing. This money should have been spent on schools, but even if it should have been spent on economic development, experience indicated it could be leveraged for much more.

SENDING SCHOOLCHILDREN TO JAIL

A 2015 report from the Center for Public Integrity showed that Virginia led the nation in sending students to jail and sent them there at three times the national average.[770] Investigators described as an example the violent overreaction to one alleged offense. When an eleven-year-old autistic child, "a small, bespectacled boy who enjoys science," kicked over a trashcan in his middle school, a police officer filed a charge of disorderly conduct against him in juvenile court. A few weeks later, the student tried to follow his schoolmates out of the classroom, breaking a "rule" imposed on him alone to wait before following. The police officer "grabbed me and tried to take me to the office," the child remembered. "I started pushing him away. He slammed me down, and then he handcuffed me."[771] "If school districts are funneling students into the criminal justice system, they are working against their central mission and abdicating their responsibility as educators," wrote *Richmond Times-Dispatch* columnist Michael Paul Williams.[772] The furthest the legislature seemed willing to go was to allow lawyers for special needs children to present evidence of their disability to the court at sentencing.[773] After the report was published, a bill to prevent students under the age of fifteen "from facing criminal charges for disorderly conduct at school" was voted down in the state legislature.[774]

STANDARDS OF LEARNING

Virginia was caught up in the national movement for standardized testing regulations, and its students took state-mandated Standards of Learning (SOLs) beginning in 1996.[775] Virginia public school students in 2016 took seventeen multiple choice tests from third through eighth grades in reading, math, science, writing, Virginia studies and civics/economics. Five additional assessments were required, though they did not have to be multiple choice.[776]

The percentage of students who passed SOLs was the basis on which schools were accredited or faced penalties.[777] The lowest 5 percent of schools were identified as "priority" schools and had to implement one of four plans:

1. "Transformation Model"—the principal was fired;
2. "Turnaround Model"— the principal and at least half the teachers were fired;
3. "Restart Model"—the school's charter was abolished and replaced;
4. "School Closure Model"—the school closed and students were sent to others.[778]

Priority schools were found in areas of the state with the highest levels of poverty and segregation, including Richmond, Norfolk and Newport News.[779] Under this system, if one school climbed out of the bottom 5 percent, another necessarily fell into it, triggering the firing of its principal, at minimum. How firing teachers would make children less poor was unexplained.

The knowledge that had to be memorized for those exams was soporific. Here are four of the seven sample test questions, picked at random, for "World History through 1500":[780]

1. What characteristic did the Persian Empire share with the Roman and Incan Empires?
    A. Uniform system of money
    B. Written system of law
    C. Monotheistic religious system
    D. Widespread road system

2. Shinto had which lasting effect on Japanese culture?
    A. Emphasis on beauty of the natural world in art
    B. Division of people into rigid social classes
    C. Adoption of examination system to select officials
    D. Focus on military devotion as the highest form of virtue

3. Which statement best supports the conclusion that the Indus Valley civilization had a centralized government?
  A. The cities had an organized pattern of streets.
  B. The farms produced annual crop surpluses.
  C. Goods were imported from coastal cities.
  D. Houses were constructed with baked bricks.

4. Which individual is described by these characteristics?
  - Creative writer and poet
  - Supporter of Renaissance humanism
  - Scholar of Greek and Roman literature
  A. Donatello
  B. Petrarch
  C. Gutenberg
  D. Raphael

If you were a student, how many of these would you guess on? Be honest. I would guess on all four.

The history standards were substantively drafted by forty-nine apparatchiks appointed by Governor George Allen in 1994. This twenty-year train wreck was foreseen at its inception by critics who excoriated its retrograde "trivial pursuit" factoids and whose hasty drafting by "politically-appointed board members writing detailed objectives is comparable to members of a hospital board performing brain surgery."[781] Modern events were not covered at all in the Standards of Learning: the most recent presidents mentioned in the "World and U.S. History" standards were Eisenhower and Truman, respectively.[782] For current schoolchildren, those historical figures lived long before their parents, or even grandparents, were born. The program for Virginia history education mentioned a tiny number of Virginians who were still living (former Governors Holton and Wilder) and whose heydays were decades ago.[783] In a Kafkaesque twist, only the very last page of the thirty-one-page "U.S. History Standards of Learning, 1865–Present" began to shed light on the major events that affected their world, such as terrorism, and which should have been the focus of inquiry and problem solving.[784] Most of the Standards of Learning material drilled after students achieved literacy was mindless and came at uncountable costs in disaffection to school and antipathy to lifelong learning.[785] Compared with 9/11, the financial crisis or the 2016 elections, the Indus Valley centralized government was patently irrelevant.

Standardized testing hurt not only students but teachers, too. An investigation in the *Richmond Times-Dispatch* shed light on teacher attrition in Richmond and adjacent Chesterfield County. Carol Marable, an elementary school teacher for twenty-seven years, stated bluntly that she was "leaving because of the pressures of SOLs and I don't think it's in the best interest of students." Lauren Harrison, who had dreamed of being a teacher her entire life, became disillusioned and left after four years.

> [She] *said she realized she needed to quit as she was taking students to the computer lab to do what was supposed to be a fun research project. Her students were more accustomed to holing up in the lab for hours taking long tests. "They asked me, 'What test are we taking today?'" Harrison said. "It broke my heart. This is what the kids think school is about. It doesn't revolve around teaching anymore and that's why I'm leaving."*

These formerly passionate educators were unequivocal about why they left.[786] The gifted students at Thomas Jefferson High School for Science and Technology and their teachers also rued standardized testing, which they said sapped creativity in the best and brightest as easily as it did in others.[787] In what jobs did people take bubble tests?

Educators had results from the decades-long social experiment of standardized tests and American education, explained New York University education expert Diane Ravitch, who had promulgated the theoretical underpinnings for standards and had since become an apostate.[788] They did not help students learn, nor did they work for evaluating teachers or principals. This "is bad science. It may even be junk science. It is inaccurate, unstable, and unreliable."[789] Even Virginia Secretary of Education Anne Holton (Governor Holton's daughter and Senator Kaine's wife) admitted that the SOLs had not worked as designed.[790]

In 2016, a series of bipartisan bills to reduce the number of standardized tests was tabled until 2017, for no evident reason. On that same day, the same Senate subcommittee voted at the behest of tourism and hotel industry lobbyists against repealing the so-called Kings Dominion law, which prohibited localities from deciding whether they could open their schools before Labor Day.[791]

When politicians ignored their constituents, parents took matters into their own hands, and a nationwide movement to opt out of standardized tests began spreading. In New York State, one in six students did not take their state tests in 2014, a phenomenon "which was essentially nonexistent just two years ago." Only a few districts in that state met the federal requirement that 95 percent of students be tested, but the districts and state did not face any repercussions.[792] Local grassroots groups, such as RVA Opt Out, were formed to encourage parents and students to exercise their freedoms and rights.[793] "Students can spend up to one-third of their time of the school year preparing for the tests and that is wrong," said Virginia Commonwealth University education professor Gabriel Reich, whose fifth-grader did not take the SOLs.[794] Virginia had 681 opt-outs in 2015, a number that was likely to increase.[795] "If a flood of students opt out, the state should wake up and get the message," cautioned a local editorial board.[796] This was not quite civil disobedience, but what social movement scholars called "resistance in everyday life," as participants faced no retaliation and parental refusal for SOLs was perfectly legal.[797]

GOVERNMENT WASTE

Education was the bedrock of the American dream and the issue that most unified Americans.[798] In Virginia, money was taken from education and given to "economic development," a genteelism that meant shoveling public money to private cronies. The cost of economic development programs in Virginia from 2002 to 2012 was $718 million.[799]

The money for corporate welfare had to come from somewhere, and public schools were a target of opportunity. All over the state, the results for children were tragic. "When we take kids on a field trip to a farm, they often don't know the difference between a cow and a dog. They've never been to a farm, or a zoo, or a beach," said Lola McDowell, a retired Richmond kindergarten teacher. "The front steps of our school are crumbling and the library floods whenever it rains. The plaster bubbles, and the paint peels. Mold grows here and there. Kids with asthma cough. Our school was built in 1929, and the lack of facility maintenance and capital improvement funding has affected our students' learning environment," said Sarah Hulcher, a Norfolk parent.[800] Prince Edward County politicians "ignored a five-year proposed capital improvement plan laid out by the school board to fix leaky roofs, replace a failing heating system, and renovate a rutted football field," Kristen Green wrote. "Yet more than a million dollars of the county's money was spent constructing a road to an undeveloped site of a hotel that may never be built."[801]

Richmond politicians who recoiled at the thought of Washington-based Common Core standards simultaneously issued destructive fiats to which generations of children and teachers were forced to adhere. Politicians were supposed to be focused like lasers on uncovering waste and bureaucracy. They could have started by abolishing not local school boards, but the Standards of Learning tests, which after twenty years had turned out to be a heartbreaking scam. Yet the consequences, visible for all with eyes to see, were denied by those responsible.

HIGHER ED

MANUFACTURING CRISES AT THE UNIVERSITY OF VIRGINIA

[President Sullivan] *understood the operations of a major research university* *"as well as anyone I have ever seen."* *—Leonard Sandridge, former UVA chief operating officer*[302]

Whatever happened, and I do not know because I was not there, it happened probably because people were trying to do the best they knew how at the time. It might not have been the right thing, but they were trying. President Sullivan is now with us. She's a good lady. She's trying her darndest to be a good president. I can assure you this board is trying to do a good job. And I would ask you to forget it and move on. *—William Goodwin, UVA rector*[303]

The University of Virginia made history in 2010 by hiring its first female president.[304] In two years, she was fired. Both happened at the hands of the board of visitors.

Membership on the board of visitors of the University of Virginia was the highest honor that could be bestowed in the state; therefore, it was a sinecure where governors appointed their biggest donors. The board of visitors could fire the university president—and it did, behind closed doors and during the summer lull—ambush her, orchestrate a resignation, suppress the facts, lie to the press, ignore the law and get away with all of it. As with the McDonnell convictions, when the old system was exposed as venal, it was immediately reconstituted. This is the story.

CLUMSY COUP

The timeline of the firing of President Teresa Sullivan begins with what we know from Peter Kiernan, former chair of the Darden (Business) School Foundation board of trustees.[805] In an internal e-mail on June 10, 2012, he wrote:

> *A number of you have asked if we were surprised by this announcement* [of the president's firing]. *Here is the truth. Several weeks ago I was contacted by two important Virginia alums about working with* [chair (rector) of the board of visitors] *Helen Dragas on this project, particularly from the standpoint of the search process and the strategic dynamism effort. It pained me to keep this information from you and from* [Dean] *Bob* [Bruner], *but I was sworn to keep the process confidential.*
>
> *Because Terry Sullivan has been such a supporter of Darden, I kept the confidence as Helen requested. I can promise you after numerous discussions with Helen, that she has been extremely thoughtful and careful in this process, with an especial eye for treating Terry with the utmost respect. Everyone involved has been a class act. And though the decisions have been difficult and painful ones, the unswerving dedication to keeping Virginia as stable as possible through this challenging time has been paramount.*
>
> *As you might expect, the decisions involving my modest role in all of this have not been entirely mine to make. As many of you know no major decision of this kind can be made at Virginia without the support and assent of the Governor. I am not sure what my future role in this process will be. Those are the facts.*[806]

Four days later, Kiernan resigned from the Darden board. He clarified in his resignation letter that "no one from Darden—not the dean, nor the faculty, nor the administration, nor the Foundation board—was involved. The conversations about President Sullivan's transition that I referred to in my e-mail were conducted through my own personal relationships and not in any official capacity."[807]

The board of visitors was brought in on the plan in the months and days before her firing.[808] Dragas met with each member one on one (except for three whom she did not meet with at all) in order to skirt open meeting laws, which required public notice and minutes when more than two board members meet. When the time came to pull the trigger, she and Kington called in board member Hunter Craig to form a quorum sufficient for accepting Sullivan's resignation.[809] Vice-Rector and Darden alum Mark Kington asked Sullivan to step down in a meeting with Dragas on June 8, 2012.[810]

STATED REASONS FOR FIRING

"According to statements from Dragas, none of the typical procedures for dismissing an employee were followed: no evidence of a poor pre-firing performance review or a failure to meet any agreed upon benchmarks; no strong or controversial public or University-wide criticisms; and no on-going communication with Sullivan that her job was in jeopardy," as the *Hook* noted.[811] Dragas claimed:

> *The Board feels strongly and overwhelmingly that we need bold and proactive leadership on tackling the difficult issues that we face. The pace of change in higher education and in health care has accelerated greatly in the last two years. We have calls internally for resolution of tough financial issues that require hard decisions on resource allocation. The compensation of our valued faculty and staff has continued to decline in real terms, and we acknowledge the tremendous task ahead of making star hires to fill the many spots that will be vacated over the next few years as our eminent faculty members retire in great numbers. These challenges are truly an existential threat to the greatness of UVA. We see no bright lights on the financial horizon as we face limits on tuition increases, an environment of declining federal support, state support that will be flat at best, and pressures on health care payors. This means that as an institution, we have to be able to prioritize and reallocate the resources we do have, and that our best avenue for increasing resources will be through passionate articulation of a vision and effective development efforts to support it. We also believe that higher education is on the brink of a transformation now that online delivery has been legitimized by some of the elite institutions.[812]*

"The rector and the board made no effort to engage with the president or the faculty on the underlying issues the rector claimed to be at stake," according to a review by the American Association of University Professors.[813] A June 21 Dragas memo that outlined the supposed crises facing the university was remarkably similar to a May 3 strategy document prepared for the board by President Sullivan herself.[814] In fact, that May, "the board adopted an operating budget that included substantial language culled from Sullivan's strategy document…yet, after Sullivan's ouster, Dragas chided the president for lacking a 'credible statement of strategic direction.'"[815]

Peter Kiernan tritely noted:

> *The decision of the Board Of Visitors to move in another direction stems from their concern that the governance of the University was not sufficiently*

tuned to the dramatic changes we all face: funding, internet, technology advances, the new economic model. These are matters for strategic dynamism rather than strategic planning. Many of the schools will face the notion of self sufficiency, steps that we at Darden and others have taken already.[816]

Bizarrely, "in a personnel review process last year, Dragas, who is immaculately tailored, told Sullivan that she received comments from several board colleagues, questioning whether her wardrobe was occasionally too informal."[817]

UNIVERSAL CONDEMNATION

From the most to least powerful at the University of Virginia, criticism boiled at the firing.

Former president Robert O'Neil, who was forced out by the board after serving the then-shortest term of any president, from 1985 to 1990, said the firing was "baffling to me." He recalled that he received nine months' notice and a prestigious academic appointment after he left office.[818]

John Casteen, whose presidency bridged the decades from O'Neil to Sullivan, galvanized faculty and protested the decision to the governor.[819]

Carl Zeithaml, the dean of the Commerce School who had filled the interim presidency, courageously and publicly stepped back three days after the promotion of a lifetime and suspended "any further negotiations with the Board regarding my status as interim president, as well as any activities associated with this role."[820]

Leonard Sandridge, a respected official who rose to advise these presidents as executive vice-president and chief operating officer over a forty-four-year career at the university, said that President Sullivan "understood the operations of a major research university 'as well as anyone I have ever seen.'"[821]

Provost John Simon lamented, "I now find myself at a defining moment, confronting and questioning whether honor, integrity and trust are truly the foundational pillars of life at the University of Virginia."[822] He threatened resignation.[823]

Hunter Rawlings, president of the Association of American Universities and former president of Cornell, said, "This is the most egregious case I have ever seen of mismanagement by a governing board."[824]

The faculty senate's executive council passed a two-line resolution unanimously:

> *Resolved, that the Faculty Senate of the University of Virginia hereby:*
> *Expresses its strong support of President Sullivan.*
> *Expresses its lack of confidence in the Rector, the Vice Rector, and the*
> *Board of Visitors.*[825]

A letter by thirty-three directors and chairs recounted that their

> *surprise and concern arise directly from the fact that we have been very*
> *pleased with the direction in which President Sullivan and her administrative*
> *team have been leading UVA and with her accomplishments thus far. She is*
> *an extraordinary academic leader, with superb administrative abilities, the*
> *heart of a faculty member, and evident strength of character.*[826]

University professor William Wulf, who had obtained the highest honors as president emeritus of the National Academy of Engineering, called the firing "the worst example of corporate governance I have ever seen."[827] He took the stunning step of e-mailing faculty and others at the University of Virginia with his public resignation:[828]

> *My judgment is that the current BOV is incompetent to govern UVa…*
> *The present BOV appointed by the Governor is 14 lawyers or corporate*
> *executives with no experience with academic governance, one part-time*
> *medic at John-Hopkins, and one CEO of a small university. Alas, they*
> *don't even seem to know much about UVA! While fond of selectively*
> *quoting Jefferson out of context, they overlook the deeply philosophical*
> *fact that Mr. Jefferson's design for UVa had *no* President or central*
> *administration—the faculty governed the University, and did so in an*
> *open collaborative way, not in secret meetings behind closed doors, with*
> *no faculty input. …I have a substantial list of distinguished current*
> *or former academic administrators that I know first hand, that are*
> *really bright and I would be happy to recommend them to serve on the*
> *BOV, and I'd even be the first contact with them—but I haven't been*
> *asked. Alas, they almost certainly didn't make major contribution to the*
> *Governor's campaign, so the chance of their selection under the current*
> *system are probably nil. BUT, it's the system needs to be changed!*

He exposed the board's reasoning:

> *Moreover, the current BOV clearly didn't even investigate the issue they expressed concern about—for example on-line presence of the University (seemingly a big deal in TS's firing), but they apparently just reacted to the hype of recent announcements by some other universities without investigating UVa's record on the subject. Well, our involvement in digital scholarship and learning goes back at least twenty years—I know because I was a principal in getting it started!*

In one of the most extraordinary moments in the history of the university, police estimated that at one time, three thousand students and faculty coalesced on the historic lawn. At the "Rally for Honor," the most venerated deans, chairs, administrators and directors—a group representing the collective conscience and institutional memory of the university—spoke against the board's hubris and called for President Sullivan's reinstatement.[829]

Expressing the rage felt by many, "Vandals spray-painted the six columns of the school's neoclassical Rotunda with the letters 'G-R-E-E-E-D.'"[830]

These are just some of countless examples of University of Virginia students, faculty, administration, alumni, donors, organizations and community members lining up in unanimous and strident opposition to the catastrophe of the board's coup d'état.[831]

On June 26, 2012, the board voted unanimously to rehire President Sullivan. At the reinstatement meeting, Dragas demonstrated her capacity for self-reflection: "I believe real progress is more possible than ever now, because there's absolutely no denying that all of the wonderful people who make up this community are as awake and engaged as ever. It is unfortunate that we had to have a near-death experience to get here, but the University should not waste the enormous opportunity at hand." However, she said, members of the board "have been the target of at times vitriolic and dishonorable communication based on a mob mentality that has been created by rumor and too little accountability from anonymous sources of information. This is plainly not the UVA way."[832] Three days later, Governor McDonnell reappointed Rector Dragas, where she would remain a member of the board until June 2016.[833] "From all accounts, she has been an incredibly good leader and strong participant on the board in helping to manage the university," said McDonnell. Nursing professor Elizabeth Friberg said, "I've never seen one person have such a negative impact on a large institution like this."[834]

At the next board meeting open to the public, roughly twenty protesters were greeted with excessive force:

With 18 armed UVA Police officers ushering protestors—and even media—outside, Dean Laushway was asked why they couldn't stay.

"If you try to come in the building, there will be consequences," said Laushway. At least five times, Laushway was asked what the consequences might be. As the question was asked again and the tension escalated, Laushway finally produced a piece of paper whose text he read aloud. He said students who failed to immediately disperse from the building might be breaking Virginia law and could face school sanctions "up to and including termination from the University."

That—and the glares of the 18 uniformed officers—dispersed the students, who reconvened moments later inside Brooks Hall. Earlier, they had announced an interest in avoiding arrest or any jeopardy to their status as students.

"We played by the rules and still we were threatened with expulsion," said protestor Dennis. "Welcome to the BOV's University of Virginia."[835]

"It's not a free speech issue," UVA spokesman Anthony Debruyn explained, using the board's rhetoric of artificial emergencies. "It was a fire, life, and safety issue."[836]

The Board of Visitors

Like so many of the issues discussed in this book, the audaciousness of corruption was plain to everyone save the beneficiaries, for whom it was moral order. The board, the *Richmond Times-Dispatch*'s state political reporter wrote, "fully reflects the intersection of influence, business, money, social cachet, and personal vanity that—depending on who's getting it in the neck—defines politics here as drawing-room comedy, melodrama, classical tragedy or intrigue. Or—as with Teresa Sullivan, ousted as U.VA president after two years—all of the above."[837] In 2012, the state's political venality had reached such seismic proportions that a straight line could be drawn from McDonnell's campaign donors to his board appointments. The line was hardly subtle, and in fact, there was no pretense left to disguise it: campaign money was the unifying factor for all members he appointed to the board prior to the presidential scandal.[838] The nonpartisan Virginia Public Access Project determined that, at one point, "123, or more than three-fourths, of 155 board members at the top 10 schools have given political money, 24 of the appointees donating at six-figure levels and higher."[839]

A cover story in the *Hook* catalogued the board's campaign donations.[840]

TABLE 8. APPOINTED POST-SCANDAL ON JUNE 29, 2012*

Name	Appointed By	Donations to Governors	Donations to UVA
A. Macdonald Caputo	Warner	0	$1,517,605
Vincent Mastracco	Warner	$25,391 to Warner $43,300 to Kaine $22,000 to McDonnell	0
Mark Kington	Warner, 2002 (Kaine did not reappoint) McDonnell, 2010**	$241,000 to Warner $0 to Kaine $157,632 to McDonnell[†]	$1,500,000[‡]
Alan Diamonstein	Warner	$2,000 to Warner $13,450 to Kaine	$64,772
Helen Dragas	Kaine	$6,000 to Kaine	$153,046[***]
Randal Kirk	Kaine	$940,000 to Kaine $300,000 to McDonnell	$60,000
Hunter Craig	McDonnell	$63,501 to McDonnell	$474,658
Stephen Long	McDonnell	$19,465 to McDonnell	$63,000

---

* Anita Kumar, "McDonnell Reappoints Dragas to U-VA Board," *Washington Post*, June 29, 2012, http://www.washingtonpost.com/local/dc-politics/mcdonnell-re-appoints-dragas-to-u-va-board/2012/06/29/gJQAD6u6BW_story.html.

** Carol Wood, "Governor Appoints Four New Members to University's Board of Visitors," *UVA Today*, July 2, 2010, https://news.virginia.edu/content/governor-appoints-four-new-members-universitys-board-visitors.

† Virginia Public Access Project, "Mark J. Kington," Data for governors and associated PACs, http://www.vpap.org/donors/10716-mark-j-kington/?start_year=all&end_year=all&contrib_type=all.

‡ Lisa Provence, "Who Are the BOV's Kington and Craig?" *Hook*, June 18, 2012, http://www.readthehook.com/104276/connections-executive-bovs-kington-and-craig.

*** Dragas donated an additional $350,000 to the University of Virginia in the year after the scandal. Jenna Johnson, "Helen Dragas Points to Positive Outcomes of U-VA Leadership Crisis," *Washington Post*, July 6, 2013, http://www.washingtonpost.com/local/education/helen-dragas-points-to-positive-outcomes-of-u-va-leadership-crisis/2013/07/06/3e0cd422-e31a-11e2-aef3-339619eab080_story.html.

Name	Appointed By	Donations to Governors	Donations to UVA
Marvin Gilliam	McDonnell	$180,000 to McDonnell	$4,817,541
Timothy Robertson	McDonnell	$84,000 to McDonnell	$1,656,445
Allison Cryor DiNardo	McDonnell	$9,000 to McDonnell	$37,348
John Nau	McDonnell	$148,678 to McDonnell	$11,723,762
George Keith Martin	McDonnell	$2,750 to McDonnell	$40,065
Hillary Hurd[2]	(student)	0	0
Frank Atkinson	McDonnell	$3,250 to McDonnell	$11,085
Victoria Harker	McDonnell	0	$34,430
Bobbie Kilberg	McDonnell	$17,133 to McDonnell*	$100
Linwood Rose	McDonnell	0	$2,300
Edward Miller[1]	McDonnell	0	$12,500
William Goodwin[2]	McDonnell	$149,500 to McDonnell**	$50,508,352
Leonard Sandridge[2]	McDonnell	0	$95,805

1. One seat is legally reserved for "a physician with administrative and clinical experience."[†] Miller is the former dean of the Johns Hopkins Medical School who resigned explosively one year before his term ended, as detailed below.[‡]

2. Non-voting.

---

* Kilberg later donated $5,000 to Bob McDonnell's legal defense fund. Virginia Public Access Project, "Donations from Kilberg, Barbara G. to Restoration Fund," http://www.vpap.org/committees/232354/donor/4472/?start_year=all&end_year=all&contrib_type=all.

** Goodwin later donated an additional $50,000 to McDonnell's Opportunity Virginia PAC. Virginia Public Access Project, "Donations from Goodwin, William H. Jr to Opportunity Virginia PAC," http://www.vpap.org/committees/184384/donor/5595/?start_year=all&end_year=all&contrib_type=all.

† Code of Virginia, "§23-70. Appointment of Visitors Generally; Number and Terms of Office," Commonwealth of Virginia, http://law.lis.virginia.gov/vacode/title23/chapter9/section23-70.

‡ Nick Anderson, "Medical Executive Quits U-VA Governing Board, Blasts Administration on Way Out," *Washington Post*, April 13, 2015, http://www.washingtonpost.com/news/grade-point/wp/2015/04/13/medical-executive-quits-u-va-governing-board-blasts-administration-on-way-out/.

It could be argued that this corruption was worse than that between Governor McDonnell and Jonnie Williams, for this was not selling access; this was selling the reins of government. The board had decision-making responsibility over billions of state dollars and tens of thousands of students and employees, giving "members power to shape public higher education in Virginia, ranging from ousting and reinstating a school president to deciding on major capital projects to holding sway over long-range planning."[841]

Philanthropists were given free rein over their own money—as a matter of principle, restricted donor funds are common—but that did not entitle the donor to spend the public's substantially greater investments, which were given year after year. Even if one accepted that power was proportional to financial contributions, the University of Virginia had an approximately $2.7 billion budget broken down by the following revenue sources:[842]

CHART 2. UNIVERSITY OF VIRGINIA BUDGET SOURCES, 2013–2014*

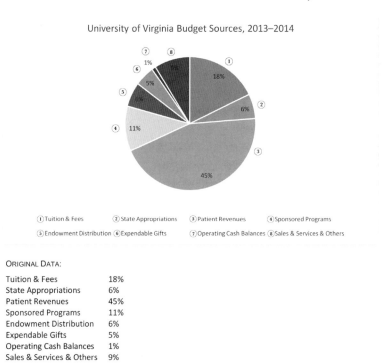

University of Virginia Budget Sources, 2013–2014

① Tuition & Fees ② State Appropriations ③ Patient Revenues ④ Sponsored Programs
⑤ Endowment Distribution ⑥ Expendable Gifts ⑦ Operating Cash Balances ⑧ Sales & Services & Others

ORIGINAL DATA:

Tuition & Fees	18%
State Appropriations	6%
Patient Revenues	45%
Sponsored Programs	11%
Endowment Distribution	6%
Expendable Gifts	5%
Operating Cash Balances	1%
Sales & Services & Others	9%

* University of Virginia, "2013–2014 Budget Summary All Divisions," May 21, 2013, http://www.virginia.edu/budget/Docs/2013-14%20Budget%20Summary.All%20 Divisions.pdf, 5. Adapted from original.

Philanthropy (Expendable Gifts) accounted for one-twentieth of the University of Virginia's revenue. If Endowment Distribution were included as well, that would add another one-seventeenth. If board representation were proportional to financial impact, then one or maybe two board seats out of seventeen would be filled by a philanthropist. Doling out almost all seats to philanthropists was grossly unrepresentative of the financial situation of the University of Virginia. Though 45 percent of revenue came from the health system, just one board member came from health care.

The two non-voting appointments that McDonnell made after the crisis contrasted remarkably. Over a five-decade career at the University of Virginia, Leonard Sandridge rose to every rank but president and earned countless accolades, including the most meritorious, the Thomas Jefferson Award.[843] He was quoted earlier as a voice of integrity criticizing the rash firing of the president. In a poignant retirement interview, "when asked what his epitaph would include if he had to choose three things (in the tradition of Thomas Jefferson's wishes for his gravestone), Sandridge said, 'If I had to settle for three things, it would be: He was honest; he worked hard; and he cared about people.'"[844]

The second appointment garnered different accolades. "If Richmond had a godfather, he'd answer to Bill Goodwin," read a profile in *Style Weekly*. "Ultimately, Goodwin derives his power from wealth. He's a billionaire, but he refuses to acknowledge he's worth more than, say, $100 million…'He's the richest guy in Richmond—probably by a wide margin,' a top local fundraiser says. That's only half the story. Goodwin makes his money then turns around and gives it back."[845] He was a generous donor to the community and to politicians, and that money was put to sometimes good and sometimes controversial ends.[846] I elsewhere praised him for his pledge of $150 million for a new pediatric hospital in Richmond, for example.[847] But Goodwin made headlines in 2004 for withdrawing a tentative commitment of $5 million to the Episcopal Church over its confirmation of a gay bishop.[848] He also got in some hot water for gifting McDonnell an extravagant $23,000 vacation and failing to disclose it.[849] He was on the witness list for the prosecution in the McDonnell trial, though he was never called to testify.[850] As of press time for this book, Goodwin's vacation gift to McDonnell was still unlisted in McDonnell's disclosure forms; Goodwin's gift disclosure form listed only a $920 gift for a 2012 McDonnell cabinet retreat.[851] Thus, Virginia faced the unusual spectacle of a board member waiting to potentially testify in the corruption trial of the governor who appointed him.

At the first board meeting after reinstatement, just one significant proposal was offered: to lengthen the rector's term from two to three years, at Goodwin's behest.[852] In September, faculty senate chair George Cohen sought answers from the board about its botched coup. Goodwin said:

> *Whatever happened, and I do not know because I was not there, it happened probably because people were trying to do the best they knew how at the time. It might not have been the right thing, but they were trying. President Sullivan is now with us. She's a good lady. She's trying her darndest to be a good president. I can assure you this board is trying to do a good job. And I would ask you to forget it and move on.*[853]

"We need to leave the past alone," he said, halting the inquiry. "The more you dig, the more you make the University look bad." New board member Bobbie Kilberg chimed in that "we agreed at our retreat that we would not be talking to the press."[854]

When a board position opened after Randal Kirk resigned in the fall of 2012, perhaps over his uncouth e-mail that "one of our nannies has two degrees from the University, by the way," McDonnell tapped Goodwin over Sandridge.[855] Goodwin asserted that "my involvement is really going smoothly. The only deterrent is the Freedom of Information Act" and public meeting laws.[856] Though he knew more about University of Virginia governance than any living person, Sandridge never became a board member or anything else with McDonnell. Governor McAuliffe appointed him to the Commission on Higher Education Board Appointments, a nonbinding advisory panel that recommended candidates for all of the state's public university boards.[857]

FINANCIAL AID UNDER ATTACK

On August 3, 2013, the board faced a difficult decision at its retreat.[858] The previous day, it had been asked to consider a proposal to end AccessUVA, a program that guaranteed poor students would graduate from the University of Virginia without debt. AccessUVA had grown since its inception from 24 percent of the undergraduate population and $11.5 million in 2005 to 33 percent and $40 million in 2013.

The financial emergency was probably not that acute, for a consultant had been hired in 2011 to evaluate the program and was reporting back now. As stated by Art & Science Group LLC, reducing financial aid would lead to fewer students of modest means enrolling at the University of Virginia. If a board member offered the global recession or tuition hikes as possible causes of the growth of the aid program, it was not reported in the minutes.

The AccessUVA program had already been cut by $4.3 million annually through stricter work-study requirements.[859] Even then, "the administrative changes do not reduce the cost of the program to the extent necessary," maintained a consultant. The proposal to be voted on would abolish the debt-free guarantee and institute a $28,000 debt ceiling in its place. The hike would increase revenue flow from its poorest students to the university by $6 million per year. Perhaps this was too drastic. The board wanted more numbers and broke for lunch.

The topic of conversation after lunch was not the radical change to the university's aid guarantees but a proposal for the state legislature to carve out exemptions for the university from the Freedom of Information Act. Dragas, who wrote that "when I was re-appointed to the board, I committed to legislators to advocate for real affordability and transparency," voted for the Freedom of Information Act gutting, as did every other board member.[860]

The board met again the next day, and any lingering issues had apparently been resolved. It voted to end the policy of graduating poorer students debt free without public meetings, consultation or feedback. As with Sullivan's dismissal, it acted while students were away for the summer. The final vote was an overwhelming 14–2, which was heralded in an Orwellian press release entitled, "Board of Visitors Reauthorizes Acclaimed AccessUVA Financial Aid Program."[861]

PUBLIC LIES

The merits of the decision were assailed. The University of Virginia had plenty of money, for example, to build a $12 million squash court and increase its marketing budget by $18 million.[862] Meanwhile, President Sullivan lamented in a university-wide e-mail, "We have known for some time that these rising costs were not sustainable."[863]

University of Virginia spokesman McGregor McCance was left to try to parry sensible inquiries with escalating mendacity. "The AccessUVa changes are a response to the dramatically escalating program costs, and an interest in putting the program on a more sustainable path for the future, while still permitting the

University to operate admission on a need-blind basis and still meeting 100 percent of demonstrated student financial need," he said. "U.VA offers very little merit aid and is committed to providing 100 percent of demonstrated need for students."[864]

Unlike other debt, student loans could not be discharged in bankruptcy, so those who bore the consequences of the board's decision responded in whatever way they could.[865] The student government unanimously endorsed a resolution calling for reversing the harsh cuts.[866] The student newspaper editorialized for the same.[867] Activists taped their mouths shut to represent students' silenced voices at the next meeting.[868] In what was becoming a habit, William Goodwin wrote to the board before its November 2013 budget meeting to "strongly suggest…that we don't include numbers of any kind."[869]

OVERFLOWING SCHOLARSHIP MONEY

Despite what the board and its spokesman claimed, the University of Virginia did, in fact, offer tens of millions of dollars in merit aid through its Jefferson Scholars program. Pursuant to its annual report, the same year that the board eliminated the debt-free guarantee was an extremely successful one for the Jefferson Scholars program. Most of the recipients of this aid were from private, out-of-state schools.[870]

TABLE 9. UNIVERSITY OF VIRGINIA JEFFERSON SCHOLARS PROGRAM*

Money raised, FY 2012–2013	$19.35 million
Operating budget, 2014	$13.1 million
Endowment distributed, 2014	4.3%
Endowment	$303 million
Number of students	128
Endowment per student, Jeff. Sch.	$2,367,188
Endowment per student, UVA**	$220,195

* Jefferson Scholars Foundation, "2013 Annual Report," http://www.jeffersonscholars.org/sites/default/files/JSF.2013.AnnualReport.pdf.
** Nick Anderson, "Top College Endowments Per Student in 2013," *Washington Post*, January 28, 2014, http://www.washingtonpost.com/local/education/top-college-endowments-per-student-in-2013/2014/01/28/ed582efe-881f-11e3-a5bd-844629433ba3_story.html.

The $6 million "saved" by hiking AccessUVA fees on the poorest one-third of the student body was almost precisely the surplus funds raised in one year by the Jefferson Scholars' $300 million endowment. Notwithstanding any additional money raised, the interest alone on a $300 million endowment could pay for all AccessUVA cuts for all time.

The beneficiaries of this largesse, going well beyond full tuition, were guaranteed an educational experience unfathomable to the general public.[871] Students began college in a week-long outdoor leadership course that included camping, climbing and games. The following summer, they took part in intensive career building and service learning. The summer after their second year, scholars traveled to and participated in one of twenty-three international study programs. Throughout their four years, students could attend exclusive lectures and networking opportunities. The total value of the scholarship was estimated at more than $125,000 for Virginia students and $240,000 for out-of-state students.[872]

When the board met, promises to the poorest students (who received admission despite the advantages accruing to wealthy students) were abandoned, and the people who were affected were blocked from input. At the same time, hundreds of millions of dollars sat idle while an opulent scholarship program raised more than enough money each year to meet its yearly budget plus 50 percent.

UVA WAS FLUSH

The Jefferson Scholars Foundation was a snapshot. What about the finances of the university as a whole? Financial documents belied any semblance of a crisis. If anything, UVA was flush. Its more than $5 billion endowment made it the nineteenth-wealthiest school in America.[873] It had by far the largest endowment of any public school in the region, including Maryland and Washington, D.C. Among public schools, it fell behind only the much larger University of Michigan and states with multi-school systems like California and Texas. It was about $1.5 billion richer than Ivy League Dartmouth, itself a notoriously wealthy school.[874]

The world-class endowment of the University of Virginia was growing fastest in the nation in 2011, the year before Sullivan was supposedly fired for financial reasons.[875] Was this an aberration? It also grew the fastest in the nation in the five-year period from 2009 to 2014 and fourth fastest in the decade from 2004 to 2014.[876] According to its own documents, "The University is one of only two public universities with top bond ratings from all three debt-rating agencies," so it could borrow money, if it ever needed to, at rates that were the lowest available to any organization.[877] It enjoyed unparalleled access to the levers of state power; it had a secure, multigenerational alumni base and attracted some of the best and brightest students and employees from across the state, nation and globe; as a nonprofit, it did not pay property taxes. Yet it was also the most miserly public school in Virginia, with the lowest percentage of Pell Grant recipients among undergraduates of the seven state schools examined.[878]

Affirmative Action

The University of Virginia collected statistics on the academic performance of its admitted classes.[879] In 2014, 89 percent of freshmen were ranked in the top tenth of their high school classes, and 97 percent were ranked in the top 20 percent. Only a few dozen were ranked in the second fifth and fifty-three in the bottom 60 percent of their class, a number that has more than quadrupled, from twelve to nineteen to forty-two to fifty-three, in four years. (Approximately 54 percent of freshmen did not have class ranks.)

What explained this jump in less-qualified matriculants? Were those 11 percent who graduated out of the top tenth beneficiaries of affirmative action or athletic scholarships?

As UVA released its matriculants, Collegiate School, a private school in Richmond with tuition well over $20,000 per year, released its matriculations every year.[880] Collegiate did not rank students, but it did indicate who graduated in the top 20 percent (*cum laude*).[881] Using that data, we can see the type of students who attended the University of Virginia.

TABLE 10. CLASS RANK OF COLLEGIATE SCHOOL MATRICULANTS TO THE UNIVERSITY OF VIRGINIA*

Year	UVA Acceptances / Total Graduates	UVA Matriculants / Total Matriculants	Top 20% Collegiate / Total to UVA	Bottom 80% Collegiate / Total to UVA
2014	35 / 122	25 / 122	14 / 25	11 / 25
2013	38 / 125	22 / 125	11 / 22	11 / 22
2012	36 / 126	23 / 126	8 / 23	15 / 23
2011	21 / 117	12 / 117	8 / 12	4 / 12
2010	29 / 130	18 / 130	8 / 18	10 / 18

It takes a little time to understand this table. In 2014, for example, nearly half of the matriculants (or eleven out of twenty-five who were in the bottom 80 percent of Collegiate graduates) were in the bottom 3 percent of the matriculants academically at the University of Virginia. In addition, thirty-five Collegiate students were accepted to the University of Virginia—or nearly one in three graduates. To put it another way, in 2012, only thirty-nine University of Virginia freshmen out of nearly two thousand matriculants did not graduate in the top 20 percent of their high school class. Fifteen students from Collegiate alone did not graduate in the top 20 percent of their high school class. (Again, there is no overlap between these groups, since Collegiate did not explicitly rank on transcripts sent to colleges. Rather, it showed an overwhelming preference of UVA admissions officers for students from at least one wealthy private school who would have placed in the lowest 3 percent of matriculants if they had been ranked.) The bottom line is that these facts indicated that money could substitute for academic success.

Many universities practiced such affirmative action for the rich, as an exposé by Pulitzer Prize–winning *Wall Street Journal* reporter Daniel Golden revealed:[882]

Even as conservative critics paint affirmative action for college-bound minorities as giving African Americans, Hispanics, and Native Americans

---

* Issues of Collegiate School's *Spark* magazine from 2010 to the present can be found at http://www.collegiate-VAorg/Page/Alumni/Spark-Magazine. Summer issues contain matriculation data.

an unfair advantage over more capable white candidates, the truth is the reverse. The number of whites enjoying preference far outweighs the number of minorities aided by affirmative action. At least one-third of the students at elite universities, and at least half at liberal arts colleges, are flagged for preferential treatment in the admissions process.[883]

It is impossible to say for sure in each of the cases, but such admissions anomalies may be due to preferences for the children of alumni. The University of Virginia was not fully desegregated until 1972; therefore, alumni admissions overwhelmingly skew white and upper class.[884] Education scholar Richard Kahlenberg reports that "while universities claim that legacy [alumni] preferences are necessary to improve fund raising, there is little empirical evidence to support the contention." The University of Virginia's national peer, the University of California at Berkeley, did not use alumni preferences, nor did a number of prestigious schools, including Oxford, Cambridge and Caltech. As another example, when "Texas A&M eliminated the use of legacy preferences, in 2004, donations took a small hit, but then they increased substantially from 2005 to 2007."[885]

Unlike affirmative action for the rich, affirmative action to redress racial discrimination arguably had some merits, yet UVA's reflection of the state's diversity was not exactly a mirror image.[886]

TABLE 11. UNIVERSITY OF VIRGINIA UNDERGRADUATE STUDENTS BY ETHNIC CATEGORY 2013–14

Ethnicity	Percent UVA*	Percent Statewide**
African American	6	19.7
American Indian or Alaskan Native	0.1	0.5
Asian	12	6.1
Hispanic	5.7	8.6

---

* University of Virginia, "Current On-Grounds Enrollment," http://www.virginia.edu/Facts/Glance_Enrollment.html.
** United States Census Bureau, "State & County QuickFacts: Virginia," http://quickfacts.census.gov/qfd/states/51000.html. Numbers for 2013.

Ethnicity	Percent UVA	Percent Statewide
Native Hawaiian or Pacific Islander	0.02	0.1
Multi-Race	4.3	2.7
White (Non-Hispanic)	71.6	63.6

The silver lining for proponents of affirmative action for racial minorities was that linking affirmative action for the rich to affirmative action for minorities could save race-based affirmative action from its detractors: those who condemned affirmative action for historically oppressed minorities could not have it both ways by simultaneously advocating for affirmative action for wealthy children.[887]

The University of Virginia was an excellent school, and parents should have been proud to send their child there. Undoubtedly, many Collegiate graduates were qualified to attend the university. However, parental wealth should not have substituted for academic achievement, and a double standard for the rich and all the rest harmed most families in the state who wished to send their children to the University of Virginia.

NOT NEED-BLIND

This was not the image the University of Virginia put forth when it asked for money. The homepage for the university's scholarship donations claimed, "To fulfill its public mission, the University of Virginia ensures that undergraduate students with strong academic credentials find the University's doors open to them, regardless of their financial circumstances. By committing to a 'need-blind' admission policy, the University can admit the best-qualified students."[888] The board also claimed the University of Virginia was need-blind—for example, in its August 2013 resolution that cut millions of dollars in financial aid.[889]

The University of Virginia did not practice need-blind admissions and instead focused on need, or its absence, among a tiny class of applicants. *U.S. News & World Report* examined the forty-six colleges and universities in the United States that claimed they were "need-blind." The University of Virginia ranked second to last in the percent of students receiving federal Pell Grants, given to students with familial income of less than about $45,000 a year.[890] Only 8 percent of

University of Virginia students received Pell Grants, while 15 percent did at neighboring University of North Carolina–Chapel Hill, for example.

Admissions spots should not have been effectively sold, but if they were to be, perhaps they should at least have been sold in the open market, and the school should have called itself plutocratic rather than public. There might have been some level of money that could make a C student attractive, and if that was the case, it was wrong to sell seats with the mere hope that wealthy parents would reciprocate. If there was to be a quid pro quo, the quo should have been determined honestly and transparently. After all, admissions seats were being sold for a wink that might have been worth nothing.

AFFIRMATIVE ATHLETES AND SPORTS SUBSIDIES

The image of the typical beneficiary of athletic scholarships that comes to mind might be a middle-class, African American man who played football or basketball. Insofar as those were the two most televised sports, the image might be plausible.[891]

A large study in 2003 found that scholar athletes in upper-class sports lagged behind their peers in SATs and, if they enrolled, in college academic performance. For example, in 2007, the University of Virginia women's rowing team averaged a 3.0 GPA, compared to 3.18 university-wide.[892]

Daniel Golden tracked down a number of University of Virginia student athletes and reported on the admissions boost that privilege provided in athletics:

> The Virginia women's crew team is given twelve admissions slots each year, more than any other sport except football. To fill these slots, Coach Sauer submits transcripts and test scores of fifty recruits to the admissions office for preapproval, prioritizing them in three categories: worthy of a full athletic scholarship, partial scholarship, or none. The office approves about forty, whom he may then offer a slot and scholarship; their actual applications for admission, submitted later, are a formality. If the office has denied a top rower, he may prod her to retake the SATs or boost her grades so he can resend her name to the admissions office. Since other universities pursue the same rowers, most enroll elsewhere, but he lands his dozen. "Most of the kids we recruit need help to get in," Coach Sauer said.[893]

The University of Virginia offered scholarships in the following sports, most of which were skewed by class and/or race:

TABLE 12. UNIVERSITY OF VIRGINIA SCHOLARSHIP SPORTS*

Men (% non-Hispanic white in Division I)**	Women (% non-Hispanic white in Division I)
Baseball (81.9)	Softball (73.6)
Basketball (27.1)	Basketball (33.6)
Cross Country (72.7)	Cross Country (74.1)
Football (41.3)	Field Hockey (79.3)[1]
Golf (72.6)[1]	Golf (62.6)
Lacrosse (84.7)[1]	Lacrosse (87.1)
Soccer (58.3)	Soccer (74.1)
Swimming and Diving (78.1)[1]	Swimming and Diving (78.8)
Tennis (45.9)[3]	Tennis (45.8)
Track and Field (56.5 indoor, 56.5 outdoor)	Track and Field (57.3 indoor, 57.4 outdoor)
Wrestling (77.7)	Rowing (76.3)[1]
Polo[2]	Polo (89.4)
	Volleyball (69.6)[1]

1. High-income sport

2. Polo is a high-income sport funded at the University of Virginia by private scholarships and private dues.[†] There were only two male NCAA polo players in the United States in 2013–14. Percentage data is for "Equestrian."

3. Tennis is a high-income sport. The ethnicity numbers were unusual in that more than 30 percent of male and female NCAA players self-identified as "nonresident alien" (international).

---

* University of Virginia Athletics, "Men's Sports, Women's Sports," http://www.virginiasports.com/ViewArticle.dbml?DB_OEM_ID=17800&KEY=&ATCLID=1139147.
** Percent white Division I data is from NCAA Race and Gender Demographics Search, 2013–2014, National Collegiate Athletic Association, "Sport Sponsorship, Participation and Demographics Search: Student-Athlete Data," http://web1.ncaa.org/rgdSearch/exec/saSearch.
† Golden, *Price of Admission*, 158–59.

The NCAA data were not broken down by school, but one could assume the University of Virginia student athletes were comparable to these nationwide percentages. Most sports teams disproportionately consisted of non-Hispanic whites, and most sports required expensive equipment, such as land, pools or horses. Basketball and football were the exceptions, not the rule. As far as the actual makeup of University of Virginia athletic scholarship recipients, the typical player was a wealthy white woman.[894]

A *USA Today* investigation discovered that all but a handful of the 230 NCAA Division I public universities subsidized their athletics programs.[895] Every Virginia university on the list did so, even those with powerhouse sports programs like Virginia basketball and Virginia Tech football. To pay for this, the University of Virginia imposed by far the highest mandatory student fees, $657 per year, of any school in a major athletic conference.[896] To put it in perspective, $657 was about eighty hours of work-study wages for scholarship teams on which work-study students would obviously not play.

TABLE 13. LIST OF VIRGINIA PUBLIC UNIVERSITY ATHLETICS REVENUE AND SUBSIDIES*

School (NCAA revenue rank)	Revenue	Subsidy	Percent Subsidy
Virginia (33)	$83,697,971	$13,235,814	16%
Virginia Tech (42)	$73,065,186	$8,110,828	11%
James Madison (63)	$43,767,486	$35,725,049	82%
Old Dominion (64)	$41,061,440	$26,733,437	65%
Virginia Commonwealth (91)	$27,957,707	$19,035,500	68%
William and Mary (109)	$23,664,928	$12,691,327	54%
George Mason (121)	$21,014,697	$17,207,354	82%
Virginia Military Institute (176)	$12,524,224	$3,982,729	32%
Norfolk State (181)	$12,134,980	$9,613,812	79%

* Steve Berkowitz, Christopher Schnaars, et al., "NCAA: Finances," *USA Today* and Indiana University National Sports Journalism Center, http://sports.usatoday.com/ncaa/finances. Only Texas, Ohio State, Louisiana State, Oklahoma, Penn State, Nebraska and Purdue athletics made net profits.

School (NCAA revenue rank)	Revenue	Subsidy	Percent Subsidy
Longwood (210)	$9,774,504	$8,416,143	86%
TOTAL	$348,623,123	$154,751,993	44%

The university also lavished its polo players with the best facilities around:

> *Alumni paid for the seventy-five acre Virginia Polo Center, considered the best college polo facility in the United States, with irrigated outdoor fields, an indoor arena, and stabling and paddocks for ponies. Alumni also underwrote the purchase of seventy ponies for between $2,500 and $60,000 apiece...UVA admissions dean John Blackburn personally reads the applications of all polo recruits, because they and their families are regarded as potential donors.*[897]

There was plenty of money for these projects and others.

STATE SALARIES

The salaries of dozens of University of Virginia employees did not reflect any sort of budget crisis. The governor made $175,000 per year, and the president of the United States made $400,000.[898] Fifteen University of Virginia employees made $400,000 per year or more, including three assistant coaches of UVA's struggling football team who made $450,000 per year. In 2013–14, more than 250 state employees made more than $250,000 per year.[899] Do assistant football coaches have more responsibilities than the commander-in-chief? They're both paid by taxpayers, after all.

PRIVATE JETS AND VANITY PROJECTS

The University of Virginia owned a private jet, an eight-seat Cessna Citation II, number N800VA, and its flight logs were available at Flight Aware.[900] On June 2, 2015, for example, the plane flew from Charlottesville to Manassas, a twenty-five-minute flight. Delegate David Ramadan estimated the used jet was worth an astonishing $2 million, while fuel use cost nearly $1,000 per hour.[901]

In the time of mass austerity purportedly requiring penny-pinching and harsh cuts to students, the board approved a $58 million renovation project for the iconic Rotunda, including a half million dollars on an unpopular paint job for the dome.[902]

REVISITING THE FIRING RATIONALES

We have seen that the university's so-called fiscal emergency was counterfeit. What about the others?

Communication

The post-scandal board appointments were ostensibly a stabilizing force. The *Washington Post* reported that "McDonnell has said he looks for board members who share his goals of reducing college costs, increasing slots for in-state students and making schools more efficient."[903] Any expectation that

Annual Performance Review of the University of Virginia President for Board of Visitors. *Rector and Visitors of the University of Virginia, "Board Meeting Minutes," August 2–3, 2013, http://www.virginia.edu/bov/meetings/13aug%20Retreat/'13%20AUG%20BOV%20RETREAT%20 MINS.pdf, pp. 9171–9172.*

cronyism would recede after the scandal proved naïve: on the contrary, the scandal exacerbated the board's venality and incompetence. By the time every member of the board had been appointed by McDonnell, fourteen of seventeen board members had contributed to his campaign, and ten had given more than $10,000.[904] In reality, McDonnell's appointments to the board were destructive. It routinely declared fiscal "emergencies" in the face of all evidence and "solved" the crises by directing cuts toward faculty and students. His board's legacy was continued privatization, cynicism and raising tuition, despite ample financial resources.

Overseeing the president was, in theory, the cornerstone of the board's work. Three years after it damaged the school community and reputation, its annual performance review of the president looked like the evaluation for an introductory course.

Faculty Recruitment

President Sullivan released a strategic plan following her reinstatement that included faculty retention as her top priority. Dragas deleted that goal, sent

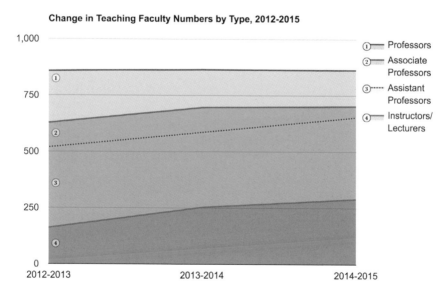

Change in Teaching Faculty Numbers by Type, 2012-2015

UVA Faculty Retention, 2012–2015. *Simone McDonnell, "University Shifts Towards Non-Tenure Track Professors," Cavalier Daily, April 9, 2015, http://www.cavalierdaily.com/article/2015/04/university-shifts-towards-non-tenure-track-professors.*

the plan back and declared that Dragas's revisions would be accepted if Sullivan did not revise hers within a week.[905] In the years following 2012, the University of Virginia substantially disinvested in its tenure-track professors, whose retention and low salaries were allegedly motivating factors in firing Sullivan. They filled the gaps with adjuncts.

Online Education

Online education was often touted as a panacea by Dragas and other dilettantes.[906] Education scholar Diane Ravitch summarized the evidence, which showed both poor results and also that even before the coup, online education in Virginia was already flourishing, in a sense, with the company K12 Inc.:

> *When K12 wanted to open a statewide online school in Virginia, it followed a politically savvy path. It made generous campaign contributions of $55,000 to the Republican Governor, Robert F. McDonnell, a staunch advocate of school choice. McDonnell pushed legislation to authorize full-time virtual schools in 2010. K12 created a partnership with rural Carroll County, taking advantage of the fact that state aid is linked to the district's affluence or poverty. Carroll County receives some $5,400 per student on state aid, and K12 is reimbursed for that amount for every student who enrolls, regardless of where he or she lives. Had K12 located in affluent Fairfax County,* The Washington Post *pointed out, the state aid would have been about half that amount. For its part, Carroll County gets a handsome reward: a $500 registration fee for every out-of-district student, plus a management fee of 6.5 percent of K12's taxpayer dollars for the school.[907]*

A *Bloomberg BusinessWeek* reporter wrote that K12 Inc. had worse results than normal public schools. The *New York Times* also investigated K12 and found "a company that tries to squeeze profits from public school dollars by raising enrollment, increasing teacher workload, and lowering standards."[908] In one instance, the company received $11,000 annually to perform speech therapy over the Internet with a special needs child for one hour per week, or about $211 per hour.

The board had offered the university's online education as a reason for firing Sullivan, so what did the board do when it had the opportunity to make UVA the leader in virtual schooling? If Dragas read the article on it she forwarded to Kington in May 2012 under the subject "why we can't wait," she would see that it said that online coursework had "no revenue stream and no business plan to sustain it."[909] This conflicted with her budget crisis rhetoric. Nevertheless, by the fall of 2012, tens of thousands of students worldwide had registered for virtual University of Virginia classes under the auspices of the for-profit online education company Coursera.[910] Three years after the crisis, UVA offered just fourteen courses online.[911] The online learning crisis rationale for firing Sullivan was, like the other explanations, a fabrication.

Transparency

McDonnell's press release after Sullivan was rehired stated that "full transparency, constant civility and open dialogue will be crucial as the university evaluates its progress in meeting the goals set by the board, president and legislature."[912] The board became more secretive, lobbied for diminished transparency and orchestrated unpopular decisions with the least public input permitted by law—and sometimes less than that.

The presidential crisis might have merited navel-gazing, but an unaccountable board had become standard operating procedure. As in 2013, a 2015 tuition hike, the highest of any of Virginia's public schools, was orchestrated behind closed doors with almost no debate.[913] The board voted to increase undergraduate tuition by $1,000 per year, plus inflation, with higher increases for particular schools, such as engineering, which was raised by an additional $2,000, and public policy, which was raised by $2,500. Simultaneously, the board trumpeted that it capped student debt at $4,000 for low-income students and $18,000 for other undergraduates.[914] This seemed like a bait-and-switch, as the board neglected to mention its substantial tuition raises over prior years.

A joint letter signed by six members of the University of Virginia chapter of the American Association of University Professors made pointed charges:

- The public was not made aware of the timing of the tuition vote.
- The public was unaware of the specifics of the tuition plan.
- The public was not able to provide input.[915]

They were ignored, as expected.

The financial, personnel and online crises offered as justifications for Sullivan's dismissal were simply untrue. Therefore, there must have been another motive.

SMOKE AND FIRE

Who was responsible?

The *Hook* fingered billionaire Paul Tudor Jones:[916]

- Jones was an influential alum who was not involved with Darden at the time, as stipulated in Kiernan's original e-mail.
- Jones spoke to Dragas for the first time in May 2012. He declined her offer of a board seat and "urged a focus on strategic planning."[917]
- He was one of McDonnell's biggest donors, contributing $100,000.[918]
- He had donated tens of millions of dollars to the University of Virginia, and it wanted more. The article quoted anonymous sources implicating Jones as fomenting the scandal, possibly in an implied quid pro quo for a $100 million donation.
- He had pushed for education reform. With Kiernan, he "helped launch the New York arm of StudentsFirst, the advocacy organization that embraces such reforms as eliminating teacher tenure, pushing merit pay, and supporting charter schools."
- Jones released an op-ed lauding the firing, one of only a few members of the community outside of the board to publicly support it.[919]
- During the 2013 gubernatorial campaign, Jones lobbied McAuliffe to alter the way board members were selected and wanted to reserve eight of seventeen slots for persons chosen by prominent alumni and donors.[920] Before Jones called him, McAuliffe received a $25,000 donation from Jeffrey Walker, the leader of the effort. After speaking with Jones, McAuliffe amended his campaign platform to pledge "proper representation on governing boards" with "alumni, staff, students, and other members of college and university communities" involved in choosing members. After the policy change, he received another $25,000.[921] In June 2015, McAuliffe appointed Walker to the board.[922]

The *Hook* issued Freedom of Information Act requests to the university "for emails connecting Dragas or Kington to UVA donors Paul Tudor

Jones, Thomas Farrell, and William Goodwin." Nothing of substance was forthcoming. However, "the UVA official fulfilling the *Hook*'s request indicated that 'several' emails that met the specifications of the request were withheld under the statutory exemptions allowing the University to conceal certain personnel, fundraising, and legal matters."[923] Those e-mails were never released, and it would have taken a successful civil lawsuit for the public to access them.[924]

The *Richmond-Times Dispatch* and other Richmond-based journalists pointed their fingers at Dominion CEO and chairman Thomas Farrell, who seemed at the center of every connection to the scandal.[925]

- Farrell was an alum and former rector not involved with Darden at the time who had close personal and professional access to Rector Dragas and Vice-Rector Kington, who fired Sullivan. Dragas and Kington were on two boards together: UVA and Dominion.[926] Dragas, Kington and Farrell were also on the Virginia Business Higher Education Council, a group that pushed for corporate education reform.[927]
- Farrell also had very close ties to McDonnell, who signed off on and supported the firing. They were friends from high school, he donated more than $135,000 to McDonnell's campaigns and he was the chairman of McDonnell's higher education reform commission.[928]
- In late 2011, Farrell presented the goals for McDonnell's higher education policy to a retreat of Virginia's public university board members, including those from UVA.[929] Among the reforms he championed were online education and more business involvement in higher education, the same dubious points Dragas pushed in her stated reasons for firing Sullivan.[930]
- Farrell was discussed as a potential president before Sullivan was hired and as one of the top candidates after she was fired.[931]
- Dominion sent two public relations officials to the University of Virginia during the crisis in order to assist in messaging. "Why those experts were needed was never explained." wrote journalist Peter Galuszka.[932]
- It was intimated that Farrell and other important University of Virginia figures were members of the secretive and powerful "Seven Society."[933]
- Farrell led the failed 2007 effort to abolish Richmond's school board, discussed in the previous chapter. In this scandal, a corporate group promoting radical educational reform issued demands, including abolition of the elected school board, in the form of an open letter to the mayor and city council. The group backed down after universal condemnation by

media, officials and citizens. The modi operandi were eerily similar—except in Richmond, the unsuccessful plan was public, while at the University of Virginia, the initially successful machinations started behind closed doors.

Journalists seemed to feel that Republican power brokers Jones, Farrell or William Goodwin, or people very much like them, were behind or had advance knowledge of the links between McDonnell and the board that could explain the firing of a president best known as a liberal labor scholar.[934] If the smoke was suffocating, the suspected arsonists were not denying it.

DARDEN WAS THE MODEL

Vice-Rector Kington wrote to Rector Dragas in a private e-mail on the day they fired President Sullivan: "As you said today, Darden is a near and visible template for much of what we seek."[935]

The Darden model had long been incubated. From 1998 to 2002, "The University of Virginia in a New Century" retreats with President Casteen and a small group of select donors explicitly included the "theme" of "adopt[ing] public/private structure like Cornell."[936] The book *Shakespeare, Einstein, and the Bottom Line: The Marketing of Higher Education* devoted a chapter to the University of Virginia's subsequent moves toward privatization.[937] In the early part of this century, a public-private fissure began to deepen within the Darden Business School, a neoclassical mosaic of red and white marble. In 2001–2, with state budgets stretched as they always were during recessions, the University of Virginia faced almost $100 million in funding cuts. The response was to effectively privatize Darden by minimizing the funds returned to the university as a whole and by sacrificing academics for proprietary executive education.

By 2003, the board had created "the most autonomous—the most 'private' school—in any American public university." The graduate programs at the School of Law and School of Commerce followed suit. In September 2012, the board directed Sullivan to "undertake a strategic plan that will examine our very purpose and reason for being."[938] Privatization was one option strongly pushed by a working group chaired by commerce dean Carl Zeithaml, whom the board had previously tapped for a brief stint as interim president. As part of this plan, state funding and oversight would end, tuition would be uniform for in-state and out-of-state students and the percentage of out-of-state students would increase.[939]

The finances of graduate business schools in general were unusual in that their clientele were well-heeled, tuition was exorbitant and pedagogy called for classrooms rather than expensive laboratories. Business schools returned money to the greater university: 24 percent of revenue at Michigan, for example, and 40 percent at Emory. For Darden, the level was just 10 percent, which bought the University of Virginia brand like a "franchise fee," noted former associate dean for administration Mark Reisler. Executive education was the moneymaker of American academia, with classes that cost over $1,000 per day and, in Darden's case, generated over half of the business school's revenue. At Darden in 2015, an executive MBA cost an eye-popping $139,300, while meeting just three days per month and two weeks per year over less than two years.[940] To serve its itinerant corporate managers, the Inn at Darden offered pedicures, spa packages and other amenities not seen at the dorms.[941] In early 2016, the board pushed a motion to increase the planned $14 million in renovations for the hotel: "$14 million is a lot of money, and if we could make it $4 or $5 million more we could really make it what I call five star rooms," said Rector William Goodwin.[942] It should be reiterated that the AccessUVA cuts foisted on the university's poorest students were roughly $6 million.

The faculty were also at the executives' beck and call. Professors were encouraged to privilege executive education over research, leading to a comparative dearth of scholarly output from Darden compared to its peer institutions. Moreover, the material specially prepared for particular companies could be withheld from the public, an abandonment of public duty that "turn[ed] Darden itself into a kind of consulting firm."

It did not have to be this way. California, for example, had a larger system, culture wars, governance issues and a professionalized, unified state university system structure with close industry relations, along with lower tuition and higher rankings.[943]

UVA's Future as "UVA, Inc."

Why austerity?

In Christopher Newfield's view:

> *Culture warriors did not openly attack the economic position of the middle class, but they did attack the university. In doing so, they created the conditions for repeated budget cuts to the core middle-class institution. More fundamentally,*

they discredited the cultural conditions of mass-middle-class development, downsized the influence of its leading institution, the university, and reduced the social and political impacts of knowledge workers overall.[944]

The board was tasked with safeguarding the mission of the school and "entrusted with the preservation of the University's many traditions, including the Honor System."[945] Yet the board "acted in disregard of its fiduciary obligations" and failed to live up to the standards expected of every student, all of whom signed an honor code renouncing lying, knowing that the only possible penalty was expulsion.[946] Seemingly everything they did harmed the well-being of the university, and every justification was evidently fraudulent. The school was even placed on accreditation warning after the catastrophic board meddling.[947] The inescapable facts were that the board conspired against the best interests of students, faculty, staff, the state and the university itself. The board was more destructive than any vandal; it did not merely paint G-R-E-E-D on treasured landmarks but also infected the University of Virginia with corruption and falsehoods.

Just like after the McDonnell trials, open and honest reassessment was jettisoned for clandestine and Machiavellian retrenchment. "There is a corporate governance problem!" wrote Dean Carl Zeithaml in an internal e-mail. "They have little or no idea what goes on in the schools. On top of it, there is essentially no oversight of the BOV and little accountability except for what the public can muster."[948] "I have been thinking about all of the positive things I could have achieved in the last year if I didn't have to deal with 'governance issues,'" said Provost John Simon.[949] The future augured poorly for UVA and well for "UVA, Inc."[950] Unlike undergraduates who copied a paper, the mandarins were not excommunicated for repeatedly and publicly lying, cheating and stealing year after year.

Mortgaging the Commonwealth

Why should the board even exist? From a managerial perspective, the board's structure was upside-down: from 1994 to 2010, only 3 percent of board members had PhDs, while 91 percent made political donations over $1,000.[951] The faculty had ample in-house knowledge to manage its own affairs; Helen Dragas, by contrast, had had one job her entire career: working for and inheriting her father's real estate company.[952] University leadership emerged from sleepless doctorate programs, faculty searches, tenure reviews and administrative gauntlets, whereupon chairs, deans, provosts and presidents were ruled by a clique of political hacks.

Perhaps the UVA community thought about it another way: which of the board's decisions were right? Edward Miller, former dean of the Johns Hopkins Medical School, resigned from the board in April 2015:

> *I do not believe I have been able to bring any of my expertise in academia, health care, or research to the University…And year after year, I have implored the administration to put an end to tuition increases that mire Virginia's students and families in a mountain of unnecessary debt. And no matter what anyone says, the latest decision to increase tuition by 23 percent over two years was not done in a transparent manner. To have such a colossal tuition hike and the plan behind it presented at the very last moment to the entire Board and the public was totally unacceptable. I don't understand why the faculty isn't protesting this time. Looking at tuition alone without addressing other issues is simply poor business management. A long-range plan is vital in order to understand the true financial status of the University, but the administration has failed to provide a viable one. With a nearly $6 billion dollar endowment and a faculty that can and should bring in more research dollars, we could have kept tuition and student aid at responsible levels. Sadly, that did not happen, and the only thing the administration has done during my time on the Board of Visitors is mortgage a significant part of the Commonwealth's academic future.[953]*

Miller was replaced by Richmond lawyer Mark Bowles, who had served on the finance committee of Governor McAuliffe's campaign.[954]

Gordon Davies, the former director of the Virginia State Council of Higher Education, stated:

> *If you look at the history of higher education, the university was controlled by, and had to fight for intellectual purity against, the church; then it had to fight against the crown; and now it's against the corporation. There has always been a tension between the university and the funding source that could control the thought. We always have to say that the earth goes around the sun even if it doesn't comport with what the Holy Father says.[955]*

For the author of *Unmaking the Public University*, defunding public education was part of the half-century backlash to the victories of post–World War II

America, which saw students, minorities, women and the middle class assert their rights in colleges and across the nation.[956] This backlash was coupled with the ascendance of a shrewd and visionary cabal of heirs and John Birch Society acolytes who affected mainstream conservatism with their own reactionary neo-conservatism, as outlined in a careful study of their internal documents.[957]

Interestingly, a leading intellectual proponent of the counter-reaction to the New Deal, Great Society, liberal institutions like labor unions and the Ford Foundation, as well as putatively liberal universities, was Richmonder Lewis Powell, a prominent lawyer, tobacco lobbyist and politician. He authored an influential memo to the director of the U.S. Chamber of Commerce in 1971 warning that "the American economic system is under attack" and beseeching corporate allies to band together in its supposed defense. "Powell's memo transformed corporate America," according to investigative journalist Jane Mayer, "prompting a new breed of wealthy ultraconservatives to weaponize their philanthropic giving in order to fight a multifront war of influence over American political thought."[958] His ideas gained even more renown when, within less than six months of writing them, he was appointed to the U.S. Supreme Court by President Nixon.[959]

The crisis at UVA was part of a multigenerational, nationwide, ideological and now predictable cycle: a disinvestment trend begun after courts opened the university's doors in the 1970s, opportunistic restructuring after every recession, perpetual tuition increases and further privatization.[960] There was no truth to the board's stated rationales for radical transformation; as we have seen, they were propagandistic. To say they wanted to transform education from a public good to a corporate finishing school would have been too much, so they invented external reasons and carried out the real work behind closed doors. Not all of this was subconscious. If what they were doing was right, why do it in secret and lie about it? Protesting students had little time, dissenting faculty had little power, but the authoritarian board had plenty of both.

The board faced a choice of ideology versus reality. Think of what happened at the university before and after its worst scandal in modern times. The board was all but unanimous and all but universally criticized in its actions; then, after false promises of reform, it continued on the same path.

In her triumphal first board meeting following reinstatement, President Sullivan addressed the saboteurs: "We are not in any financial crisis."[961]

What crisis, then?

The University of Virginia was in a crisis wholly manufactured by its board of visitors.

THE COMMODIFICATION
OF GOVERNMENT

As long as politics is the shadow cast on society by big business, the attenuation
of the shadow will not change the substance.
—*John Dewey*[962]

The month after the McDonnells were sentenced to prison, Senator
William Stanley bragged without irony about the legislative activity in the
2015 session: "You've got Joe Morrissey, cat bills and the Governor falling
off a horse."[963]

What was the Virginia Way?[964]

Virginia's politicians were greedy, entitled and lazy; they were ignorant
of public policy because they marched to the tune of lobbyists; federal
programs drove Virginia's economy, funded the Virginia Way and allowed
politicians conceit; they enriched themselves on the public dole while
denying necessary investments in the state's destitute schools; conflicts of
interest could not, by definition, exist under Virginia's political philosophy,
so corruption could not end.

It was remarkable that such a system could survive at all. The world routinely
rended, yet the Virginia Way endured like a horseshoe crab. This took unending
cognitive dissonance. Politicians simultaneously believed that government hurt
and helped business, business needed and did not need government help,
power signified merit, graft was moral, government could not create jobs
and politicians worked for the government, benefits bred dependency and
politicians' benefits were necessary. Avarice synthesized these paradoxes.

Bipartisan. Free market Republicans and populist Democrats might have rebelled against the conflation of business and politics. This was not the case in Virginia, where Republicans and Democrats differed on social issues only. In economic policy, whether an R or D abutted a name was irrelevant, and there was only one party: the money party. Senate Democratic leader Dick Saslaw expressed his perceived role in a debate with his Republican counterpart as if they were in a contest: "Go ask Dominion, go ask any of these companies—beer and wine wholesalers, banks, the development community—every one of them will tell you, they will tell you I'm the most pro-business senator."[965] Bipartisanship also extended to self-enrichment, including the jaw-dropping $300 million the legislature appropriated itself for a new office building that passed 38–1 in the Senate and 91–3 in the House and the simultaneous absence of any ethics reform.[966]

Pay-to-play. The fount of Virginia corporate power seemed enigmatic. Dominion, a state electric monopoly, and Altria, which controlled half the nation's cigarette market, were by no means the largest businesses in Virginia or even Richmond, yet they were the two dominant players, essentially writing the state's energy and tobacco policies.[967] This puzzle could be solved by looking at their campaign contributions: Dominion and Altria were the two largest contributors to statewide politics over the past twenty years.[968] Large campaign contributions, which purchased access and obeisance, did not differ functionally from the McDonnell bribes, except that campaign contributions were greater by an order of magnitude. In Virginia, "corporations [were] vast, wealthy powers unto themselves, controlling their servants in Richmond with measured sops mistaken for beneficence," and government was "a wholly owned subsidiary."[969]

Not "pro-business." Importantly, this differed from a pro-business climate, since the more money Dominion and Altria made, the worse off the state's businesses and people were. This was also not a big, or small, or Virginia business agenda, as we have seen contributors from businesses of all sizes game the system to procure favors for themselves and not for others—from Jonnie Williams's insane ploy to test irradiated tobacco on state employees to a con man's fake veterans' charity, for-profit education leeches, an establishment law firm, a global professional sports team, shell companies in southwest Virginia and operations based in other states and countries.

Authoritarian. In the Tenth Amendment, "The powers not delegated to the United States by the Constitution, nor prohibited by it to the States, are reserved to the States, respectively, or to the people." States could either be "home rule" or "Dillon's rule." Under home rule, local government could act except when prohibited by the state; under Dillon's rule, local government could act only when permitted by the state.[970] Virginia was a Dillon's rule state that reserved all power to itself. Did citizens want to expand gun rights, increase the minimum wage or open school before Labor Day? They needed the legislature to grant permission. Should decision-making have been closest to the people? Was that government best that governed least? Virginia politicians railed against out-of-touch D.C. bureaucrats while fortifying the federalism that benefited themselves. In one example, the legislature "passed a state law in 2003 granting permission requested by some school districts to display on their school buses decals of American flags 'no larger than 100 square inches.'"[971]

Anti-capitalist. Politicians catechized capitalism as promoting competition and innovation. The Virginia Way slandered meaningful business competition, and the invisible hand was replaced by a hands-out rush to Uncle Sam.

Operated by a minuscule number of people. Supreme Court justice Louis Brandeis warned, "We may have democracy, or we may have wealth concentrated in the hands of a few, but we cannot have both."[972] The slogan that "the 1%" harm "the other 99%" did not describe Virginia.[973] Virginia's elitist sector was much smaller; a few dozen politicians, CEOs and mandarins dictated economic policy in the state.

Anti-Jeffersonian. The function of government was anathema to the ideals of democracy and freedom worshiped in prose by Thomas Jefferson, Virginia's proudest son. A statue of him greeted visitors in the Capitol atrium under a ceiling that bore his quote, "The most sacred of the duties of a government [is] to do equal and impartial justice to all its citizens." The back pedestal read:

Presented to our fellow Virginians by

The Thomas F. Farrell II Family
The William H. Goodwin Jr. Family
The Brenton S. Halsey Family
May 4, 2012

CONCLUSION

Within two months of the plaque's dedication, the president of Jefferson's university was fired in a backroom coup.

Participants acted as if they were above the law. Even after the McDonnell indictments in January 2014, lawmakers and lobbyists continued to flout the law. At two posh events followed by a reporter in February, thirty-two legislators attended and only two subsequently disclosed it. One of the events was paid for by nine lobbying firms, only two of which disclosed their funding roles.[974] In March, Governor McAuliffe's PAC sent out a solicitation quite literally selling access to the governor.[975] For $10,000, donors could purchase two "roundtable discussions," one with "policy experts" and the other with the governor, while $100,000 donors received a "private dinner with Governor McAuliffe, Mrs. McAuliffe, and special guest."[976] The invitation was recalled after media scrutiny.[977] No one but the McDonnells faced any charges.

Class-based. The government taxed people, not businesses, and tax collectors shoveled piles of cash into corporate steam engines.[978] If taxes needed to be raised—and the existence of the Virginia Way required government—they were raised on people outside of it. This exposed citizens to budget cuts and increased electricity, gasoline and sales taxes and tuition in order to support favored businesses and the ruling class. The income tax was misaligned: citizens reached the top bracket at just $17,000 annual income.[979] Schools and universities were sacrificed in slow motion for decades. Those few who held the keys to power that could have accomplished so much good instead chose to enrich themselves beyond any fortunes they could ever spend.

TABLE 14. SOURCES OF VIRGINIA GENERAL FUND
(NON-EARMARKED) REVENUE, 2014*

Tax	Percent
Individual Income Tax	68%
Sales and Use Tax	19%
All Other Taxes	8%
Corporate Income Tax	5%

* Virginia Department of Taxation, "Annual Report: Fiscal Year 2014," http://www.tax.virginia.gov/sites/tax.virginia.gov/files/Annual_Report_FY_2014_03302015.pdf.

Nontransparent. Curiously, though the idea of the Virginia Way presumed complete transparency, open government laws were harshly criticized and avoided at all costs. When citizens and journalists exposed the Virginia Way, there was a disdainful and mendacious backlash. When the uproar died down, the Virginia Way resumed unabated.

Richmond-centric. Richmond was the locus of political power, and by and large, Richmonders ran the state. Richmond corporations, politicians, donors and media had a disproportionate sway over state issues. Politicians may have had their own local constituencies, but the Richmond-based business class was every politician's constituency. Voters felt that the Richmond business-political machine did not care about them. They were right.

Sold cheaply. The biggest donor in Virginia politics was William Goodwin, who donated about $200,000 per year, which was certainly not cheap, but his typical contributions to individual politicians of $1,000 to $5,000 were not out of reach for many Virginians.[980] We saw earlier that the largest corporate donor bought politicians for around $6,000 per year.

Objectively broken. Outside observers did not share in the illusion of clean government. One group summarized that the findings of

> *a 2012 survey by the nonprofit Center for Public Integrity, Public Radio International and Global Integrity on honest government in the states gave Virginia grades of "F" for legislative accountability and campaign financing. A lack of laws and effective regulation to keep legislators from using public funds for themselves, ineffective regulations about the gifts legislators get, their financial disclosures, the work legislators do when they leave office and granting jobs or favors to family or cronies help put Virginia near the bottom when it comes to the risk of corruption, as does the lack of any limits on campaign donations, the survey said.[981]*

The State Integrity Investigation ranked Virginia forty-seventh out of fifty in its corruption risk report card, earning an overall grade of F.[982] In another report, Virginia ranked fiftieth out of the fifty-one states plus D.C. on the health of its democracy, with F grades on ballot accessibility and state government representation and a D- on political corruption.[983] In 2013, the nonpartisan group Representation 2020 ranked Virginia dead last among the states in gender equity of elected officials.[984] The wealthiest areas of Virginia were funded by federal largesse, while the poorest did not have much federal investment: when comparing the lowest-, average- and highest-paid workers in America, "Virginia is now the most unequal state in the country, and is more unequal than at any time on record."[985]

ANTECEDENTS

This book circumscribed the long history of Virginia, which has been covered thoroughly elsewhere and was not as germane to Virginians' lives as the present day. Brent Tarter, founding editor of the Library of Virginia's *Dictionary of Virginia Biography*, in his brilliant study on the history of Virginia government, wrote:

> *Virginia's political culture has almost always exhibited an inhospitality to changes because the people in charge contrived and protected institutions and practices that worked to their advantage. As a result the state's constitutions and laws have created undemocratic institutions and practices that are also resistant to change. An unexamined reverence for the Spirit of Virginia* [revisionist history] *that Douglas Southall Freeman, Virginius Dabney, and others propagated in the twentieth century allowed a mythic version of the past to constrict the range of options that the state's political leaders contemplated. That reverence, more importantly, either blinded them and the larger public to the undemocratic features of their government or allowed them to ignore or accept those features as if they were part of the inevitable natural order of things.*[986]

Virginia politicians so frequently recalled Washington, Jefferson and Madison that their selective histories became catechisms—but the true founder of modern Virginia politics was U.S. Senator Harry Byrd, whose statue and legacy shadowed Capitol Square like a ghost yet who was so despised by the public that his name was stripped from Richmond-area Harry F. Byrd, now Quioccasin, Middle School in 2016.[987]

In Robert Caro's profile of Byrd, who from the 1920s through the 1960s dominated Virginia more than any politician before or since, we can see the arrogance, contempt, elitism, incompetence, sarcasm and faux gentility that characterized today's politicians and businesspeople.

"The Byrd Machine is genteel," the liberal Reporter *magazine had to admit. "There are no gallus-snapping or banjo-playing characters in Virginia politics." Its hallmark was courtliness, not the demagoguery prevalent in other southern states. "Virginia breeds no Huey Longs or Talmadges,"* John Gunther *wrote in* Inside U.S.A. *"The Byrd Machine is the most urbane and genteel dictatorship in America."*

"He hated public debt with a holy passion," [U.S. Senator Paul] *Douglas was to write of Byrd. "With little or no sympathy for poor people, and instinctively on the side of the rich and powerful, of whom he was one, he nevertheless had a certain rugged personal honesty and a genial air of courtesy towards his opponents, except when severely pressed…"*

While he ran the [Senate Finance C]*ommittee graciously, however, he ran it unyieldingly. "He had a habit of slapping" a fellow senator on the back and laughing, "as if they were both enjoying a good joke," while he was denying a request…*

His economic philosophy was a businessman's philosophy. No one ever called him a reader or a particularly deep thinker, or even a man with more than a surface understanding.[988]

Key wrote in his masterpiece:

Of all the American states, Virginia can lay claim to the most thorough control by an oligarchy. Political power has been closely held by a small group of leaders who, themselves and their predecessors, have subverted democratic institutions and deprived most Virginians of a voice in their government. The Commonwealth possesses characteristics more akin to those of England at about the time of the Reform Bill of 1832 than to those of any other state of the present-day South. It is a political museum piece. Yet the little oligarchy that rules Virginia demonstrates a sense of honor, an aversion to open venality, a degree of sensitivity to public opinion, a concern for efficiency in administration, and, so long as it does not cost much, a feeling of social responsibility… [Byrd formed] *an autocratic machine which may long outlive him.*[989]

In the early twenty-first century, the Virginia Way was the descendant of Harry Byrd's machine made bipartisan, yet was more venal than Key had found in the mid-twentieth.

WHOSE COMMONWEALTH WERE THEY PRESERVING?

State Senator John Chichester, whose definition of the Virginia Way began this book, concluded his essay:

> *We can all think of crucial junctures in our history. And while by today's standards, all of the original choices were not correct, they were ultimately corrected so that our way of life did not depart significantly from the traces in which we walk.*
>
> *We can take comfort in the lessons of Virginia history. At those crucial points in our journey, Virginia's political leaders will reach deep and find fortitude and courage. They will coalesce and make that unpopular choice, if it truly is necessary to preserve the treasure that is our Commonwealth.*[990]

People may say that politicians failed their voters, but that would be a misconception, for the Virginia Way was working exactly as designed: it benefited the architects. When that is understood, the existential dilemmas of, Reassessment or retrenchment? Reality or ideology? became much easier to answer. If government was for sale, then society would naturally reflect the values of the ultra-wealthy rather than the majority of citizens who chose to dedicate their lives to family, religion, science, service or pursuits other than accumulation. Far from being anomalous, the McDonnell corruption scandal was a microcosm for the operation of Virginia politics and government writ large. Power does not necessarily corrupt; power *reveals*.[991]

The Capitol was built atop one of Richmond's Romanesque hills and was visible from every station, its height surpassed only by churches until it was enveloped by corporate monoliths.[992] Through the only remaining slit of green space between the skyscrapers, citizens can now see the billowing Dominion smokestacks in east Chesterfield County of the most polluting power plant in Virginia.[993] "This corridor has the county's 10 poorest schools, which are in structural decline," writes a local reporter. "These ZIP codes also feature the highest concentration of air pollution in the metro area, according to a Virginia chapter of the Sierra Club report released in July. Children in this area are subjected to asthma triggers from power plants, such as ammonia, hydrochloric acid and sulfuric acid."[994]

What if they were your children?

The Virginia Way cannot change as long as politicians' self-conceptions hinge on their own righteousness, for if there can be no fall, there can be no catharsis. Virginia government can shine if its political and economic powers would act in the public interest rather than their own. But now, Virginia government is neither capitalist, nor communist, but commodified.

METHODOLOGY AND LITERATURE REVIEW

This book is written for multiple audiences so that all may read it, including high school, college and graduate students, as well as professional audiences. I agree with the sentiment of the authors of *The Tea Party and the Remaking of Republican Conservatism*: "Using vivid English and avoiding dry academic jargon are things we strive to do. Still, make no mistake, we are social scientists; our research is carefully grounded in the best evidence we can find. The footnotes are there for anyone who wants to look closely."[995]

METHODOLOGY

I read every book on Virginia politics in the Library of Virginia's catalogue that covered any period over the last twenty-five years (1990–2015) and utilized the news aggregator at the Virginia Public Access Project (http://vpap.org/vanews) to read every article on Virginia politics published over a span of three and a half years (July 1, 2012, to January 1, 2016) in the only newspapers to maintain full- or part-time state political reporters in Virginia (*Daily Press*, *Richmond Times-Dispatch*, *Roanoke Times*, *Virginian-Pilot*, *Washington Post*), which were also the top four and seventh-largest state newspapers by circulation.[996]

I selected six comprehensive themes for describing the functioning of Virginia politics and government: the executive, the legislature, corporations, health, K-12 education and higher education. These themes represented the fundamental ways that Virginians were affected by their state government, and I chose the most newsworthy and consequential case studies in each category from 2012 to 2015:

1) the McDonnells' trials, which served as an introduction and case study for the most powerful executive branch politician;
2) the legislature, which provided the political backdrop and case study for the most powerful branch of government;
3) the corporate-political nexus vis-à-vis Dominion, by far the most powerful player in Virginia politics;
4) policymaking in public health as it related to the other five topics;
5) local government, particularly K-12 education and economic development in the state capital; and
6) higher education, focusing on the state's flagship university and its management by the board of visitors of the University of Virginia.

Having targeted research areas, I read every academic journal article on Virginia politics published from January 1, 2012, to January 1, 2016, and relating to that same time period found by Google Scholar searches of "Virginia" and either "Bob McDonnell," "Terry McAuliffe" or "Teresa Sullivan." Out of roughly 250 total hits, 30 or so were relevant. Given the nature of academic publishing, the scholarly literature on very recent events was sparse.

I then searched journals that may have a more parochial focus on Virginia. I searched for articles with "Virginia" in the title in Virginia law reviews from January 1, 2010, to January 1, 2016, at the law schools of the University of Richmond (four journals), University of Virginia (ten), Washington and Lee (four) and William and Mary (six). In addition, I examined every article published since 2000 in the University of Virginia's *Virginia News Letter*. Few of these returned topical hits, as expected (e.g., *University of Virginia Sports & Entertainment Law Journal*, *Washington and Lee German Law Journal*), with the exceptions of the *University of Richmond Law Review*, which published an annual compendium of the past Virginia legislative session; *Virginia News Letter*; and the *William and Mary Environmental Law & Policy Review*.

LITERATURE REVIEW

There are no books that describe Virginia politics and government in 2016 and too few that describe it at any time. In my opinion, the best book on modern Virginia politics is Dinan's *The Virginia State Constitution*.[997] In examining the meaning of the Virginia Constitution, he chronicles present legislation and litigation, and his book is an excellent starting point for understanding all three branches of government. He misses, unfortunately, the political operation of government and economics that this book reveals.

Kidd's superb edited volume, *Government and Politics in Virginia: The Old Dominion at the 21st Century*, crucially comprehends that government and politics are indivisible, especially in the chapters authored by Kidd himself.[998] That book recommends much to the structure of this book, including a government-politics-policy synthesis, a case study format, overall readability and audience, clear figures and appropriate survey of subject matter (e.g., legislature, governor, campaigns) grounded in contemporary events. This book improves on Kidd's with its timeframe (i.e., nearly two decades later), consistent tone (as opposed to multiple authors often reproducing material) and scholarly grounding (hundreds as compared to five to thirty-two footnotes per chapter). Much the same can be said about Morris and Sabato's decade-older work.[999]

Atkinson made a strong contribution to the history of the 1990s with his 2006 *Virginia in the Vanguard*.[1000] He is a good historian. Despite his efforts, Atkinson reveals his partisanship when we move to the modern, two-party era, the era that most interests me. Atkinson was legal counsel and policy director for Republican governor George Allen in the 1990s and worked for Bob McDonnell, in addition to holding a slew of board appointments and advisories at the University of Virginia and George Mason University. He has a frontline role in the Virginia Way, while his history attempts a bird's-eye view. He is currently the head of lobbying for the McGuireWoods law firm, which sober reporters have taken to calling Virginia's "shadow government."[1001] Maintaining objectivity might be impossible, as he acknowledged. He also acknowledged that he did not give "the same degree of descriptive detail and analysis" to the years after 2000.[1002]

Two more recent books, *Governing Virginia* and *Virginia Government: Institutions and Policies*, fill some of this void.[1003] They are shorter works with aims of being course primers and are snapshots that should be judged as such. *Governing Virginia* is a collection of essays from politicians and government functionaries. It is useful as a window into their minds, but readers must look between the lines to perceive their refractions. They both describe a sanitized version of three branches of coequal government. In this, they fall short. Political science should be honest, and state government does not operate in the ways they contend.

Wallenstein's impressive history of Virginia, *Cradle of America*, devotes two and a half pages to Virginia history after 2007, as does Rozell's chapter on Virginia in *The New Politics of the Old South: An Introduction to Southern Politics*.[1004] Tarter's brilliant work, *The Grandees of Government*, is well worth reading for those who find this book appealing, yet again, it does not take readers to the present day or with much substance into the past several decades.[1005]

Two others merit mentioning for their elucidations of Virginia political campaigns. Half of *Netroots Rising* is devoted to the emerging Internet-linked activists who formed the nexus of Jim Webb's successful 2006 challenge to incumbent U.S. Senator George Allen.[1006] *Swing County* details the Obama campaign's historic victory in Virginia through the eyes of high-level Loudon County volunteers.[1007] Both of these are worth reading for those interested in statewide electoral politics. Federal campaigns are not a focus of this book, one of whose theses is that most Democrats and Republicans in the state legislature are similar in their economic policy prescriptions.

Going back a bit further, *Second Coming: The New Christian Right in Virginia Politics* was published in 1996.[1008] The resurgence of political evangelism is in vogue with the wax and wane of national Republican politics.

When Hell Froze Over is possibly the best book ever written on Virginia politics since the formation of the two-party system after desegregation.[1009] Yancey gets behind the scenes of the historic Wilder campaign for lieutenant governor in 1985, which presaged the first popular election of an African American governor in the United States four year later, itself chronicled in the lesser *Claiming the Dream* and *Virginia's Native Son*.[1010] Playing underdog, the Wilder campaign set off on a historic station wagon tour of Virginia, with eccentric wunderkind Paul Goldman managing it all with folders crammed full of crumpled loose-leafs. An insightful take on Henry Howell's liberal gubernatorial campaign in the 1970s is Garrett Epps's *The Shad Treatment*, a semi-autobiographical novel of a Richmonder's struggle to fight the city's reactionary politics and its mummified upper crust.[1011]

Authors have produced several biographies of varying merit. The best is *Mark Warner the Dealmaker*, based on extensive interviews summarizing his business and gubernatorial career, though from time to time it ventures into hagiography.[1012] There is *Starting Over*, a sycophantic biography of Governor Allen, and *Opportunity Time*, a soporific memoir from the governor who served from 1970 to 1974.[1013] Governor Wilder recently released his own memoirs, which lack substance.[1014]

Strong histories of Richmond can be found, but they touch on modern politics barely or not at all. Reverend Campbell's *Richmond's Unhealed History* provides a critical look at the forces that shape current Richmond, from the founding through war and desegregation to the current dichotomy of poverty and plenty.[1015] Two books on Richmond infrastructure reveal more than their titles indicate: *Nonesuch Place*, which documents the construction of the city's major landmarks, and *Built by Blacks*, which memorializes African American contributions and injustice and has a good chapter on urban development.[1016] *Rights for a Season* introduces original research on the Richmond civil rights movement but culminates with the election of Richmond's first African American mayor in the 1970s.[1017]

Three strong works concentrate on specific aspects of Virginia power. *Five Miles Away, a World Apart*, written by a Harvard professor and former clerk to U.S. Supreme Court Chief Justice William Rehnquist, compares Richmond's Freeman and Thomas Jefferson High Schools within the context of American education law.[1018] The book deserves much more attention than it receives. *Thunder on the Mountain* excoriates Massey Energy, formerly headquartered in Richmond, for its reckless safety and environmental records.[1019] *Virginia Climate Fever* is a first-rate look at science and public policy but only touches on modern politics.[1020] *Something Must Be Done About Prince Edward County* is an engaging history of local education in that Virginia locale over the past sixty years.[1021]

Other books deal with Virginia only in part, such as *The Price of Admission*'s chapter on the University of Virginia or anecdotes from *Blue Dixie* and *Still Fighting the Civil War*.[1022] *Factory Man* studies the Bassett furniture family of Galax in the context of globalization but leaves little room for the state capital.[1023]

A schism exists between state historians and journalists. The historians see little wrong, and the reporters see a little wrong everyday. It is bizarre that any schism looms whatsoever. Scribes of "the first rough draft of history" are the backbone of this book.[1024] Notwithstanding the dearth of serious political books, the state's journalism is prolific. Articles appear virtually every day that critique the inner workings of a sclerotic political-economic system. The McDonnell bribery scandal may never have been revealed were it not for the gumption of investigative journalist Rosalind Helderman of the *Washington Post*. She and her colleagues Jenna Portnoy, Laura Vozzella and Matt Zapotosky saw an oddball case of a governor's embezzling chef and "followed the money" through his boss's indictments, trials and convictions.[1025] A number of other reporters at the *Post* keep politicians minimally honest. Though the *Post* comes from the other partisan viewpoint of the *Richmond Times-Dispatch*, they have much in common. *Style Weekly* is less rhetorically constrained and has excellent long-form pieces. That and the *Richmond Free Press* form a triumvirate that covers local Richmond news well. The *Daily Press*, *Virginian-Pilot* and *Roanoke Times* have crack reporters covering state politics. There are many other organizations, including the TV news affiliates, Associated Press and VCU Capital News Service, that have more ephemeral yet still important presences in the capital. With 140 legislators to cover, every reporter makes a difference.

Virginia has active political blogs, and I rely on three: Bearing Drift (Republican), Blue Virginia (Democratic) and The Bull Elephant (Tea Party), as well as the news aggregators at the nonpartisan Virginia Public Access Project.

Royalties and Fair Use

I am not receiving any royalties or other income from this book; rather, I am donating them to Richmond's public schools, which does not imply their endorsement. I wrote the book because the public has a right to know the truth about its government.

I disagree with restricting the free market of ideas by government copyright, but I appreciate that publishers have to stay in business; thus, I grant all permissions for others to quote from and otherwise use this work to the maximum extent permitted by law and by my publisher.

ACKNOWLEDGEMENTS

I want to thank first the journalists whose fortitude made this book possible. I want to single out those who have worked in Virginia politics newsrooms in no particular order: Jeff Schapiro, Olympia Meola, Markus Schmidt, Graham Moomaw, Ned Oliver, Tammie Smith, Michael Paul Williams, A. Barton Hinkle and Todd Culbertson at the *Richmond Times-Dispatch*; Jeremy Lazarus at the *Richmond Free Press*; Rosalind Helderman, Matt Zapotosky, Laura Vozzella and Jenna Portnoy at the *Washington Post*; Travis Fain and Dave Ress at the *Daily Press*; Dwayne Yancey of the *Roanoke Times*; Alan Suderman of the Associated Press; Peter Galuszka and Edwin Slipek of *Style Weekly*; and James Bacon, Lowell Feld, Norman Leahy and Jeanine Martin at Bacon's Rebellion, Blue Virginia, Bearing Drift and The Bull Elephant, respectively. The work of each of these authors was critical for formulating this book. Their management and staffs who work behind the bylines deserve praise for calling politicians to account.

I owe a particular debt of gratitude to the staff of the *Charlottesville Hook* (now *C-Ville Weekly*) for telling the truth about the malady that gripped the University of Virginia.

The section on the reality of child labor exploitation in Virginia tobacco fields was all due to the research of Human Rights Watch, and I thank it for its compassion.

I owe more than I can say to those teachers who gave me the tools to create with words, think analytically and dream: Yvonne Pinckney of St. Stephen's Preschool; Blair Chewning, John Coates, Ann Griffin and Neil

Weiser of Collegiate School; David Schaad and Todd Woerner of Duke University; Wilma Dunaway, her husband Don, George Simmons and Peter Wallenstein of Virginia Tech; and Michael Dancisak and Raj Ettarh of Tulane University.

I wish to thank the team at The History Press, particularly J. Banks Smither for his tireless professionalism, optimism and guidance, and the staff at the Library of Virginia for their dedication and expertise. Thanks also to my friends Taylor Beck, Libby Boudreau, Katie Branch, Max Comess, Greg Rosenberg, Billy Schirmer and Liz Sweet for being your kind selves and Bumi, Lola, Scout and Surya for being so sweet.

Most importantly, I want to thank my family in Virginia and Texas— including my extended family: the Fountains, Cottrells, Stuart Fletcher Trope and Russ Sterling—for believing in me, and especially Mom, to whom this book is dedicated.

I hope this book will make our government better reflect all its citizens' values and thus help our state's wonderful people and beautiful animals.

NOTES

Introduction

1. Matt Zapotosky, "Appeals Judges Pepper McDonnell with Skeptical Questions," *Washington Post*, May 12, 2015, http://www.washingtonpost.com/local/virginia-politics/what-to-expect-from-oral-arguments-over-bob-mcdonnells-appeal/2015/05/11/32796f76-f35d-11e4-b2f3-af5479e6bbdd_story.html.

2. John Chichester, "The Virginia Way," in Morgan and Giesen, *Governing Virginia*, 229.

3. Caro, *Passage of Power*, xiv (italics in original).

4. Michael Duffy, "Karl Rove Won't Rule Out Donald Trump Nomination," *Time*, December 2, 2015, http://time.com/4132504/karl-rove-donald-trump; Rachel Weiner, "In Virginia, the GOP Establishment Battles Back—for the White House," *Washington Post*, June 10, 2015, https://www.washingtonpost.com/local/virginia-politics/in-virginia-the-gop-establishment-battles-back--for-the-white-house/2015/06/10/89289e52-0a4e-11e5-95fd-d580f1c5d44e_story.html.

5. H. Brevy Cannon, "U. VA Experts: 2012 Election Shows Virginia Is Demographic Bellwether for Nation," *UVA Today*, November 7, 2012, http://news.virginia.edu/content/uva-experts-2012-election-shows-virginia-demographic-bellwether-nation.

6. Mark Rozell, "Virginia: From Red to Blue?" in Bullock and Rozell, *New Politics of the Old South*, 137–55.

7. Virginia Board of Elections, "Official Results—General Election—November 5, 2013," http://elections.virginia.gov/Files/Electionresults/2013/November-5/electionresults.virginia.gov/resultsSWde2d.html?eid=7&type=SWR&map=CTY; M.V. Hood, Quentin Kidd and Irwin Morris, "Race and the Tea Party in the Old Dominion: Split-Ticket Voting in the 2013 Virginia Elections," *PS: Political Science and Politics* 48, no. 1 (2015): 109.

8. Rockefeller Institute of State Government, Brookings Institution and Fels Institute of Government, "Virginia: Baseline Report: State-Level Field Network Study of the Implementation of the Affordable Care Act," January 2015, http://www.rockinst.org/aca/states/Virginia/2015-01-Virginia_Baseline_Report.pdf, p. 5.

9. GovTrack, "Members of Congress: Virginia," https://www.govtrack.us/congress/members/VA.

10. Sam Frizell and Zeke Miller, "What Hillary Clinton Learned from This 2013 Campaign," *Time*, June 30, 2015, http://time.com/3940783/hillary-clinton-terry-mcauliffe-robby-mook.

11. Trevor Baratko, "Clinton Touches on Race, Gun Control and Gay Rights at Virginia Rally," *Loudon Times-Mirror*, June 27, 2015, http://www.loudountimes.com/news/article/clinton_touches_on_race_gun_control_and_gay_rights_at_virginia_rally432; Associated Press, "Candidates Talk Guns at Virginia Tech Debate," *Martinsville Bulletin*, October 25, 2013, http://www.martinsvillebulletin.com/news/local/candidates-talk-guns-at-virginia-tech-debate/article_b0d6143e-eb88-5bbf-a38a-5982ca276010.html.

12. Moser, *Blue Dixie*, 11.

13. Amy Chozick, "Hillary Clinton Visits Virginia, a Bellwether State in 2016 Race," *New York Times*, June 26, 2015, http://www.nytimes.com/politics/first-draft/2015/06/26/hillary-clinton-visits-virginia-a-bellwether-state-in-2016-race/?partner=rssnyt&emc=rss&_r=0; Frizell and Miller, "What Hillary Clinton Learned"; Baratko, "Clinton Touches on Race."

14. Coyle, *Roberts Court*, 275; Toobin, *Oath*, 184–85.

15. Editorial Board, "Big Money's Corrosive Spread," *Washington Post*, May 9, 2015, http://www.washingtonpost.com/opinions/big-moneys-corrosive-spread/2015/05/09/6ee308c6-f594-11e4-bcc4-e8141e5eb0c9_story.html.

16. Martin Gilens and Benjamin Page, "Testing Theories of American Politics: Elites, Interest Groups, and Average Citizens," *Perspectives on Politics* 12, no. 3 (September 2014): 576–77, http://journals.cambridge.org/download.php?file=%2FPPS%2FPPS12_03%2FS1537592714001595a.pdf&code=bbcd58f7e38be2c58a9e7b504bdd5319.

17. Nicholas Confessore, Sarah Cohen and Karen Yourish, "Small Pool of Rich Donors Dominates Election Giving," *New York Times*, August 1, 2015, http://www.nytimes.com/2015/08/02/us/small-pool-of-rich-donors-dominates-election-giving.html?_r=0; Peter Olsen-Phillips, Russ Choma, Sarah Bryner and Doug Weber, "The Political One Percent of the One Percent: Megadonors Fuel Rising Cost of Elections in 2014," Sunlight Foundation, April 30, 2015, http://sunlightfoundation.com/blog/2015/04/30/the-political-one-percent-of-the-one-percent-megadonors-fuel-rising-cost-of-elections-in-2014; Andrew Cain, "Jeb Bush Speaks at Republican Fundraiser in Richmond," *Roanoke Times*, February 17, 2015, http://www.roanoke.com/news/virginia/jeb-bush-speaks-at-republican-fundraiser-in-richmond/article_af10c896-c1ca-5f0e-8ad7-9115b6c359d1.html; Gabriel de Benedetti, "Hillary Clinton to Headline Virginia Event," *Politico*, May 13, 2015, http://www.politico.com/story/2015/05/hillary-clinton-virginia-democratic-party-dinner-campaign-speech-2016-117913.html;

Alan Suderman, "Chris Christie Set to Meet with Top Virginia Donors," *Virginian-Pilot*, Associated Press, February 19, 2015, http://hamptonroads.com/2015/02/chris-christie-set-meet-top-virginia-donors.

18. Tarini Parti, "Jeb Bush Aids Down-Ballot Republicans," *Politico*, February 16, 2015, http://www.politico.com/story/2015/02/jeb-bush-virginia-republicans-115239.html; Cain, "Jeb Bush Speaks at Republican Fundraiser."

19. Alan Rappeport and Patrick Healy, "Who Might Hillary Clinton's Running Mate Be if She's the Nominee?" *New York Times*, April 23, 2016, http://www.nytimes.com/interactive/2016/04/24/us/politics/hillary-clinton-running-mate.html?smid=pl-share&_r=0; Anita Kumar, "McDonnell Tops Hypothetical Vice Presidential Contenders List," *Washington Post*, March 8, 2012, http://www.washingtonpost.com/blogs/virginia-politics/post/mcdonnell-tops-hypothetical-vice-presidential-contenders-list/2012/03/08/gIQAeE8XzR_blog.html.

20. Lowell Feld, "Is Gov. McAuliffe Really 'Getting Everything He's Asking For' from GOP-Controlled Gen. Assembly?" Blue Virginia, April 5, 2015, http://www.bluevirginia.us/diary/13128/is-gov-mcauliffe-getting-everything-hes-asking-for.

21. Jeff Schapiro, "Dealmaker-in-Chief Does Business with Dominion," *Richmond Times-Dispatch*, February 10, 2015, http://www.richmond.com/news/virginia/government-politics/jeff-schapiro/article_0ca099b5-fef3-5af7-8d5b-d07163d9d8ee.html.

22. Laura Vozzella, "McAuliffe Suddenly Seems Chummy with Virginia's GOP Lawmakers," *Washington Post*, April 4, 2015, http://www.washingtonpost.com/local/virginia-politics/mcauliffe-suddenly-seems-chummy-with-virginias-gop-lawmakers/2015/04/04/f7ff5548-d8d3-11e4-b3f2-607bd612aeac_story.html.

23. James Madison, Federalist No. 51, http://www.constitution.org/fed/federa51.htm.

24. Jeff Schapiro, "Governor, Legislature—A Clash of Constitutional Perogatives," *Richmond Times-Dispatch*, April 20, 2016, http://www.richmond.com/news/virginia/government-politics/jeff-schapiro/article_620bfb6d-d897-5f30-8c3e-b7470c27089a.html.

25. James Madison, Federalist No. 48, http://www.constitution.org/fed/federa48.htm; Dinan, *Virginia State Constitution*, 113–38.

26. Chris Cillizza, "Veepstakes 2012: The Inaugural Edition," *Washington Post*, March 23, 2012, http://www.washingtonpost.com/blogs/the-fix/post/veepstakes-2012-the-inaugural-edition/2012/03/22/gIQAAAbKUS_blog.html; Kumar, "McDonnell Tops Hypothetical Vice Presidential Contenders List"; Alexander Burns, "Bob McDonnell the Survivor," *Politico*, October 9, 2013, http://www.politico.com/story/2013/10/bob-mcdonnell-virginia-governor-survivor-98104.html.

27. Rosalind Helderman, Matt Zapotosky and Justin Jouvenal, "Prosecutor Spars with McDonnell During Questioning," *Washington Post*, August 25, 2014, http://www.washingtonpost.com/local/virginia-politics/prosecutor-spars-with-mcdonnell-during-questioning/2014/08/25/0f4b51ae-2c70-11e4-994d-202962a9150c_story.html.

28. A note about this section: I have chosen not to recount some of the tawdrier aspects of the McDonnell case. First, I do not wish to bring the other members of the McDonnell family into the story. They have been through more than most and were never charged with any crimes. Secondly, I do not want to record the human frailties that surround this case. I see no public purpose in doing so.

29. Kurt Eichenwald, "The Funny-Money Man Behind McDonnell's Fall," *Newsweek*, January 23, 2014, http://www.newsweek.com/2014/01/24/funny-money-man-behind-mcdonnells-fall-245100.html.

30. Rosalind Helderman and Laura Vozzella, "VA Gov. McDonnell on Two-Way Street with Chief Executive of Struggling Company," *Washington Post*, March 30, 2013, http://www.washingtonpost.com/local/dc-politics/va-gov-mcdonnell-in-close-relationship-with-owner-of-struggling-company/2013/03/30/43f34fb8-97ea-11e2-814b-063623d80a60_story.html.

31. Peter Galuszka, "A Chemical Romance," *Style Weekly*, July 16, 2013, http://www.styleweekly.com/richmond/a-chemical-romance/Content?oid=1920271.

32. A. Barton Hinkle, "Handouts Corrupt All Governors," *Richmond Times-Dispatch*, August 31, 2014, http://www.richmond.com/opinion/our-opinion/bart-hinkle/article_f2fbf4a5-a760-5674-8c67-c88edc5b07d0.html.

33. McDonnell indictment, https://localtvwtvr.files.wordpress.com/2014/01/mcdonnell-indictment.pdf. The narrative in this section and the next ("Quid Pro Quo" and "Cover-up") is based directly on the indictment, unless otherwise cited. For the sake of clarity and brevity, this chapter will refer to Governor Bob McDonnell as "Bob," First Lady Maureen McDonnell as "Maureen" and both of them together as "the McDonnells." Bob's sister is also named Maureen McDonnell, but she is not mentioned in this book.

34. Associated Press, "Chef to Virginia Gov. Bob McDonnell Leaves Job Amid Probe," *CBS DC*, March 23, 2012, http://washington.cbslocal.com/2012/03/23/chef-to-virginia-gov-bob-mcdonnell-resigns-amid-probe.

35. Staff, "Key Events in the McDonnell Corruption Case," *Richmond Times-Dispatch*, January 6, 2015, http://www.richmond.com/news/local/government-politics/article_9ee747e6-e739-5156-82d8-9628e317be8c.html.

36. Rosalind Helderman and Laura Vozzella, "VA Gov. McDonnell on Two-Way Street with Chief Executive of Struggling Company," *Washington Post*, March 30, 2013, http://www.washingtonpost.com/local/dc-politics/va-gov-mcdonnell-in-close-relationship-with-owner-of-struggling-company/2013/03/30/43f34fb8-97ea-11e2-814b-063623d80a60_story.html.

37. Bob Lewis, "McDonnell Repays Loans, Apologizes," *Northern Virginia Daily*, July 23, 2013, http://www.nvdaily.com/news/2013/07/mcdonnell-repays-loans-apologizes; *Northern Virginia Daily*, "McDonnell Says He Will Return Remaining Donor's Gifts," July 30, 2013, http://www.nvdaily.com/news/2013/07/gov-mcdonnell-says-he-will-return-remaining-donors-gifts; *Northern Virginia Daily*, "McDonnell: Daughter Returned Wedding Gift," July 31, 2013, http://www.nvdaily.com/news/2013/07/mcdonnell-daughter-returned-wedding-gift.

38. Helderman and Vozzella, "VA Gov. McDonnell on Two-Way Street."

39. Virginia Public Access Project, "Bob McDonnell: Conflicts of Interest Disclosure: Overview: 2013," http://www.vpap.org/candidates/5666/conflicts_disclosure.

40. Rosalind Helderman and Carol Leonnig, "McDonnell Rejected Plea Offer to Face One Felony, Spare Wife Any Charges, Avoid Trial," *Washington Post*, January 23, 2014, http://www.washingtonpost.com/politics/gov-mcdonnell-rejected-plea-offer-to-face-one-felony-spare-wife-any-charges-avoid-trial/2014/01/23/96b53a62-83bd-11e3-8099-9181471f7aaf_story.html.

41. Frank Green, "Former Star Scientific CEO Williams Lands Immunity," *Roanoke Times*, July 12, 2014, http://www.roanoke.com/news/virginia/former-star-scientific-ceo-williams-lands-immunity/article_5a2f6878-fe6c-5b84-9dbc-077c444bf104.html.

42. Rosalind Helderman, Carol Leonnig and Sari Horwitz, "Prosecutors Were Ready to Charge VA Gov. McDonnell, but Final Decision Delayed by Justice Officials," *Washington Post*, December 18, 2013, http://www.washingtonpost.com/local/dc-politics/prosecutors-were-ready-to-charge-va-gov-mcdonnell-but-final-decision-delayed-by-justice-officials/2013/12/18/32260fa6-67fa-11e3-a0b9-249bbb34602c_story.html.

43. McDonnell indictment, https://localtvwtvr.files.wordpress.com/2014/01/mcdonnell-indictment.pdf.

44. Rosalind Helderman, Carol Leonnig and Sari Horwitz, "Former VA Gov. McDonnell and Wife Charged in Gifts Case," *Washington Post*, January 21, 2014, http://www.washingtonpost.com/local/virginia-politics/former-va-gov-mcdonnell-and-wife-charged-in-gifts-case/2014/01/21/1ed704d2-82cb-11e3-9dd4-e7278db80d86_story.html.

45. Ibid.

46. Personal observation, August 2014.

47. Patrick Wilson, "McDonnell and Wife Seen Together at Virginia Beach Show," *Virginian-Pilot*, June 19, 2015, http://hamptonroads.com/2015/06/mcdonnell-and-wife-seen-together-virginia-beach-show.

48. Olympia Meola, Jim Nolan and Frank Green, "Prosecutor Attacks McDonnell's Version of Events," *Roanoke Times*, August 25, 2014, http://www.roanoke.com/news/politics/prosecutor-attacks-mcdonnell-s-version-of-events/article_1e0aa537-775a-5499-92e5-d014ae623f76.html.

49. Ned Oliver, "Legal Stylings," *Style Weekly*, May 27, 2014, http://www.styleweekly.com/richmond/the-governors-shade-good-hair-goes-gray/Content?oid=2079464.

50. Rosalind Helderman, Matt Zapotosky and Justin Jouvenal, "Prosecutor Spars with McDonnell During Questioning," *Washington Post*, August 25, 2014, http://www.washingtonpost.com/local/virginia-politics/prosecutor-spars-with-mcdonnell-during-questioning/2014/08/25/0f4b51ae-2c70-11e4-994d-202962a9150c_story.html.

51. Frank Green, "Judge Tosses Out One of Maureen McDonnell's Convictions," *Richmond Times-Dispatch*, December 1, 2014, http://www.richmond.com/news/virginia/article_4a21bd65-3b55-5948-b6a3-426492a1e56f.html.

52. Rosalind Helderman and Matt Zapotosky, "Ex-VA Governor Robert McDonnell Guilty of 11 Counts of Corruption," *Washington Post*, September 4, 2014, http://www.washingtonpost.com/local/virginia-politics/mcdonnell-jury-in-third-day-of-deliberations/2014/09/04/0e01ff88-3435-11e4-9e92-0899b306bbea_story.html.

53. Peter Galuszka, "Gift-Gate: Star Scientific, Jonnie Williams & a Governor in Hot Water," *Hook*, July 18, 2013, http://www.readthehook.com/109891/here-comes-jonnie-mcdonnell-gifts-keep-giving.

54. Staff, "Verdicts in the McDonnell Trial," *Richmond Times-Dispatch*, September 4, 2014, http://www.richmond.com/news/state-regional/virginia-politics/

verdicts-in-the-mcdonnell-trial/article_9e1b84d2-3385-11e4-9388-0017a43b2370.html.

55. Matt Zapotosky, "Appeals Judges Pepper McDonnell Defense with Skeptical Questions," *Washington Post*, May 12, 2015, http://www.washingtonpost.com/local/virginia-politics/what-to-expect-from-oral-arguments-over-bob-mcdonnells-appeal/2015/05/11/32796f76-f35d-11e4-b2f3-af5479e6bbdd_story.html.

56. Patrick Wilson, "Letters of Support Pour in for Bob McDonnell," *Virginian-Pilot*, December 24, 2014, http://hamptonroads.com/2014/12/letters-support-pour-bob-mcdonnell.

57. George Will, "Virginia's Former Governor Faces Prison over Politics," *Washington Post*, January 6, 2016, https://www.washingtonpost.com/opinions/virginias-former-governor-faces-prison-over-politics/2016/01/06/2af3ff74-b3e6-11e5-9388-466021d971de_story.html.

58. *McCutcheon v. Federal Election Commission*, 572 US Supreme Court, 2014, pp. 2–3, http://www.supremecourt.gov/opinions/13pdf/12-536_e1pf.pdf. Chief Justice Roberts's opinion was joined by Justices Alito, Kennedy and Scalia; Justice Thomas wrote his own concurring opinion.

59. "Brief for Members and Former Members of the Virginia General Assembly as *Amici Curiae* in Support of Appellant," United States Court of Appeals for the Fourth Circuit, Record Number 15-4019, http://valawyersweekly.com/files/2015/03/Amicus-of-General-Assembly.pdf. The brief was signed by the following legislators: fourteen current senators, one former senator, nineteen current delegates and five former delegates; Chemerinsky, *Constitutional Law*, 402.

60. Wilder, *Son of Virginia*, 168.

61. Shaun Kenney, "Slow News Day at the Virginia Pilot [*sic*], Eh?" *Bearing Drift*, April 1, 2015, http://bearingdrift.com/2015/04/01/slow-news-day-at-the-virginia-pilot-eh.

62. Val Thompson, "Former Republican Spokesman Calls on McDonnell to Resign," July 17, 2013, http://www.newsplex.com/home/headlines/Former-Republican-Spokesman-Calls-for-McDonnell-to-Resign-215900741.html.

63. Travis Fain, "Former AG Troy: McDonnell 'Not Even Ethically' Wrong," *Daily Press*, May 13, 2015, http://www.dailypress.com/news/politics/shad-plank-blog/dp-former-ag-troy-mcdonnell-not-even-ethically-wrong-20150513-post.html.

64. Tracy Sears, "State Will Not Pursue Charges Against Former Gov. McDonnell," WTVR-CBS, January 28, 2014, http://wtvr.com/2014/01/28/state-will-not-pursue-charges-against-former-gov-mcdonnell.

65. Andrew Cain, "Six Former Attorneys General Back McDonnell's Release Pending Appeal," *Roanoke Times*, January 16, 2015, http://www.roanoke.com/news/six-former-attorneys-general-back-mcdonnell-s-release-pending-appeal/article_4d5534b8-d43a-5c18-97a3-c304d02935a8.html.

66. Catalina Camia, "Poll: 68% of Virginia Voters Agree with McDonnell Guilty Verdict," *USA Today*, September 9, 2014, http://onpolitics.usatoday.com/2014/09/09/bob-mcdonnell-guilty-verdict-virginia-poll.

67. Wilson, "McDonnell and Wife Seen Together."

CHAPTER 1

68. Freire, *Pedagogy of the Oppressed*, 156.

69. Olympia Meola, "GOP Panel Picks Peter Farrell to Run for Janis' House Seat," *Richmond Times-Dispatch*, August 24, 2011, http://m.richmond.com/archive/gop-panel-picks-peter-farrell-to-run-for-janis-house/article_71a52a72-0b46-55bc-8ea0-185dd53675ba.html?mode=jqm; Jeff Schapiro, "Brat in Step with Right; Out of Step with Everyone Else," *Richmond Times-Dispatch*, October 14, 2015, http://www.richmond.com/news/virginia/government-politics/jeff-schapiro/article_35921b24-00e1-5057-a8a5-c1a68c55d84b.html.

70. Jeff Schapiro, "Farrell Takes to the Political Stage," *Richmond Times-Dispatch*, September 25, 2011, http://www.richmond.com/archive/article_23a34058-4324-5a84-8cb3-befe30dac994.html; Dave Ress, "The Virginia Way, Part 7: Networking and Career-Building in the Capitol," *Daily Press*, November 21, 2014, http://www.dailypress.com/news/politics/dp-virginiaway-part-7--career-20141121-story.html#page=1; Jo Ann Frohman, "The Gray Era Ends: Power Brokers for Half a Century Grays Held Sway When Old Boys Ran Old Dominion," *Daily Press*, July 14, 1991, http://articles.dailypress.com/1991-07-14/news/9107140001_1_virginia-senate-gray-era-ends-favor.

71. Editorial Board, "House of Delegates: Mock the Vote," *Richmond Times-Dispatch*, September 29, 2011, http://www.richmond.com/news/article_41ffa15f-468d-55d0-9392-66e33a64157e.html.

72. Jeff Schapiro, "Farrell Takes to the Political Stage," *Richmond Times-Dispatch*, September 25, 2011, http://www.richmond.com/archive/article_23a34058-4324-5a84-8cb3-befe30dac994.html.

73. Olympia Meola, "Five Voters Pick Two Nominees for House of Delegates," *Richmond Times-Dispatch*, September 21, 2011, http://www.richmond.com/archive/article_538fdf39-a8d2-5d15-81a8-fd3e6ee58940.html.

74. Virginia Public Access Project, "Peter Farrell: Conflicts of Interest Disclosure: Personal Liabilities: 2010–2014," http://vpap.org/candidates/205491/conflicts_disclosure/personal_liabilities/?sei_period=11.

75. Jenna Portnoy, "VA Delegate and Son of Dominion Resources CEO Says He Is His Own Man," *Washington Post*, February 9, 2015, http://www.washingtonpost.com/local/virginia-politics/va-delegate-and-son-of-dominion-resources-ceo-says-he-is-his-own-man/2015/02/08/a884ef14-abc9-11e4-9c91-e9d2f9fde644_story.html. Steve Thomas is not related to me.

76. Staff, "Capitol Briefs: Henrico's Farrell Withstands Good-Natured Ribbing," *Richmond Times-Dispatch*, February 17, 2012, http://www.richmond.com/news/article_f514c57d-5dac-51c5-a845-135dd0838a58.html.

77. Dave Ress, "The Virginia Way, Politics, Power, and Profit" (Series), *Virginian-Pilot*, November 16–23, 2014, http://www.dailypress.com/news/watchdog/dp-nws-virginia-way-story-gallery-storygallery.html.

78. All quotations in this list are from Dave Ress, "The Virginia Way, Part 1: A Part-Time Legislature with Full-Time Rewards," *Virginian-Pilot*, November 16, 2014, http://www.dailypress.com/news/politics/dp-nws-virginiaway-overview-20141116-story.html#page=2.

79. Ibid.

80. Michael Martz, "State Budget Deal: 3% Raise for State Employees, Faculty; 2% for Teachers," *Richmond Times-Dispatch*, March 10, 2016, http://www.richmond.com/news/virginia/government-politics/general-assembly/article_e4a5f052-1814-5513-a6e2-f3c5d2baf6ee.html.

81. Office of the Attorney General, "Attorney General Personal Use Explanation," Commonwealth of Virginia, http://elections.virginia.gov/Files/CandidatesAndPACs/LawsAndPolicies/AttorneyGeneralPersonalUseExplanation.pdf.

82. Editorial Board, "Half-Measures of Ethics in Virginia," *Washington Post*, April 19, 2015, http://www.washingtonpost.com/opinions/half-measures-on-ethics-in-virginia/2015/04/19/26e9f612-e534-11e4-81ea-0649268f729e_story.html.

83. Dave Ress, "The Virginia Way, Part 3: The Big Money in Running—Even Unopposed," *Daily Press*, November 18, 2014, http://www.dailypress.com/news/politics/dp-nws-virigniaway-campaign-20141118-51-story.html#page=2.

84. Associated Press, "Panel Members: VA Lawmakers Need a Raise, Maybe Fundraising Rules," *Daily Press*, June 3, 2015, http://www.dailypress.com/news/politics/dp-panel-members-va-lawmakers-need-a-raise-maybe-fundraising-rules-20150603-story.html.

85. Quentin Kidd and Meyrem Baer, "Virginia's Ethics Rules for Public Officials: The Need for Reform," *Virginia News Letter* 90, no.1 (January 2014): 3, http://www.coopercenter.org/sites/default/files/publications/Virginia%20News%20Letter%202014%20Vol.%2090%20No%201.pdf.

86. Alan Suderman, "The Virginia Way: Corporate Money for Personal Niceties," *Daily Press*, February 20, 2016, http://www.dailypress.com/news/politics/dp-the-virginia-way-corporate-money-for-personal-niceties-20160219-story.html.

87. Ibid.

88. Virginia House of Delegates Bill 578, "Campaign Finance; Statewide and General Assembly Candidates; Personal Use of Campaign Funds; Penalty," 2014, http://leg1.state.VAus/cgi-bin/legp504.exe?151+sum+HB578.

89. Graham Moomaw, "House Panel Punts on Bill to Ban Personal Use of Campaign Funds," *Richmond Times-Dispatch*, February 5, 2016, http://www.richmond.com/news/virginia/government-politics/article_61bee09f-d75d-5c9d-91cc-ffaebb150796.html.

90. Jenna Portnoy, "In Post-McDonnell Scandal VA, Pols Take Another Stab at Ethics Reform," *Washington Post*, February 17, 2015, http://www.washingtonpost.com/local/virginia-politics/in-post-mcdonnell-scandal-va-pols-take-another-stab-at-ethics-reform/2015/02/17/0b282f7c-b15c-11e4-886b-c22184f27c35_story.html.

91. Associated Press, "Howell Raises $550,000 in Final Weeks of Primary," *Fredericksburg Free Lance-Star*, June 1, 2015, http://www.fredericksburg.com/news/virginia/howell-raises-in-final-weeks-of-primary/article_192f74f2-08ac-11e5-945c-9f2563f94693.html.

92. Dave Ress, "Donors Love General Assembly Incumbents," *Daily Press*, June 5, 2015, http://www.dailypress.com/news/politics/dp-nws-campaign-finance-20150605-story.html.

93. Patrick Wilson, "Incumbents Enjoy Donations' Edge; Cash Doesn't Stop When They're Unopposed," *Virginian-Pilot*, June 3, 2015, http://hamptonroads.com/2015/06/incumbents-enjoy-donations-edge-cash-doesnt-stop-when-theyre-unopposed.

94. Ress, "The Virginia Way, Part 3."

95. National Conference of State Legislatures, "State Limits on Contributions to Candidates," October 2013, http://www.ncsl.org/Portals/1/documents/legismgt/Limits_to_Candidates_2012-2014.pdf; Federal Election Commission, "Contribution Limits 2013–14," http://www.fec.gov/pages/brochures/contriblimits.shtml.

96. Dan Casey, "Cuccinelli Lawsuit Sheds Light on Political Hypocrisy," *Roanoke Times*, May 30, 2015, http://www.roanoke.com/news/columns_and_blogs/columns/dan_casey/casey-cuccinelli-lawsuit-sheds-light-on-political-hypocrisy/article_68d13960-094d-5c91-942f-8a609487c98a.html.

97. Tory Newmyer, "The Big Political Player You've Never Heard Of," *Fortune*, January 10, 2011, http://fortune.com/2011/01/10/the-big-political-player-youve-never-heard-of; Alison Fitzgerald, "Koch, Exxon Mobil Among Corporations Helping Write State Laws," *Bloomberg Business*, July 21, 2011, http://www.bloomberg.com/news/articles/2011-07-21/koch-exxon-mobil-among-corporations-helping-write-state-laws; Mechelle Hankerson, "Conservative Organization Has a Gift for Writing Laws," *Daily Press*, March 17, 2012, http://articles.dailypress.com/2012-03-17/news/dp-nws-cns-alec-influence-20120317_1_castle-doctrine-progressva-state-legislators.

98. Anita Kumar, "Virginia House Speaker William Howell Said Conservative Group ALEC Is 'Under Attack' by Liberals," *Washington Post*, April 12, 2012, http://www.washingtonpost.com/local/dc-politics/virginia-house-speaker-william-howell-said-conservative-group-alec-is-under-attack-by-liberals/2012/04/12/gIQAD5hrDT_story.html.

99. Mechelle Hankerson, "Conservative Organization Has a Gift for Writing Laws," Capital News Service, March 17, 2012, http://articles.dailypress.com/2012-03-17/news/dp-nws-cns-alec-influence-20120317_1_castle-doctrine-progressva-state-legislators.

100. American Legislative Exchange Council, "Board of Directors," http://www.alec.org/about-alec/board-of-directors; Editorial Board, "The Big Money Behind State Laws," *New York Times*, February 12, 2012, http://www.nytimes.com/2012/02/13/opinion/the-big-money-behind-state-laws.html?_r=0.

101. Kumar, "Virginia House Speaker William Howell."

102. Dave Ress, "The Virginia Way, Part 8: Disclosure Rules Are Lax, and Reports Are Hard to Find," *Daily Press*, November 23, 2014, http://www.dailypress.com/news/politics/dp-nws-virginiaway-part-8-disclosure-20141123-story.html#page=1.

103. Quentin Kidd and Meyrem Baer, "Virginia's Ethics Rules for Public Officials: The Need for Reform," *Virginia News Letter* 90, no.1 (January 2014): 2, http://www.coopercenter.org/sites/default/files/publications/Virginia%20News%20Letter%202014%20Vol.%2090%20No%201.pdf;

David Poole, "Virginia's Slow Progress on Campaign Finance Reform," *Virginia News Letter* 76, no. 8 (December 2000), http://www.coopercenter.org/sites/default/files/publications/Virginia%20News%20Letter%202000,%20Vol.%2076,%20No.%208.pdf.

104. Dave Ress, "The Virginia Way, Part 6: Giving Gifts, and Gaining Influence?" *Daily Press*, November 20, 2014, http://www.dailypress.com/news/politics/dp-nws-virginiaway-part-6-gifts-20141120-story.html#page=1.

105. Rachel DePompa, "Key Figures Disclose New Gifts on Public Record," WWBT-NBC, July 9, 2013, http://www.nbc12.com/story/22787395/12-investigates-key-figures-disclose-new-gifts-on-public-record.

106. Matt Zapotosky and Rosalind Helderman, "McDonnell Prosecutors Allege Undisclosed Gifts from People Other than Williams," *Washington Post*, June 23, 2014, http://www.washingtonpost.com/local/crime/mcdonnell-prosecutors-allege-undisclosed-gifts-from-people-other-than-williams/2014/06/23/b4b43736-fae4-11e3-b1f4-8e77c632c07b_story.html.

107. Terry Brooks, "Onzlee Ware Resigns," RealRadio804.com, November 15, 2013, http://realradio804.com/onzlee-ware-resigns.

108. Ress, "Virginia Way, Part 2." This section is based on this article, unless otherwise noted.

109. Bloomberg Business, "William C. Wampler Jr., Executive Profile," http://www.bloomberg.com/research/stocks/people/person.asp?personId=12108740&ticker=BSET&previousCapId=253995&previousTitle=BASSETT%2520FURNITURE%2520INDS; Our Campaigns, "Oder, G. Glenn: Candidate Details," http://www.ourcampaigns.com/CandidateDetail.html?CandidateID=48192.

110. Ress, "The Virginia Way, Part 7."

111. McGuireWoods, "Richard Rathborne Hobson," http://www.mcguirewoods.com/People/H/Richard-Rathborne-Hobson.aspx; "Preston Bryant Jr.," http://www.mcguirewoods.com/People/B/Preston-Bryant-Jr.aspx; "Heather L. Martin," http://www.mcguirewoods.com/People/M/Heather-L-Martin.aspx.

112. Ibid., "Frank B. Atkinson," http://www.mcguirewoods.com/People/A/Frank-B-Atkinson.aspx.

113. Ibid., "Tyler W. Bishop," http://www.mcguirewoods.com/People/B/Tyler-W-Bishop.aspx.

114. Ibid., "Mark T. Bowles," http://www.mcguirewoods.com/People/B/Mark-T-Bowles.aspx.

115. Ibid., "Richard Cullen," http://www.mcguirewoods.com/People/C/Richard-Cullen.aspx.

116. Ibid., "James W. Dyke Jr.," http://www.mcguirewoods.com/People/D/James-W-Dyke-Jr.aspx.

117. Ibid., "Stephen A. Horton," http://www.mcguirewoods.com/People/H/Stephen-A-Horton.aspx.

118. Ibid., "Generra J. Peck," http://www.mcguirewoods.com/People/P/Generra-J-Peck.aspx.

119. Ibid., "Michael P. Reynold," http://www.mcguirewoods.com/People/R/Michael-P-Reynold.aspx.

120. Ibid., "Andrew M. Smith," http://www.mcguirewoods.com/People/S/Andrew-M-Smith.aspx.
121. Ibid., "Michael E. Thomas," http://www.mcguirewoods.com/People/T/Michael-E-Thomas.aspx. No relation to this author.
122. Ibid., "Anne T. Obenshain," http://www.mcguirewoods.com/People/O/Anne-T-Obenshain.aspx; Laura Vozzella, "Attorney General Candidate Mark Obenshain Carries Bulk of GOP's Hopes in Virginia Races," *Washington Post*, October 26, 2013, http://www.washingtonpost.com/local/virginia-politics/attorney-general-candidate-mark-obenshain-carries-bulk-of-gops-hopes-in-virginia-races/2013/10/26/f653cb3c-3d1d-11e3-b7ba-503fb5822c3e_story.html; Jeff Schapiro, "Name from the Past in Fight for the Future," *Richmond Times-Dispatch*, January 27, 2015, http://www.richmond.com/news/virginia/government-politics/jeff-schapiro/article_6b0c5d18-ea8b-5e31-87ef-39339897993c.html.
123. Ress, "Virginia Way, Part 5."
124. Carl Tobias, "Reconsidering Virginia Judicial Selection," *University of Richmond Law Review* 43 (2008): 37–49, http://scholarship.richmond.edu/cgi/viewcontent.cgi?article=1779&context=law-faculty-publications.
125. Ashley Delja, "Across Four Aprils: School Finance Litigation in Virginia," *Brigham Young University Education and Law Journal* (2004): 191–247, http://digitalcommons.law.byu.edu/cgi/viewcontent.cgi?article=1183&context=elj.
126. Ress, "Virginia Way, Part 4." All quotes in this section are from this article.
127. Michael Sluss, "McDonnell Cuts Public Broadcasting Further," *Daily Press*, May 4, 2011, http://articles.dailypress.com/2011-05-04/news/ro-mcdonnell-cuts-public-broadcasting20110504_1_bob-mcdonnell-state-funding-budget-bill.
128. Anita Kumar and Rosalind Helderman, "McDonnell Signs Budget Bill, Reduces Money for Public Broadcasting," *Washington Post*, May 3, 2011, http://www.washingtonpost.com/blogs/virginia-politics/post/mcdonnell-signs-budget-bill-reduces-money-for-public-broadcasting/2011/05/03/AFPWEUhF_blog.html.
129. VirginiaBusiness.com, "McDonnell Signs Film Tax Credit Legislation," June 14, 2010, http://www.virginiabusiness.com/news/article/mcdonnell-signs-film-tax-credit-legislation; Virginia Senate Bill 257, "Motion Picture Film Production: Provides Income Tax Credits to Any Company with Qualifying Expenses," 2010, http://leg1.state.VAus/cgi-bin/legp504.exe?ses=101&typ=bil&val=sb257; Julian Walker, "McDonnell Touts Film Incentives," *Virginian-Pilot*, June 14, 2010, http://hamptonroads.com/2010/06/mcdonnell-touts-film-incentives.
130. Sandy Hausman, "Lincoln Biopic: Virginia's Hollywood Incentives Get Closer Look," Virginia Public Radio, December 2, 2011, http://wamu.org/news/11/12/02/lincoln_biopic_virginias_hollywood_incentives_get_closer_look.
131. Ibid.
132. Mendell, *Obama*, 305–12.
133. Joshua Huffman, "Tea Party Releases Scorecard," *Virginia Conservative*, March 18, 2013, https://virginiaconservative.wordpress.com/2013/03/18/tea-party-releases-score-card.
134. Portnoy, "VA Delegate and Son."

135. Thomas Heath, "Dominion Resources CEO, Pens, Funds, Produces Civil War Film about VMI Cadets," *Washington Post*, May 18, 2014, https://www.washingtonpost.com/business/economy/dominion-resources-ceo-pens-funds-produces-civil-war-film-about-vmi-cadets/2014/05/18/099854a2-dab6-11e3-b745-87d39690c5c0_story.html.

136. Ibid.

137. Indiegogo, "Field of Lost Shoes," https://www.indiegogo.com/projects/field-of-lost-shoes#/story.

138. Alan Suderman, "VA Lawmaker, Father Benefit from Film Tax Credit," WAVY-TV, November 17, 2014, http://wavy.com/2014/11/17/va-lawmaker-father-benefit-from-film-tax-credit.

139. National Park Service, "Tredegar Iron Works," United States Department of the Interior, http://www.nps.gov/nr/travel/richmond/tredegar.html; Dominion Virginia Power, "Customer Service," https://www.dom.com/residential/dominion-virginia-power/contact-us/customer-service.

140. Suderman, "VA Lawmaker."

141. Ibid.

142. VMI News, "Red Carpet Screening," April 14, 2014, http://vminews.tumblr.com/post/82706602286/red-carpet-screening-april-14-2014-more-than.

143. John Ramsey, "'Field of Lost Shoes' Screened to Private Audiences in Richmond," *Richmond Times-Dispatch*, April 14, 2014, http://www.richmond.com/news/local/city-of-richmond/field-of-lost-shoes-screened-to-private-audiences-in-richmond/article_123a382f-e08f-5f66-847b-18caf5 2f1372.html.

144. Frank Scheck, "'Field of Lost Shoes': Film Review," *Hollywood Reporter*, September 25, 2014, http://www.hollywoodreporter.com/review/field-lost-shoes-film-review-735700.

145. Internet Movie Database, "Field of Lost Shoes: Full Credits," http://www.imdb.com/title/tt2477218/fullcredits; "Box Office / Business for Field of Lost Shoes," http://www.imdb.com/title/tt2477218/business?ref_=ttfc_ql_4; *The Spark*, Collegiate School Alumni Magazine (Winter 2014): 43, http://issuu.com/collegiateva/docs/finalspark_winter14_sm.

146. Jim Bacon, "More Money for Millionaires," Bacon's Rebellion, November 17, 2014, http://www.baconsrebellion.com/2014/11/more-money-for-millionaires.html.

147. Editorial Board, "Cut!" *Richmond Times-Dispatch*, November 24, 2014, http://www.richmond.com/zzstyling/view-editorial/article_fb5d41d8-9a36-5eaa-b48b-a7d024177531.html.

148. Suderman, "VA Lawmaker."

149. Ress, "Virginia Way, Part 4."

150. Virginia General Assembly, "Senate and House Page Programs," Commonwealth of Virginia, http://capclass.virginiageneralassembly.gov/PagePrograms/PagePrograms.html.

151. David Kidd, "Virginia's Long-Running Page Program Perseveres," *Governing Magazine* (January 2015), http://www.governing.com/topics/politics/gov-

virginia-page-program.html; Melinda Williams, "The Legs of the General Assembly," *Southwest Times*, April 6, 2015, http://www.southwesttimes.com/2015/04/the-legs-of-the-general-assembly.

152. Chad Pergram, "House Page Program to End After Nearly 200 Years," Fox News, August 8, 2011, http://www.foxnews.com/politics/2011/08/08/house-page-program-to-end-after-nearly-200-years.

153. Office of Senator Mark Warner, "Requirements for Page Selection," United States Senate, http://www.warner.senate.gov/public//index.cfm?p=requirements-for-page-selection.

154. Office of the Governor, "2015 Governor's Fellows Program," Commonwealth of Virginia, https://governor.virginia.gov/the-administration/governors-fellows-program.

155. Division of Capitol Police, Homepage, Commonwealth of Virginia, http://www.vcp.state.VAus.

156. Travis Fain, "McAuliffe, Lawmakers in Tiff Over Office Building," *Daily Press*, July 9, 2014, http://articles.dailypress.com/2014-07-09/news/dp-nws-gab-construction-20140709_1_mcauliffe-house-appropriations-chairman-s-house-republicans.

157. Laura Vozzella and Rachel Weiner, "Virginia Budget Plans Include New Office Building for Lawmakers," *Washington Post*, February 14, 2014, http://www.washingtonpost.com/local/virginia-politics/virginia-budget-plans-include-new-office-building-for-lawmakers/2014/02/13/91093844-94d3-11e3-83b9-1f024193bb84_story.html.

158. Fain, "McAuliffe, Lawmakers in Tiff."

159. Lauren McClellan, "General Assembly Building New Offices," Capital News Service, April 25, 2014, http://www.virginiabusiness.com/news/article/general-assembly-building-new-offices.

160. Office of the Governor, "Statement of Governor Terence McAuliffe on 2015–16 Budget Actions," Commonwealth of Virginia, June 20, 2014, https://governor.virginia.gov/newsroom/newsarticle?articleId=5216.

161. McClellan, "General Assembly Building New Offices."

162. Michael Martz, "$2.1 Billion Bond Bill Ties New Capital Spending to Completing Capitol Square Project," *Richmond Times-Dispatch*, March 12, 2016, http://www.richmond.com/news/virginia/government-politics/general-assembly/article_9b7a2130-11ed-541b-92b0-13f014a21956.html.

163. Portnoy, "Post-McDonnell Scandal VA."

164. Associated Press, "In Virginia General Assembly, Many Bills Die by Stealth," *Fredericksburg Free Lance-Star*, February 25, 2015, http://www.fredericksburg.com/news/virginia/in-virginia-general-assembly-many-bills-die-by-stealth/article_bfbd12c0-bd25-11e4-a211-af13f90df680.html. Similar nonpartisan redistricting bills were voted down by a 4–3 House subcommittee vote in 2016. See Jim Nolan and Andrew Cain, "House Panel Defeats Redistricting Bills; Senate Panel Advances Party Registration," *Richmond Times-Dispatch*, February 3, 2016, http://www.richmond.com/news/virginia/government-politics/article_28f1e94d-d24a-57a6-ba48-5044e56f214a.html.

165. Associated Press, "In Virginia General Assembly."

166. Virginia Senate Bill 1399, "Political Candidates; Repeals Personal Income Tax Credit for Contributions," 2015, http://lis.virginia.gov/cgi-bin/legp604.exe?151+sum+SB1399.

167. Virginia House Bill 1310, "Taxes on Electronic Cigarettes and Other Vapor Products," 2015, http://lis.virginia.gov/cgi-bin/legp604.exe?151+sum+HB1310.

168. Virginia House Bill 1327, "Elections; Assistance for Certain Voters," 2015, http://lis.virginia.gov/cgi-bin/legp604.exe?151+sum+HB1327.

169. Virginia House Bill 1354, "Animal Cruelty Conviction List; Established," 2015, http://lis.virginia.gov/cgi-bin/legp604.exe?151+sum+HB1354.

170. Virginia House Bill 1385, "Sexual Orientation Change Efforts; Prohibited," 2015, http://lis.virginia.gov/cgi-bin/legp604.exe?151+sum+HB1385.

171. Virginia House Bill 1441, "Child Abuse or Neglect, Suspected; Person Required to Report, Training Program Required," 2015, http://lis.virginia.gov/cgi-bin/legp604.exe?151+sum+HB1441.

172. Virginia House Bill 1406, "Driving on a Suspended or Revoked License; Causing Death of Another Person, Penalty," 2015, http://lis.virginia.gov/cgi-bin/legp604.exe?151+sum+HB1406.

173. Staff, "General Assembly Briefs," *Richmond Times-Dispatch*, February 12, 2016, http://www.richmond.com/news/virginia/government-politics/article_746553a5-351b-5f75-bb37-9fcbb3ca5c04.html.

174. Transparency Virginia, "The Virginia General Assembly: The Case for Improved Transparency," April 14, 2015, https://transparencyvirginia.files.wordpress.com/2015/04/transparencyvareportreleased.pdf, 10.

175. Ibid., 18.

176. Associated Press, "In Virginia General Assembly."

177. Transparency Virginia. "Virginia General Assembly," 18.

178. Jim Nolan, "By the Numbers: How Bills Fared in 2016 VA General Assembly," *Richmond Times-Dispatch*, April 6, 2016, http://www.richmond.com/news/virginia/article_bf0874d0-c4d8-5ec5-b027-84b5d67baa23.html.

179. Editorial Board, "Virginia Needs an Effective FOIA, Real Reform to Protect Public's Right to Know," *Daily Press*, June 2, 2015, http://www.dailypress.com/news/opinion/editorials/dp-edt-foia-reform-editorial-20150603-20150602-story.html. For lists of general record and meeting exemptions, see Virginia Freedom of Information Advisory Council, "General Exemptions," Commonwealth of Virginia, http://foiacouncil.dls.virginia.gov/Applicability_Exemptions/General_Exemptions.htm.

180. Julian Walker, "Document Seekers Stymied by 'Working Papers' Rule," *Virginian-Pilot*, March 19, 2011, http://hamptonroads.com/2011/03/document-seekers-stymied-working-papers-rule.

181. Travis Fain, "Evidence Fight Points to Secret Redistricting Talks in Virginia," *Daily Press*, April 30, 2015, http://www.dailypress.com/news/dp-nws-house-secret-emails-20150428-story.html.

182. Megan Rhyne, "End FOIA's Working-Paper Exemption," *Suffolk News-Herald*, March 17, 2015, http://www.suffolknewsherald.com/2015/03/17/end-foias-

working-papers-exemption; Travis Fain, "FOIA Group Agrees to Look at 'Working Papers' Exemption," *Daily Press*, June 18, 2015, http://www.dailypress. com/news/politics/dp-nws-foia-stuff-20150618-story.html.

183. Ress, "Virginia Way, Part 8."

184. Virginia House Bill 174, "Virginia Freedom of Information Act; Administrative Investigations; Local Inspectors General," 2013, https://leg1.state.VAus/cgi-bin/legp504.exe?141+sum+HB174.

185. Editorial Board, "Virginia Supreme Court's Executive Secretary Should Honor FOIA, Transparency," *Daily Press*, May 18, 2015, http://www.dailypress. com/news/opinion/editorials/dp-edt-supreme-court-foia-editorial-20150519-20150518-story.html.

186. Dave Ress, "Virginia Supreme Court Administrators Say FOIA Doesn't Apply to Them," *Daily Press*, May 15, 2015, http://www.dailypress.com/news/politics/dp-nws-foia-court-20150515-story.html.

187. Graham Moomaw, "Manuals for Prisoner Executions Can Be Kept Secret, Virginia Supreme Court Rules," *Richmond Times-Dispatch*, September 17, 2015, http://www.richmond.com/news/local/crime/article_6fd1a35e-4335-5014-9c4f-9b9e89182d19.html.

188. Cameron Vigliano, "FOIA Lawsuit Against City of Richmond Can Proceed," RVA News, February 3, 2015, http://rvanews.com/news/foia-lawsuit-against-city-of-richmond-can-proceed/121771.

189. Dave Ress, "FOIA Bills—Some Whittle Away at Disclosure, but Others at Secrecy," *Daily Press*, January 9, 2015, http://www.dailypress.com/news/politics/shad-plank-blog/dp-foia-bills-some-whittle-away-at-disclosure-but-others-at-secrecy-20150109-post.html; Fain, "FOIA Group Agrees to Look."

190. Hawes Spencer, "Dragas to Simon: 'Quite an Unhelpful Comment,'" *Hook*, July 5, 2012, http://www.readthehook.com/104458/dragas-simon-quite-unhelpful-comment.

191. Graham Moomaw and Michael Martz, "FOIA Open Record Rules Don't Always Apply to Economic Development," *Roanoke Times*, March 14, 2015, http://www.roanoke.com/news/virginia/foia-open-record-rules-don-t-always-apply-to-economic/article_6a8d46a3-781d-5942-84d7-44e1f7945bb2.html.

192. Elisabeth Hulette, "Family Sues VA Beach After Records on Son's Death Are Withheld," *Virginian-Pilot*, June 28, 2015, http://hamptonroads.com/2015/06/family-sues-va-beach-after-records-sons-death-are-withheld.

193. Larry Sabato, Kyle Kondik and Geoffrey Skelley, "The 2016 Results We Can Already Predict," *Politico Magazine*, May 3, 2015, http://www.politico.com/magazine/story/2015/05/2016-predictions-117554.html.

194. Editorial Board, "Gerrymandering and Secrecy Add Up to Trouble," *Richmond Times-Dispatch*, May 10, 2015, http://www.richmond.com/opinion/our-opinion/article_99590af9-3c92-5e65-9063-6c8a7efb30c6.html.

195. Kenneth Stroupe, "Gerrymandering's Long History in Virginia: Will This Decade Mark the End?" *Virginia News Letter* 85, no. 1 (February 2009): 6, http://www.coopercenter.org/sites/default/files/publications/vanl0209_0.pdf.

196. GovTrack, "Members of Congress: Virginia."

197. Tarini Parti, "Court Strikes Down VA Congressional Map," *Politico*, October 7, 2014, http://www.politico.com/story/2014/10/court-strikes-down-va-congressional-map-111677.html.

198. Karl Rove, "The GOP Targets State Legislatures," *Wall Street Journal*, March 4, 2010, http://www.wsj.com/articles/SB10001424052748703862704575099670689398044.

199. United States Census Bureau, "Census Redistricting Data Program," http://www.census.gov/rdo.

200. Fresh Air, "The Multimillionaire Helping Republicans Win N.C.," National Public Radio, October 6, 2011, http://www.npr.org/2011/10/06/141078608/the-multimillionaire-helping-republicans-win-n-c.

201. Olga Pierce, Justin Elliott and Theodoric Meyer, "How Dark Money Helped Republicans Hold the House and Hurt Voters," ProPublica, December 21, 2012, http://www.propublica.org/article/how-dark-money-helped-republicans-hold-the-house-and-hurt-voters.

202. Jane Mayer, "State for Sale," *New Yorker*, October 10, 2011.

203. Glenn Thrush, "Obama's States of Despair: 2010 Losses Still Haunt," *Politico*, July 26, 2013, http://www.politico.com/story/2013/07/obamas-states-of-despair-2010-losses-still-haunt-94775.html; Erin Kelly, "Warner Wins Close VA Senate Race; Gillespie Concedes," *USA Today*, November 7, 2014, http://www.usatoday.com/story/news/politics/2014/11/07/warner-gil.

204. Gregory Giroux, "Republicans Win Congress as Democrats Get Most Votes," Bloomberg Business, March 18, 2013.

205. Staff, "House Map: Election 2012," *New York Times*, http://elections.nytimes.com/2012/results/house.

206. Giroux, "Republicans Win Congress."

207. Tom Coburn and John Hart, *Breach of Trust*, 183–84.

208. John Dinan, *Virginia State Constitution*, 97.

209. Bill Bartel, "Plan Would Shift Rep. Forbes' District Away from His Base," *Virginian-Pilot*, April 14, 2011, http://hamptonroads.com/2011/04/plan-would-shift-repforbes-district-away-his-base.

210. Bill Bartel, "For Now, Scott Stays Out of Redistricting Battle," *Virginian-Pilot*, June 1, 2015, http://hamptonroads.com/2015/05/now-scott-stays-out-redistricting-legal-battle.

211. Andrew Cain and Frank Green, "Three-Judge Panel Rules Virginia Must Redraw Congressional Map," *Richmond Times-Dispatch*, June 5, 2015, http://www.richmond.com/news/virginia/government-politics/articl_14c2537e-255b-5452-9c16-e23f545158e6.html.

212. Bill Bartel and Bill Sizemore, "Court Rejects Boundaries of Bobby Scott's 3rd District," *Virginian-Pilot*, October 8, 2014, http://hamptonroads.com/2014/10/court-rejects-boundaries-bobby-scotts-3rd-district.

213. Andrew Cain, "Forbes Leaving 4th District to Run for Congress in 2nd District," *Richmond Times-Dispatch*, http://www.richmond.com/news/virginia/government-politics/article_3fae0afa-2123-5ecc-bfbb-7c9ea5738e58.html.

214. Laura Vozzella and Errin Haines, "VA Republicans' Redistricting Maneuver Draws Criticism," *Washington Post*, January 22, 2013, http://www.washingtonpost.com/local/va-politics/va-republicans-move-on-redistricting-draws-criticism/2013/01/22/f7645ee8-64b9-11e2-9e1b-07db1d2ccd5b_print.html.

215. Bill Sizemore and Julian Walker, "GOP Senate Redistricting Plan Killed by House Speaker," *Virginian-Pilot*, February 7, 2013, http://hamptonroads.com/2013/02/gop-senate-redistricting-plan-killed-house-speaker-0.

216. Geoffrey Skelley, "Virginia's Redistricting History: What's Past Is Prologue," Sabato's Crystal Ball: University of Virginia Center for Politics, June 18, 2015, http://www.centerforpolitics.org/crystalball/articles/virginias-redistricting-history-whats-past-is-prologue.

217. Editorial Board, "Time to Redraw Districts to Reflect Virginia's Electoral Reality," *Fredericksburg Free Lance-Star*, June 11, 2015, http://www.fredericksburg.com/opinion/editorials/editorial-tme-to-redraw-districts-to-reflect-virginia-s-electoral/article_8bd32216-95e9-5e43-b6b0-9ece02abe0bb.html.

218. Christopher Ingraham, "One Easy Way to End Gerrymandering: Stop Letting Politicians Draw Their Own Districts," *Washington Post*, June 2, 2014, http://www.washingtonpost.com/blogs/wonkblog/wp/2014/06/02/one-easy-way-to-end-gerrymandering-stop-letting-politicians-draw-their-own-districts; Editorial Board, "Gerrymandering Endures, Thanks to the General Assembly," *Staunton News Leader*, July 1, 2015, http://www.newsleader.com/story/opinion/editorials/2015/07/01/gerrymandering-endures-thanks-general-assembly/29554113.

219. Lowell Feld, http://www.bluevirginia.us/diary/12974/how-many-seats-could-virginia-dems-gain-in-the-house-of-delegates-in-2015. Feld runs and blogs at Blue Virginia (http://www.bluevirginia.us) and is a co-author of *Netroots Rising*.

220. Travis Fain, "Virginia House of Delegates Districts Challenged in Lawsuit," *Daily Press*, December 31, 2014, http://www.dailypress.com/news/politics/dp-nws-virginia-house-gerrymander-20141231-storty.html; Jenna Portnoy, "Federal Lawsuit Filed to Challenge Virginia's State Electoral Districts," *Washington Post*, January 1, 2015, http://www.washingtonpost.com/local/virginia-politics/federal-lawsuit-filed-to-challenge-virginias-state-electoral-districts/2015/01/01/ac924ba4-911d-11e4-a412-4b735edc7175_story.html.

221. Travis Fain, "Toscano Calls for Redistricting Openness, but Seems to Have Protected His Own Privilege," *Daily Press*, May 6, 2015, http://www.dailypress.com/news/politics/shad-plank-blog/dp-toscano-calls-for-redistricting-openness-but-seems-to-have-protected-his-own-privilege-20150506-post.html.

222. Staff, "Six Current, Former VA Senators Found in Contempt for Refusing to Surrender Redistricting Records," *Richmond Times-Dispatch*, April 8, 2016, http://www.richmond.com/news/virginia/government-politics/article_6cd01699-7c61-53a4-a7e5-0c3635a8dcca.html.

223. Travis Fain, "Another Lawsuit Coming in Virginia Redistricting Fight," *Daily Press*, June 10, 2015, http://www.dailypress.com/news/politics/dp-nws-redistricting-lawsuit-20150610-story.html; Virginia Constitution, Article II, Section 6, in Dinan, *Virginia State Constitution*, 95.

224. Associated Press, "Defense Says Partisan Politics, Not Race, Drove VA Redistricting," *Richmond Times-Dispatch*, July 7, 2015, http://www.richmond.com/news/virginia/government-politics/article_151fe780-d689-5ffb-8f96-7976f2887863.html.

225. Associated Press, "GOP Delegate Jones Defends 2011 House Redistricting," *Richmond Times-Dispatch*, July 8, 2015, http://www.richmond.com/news/virginia/government-politics/article_14bb4f54-59af-523f-8d65-ade7353743fc.html.

226. Andrew Cain, "122 Legislators Sought Re-Election Tuesday; They All Won," *Richmond Times-Dispatch*, November 4, 2015, http://www.richmond.com/news/virginia/government-politics/article_fcaec32d-9cea-525f-a04e-65109350396a.html.

227. Editorial Board, "The 2015 Election Is Really About 2017—and Beyond," *Roanoke Times*, October 9, 2015, http://www.roanoke.com/opinion/editorials/our-view-the-election-is-really-about---/article_8225d01b-1f1a-521e-9fcf-3097c2253ce1.html.

228. Editorial Board, "Another Wasted Election," *Richmond Times-Dispatch*, May 19, 2015, http://www.richmond.com/opinion/our-opinion/article_25ffbc97-b217-5c8a-8124-f2b33f8d4ccd.html.

229. Jeff Schapiro, "New Front Opens in Legal Fight Over Gerrymandering," *Richmond Times-Dispatch*, June 10, 2015, http://www.richmond.com/news/virginia/government-politics/jeff-schapiro/article_784cffac-a447-53c0-afba-e97ecb83aa5d.html.

230. Editorial Board, "Soviet-Style Elections," *Roanoke Times*, June 7, 2015, http://www.roanoke.com/opinion/editorials/our-view-soviet-style-elections/article_1f171420-f0bd-5cfc-8ce2-4edca989ef62.html.

231. Jeff Schapiro, "Low Primary Turnout Would Have Thrilled Byrd," *Richmond Times-Dispatch*, June 17, 2015, http://www.richmond.com/news/virginia/government-politics/jeff-schapiro/article_88d60bd4-40c3-526a-8450-351d11c8ccff.html.

232. Virginia Department of Elections, "Registration/Turnout Statistics: November General Elections 1976–Present," http://elections.virginia.gov/index.php/resultsreports/registration-statistics/registrationturnout-statistics.

233. Jim Nolan, "Low Turnout Exposed Incumbents Vulnerable to Upsets," *Richmond Times-Dispatch*, June 10, 2015, http://www.richmond.com/news/virginia/government-politics/article_c88ed57b-407a-5932-b4e7-34301a6349c0.html.

234. Markus Schmidt, "Light Turnout Expected During June Primaries," *Richmond Times-Dispatch*, May 18, 2015, http://www.richmond.com/news/virginia/government-politics/article_0c5587e1-eb08-541b-9fbc-969945ee2dfa.html.

235. Alicia Petska, "Bill Targeting 'Incumbent Protection Act' Dies in Committee," *Roanoke Times*, February 10, 2016, http://www.roanoke.com/news/politics/general_assembly/bill-targeting-incumbent-protection-act-dies-in-committee/article_cb1e2f22-0207-5354-b0fb-25dc8a07a552.html.

236. John Fredericks, "Virginia's New Senator Stooge," *Roanoke Times*, April 12, 2015, http://www.roanoke.com/opinion/commentary/fredericks-virginia-s-new-senator-stooge/article_ff207eae-a56a-5c93-bfb1-d15b6d6d4e4c.html.

237. Carmen Forman and Laurence Hammack, "Smith Out, Edwards in with 2 Contested State Senate Races in Roanoke Region," *Roanoke Times*, March 16, 2015, http://www.roanoke.com/news/local/bedford_county/smith-out-edwards-in-with-contested-state-senate-races-in/article_16db9f66-a739-513d-926b-6112fe53c661.html.

238. Carmen Forman, "Suetterlein Only Republican to File for Ralph Smith's Senate Seat by Deadline," *Roanoke Times*, March 18, 2015, http://www.roanoke.com/news/suetterlein-only-republican-to-file-for-ralph-smith-s-senate/article_adfa92fe-a03c-5763-891f-5cda3ff4f8ad.html.

239. Virginia Public Access Project, "State Senate District 19: District Profile," http://www.vpap.org/offices/state-senate-19/district.

240. Petska, "Bill Targeting 'Incumbent Protection Act.'"

241. Larry Sabato, "Off-Off-Year Elections," Sabato's Crystal Ball: University of Virginia Center for Politics, June 18, 2009, http://www.centerforpolitics.org/crystalball/articles/ljs2009061801.

242. Quentin Kidd, "Virginia's Off-Off-Year Elections," William and Mary Election Law Society, http://electls.blogs.wm.edu/2009/11/16/virginias-off-off-year-elections; Jeff Schapiro, "Low Primary Turnout Would Have Thrilled Byrd," *Richmond Times-Dispatch*, June 17, 2015, http://www.richmond.com/news/virginia/government-politics/jeff-schapiro/article_88d60bd4-40c3-526a-8450-351d11c8ccff.html.

243. Dave Ress, "Are Virginia's Odd Year Elections Facing Challenges?" *Daily Press*, January 12, 2015, http://www.dailypress.com/news/politics/shad-plank-blog/dp-virginia-politics-are-virginias-odd-year-elections-facing-challenges-20150112-post.html.

244. Virginia House of Delegates Joint Resolution 547, "Constitutional Amendment (First Resolution); Establishes Uniform Schedule for General Elections," 2015, http://leg1.state.vaus/cgi-bin/legp504.exe?151+sum+HJ547. Bill cited in Ress, "Are Virginia's Odd Year Elections Facing Challenges?"

245. Dave Ress, "Looking at GOP Effect in Virginia's Off-Off-Year Elections," *Daily Press*, March 20, 2015.

246. Editorial Board, "Mr. Howell's Voting Flip-Flop in Virginia," *Washington Post*, May 27, 2015, http://www.washingtonpost.com/opinions/mr-howells-voting-flip-flop/2015/05/27/0fa58cbc-04a8-11e5-bc72-f3e16bf50bb6_story.html.

247. Christopher Ingraham, "7 Papers, 4 Government Inquiries, 2 News Investigations and 1 Court Ruling Proving Voter Fraud Is Mostly a Myth," *Washington Post*, July 19, 2014, http://www.washingtonpost.com/blogs/wonkblog/wp/2014/07/09/7-papers-4-government-inquiries-2-news-investigations-and-1-court-ruling-proving-voter-fraud-is-mostly-a-myth.

248. Justin Levitt, "A Comprehensive Investigation of Voter Impersonation Finds 31 Credible Incidents Out of One Billion Ballots Cast," *Washington Post*, August 6, 2014, http://www.washingtonpost.com/blogs/wonkblog/wp/2014/08/06/a-comprehensive-investigation-of-voter-impersonation-finds-31-credible-incidents-out-of-one-billion-ballots-cast.

249. Frank Green, "State Official Says He's Unaware of Any Voter Impersonation in Last 20 Years," *Richmond Times-Dispatch*, February 27, 2016, http://www.richmond.com/news/article_b8a007a7-0ca1-59ca-8811-4d8c46892381.html.

250. Matt Laslo, "Virginia's Voter ID Laws," WVTF Radio, October 7, 2014, http://wvtf.org/post/virginias-voter-id-laws.

251. Perkinson, *Texas Tough*, 335–37.

252. Tammie Smith, "Police Veterans Urge New Approach to War on Drugs," *Richmond Times-Dispatch*, May 12, 2015, http://www.richmond.com/life/health/article_6f55fe57-86b2-545d-905f-a12c50c996c1.html.

253. Sean Gorman, "Webb Says U.S. Has 5 Percent of World's Population, 25 Percent of Its 'Known' Prisoners," *Richmond Times-Dispatch* and Politifact, December 15, 2014, http://www.politifact.com/virginia/statements/2014/dec/15/jim-webb/webb-says-us-has-5-percent-worlds-population-25-pe.

254. Jenna Portnoy, Laura Vozzella and Matt Zapotosky, "McAuliffe Creates Commission to Study Bringing Parole Back to Virginia," *Washington Post*, June 24, 2015, http://www.washingtonpost.com/local/virginia-politics/mcauliffe-creates-commission-to-study-bringing-parole-back-to-virginia/2015/06/24/1a10c106-1a7b-11e5-bd7f-4611a60dd8e5_story.html?hpid=z2.

255. Christopher Uggen, Sarah Shannon and Jeff Manza, "State-Level Estimates of Felon Disenfranchisement in the United States, 2010," The Sentencing Project, July 2012, http://www.sentencingproject.org/doc/publications/fd_State_Level_Estimates_of_Felon_Disen_2010.pdf.

256. Louis Hansen, "VA Felons Face Slew of Hurdles to Regain Voting Rights," *Virginian-Pilot*, October 8, 2012, http://hamptonroads.com/2012/10/va-felons-face-slew-hurdles-regain-voting-rights.

257. Uggen, Shannon and Manza, "State-Level Estimates."

258. Ibid.

259. Ibid.

260. Louis Hansen, "VA Felons Face Slew of Hurdles to Regain Voting Rights," *Virginian-Pilot*, October 8, 2012, http://hamptonroads.com/2012/10/va-felons-face-slew-hurdles-regain-voting-rights.

261. Dinan, *Virginia State Constitution*, 90–91.

262. Travis Fain, "McAuliffe Widens Felon Voting Rights Restoration," *Daily Press*, June 23, 2015, http://www.dailypress.com/news/politics/dp-nws-mcauliffe-felon-voting-20150623-story.html.

263. Jeremy Lazarus, "Governor 'Bans the Box' for State Job Applications," *Richmond Free Press*, April 9, 2015, http://richmondfreepress.com/news/2015/apr/09/governor-bans-box-state-job-applications.

264. Jenna Portnoy, "McAuliffe 'Bans the Box' on State Job Applications," *Washington Post*, April 3, 2015, http://www.washingtonpost.com/local/virginia-politics/mcauliffe-bans-the-box-on-state-job-applications/2015/04/03/55a904d0-da16-11e4-ba28-f2a685dc7f89_story.html.

265. Portnoy, Vozzella and Zapotosky, "McAuliffe Creates Commission"; Editorial Board, "Virginia Governor Makes Voting Rights Restoration a Bit Easier," *Fredericksburg Free Lance-Star*, June 30, 2015, http://www.fredericksburg.com/opinion/editorials/editorial-virginia-governor-makes-voting-rights-restoration-a-bit-easier/article_dc6aa01d-4d26-575a-bf4a-386374ae4edc.html.

266. Jim Nolan, "Assembly Republicans Sue McAuliffe Over Mass Rights Restoration Order," *Richmond Times-Dispatch*, May 24, 2016, http://www.richmond.com/news/virginia/article_8e5e5066-5c6b-514a-b0f3-ea9b68469bc1.html.

267. Atkinson, *Virginia in the Vanguard*, 131.

268. Larry Sabato, "Virginia Votes 1999–2002," University of Virginia Center for Politics, 41, http://www.centerforpolitics.org/downloads/vavote3.pdf.

269. Lynch, *Starting Over*, 219.

270. Feld and Wilcox, *Netroots Rising*, 95–96.

271. Ibid., 96–105.

272. Ibid., 119–20.

273. Tim Craig and Michael Shear, "Allen Quip Provokes Outrage, Apology," *Washington Post*, August 15, 2006, http://www.washingtonpost.com/wp-dyn/content/article/2006/08/14/AR2006081400589.html.

274. Jordan Fabian, "Allen's 'Macaca' Moment Remains Close," *Hill*, April 7, 2011, http://thehill.com/homenews/senate/154755-macaca-moment-remains-close-to-surface-for-allen; Ben Pershing, "How Tim Kaine Won the VA Senate Race," *Washington Post*, November 7, 2012, http://www.washingtonpost.com/local/virginia-politics/how-tim-kaine-won-the-va-senate-race/2012/11/06/c425d3d8-27b3-11e2-b2a0-ae18d6159439_story.html; Kate Nocera, "Virginia Senate Election Results 2012: Tim Kaine Beats George Allen," *Politico*, November 6, 2012, http://www.politico.com/news/stories/1112/83445.html, ck cates-congresss-to-do-list.

275. Gary Robertson, "Party Crasher," *Richmond Magazine*, May 6, 2014, http://richmondmagazine.com/news/features/dave-brat-republican-primary.

276. Steve Albertson, "Tuesday Night's Winners and Losers," Bull Elephant, June 11, 2014, http://thebullelephant.com/tuesday-nights-winners-losers.

277. CNN Transcripts, "Eric Cantor Loses GOP Primary and Seat in Congressional Upset; Immigration on the Front Lines of Battles in Arizona," CNN, June 10, 2014, http://www.cnn.com/TRANSCRIPTS/1406/10/cnnt.02.html.

278. Steven Shepard, "GOP Pollsters Missed Big in Virginia," *Politico*, June 12, 2014, http://www.politico.com/story/2014/06/eric-cantor-gop-polls-virginia-primary-107777.html.

279. Steve Albertson, "Brat, Gillespie Score Wins in 7th District Straw Poll," Bull Elephant, May 12, 2014, http://thebullelephant.com/brat-gillespie-score-wins-7th-district-straw-poll.

280. Mark Barabak, "The Earthquake that Toppled Eric Cantor: How Did It Happen?" *Los Angeles Times*, June 11, 2014, http://www.latimes.com/nation/politics/politicsnow/la-pn-earthquake-toppled-cantor-20140611-story.html.

281. Jeremy Peters, "Potent Voices of Conservative Media Propelled Cantor Opponent," *New York Times*, June 11, 2014, http://www.nytimes.com/2014/06/12/us/dave-brat-was-aided-by-laura-ingraham.html.

282. Joe Schaeffer, "VA Conservative Blogger Tom White Called the Cantor Defeat," Newsmax, June 12, 2014; Steve Albertson, "Looking Back at the Only Poll that Picked Dave Brat to Win," Bull Elephant, June 14, 2014, http://thebullelephant.com/looking-back-at-poll-picked-brat-win.

283. Peter Grier, "Eric Cantor Loss; What Happened There?" *Christian Science Monitor*, June 11, 2014.

284. Alex Altman, "A National Leader Falls in a Local Rebellion," *Time*, June 11, 2014, http://time.com/2858234/eric-cantor-dave-brat-virginia-tea-party.

285. Jamie Radtke, "Top Ten Reasons Eric Cantor Lost," Bull Elephant, June 11, 2014, http://thebullelephant.com/top-ten-reasons-eric-cantor-lost. This post is the best analysis of the Cantor-Brat election.

286. Reid Epstein, "David Brat Pulls Off Cantor Upset Despite Raising Just $231,000," *Wall Street Journal*, June 10, 2014, http://www.wsj.com/articles/david-brat-beats-eric-cantor-despite-raising-just-231-000-1402455265.

287. Frank Thorp, "Eric Cantor Blew $168K at Steak Houses; Brat Spent $122K Overall," NBC News, June 11, 2014, http://www.nbcnews.com/politics/elections/eric-cantor-blew-168k-steak-houses-brat-spent-122k-overall-n128126.

288. Paul Steinhauser and Dierdre Walsh, "Cantor 'Earthquake' Rattles Capitol Hill," CNN, June 11, 2014, http://www.cnn.com/2014/06/11/politics/cantor-upset-analysis. Ellipsis in original.

289. Steve Albertson, "Tuesday Night's Winners and Losers," Bull Elephant, June 11, 2014, http://thebullelephant.com/tuesday-nights-winners-losers.

290. Staff, "How Did Virginia Underdog David Brat Beat DC Political Player Eric Cantor?" Fox News, June 11, 2014, http://www.foxnews.com/politics/2014/06/11/how-did-virginia-underdog-david-brat-beat-dc-political-player-eric-cantor.

291. Rebecca Shabad, "Congress Faces Looming Deadlines amid Chaos of House Speaker Election," CBS News, October 8, 2015, http://www.cbsnews.com/news/race-for-speaker-chaos-complicates-congresss-to-do-list; Rick Klein, "ANALYSIS: Why the House Speaker Drama Should Scare You," ABC News, October 9, 2015, http://abcnews.go.com/Politics/analysis-house-speaker-drama-scare/story?id=34374085.

CHAPTER 2

292. Patrick Madden, "Has Dominion's Political Power Clouded the Fight over Coal Ash?" WAMU, March 14, 2016, http://wamu.org/news/16/03/14/has_dominions_political_power_clouded_the_fight_over_coal_ash. Bracketed text in original.

293. Patrick Wilson, "Foes of Dominion Bill Are Mainly Outside Legislature," *Virginian-Pilot*, February 6, 2015, http://hamptonroads.com/2015/02/foes-dominion-bill-are-mainly-outside-legislature.

294. William Howell and Thomas Norment, "Rebuilding Trust, Our Pledge to Virginians," *Richmond Times-Dispatch*, September 9, 2014, http://www.richmond.com/opinion/their-opinion/guest-columnists/article_9eb7231c-9721-5cc4-835b-edda6d7f9107.html.

295. Carolyn Shapiro, "Dominion's Plan to Give Refunds to Customers OK'd," *Virginian-Pilot*, March 12, 2010, http://hamptonroads.com/2010/03/dominions-plan-give-refunds-customers-okd; Matt Leonard, "Law Could Lead to Spike in Electric Bill," *Staunton News Leader*, January 25, 2015, http://www.newsleader.com/story/news/2015/01/25/law-lead-spike-electric-bill/22327531.

296. Jenna Portnoy, "VA Bill Would Put a Pause on Dominion Audits Linked to Refunds or Rate Reductions," *Washington Post*, January 28, 2015, http://www.

washingtonpost.com/local/virginia-politics/va-bill-would-put-a-pause-on-dominion-audits-linked-to-refunds-or-rate-reductions/2015/01/28/2eb21e4a-a64d-11e4-a2b2-776095f393b2_story.html.

297. Virginia Public Access Project, "Frank Wagner: All Years: All Donations from Dominion," http://www.vpap.org/candidates/5699/donor/120206/?page=1&end_year=all&start_year=all&contrib_type=all.

298. Ibid., "Frank Wagner: 2014: Conflicts of Interest Disclosure, Securities, Mutual Funds, Investments," http://www.vpap.org/candidates/5699/conflicts_disclosure/securities/?sei_period=16.

299. Editorial Board, "Elections: Virginia's Incumbency Racket," *Richmond Times-Dispatch*, June 8, 2015, http://www.richmond.com/opinion/our-opinion/article_f21e87b3-8bee-565d-aa02-dc08d4cde76b.html.

300. Virginia Public Access Project, "Frank Wagner: 2014: Conflicts of Interest Disclosure, Securities, Mutual Funds, Investments," http://www.vpap.org/candidates/5699/conflicts_disclosure/securities/?sei_period=16.

301. Anne VanderMey and Nicolas Rapp, "Who Needs a Blind Trust?" *Fortune*, October 22, 2014, http://fortune.com/2012/10/22/who-needs-a-blind-trust.

302. Jim Nolan, "44 Legislators Hold at Least $5,000 in Stock in Companies that Lobby General Assembly," *Richmond Times-Dispatch*, April 15, 2016.

303. Associated Press, "VA Beach Senator Says He's Sold Dominion Shares," *Virginian-Pilot*, February 4, 2015, http://hamptonroads.com/2015/02/va-beach-senator-says-hes-sold-dominion-shares.

304. Bill Sizemore and Alan Suderman, "With Ethics Overhaul Advancing, Norment Points to Media," *Daily Press*, February 4, 2015, http://www.dailypress.com/news/politics/dp-with-ethics-overhaul-advancing-norment-points-to-media2-20150204-story.html.

305. Editorial Board, "Another Ethics Charade in Richmond," *Virginian-Pilot*, February 12, 2015.

306. Bill Sizemore and Alan Suderman, "With Ethics Overhaul Advancing, Norment Points to Media," *Daily Press*, February 4, 2015, http://www.dailypress.com/news/politics/dp-with-ethics-overhaul-advancing-norment-points-to-media2-20150204-story.html.

307. Laura Vozzella, Jenna Portnoy and Rachel Weiner, "Virginia Senate Republicans Were Set to Sink Ethics Bill," *Washington Post*, February 28, 2015, http://www.washingtonpost.com/local/virginia-politics/virginia-senate-republicans-were-set-to-sink-ethics-bill/2015/02/28/05729c98-bec7-11e4-bdfa-b8e8f594e6ee_story.html.

308. Ibid.

309. Travis Fain and Dave Ress, "Ethics Reforms Clear Chambers, Now to Negotiate," *Daily Press*, February 10, 2015, http://www.dailypress.com/news/politics/dp-nws-ga-ethics-bills-20150210-story.html.

310. Virginia Public Access Project, "John Watkins: 2014: Gifts Disclosed by Candidate," http://www.vpap.org/gifts/recipient/5702-john-watkins/disclosed_by_candidate/?start_year=2014&end_year=2014; Virginia Public Access Project, "John Watkins: 2014: Conflicts of Interest Disclosure, Securities,

Mutual Funds, Investments," http://www.vpap.org/candidates/5702/conflicts_disclosure/securities/?sei_period=16. It would be hard to judge how many millions he has, as the top disclosure bracket in which seven of his investments fall caps out at a limitless "more than $250,000."

311. Editorial Board, "Another Ethics Charade in Richmond," *Virginian-Pilot*, February 12, 2015, http://hamptonroads.com/2015/02/another-ethics-charade-richmond.

312. Editorial Board, "Virginia Senate's Treatment of the Press Boggles the Mind," *Richmond Times-Dispatch*, February 9, 2016, http://www.richmond.com/opinion/our-opinion/article_8a13757e-6d34-5297-b5f6-a26f22344fe8.html.

313. Staff, "Norment Bars Reporters from Floor of State Senate," *Richmond Times-Dispatch*, January 13, 2016, http://www.richmond.com/news/virginia/government-politics/article_0eabdd10-eed7-587b-afdb-fbf51e14eb2e.html.

314. Andrew Cain, "Norment Announces Press Will Return to Senate Floor Monday," *Richmond Times-Dispatch*, January 30, 2016, http://www.richmond.com/news/virginia/government-politics/article_c0925d03-f3dd-59bd-adb2-24bbad4f7b29.html; *Richmond Times-Dispatch*, "Reporters Return to Senate Floor—With New Desks," February 2, 2016, http://www.richmond.com/news/virginia/government-politics/article_4180b83f-c500-53bb-860c-9d80ead68b5e.html.

315. Quentin Kidd and Meyrem Baer, "Virginia's Ethics Rules for Public Officials: The Need for Reform," *Virginia News Letter* 90, no.1 (January 2014): 1, http://www.coopercenter.org/sites/default/files/publications/Virginia_News_Letter_2014_Vol._90_No_1.pdf.

316. Dennis Atwood, "Dominion Power Short-Circuits Virginia Governance and Environment," *Roanoke Times*, April 1, 2015, http://www.roanoke.com/opinion/atwood-dominion-power-short-circuits-virginia-governance-and-environment/article_892c0f61-c6fe-52fa-b490-39951e58352d.html.

317. King, *Dominion's First Century*, 114.

318. Ibid., 109–10.

319. Ibid., 108.

320. Peter Galuszka, "Dominion's Clever Legerdemain," Bacon's Rebellion, March 19, 2015, http://www.baconsrebellion.com/2015/03/dominions-clever-legerdemain.html.

321. Peter Bacqué, "Chesterfield Power Station Emits Greatest Amount of Carbon Emissions in the State," *Richmond Times-Dispatch*, September 11, 2013, http://www.richmond.com/news/local/city-of-richmond/article_56b67d22-a3af-5218-87e1-99adccae0ea1.html.

322. Dominion, "Chesterfield Power Station," https://www.dom.com/corporate/what-we-do/electricity/generation/fossil-fueled-power-stations/chesterfield-power-station.

323. Jenna Portnoy, "McAuliffe Backs 550-Mile Natural Gas Pipeline, Disappointing Environmentalists," *Washington Post*, September 2, 2014, http://www.washingtonpost.com/local/virginia-politics/mcauliffe-backs-550-mile-natural-gas-pipeline-disappointing-environmentalists/2014/09/02/e1bd59c6-32a5-11e4-a723-fa3895a25d02_story.html.

324. John Ramsey, "VA Attorney General's Office Says Dominion Should Abandon Third North Anna Reactor," *Richmond Times-Dispatch*, October 22, 2015, http://www.richmond.com/news/virginia/article_ecee574f-77af-5d7f-8b7f-7cf5de60e130.html.

325. Environmental Protection Agency, "Fact Sheet: Clean Power Plan & Carbon Pollution Standards Key Dates."

326. Coral Davenport, "Judges Skeptical of Challenge to Proposed E.P.A. Rule on Climate Change," *New York Times*, April 16, 2015, http://www.nytimes.com/2015/04/17/us/legal-battle-begins-over-obama-bid-to-curb-greenhouse-gases.html.

327. Alan Neuhauser, "EPA Sets Stage to Limit Aircraft Emissions," *U.S. News & World Report*, June 10, 2015, http://www.usnews.com/news/articles/2015/06/10/epa-sets-stage-to-limit-aircraft-emissions.

328. Business Wire, "New Study Released on the Hidden Cost of Harmful Pollution to Downwind Employers and Businesses," Bloomberg, December 8, 2010, http://www.bloomberg.com/apps/news?pid=newsarchive&sid=a_0c63a8Ezaw.

329. Environmental Protection Agency, "Benefits and Costs of the Clean Air Act: Second Prospective Study—1990 to 2020," http://www.epa.gov/air/sect812/prospective2.html.

330. Prue Salasky, "Virginia Groups Urge Better Air Quality," *Daily Press*, June 30, 2015, http://www.dailypress.com/health/dp-nws-air-quality-asthma-20150630-story.html.

331. Jeff Schapiro, "Ex-Regulators Uneasy with Dominion Power Play," *Richmond Times-Dispatch*, February 14, 2015, http://www.richmond.com/news/virginia/government-politics/jeff-schapiro/article_3a89d699-67a5-537c-b92e-ab70860059b9.html.

332. Virginia Senate Joint Resolution 323, "Commending Dominion Resources, Inc.," 2015, http://lis.virginia.gov/cgi-bin/legp604.exe?151+ful+SJ323ER. Accessed May 14, 2016.

333. Robert Chesley, "Welcome to the State of Dominion, Where One Utility Calls All the Shots," *Virginian-Pilot*, February 17, 2015, http://hamptonroads.com/2015/02/welcome-state-dominionwhere-one-utility-calls-all-shots.

334. Jacob Geiger, "Dominion Donations Show It's a Power Company in Virginia Politics," *Roanoke Times*, February 14, 2015; Jeff Schapiro, "Unforeseen Consequences of Dominion's 'Power' Politics," *Richmond Times-Dispatch*, February 3, 2015, http://www.richmond.com/news/virginia/government-politics/jeff-schapiro/article_2660e707-afcb-5908-bed3-202626acc532.html.

335. Alan Suderman, "Dominion Power Turning Customers' Bills into Politically Connected Donations," *Virginian-Pilot*, Associated Press, August 22, 2015.

336. Associated Press, "Critics Say Dominion Trying to Avoid Lower Rates," *Fredericksburg Free Lance-Star*, February 11, 2015, http://www.fredericksburg.com/news/virginia/critics-say-dominion-trying-to-avoid-lower-rates/article_baf74c20-b211-11e4-ab03-bfa6965a514f.html.

337. Amy Gardner, "McAuliffe's Claim of Not Taking Money from Dominion Doesn't Include Executives," *Washington Post*, May 20, 2009, http://www.washingtonpost.com/wp-dyn/content/article/2009/05/19/AR2009051903518.html.

338. Virginia Public Access Project, "McAuliffe for Governor—Terry: Donations from Dominion, 2010–2013," http://www.vpap.org/committees/156114/donor/120206/?start_year=2010&end_year=2013&contrib_type=A.

339. Associated Press, "Dominion Gets Its Way in 2015 Legislature," *Fredericksburg Free Lance-Star*, March 1, 2015, http://www.fredericksburg.com/news/virginia/dominion-gets-its-way-in-legislature/article_ee244501-f5f9-5d08-a889-9a777eb4b929.html.

340. Jeff Schapiro, "Dealmaker-in-Chief Does Business with Dominion," *Richmond Times-Dispatch*, February 10, 2015, http://www.richmond.com/news/virginia/government-politics/jeff-schapiro/article_0ca099b5-fef3-5af7-8d5b-d07163d9d8ee.html.

341. Virginia Senate Bill 1349, "Electric Utility Regulation; Suspension of Regulatory Reviews of Utility Earnings," 2015, http://leg1.state.vaus/cgi-bin/legp504.exe?151+cab+HC10211SB1349+RCSB2.

342. Jacob Geiger, "Dominion Donations Show It's a Power Company in Virginia Politics," *Roanoke Times*, February 14, 2015, http://www.roanoke.com/news/politics/general_assembly/dominion-donations-show-it-s-a-power-company-in-virginia/article_f1d230ea-6664-5912-80ad-980a5808a570.html; Rachel Weiner, "New VA Law Shields Dominion Power from Financial Reviews," *Washington Post*, February 24, 2015, http://www.washingtonpost.com/local/virginia-politics/new-va-law-shields-dominion-power-from-financial-reviews/2015/02/24/9cd64026-bc51-11e4-b274-e5209a3bc9a9_story.html.

343. Jenna Portnoy, "VA Legislature Passes Bill."

344. Jeff Schapiro, "VA Corporate Cops Urged to Man Up—By One of Their Own," *Richmond Times-Dispatch*, December 20, 2015, http://www.richmond.com/news/virginia/government-politics/jeff-schapiro/article_0642f7c1-96f2-5caf-b63b-eb556d1c0922.html.

345. Vozzella, Portnoy and Weiner, "Virginia Senate Republicans Were Set to Sink Ethics Bill," *Washington Post*, February 28, 2015, http://www.washingtonpost.com/local/virginia-politics/virginia-senate-republicans-were-set-to-sink-ethics-bill/2015/02/28/05729c98-bec7-11e4-bdfa-b8e8f594e6ee_story.html.

346. Editorial Board, "Virginia's Toothless Ethics Reform," *Washington Post*, March 4, 2015, http://www.washingtonpost.com/opinions/virginias-toothless-ethics-reform/2015/03/04/eca06542-c29a-11e4-9271-610273846239_story.html. Unless noted, all quotes in this list are from this source.

347. Travis Fain, "Ethics Reform Delays Virginia General Assembly Again," *Daily Press*, April 15, 2015, http://www.dailypress.com/news/politics/dp-nws-ga-session-20150415-story.html-page=1; Patrick Wilson, "Lobbyists Take Changes to Gift Law in Stride," *Virginian-Pilot*, May 11, 2015, http://hamptonroads.com/2015/05/lobbyists-take-changes-gifts-law-stride.

348. Patrick Wilson, "Virginia Lawmakers Should Be Barred from Ethics Panel, Former Top Official Says," *Virginian-Pilot*, June 4, 2015, http://hamptonroads.com/2015/06/virginia-lawmakers-should-be-barred-ethics-panel-former-top-official-says; *Virginian-Pilot*, "Lobbyists Take Changes to Gift Law in Stride," May 11, 2015, http://hamptonroads.com/2015/05/lobbyists-take-changes-gifts-law-stride.

349. Graham Moomaw, "Ethics Lawyer: 'Common Interest' in Sports Clears Va. Officials to Accept Free Tickets," *Richmond Times-Dispatch*, April 27, 2016, http://richmond.com/news/virginia/government-politics/article_a2dd69c1-b229-513c-90a1-9611aacd189a.html.

350. Editorial Board, "Terry McAuliffe's Ethics Rules Turn Elastic," *Richmond Times-Dispatch*, February 5, 2016, http://www.richmond.com/opinion/our-opinion/article_b74e97c2-647e-5e3b-9d9c-36e6f843f425.html.

351. Dave Ress, "Year in Review: The Virginia Way Ain't What It Used to Be," *Daily Press*, December 20, 2014, http://www.dailypress.com/news/dp-nws-top-virginia-way-20141220-story.html.

352. Editorial Board, "Virginia Desperately Needs Substantive Ethics Rules to Curb Abuse by Elected Officials," *Daily Press*, May 11, 2015, http://www.dailypress.com/news/opinion/editorials/dp-edt-ethics-reform-editorial-20150512-20150511-story.html.

353. Kerry Dougherty, "State Wouldn't Need Lobbying Laws if Lawmakers Had More Integrity," *Virginian-Pilot*, May 13, 2015, http://hamptonroads.com/2015/05/state-wouldnt-need-lobbying-laws-if-lawmakers-had-more-integrity.

354. Jeff Schapiro, "What If Dominion's Money Wasn't Flooding the System?" *Richmond Times-Dispatch*, March 17, 2015, http://www.richmond.com/news/virginia/government-politics/jeff-schapiro/article_8c8d98f6-7345-5897-8476-d6aaff45695d.html.

355. Paul Starr, *Remedy and Reaction*, 218–19.

356. Nichols and McChesney, *Dollarocracy*, 97.

357. Virginia Public Access Project, "Dominion: Campaign Contributions, 2014," http://www.vpap.org/donors/120206-dominion/?start_year=2014&end_year=201; "Dominion: Gifts/Entertainment Provided to Legislative or Executive Officials, 2014," http://www.vpap.org/gifts/gifter/120206-dominion/disclosed_by_candidate.

358. Megan Wilson, "Court Upholds Political Contribution Ban for Federal Contractors," *Hill*, July 7, 2015, http://thehill.com/business-a-lobbying/247079-court-upholds-political-giving-ban-for-contractors; Schapiro, "What If Dominion's Money Wasn't Flooding the System?"

359. Madden, "Has Dominion's Political Power Clouded the Fight over Coal Ash?" WAMU, March 14, 2016, http://wamu.org/news/16/03/14/has_dominions_political_power_clouded_the_fight_over_coal_ash. Bracketed text in original.

360. Patrick Wilson, "Lobbyists Take Changes to Gift Law in Stride," *Virginian-Pilot*, May 11, 2015, http://hamptonroads.com/2015/05/lobbyists-take-changes-gifts-law-stride.

361. Virginia Public Access Project, "Dominion: Gifts/Entertainment Provided to Legislative or Executive Officials, 2014," http://www.vpap.org/gifts/gifter/120206-dominion/disclosed_by_candidate.

362. Patrick Wilson, "Foes of Dominion Bill Are Mainly Outside Legislature," *Virginian-Pilot*, February 6, 2015, http://hamptonroads.com/2015/02/foes-dominion-bill-are-mainly-outside-legislature.

363. Associated Press, "Dominion Gets Its Way in 2015 Legislature," *Fredericksburg Free Lance-Star*, March 1, 2015, http://www.fredericksburg.com/news/virginia/dominion-gets-its-way-in-legislature/article_ee244501-f5f9-5d08-a889-9a777eb4b929.html.

364. Patrick Wilson, "Records: Norment Admitted to Relationship with Lobbyist," *Virginian-Pilot*, April 3, 2015, http://hamptonroads.com/2015/04/records-norment-admitted-relationship-lobbyist.

365. Travis Fain, "Norment Won't Discuss Lobbyist Relationship," *Daily Press*, April 3, 2015, http://www.dailypress.com/news/dp-nws-norment-lobbyist-20150403-story.html.

366. Jenna Portnoy, "Federal Investigators Reviewed Top VA Lawmaker's Relationship with Lobbyist," *Washington Post*, April 23, 2015, http://www.washingtonpost.com/local/virginia-politics/federal-investigators-reviewed-top-va-lawmakers-relationship-with-lobbyist/2015/04/23/149d2812-e87c-11e4-aae1-d642717d8afa_story.html.

367. Patrick Wilson, "Norment Sponsored Bills Pushed by Beach Lobby Firm," *Virginian-Pilot*, April 25, 2015, http://hamptonroads.com/2015/04/norment-sponsored-bills-pushed-beach-lobby-firm.

368. Dave Ress and Travis Fain, "Feds Looked Hard, Found Nothing on Lawmaker Norment," *Daily Press*, April 24, 2015, http://www.dailypress.com/news/politics/dp-nws-norment-lobbyist-20150424-story.html.

369. Portnoy, "Federal Investigators Reviewed."

370. William Howell and Thomas Norment, "Rebuilding Trust, Our Pledge to Virginians," *Richmond Times-Dispatch*, September 9, 2014, http://www.richmond.com/opinion/their-opinion/guest-columnists/article_9eb7231c-9721-5cc4-835b-edda6d7f9107.html.

371. Jenna Portnoy, "Virginia Lawmaker Facing Sex Charges Denies Wrongdoing," *Washington Post*, June 30, 2014, http://www.washingtonpost.com/local/virginia-politics/virginia-lawmaker-facing-sex-charges-denies-wrongdoing/2014/06/30/88e6e130-0084-11e4-8fd0-3a663dfa68ac_story.html; Mark Robinson, "Joe Morrissey Is on Trial. Again," *Richmond Magazine*, December 8, 2014, http://richmondmagazine.com/news/features/joe-morrissey-trials.

372. Scott Wise, "'OMG, I Just F***ed My Boss!' Morrissey Drops F-Bomb on Live TV," WTVR-CBS, July 1, 2014, http://wtvr.com/2014/07/01/joe-morrissey-fbomb.

373. Bill McKelway, "Del. Morrissey Sentenced to 12 Months for Sexual Delinquency of a Minor," *Roanoke Times*, December 12, 2014, http://www.roanoke.com/news/virginia/del-morrissey-sentenced-to-months-for-sexual-delinquency-of-a/article_97d8fbb4-2adb-5db7-aa89-19db59c1a3d5.html.

374. Sandra Jones, "Delegate Joe Morrissey Sentenced to Jail After Entering Plea to Reduced Charges in Case Involving Teen Staffer," WTVR-CBS, December 12, 2014, http://wtvr.com/2014/12/12/joseph-morrissey-alford-plea.

375. Bill McKelway, "Del. Morrissey Sentenced to 12 Months for Sexual Delinquency of a Minor," *Roanoke Times*, December 12, 2014, http://www.roanoke.com/news/virginia/del-morrissey-sentenced-to-months-for-sexual-delinquency-of-a/article_97d8fbb4-2adb-5db7-aa89-19db59c1a3d5.html.

376. Rachel Weiner, "Del. Joe Morrissey Hasn't Decided Whether or Not He Will Resign from General Assembly," *Washington Post*, December 14, 2014, http://www.washingtonpost.com/local/virginia-politics/del-joe-morrissey-hasnt-decided-whether-or-not-he-will-resign-from-general-assembly/2014/12/14/ee24b326-83a4-11e4-b9b7-b8632ae73d25_story.html.

377. Rachel Weiner, "Expulsion of Convicted VA Lawmaker from House Would Be First Since Reconstruction," *Washington Post*, December 16, 2014, http://www.washingtonpost.com/local/virginia-politics/expulsion-of-convicted-va-lawmaker-from-house-would-be-first-since-reconstruction/2014/12/16/90d8bc14-855a-11e4-a702-fa31ff4ae98e_story.html.

378. Markus Schmidt, "Joe Morrissey to Run as Independent for House Seat," *Roanoke Times*, December 23, 2014, http://www.roanoke.com/news/politics/joe-morrissey-to-run-as-independent-for-house-seat/article_3de11501-0de2-53a5-94d3-4e82e84ae952.html.

379. Jenna Portnoy, "Morrissey, in Midst of Six-Month Jail Term, Wins Special Election to Virginia House," *Washington Post*, January 13, 2015, http://www.washingtonpost.com/local/virginia-politics/morrissey-in-midst-of-six-month-jail-term-wins-special-election-to-virginia-house/2015/01/13/8676f33a-9b2b-11e4-a7ee-526210d665b4_story.html; Rachel Weiner, "Democrats Pick New Candidate for Morrissey's Henrico County House Seat," *Washington Post*, December 22, 2014, http://www.washingtonpost.com/local/virginia-politics/democrats-pick-new-candidate-for-joe-morrisseys-seat/2014/12/22/f7a5e598-89ec-11e4-8ff4-fb93129c9c8b_story.html.

380. Editorial Board, "Del. Joseph Morrissey Is an Embarrassment to Virginia's General Assembly," *Washington Post*, January 15, 2015, http://www.washingtonpost.com/opinions/del-joseph-morrissey-is-an-embarrassment-to-virginias-general-assembly/2015/01/15/92e1bcd6-9c3e-11e4-a7ee-526210d665b4_story.html.

381. Associated Press, "Morrissey Opposes Ban on Porn in Jail," *Fredericksburg Free Lance-Star*, February 5, 2015, http://www.fredericksburg.com/news/va_md_dc/morrissey-opposes-ban-on-porn-in-jail/article_1f139041-3d89-5cbd-b9f4-1d01ac7d9376.html.

382. Associated Press, "Jailed Virginia Lawmaker Charged with Forgery, Perjury," *Chicago Tribune*, January 21, 2015, http://www.chicagotribune.com/news/nationworld/chi-virginia-lawmaker-perjury-forgery-20150121-story.html.

383. Jeremy Lazarus, "Judge Throws out Felony Charges Against Morrissey," *Richmond Free Press*, April 2, 2015, http://richmondfreepress.com/news/2015/apr/02/judge-throws-out-felony-charges-against-morrissey.

384. Markus Schmidt, "Virginia Democrats Now Wary of Expelling Del. Joe Morrissey," *Roanoke Times*, January 15, 2015, http://www.roanoke.com/news/politics/virginia-democrats-now-wary-of-expelling-del-joe-morrissey/article_30e042d7-f15d-5374-86a9-762c90a6fc54.html.

385. Ned Oliver, "Morrissey Plans to Make Mayoral Campaign Official at Event Next Week," *Richmond Times-Dispatch*, March 25, 2016, http://www.richmond.com/news/local/city-of-richmond/article_b0489d2c-5a69-54d0-9a3b-c116261ba0b9.html.

386. Dave Webster, "Did Morrissey Outsmart the Democrats?" The Bull Elephant, January 14, 2015, http://thebullelephant.com/did-morrissey-outsmart-the-democrats.

387. Sam Robinson, "So Much Up in the Air: The Carbon Dioxide Debate and Coal Plant Permitting in Virginia," *William & Mary Environmental Law and Policy Review* 35, no. 1 (2010): 269–302, http://scholarship.law.wm.edu/cgi/viewcontent.cgi?article=1512&context=wmelpr.

388. John Reid Blackwell, "Dominion Customers to See Rates Drop After SCC Ruling," *Roanoke Times*, November 26, 2013, http://www.roanoke.com/business/news/dominion-customers-to-see-rates-drop-after-scc-ruling/article_d1e7dc40-b329-57fb-835a-2a2bde5fe5b0.html. Ellipsis in original.

389. Alan Suderman, "Dominion Power Turning Customers' Bills into Politically Connected Donations," *Virginian-Pilot*, Associated Press, August 22, 2015, http://hamptonroads.com/2015/08/dominion-power-turning-customers-bills-politically-connected-donations.

390. TheStreet Transcripts, "Dominion Resources (D) Earnings Report: Q1 2015 Conference Call Transcript," TheStreet, May 4, 2015, http://www.thestreet.com/story/13137285/7/dominion-resources-d-earnings-report-q1-2015-conference-call-transcript.html. Accessed May 14, 2016. Errors in original.

391. Heidi King, *Dominion's First Century*, 76.

392. John Reid Blackwell, "Most Local CEOs Saw Their Compensation Increase Last Year," *Richmond Times-Dispatch*, June 27, 2015, http://www.richmond.com/business/local/article_d2540567-1808-5804-9c04-38bfcaac29d3.html.

393. Equilar, "Equilar 200 Highest-Paid CEO Rankings," http://www.equilar.com/publications/51-200-highest-paid-CEO-rankings-2015.html.

394. United States Census Bureau, "State & County QuickFacts," http://quickfacts.census.gov/qfd/states/00000.html.

395. Michael Felberbaum, "Dominion Resources CEO Farrell Made $17.3M in 2014," *Daily Press*, April 1, 2015, http://www.dailypress.com/business/us-dominion-executive-compensation-20150401-story.html.

396. Gretchen Morgenson, "Despite Federal Regulation, C.E.O.-Worker Pay Gap Data Remains Hidden," *New York Times*, April 10, 2015, http://www.nytimes.com/2015/04/12/business/despite-federal-regulation-ceo-worker-pay-gap-data-remains-hidden.html.

397. Olympia Meola, "Virginia's Salary for Governor Tied for Fifth Among States," *Richmond Times-Dispatch*, July 7, 2013, http://www.richmond.com/news/virginia/article_11f331bf-ff95-52f1-8191-3f13b2333bed.html.

398. Wall Street Journal online, "Dominion Resources Stock Price & News," http://quotes.wsj.com/D. Interactive table.

399. Bill McKibben, "How Mankind Blew the Fight Against Climate Change," *Washington Post*, June 9, 2015, http://www.washingtonpost.com/opinions/the-perils-of-engagement/2015/06/05/1d3392ea-094c-11e5-9e39-0db921c47b93_story.html?hpid=z6.

400. Lindley Estes, "Mary Washington Board Approves Divestment Goals," *Fredericksburg Free Lance-Star*, April 15, 2016, http://www.fredericksburg.com/news/education/mary-washington-board-approves-divestment-goals/article_bb9fa4ac-0318-11e6-802b-1f3bfebaedb0.html.

401. Mark Bowes, Rex Springston and John Ramsey, "Explosions Rock City's Electrical Grid," *Richmond Times-Dispatch*, July 24, 2015, http://www.richmond.com/news/local/city-of-richmond/article_da679075-1435-5c4c-a81d-66a5c6f0af5d.html?_dc=566076481249.1835; Alix Bryan, Jerrita Patterson and Shelby Brown, "Multiple Underground Explosions Close Parts of Broad

Street," WTVR-CBS, July 3, 2014, http://wtvr.com/2014/07/02/multiple-explosions-close-broad-street-downtown; Staff, "'Boom Like Thunder,' Fire and Smoke Downtown After Transformer Explodes," WTVR-CBS, http://wtvr.com/2015/07/24/loud-booms-black-smoke-reported-downtown; Rober Sorrell, "Underground Explosions in Richmond Result in Court Closures Across Virginia," *Bristol Herald-Courier*, July 24, 2015, http://www.heraldcourier.com/news/underground-explosions-in-richmond-result-in-court-closures-across-virginia/article_51823686-323d-11e5-90b0-8fce3c3af176.html.

402. American Council for an Energy-Efficient Economy, "State Scorecard Rank," http://database.aceee.org/state-scorecard-rank.

403. CERES, "First-of-Its-Kind Report Ranks U.S. Electric Utility Companies' Renewable Energy Efficiency Performance," July 24, 2014, http://www.ceres.org/press/press-releases/first-of-its-kind-report-ranks-u.s.-electric-utility-companies2019-renewable-energy-energy-efficiency-performance.

404. John Ramsey, "Virginia Solar Power Development Lags Neighboring States," *Richmond Times-Dispatch*, August 9, 2015, http://www.richmond.com/news/virginia/article_8e545711-1356-52f2-9600-6c16035bfeca.html.

405. King, *Dominion's First Century*, 7.

406. Department of Energy data tabulated at Jordan Wifrs-Brock, "Data: Explore 15 Years of Power Outages," Inside Energy, http://insideenergy.org/2014/08/18/data-explore-15-years-of-power-outages.

407. Public Service Enterprise Group, "Awards and Recognition," https://www.pseg.com/family/about/awards.jsp.

408. PA Consulting, "PA Consulting Group Honours North American Utilities for Excellence in Reliability at the 2015 ReliabilityOne™ Awards Ceremony," http://www.paconsulting.com/introducing-pas-media-site/releases/pa-consulting-group-honours-north-american-utilities-for-reliability-excellence-at-2015-reliabilityone-awards-23-october-2015.

409. JD Power, "2015 Electric Utility Residential Customer Satisfaction Study," http://www.jdpower.com/press-releases/2015-electric-utility-residential-customer-satisfaction-study.

410. Patrick Wilson, "Foes of Dominion Bill Are Mainly Outside Legislature," *Virginian-Pilot*, February 6, 2015, http://hamptonroads.com/2015/02/foes-dominion-bill-are-mainly-outside-legislature.

411. John Ramsey, "Dominion Virginia Power Plans to Spend $9.5 Billion on Infrastructure and Upgrades," *Richmond Times-Dispatch*, January 14, 2016, http://www.richmond.com/business/article_70f63589-e725-5eea-9a35-00caddd79d1e.html.

412. United States Energy Information Administration, "Table 5.6.A. Average Retail Price of Electricity to Ultimate Customers by End-Use Sector: All Sectors," March 2015, http://www.eia.gov/electricity/monthly/epm_table_grapher.cfm?t=epmt_5_6_a.

413. Ibid., "State Profile and Energy Estimates: Washington," http://www.eia.gov/state/?sid=wa#tabs-5; Washington Public Utility Districts Association, "History of PUDS in Washington," http://www.wpuda.org/pud-history.cfm.

414. Duncan Adams, "From Thorny to Thornier: Pipeline Companies Tap State Law to Gain Access to Properties," *Roanoke Times*, May 8, 2015, http://www.roanoke. com/news/local/franklin_county/from-thorny-to-thornier-pipeline-companies-tap-state-law-to/article_c7975fcf-4257-5467-bf18-ed633a89d21c.html.

415. Code of Virginia § 56-49.01, "Natural Gas Companies; Right of Entry Upon Property," http://leg1.state.VAus/cgi-bin/legp504.exe?000+cod+56-49.01.

416. Ballotopedia, "Virginia Eminent Domain Amendment, Question 1 (2012)," http://ballotpedia.org/Virginia_Eminent_Domain_Amendment,_Question_1_%282012%29.

417. Chemerinsky, *Constitutional Law*, 656–82.

418. Jeff Schapiro, "Name from the Past in Fight for the Future," *Richmond Times-Dispatch*, January 27, 2015, http://www.richmond.com/news/virginia/government-politics/jeff-schapiro/article_6b0c5d18-ea8b-5e31-87ef-39339897993c.html.

419. Dinan, *Virginia State Constitution*, 69.

420. A. Barton Hinkle, "Should Dominion Get to Walk All Over Property Rights?" *Richmond Times-Dispatch*, January 6, 2015, http://www.richmond.com/opinion/our-opinion/article_5ae34be2-5e7d-55c4-a8eb-65f841107345.html.

421. Elana Schor, "Pipeline Politics: Virginia's Keystone?" *Politico*, May 3, 2015, http://www.politico.com/story/2015/05/virginia-keystone-pipeline-natural-gas-117578.html. The 550-mile pipeline is an investment of a consortium of energy companies, and Dominion is the largest investor. A second spur would run from North Carolina to Virginia.

422. Duncan Adams, "Mountain Valley Pipeline Considers Alternative Routes," *Roanoke Times*, February 2, 2015, http://www.roanoke.com/news/local/giles_county/mountain-valley-pipeline-considers-alternative-routes/article_d2e79f0c-63ce-546b-93b0-f924f65b0d77.html.

423. Adams, "From Thorny to Thornier."

424. Editorial Board, "The Governor and the Pipeline," *Roanoke Times*, July 28, 2015, http://www.roanoke.com/opinion/editorials/our-view-the-governor-and-the-pipeline/article_24cf940d-b61c-59f7-a0b7-1aa7e30a9a93.html.

425. Jenna Portnoy, "McAuliffe Backs 550-Mile Natural Gas Pipeline, Disappointing Environmentalists," *Washington Post*, September 2, 2014, http://www.washingtonpost.com/local/virginia-politics/mcauliffe-backs-550-mile-natural-gas-pipeline-disappointing-environmentalists/2014/09/02/e1bd59c6-32a5-11e4-a723-fa3895a25d02_story.html.

426. Preston Knight, "Pipeline Protest Planned," *Harrisonburg Daily News-Record*, October 31, 2014.

427. Michael Martz, "Dominion to Withdraw Lawsuits Against Landowners Over Pipeline Surveys—and Start Over," *Richmond Times-Dispatch*, April 7, 2015, http://www.richmond.com/news/virginia/government-politics/article_c6c9ac9b-5bea-5ba1-8739-e1b11e7fb24c.html.

428. Rachel Smith, "Real Estate Agents: Proposed Pipeline Already Affecting Sales," *Lynchburg News & Advance*, May 18, 2015, http://www.newsadvance. com/work_it_lynchburg/news/real-estate-agents-proposed-pipeline-

already-affecting-sales/article_486d8e38-fcf5-11e4-b10b-5bfa67606
fa1.html.

429. Michael Martz, "Wintergreen Says Pipeline Proposal Could Slow Resort's Revitalization," *Richmond Times-Dispatch*, February 7, 2016, http://www.richmond. com/news/virginia/article_efe8628b-a0e0-553d-a0d9-c67513741a3e.html.

430. Duncan Adams, "Franklin County Residents in Pipeline's Path Worry about Their Future," *Roanoke Times*, February 29, 2016, http://www.roanoke.com/ business/news/franklin-county-residents-in-pipeline-s-path-worry-about-their/ article_2c5993e7-2b47-57d2-b3f0-d0bad1c289a2.html.

431. Ibid.; R.J. Tracy, "Pipeline Is No Nice Walk Through a Cornfield," *Roanoke Times*, May 18, 2015, http://www.roanoke.com/opinion/tracy-pipeline-is-no-nice-walk-through-a-cornfield/article_21921c03-0bcc-5fa9-ab87-fbdf3c3bfdc6.html.

432. Bob Stuart and Rachael Smith, "ACP: Dominion Puts Price on Pipeline Connections," *Waynesboro News Virginian*, May 2, 2015, http://www.dailyprogress. com/newsvirginian/news/local/acp-dominion-puts-price-tag-on-pipeline-connections/article_7a753956-f13a-11e4-83f2-3ffeed7e9fce.html.

433. Duncan Adams, "Pipeline Turnabout: Gas Could Be Sent to India," *Roanoke Times*, June 25, 2015, http://www.roanoke.com/news/local/pipeline-turnabout-gas-could-be-sent-india/article_27512cb7-f09a-56ea-8e3b-ca388a55df6d.html.

434. Ibid., "Pipeline Contractors Face Trespassing Charges in Craig County," *Roanoke Times*, May 28, 2015, http://www.roanoke.com/news/local/pipeline-contractors-face-trespassing-charges-in-craig-county/article_891a351b-553c-58c1-816f-12747259ba4f.html.

435. Elana Schor, "Pipeline Politics: Virginia's Keystone?" *Politico*, May 3, 2015, http://www.politico.com/story/2015/05/virginia-keystone-pipeline-natural-gas-117578.html; Adams, "From Thorny to Thornier."

436. Staff, "General Assembly Briefs," *Richmond Times-Dispatch*, February 9, 2016, http://www.richmond.com/news/virginia/government-politics/article_2340c8da-2d27-5ae4-b82a-8ad419ad2f7b.html.

437. Associated Press, "Critics Say Dominion Trying to Avoid Lower Rates," *Fredericksburg Free Lance-Star*, February 11, 2015, http://www.fredericksburg. com/news/virginia/critics-say-dominion-trying-to-avoid-lower-rates/article_baf74c20-b211-11e4-ab03-bfa6965a514f.html.

438. Patrick Wilson, "Lobbyists Take Changes to Gift Law in Stride," *Virginian-Pilot*, May 11, 2015, http://hamptonroads.com/2015/05/lobbyists-take-changes-gifts-law-stride.

439. Rachel Weiner, "New VA Law Shields Dominion Power from Financial Reviews," *Washington Post*, February 24, 2015, http://www.washingtonpost.com/ local/virginia-politics/new-va-law-shields-dominion-power-from-financial-reviews/2015/02/24/9cd64026-bc51-11e4-b274-e5209a3bc9a9_story.html.

440. Associated Press, "Critics Say Dominion Trying to Avoid Lower Rates," *Fredericksburg Free Lance-Star*, February 11, 2015, http://www.fredericksburg. com/news/virginia/critics-say-dominion-trying-to-avoid-lower-rates/article_baf74c20-b211-11e4-ab03-bfa6965a514f.html.

441. Jacob Geiger, "Governor, Energy Companies Say They Want More Lenient Clean Power Plan," *Richmond Times-Dispatch*, April 14, 2015, http://www.richmond.com/business/local/article_8af01526-75df-5543-ae69-ded8609c3c8f.html.

442. Thomas Farrell and John Luke, "Let's GO Virginia," *Richmond Times-Dispatch*, July 26, 2015, http://www.richmond.com/opinion/their-opinion/guest-columnists/article_79a2d9f9-f041-528d-9892-3642dab0f767.html.

443. John Ramsey and Rex Springston, "U.S. Plan to Reduce Carbon Dioxide Emissions Eases the Requirement for Virginia," *Richmond Times-Dispatch*, August 4, 2015, http://www.richmond.com/news/virginia/article_d7d572b2-184f-5f50-9ba0-8e2818ee115b.html; Adam Liptak and Coral Davenport, "Supreme Court Deals Blow to Obama's Efforts to Regulate Coal Emissions," *New York Times*, February 9, 2016, http://www.nytimes.com/2016/02/10/us/politics/supreme-court-blocks-obama-epa-coal-emissions-regulations.html.

444. John Ramsey, "Dominion Plans Three New Solar Farms," *Richmond Times-Dispatch*, October 2, 2015, http://www.richmond.com/business/article_091ce695-c1ad-5116-b417-5da0d741fa6a.html; *Richmond Times-Dispatch*, "Amazon Moving Forward on Accomack Solar Farm," September 29, 2015, http://www.richmond.com/business/article_e51b04b5-2896-59d9-af83-0ffbc4e825d0.html.

445. Travis Fain, "Dominion Gets Nod for New Plant, Higher Charges," *Daily Press*, March 31, 2016, http://www.dailypress.com/news/politics/dp-nws-dominion-gas-20160330-story.html.

446. Bill McKibben and Mike Tidwell, "Will McAuliffe Honor Paris or Dominion?" *Virginian-Pilot*, February 8, 2016, http://pilotonline.com/opinion/columnist/guest/bill-mckibben-mike-tidwell-will-mcauliffe-honor-paris-or-dominion/article_4b640eb6-1b37-5a99-89d4-e83f430f8939.html.

447. Doug Domenech, "The EPA's Carbon Rule Will Hurt Virginia," *Richmond Times-Dispatch*, February 7, 2016, http://www.richmond.com/opinion/their-opinion/guest-columnists/article_ee6c14ba-7b3b-52e2-b3ff-bb58dd9711f6.html.

448. Peter Galuszka, "Dominion's Clever Legerdemain," *Bacon's Rebellion*, March 19, 2015, http://www.baconsrebellion.com/2015/03/dominions-clever-legerdemain.html.

449. *Amicus Curiae Brief of Dominion Resources, Inc. in West Virginia v. EPA, DC Circuit Court of Appeals*, USCA Case #15-1363, Document #1606771, April 1, 2016.

450. Jeff Schapiro, "Ex-Regulators Uneasy with Dominion Power Play," *Richmond Times-Dispatch*, February 14, 2015, http://www.richmond.com/news/virginia/government-politics/jeff-schapiro/article_3a89d699-67a5-537c-b92e-ab70860059b9.html.

451. Robert McIntyre et al., "The Sorry State of Corporate Taxes: What Fortune 500 Firms Pay (or Don't Pay) in the USA and What They Pay Abroad—2008 to 2012," Citizens for Tax Justice, February 2014, pp. 26–27, http://www.ctj.org/corporatetaxdodgers/sorrystateofcorptaxes.pdf.

452. Heidi King, *Dominion's First Century*, 79.

453. Associated Press, "Critics Say Dominion Trying to Avoid Lower Rates," *Fredericksburg Free Lance-Star*, February 11, 2015, http://www.fredericksburg.

com/news/virginia/critics-say-dominion-trying-to-avoid-lower-rates/article_baf74c20-b211-11e4-ab03-bfa6965a514f.html.

454. Rachel Weiner, "Bill Passed by VA Legislators May Help Dominion Power Avoid Rebates or Rate Cuts," *Washington Post*, February 27, 2014, http://www.washingtonpost.com/local/virginia-politics/2014/02/27/9b04f42a-9d9b-11e3-b8d8-94577ff66b28_story.html.

455. Virginia Senate Bill 459, "Electric Utility Regulation; Recovery of Nuclear Costs; Rate Adjustment Clauses," 2014, https://leg1.state.VAus/cgi-bin/legp504.exe?141+sum+SB459.

456. Virginia House Bill 848, "Electric Utility Regulation; Recovery of Costs of New Underground Distribution Facilities," 2014, https://leg1.state.VAus/cgi-bin/legp504.exe?141+sum+HB848.

457. Associated Press, "Bills of Note that Passed in the 2014 General Assembly Session," *Loudon Times-Mirror*, March 10, 2014, http://www.loudountimes.com/news/article/bills_of_note_that_passed_in_2014_general_assembly_session654.

458. Dave Ress, "Newport News Shipbuilding Among Businesses Facing Dominion Virginia Power Over Accounting Issue," *Daily Press*, February 4, 2014, http://articles.dailypress.com/2014-02-04/news/dp-nws-ga-power-0205-20140204_1_dominion-virginia-power-third-nuclear-plant-accounting-issue.

459. Zachary Reid, "Richmond School Board Approves $271 Million Budget," *Richmond Times-Dispatch*, May 27, 2015, http://www.richmond.com/news/local/city-of-richmond/article_6aa45336-4b74-5a2c-ba1b-64d0e6b01c0b.html.

460. Stiglitz, *Freefall*, 238–39.

461. Wolin, *Managed Democracy*.

462. Local Government Employee Salary Database, 2013, *Richmond Times-Dispatch*, Salary for director of Public Utilities, http://www.richmond.com/data-center/salaries-local-government-employees-2013/?appon=0320844857356878212450172880949205525642150505881069338855898494057320090821044893079834125540408354022481 0.

463. Pope Francis, "Encyclical Letter Laudato Si' of the Holy Father Francis on Care for Our Common Home," http://w2.vatican.va/content/francesco/en/encyclicals/documents/papa-francesco_20150524_enciclica-laudato-si.html. See also Scully, *Dominion*, 15–16.

464. Roanoke College Public Relations Office, "Roanoke College Poll Finds Virginians Support Ethics Reform," *Roanoke Times*, January 22, 2015, http://www.roanoke.com/community/sosalem/roanoke-college-poll-finds-virginians-support-ethics-reforms/article_84565b7a-6ee3-586e-9a21-6addb637ef70.html; Quentin Kidd, "Virginians Think McDonnell Prison Sentence Fair; Back Gift Ban, Redistricting Reform, Reporting Campus Rape to Police, Looser Marijuana Laws," Christopher Newport University, January 27, 2014, https://lintvwavy.files.wordpress.com/2015/01/jan-27-2015-report.pdf.

465. Gayla Mills, "The Crowded Halls of Power," *Style Weekly*, April 7, 2015, http://www.styleweekly.com/richmond/the-crowded-halls-of-power/Content?oid=2194168.

CHAPTER 3

466. Ibid., 62. Bracketed text in original.

467. Asthma and Allergy Foundation of America, "Asthma Capitals 2015: The Most Challenging Places to Live with Asthma," 2015, http://www.aafa.org/pdfs/2015_AC_PublicList.pdf.

468. Ibid.,"There's More to Asthma than Meets the Air," http://aafa.org/display.cfm?id=7&sub=100&cont=896.

469. Ibid., "Asthma Capitals 2015: The Most Challenging Places to Live with Asthma," 2015, http://www.aafa.org/pdfs/2015_AC_PublicList.pdf.

470. Bob Marshall, "More Medicaid Doesn't Mean More Care," *Richmond Times-Dispatch*, December 26, 2013, http://www.richmond.com/opinion/their-opinion/article_2364e75f-10a3-58b7-92f5-feae1dda6318.html.

471. K. Baicker et al., "The Oregon Experiment—Effects of Medicaid on Clinical Outcomes," *New England Journal of Medicine* 368 (2013): 1713–22, http://www.nejm.org/doi/full/10.1056/NEJMsa1212321.

472. I made this point in a letter to the editor, "Misquoting Report Deceives Constituents," *Richmond Times-Dispatch*, January 3, 2014, http://www.richmond.com/opinion/your-opinion/letters-to-the-editor/article_97f3ab86-119c-5e6b-8aa2-221f5105b050.html.

473. Todd Datz, "Expanding Medicaid to Low-Income Adults Leads to Improved Health, Fewer Deaths," Harvard School of Public Health, July 25, 2012, http://www.hsph.harvard.edu/news/press-releases/medicaid-expansion-lower-mortality; Louis Jacobson, "Politifact: Ted Cruz Says Expanding Medicaid 'Will Worsen Health Care Options for the Most Vulnerable,'" *Tampa Bay Times and Politifact*, April 8, 2013, http://www.politifact.com/truth-o-meter/statements/2013/apr/08/ted-cruz/ted-cruz-says-expanding-medicaid-will-worsen-healt; Julia Paradise and Rachel Garfield, "What Is Medicaid's Impact on Access to Care, Health Outcomes, and Quality of Care? Setting the Record Straight on the Evidence," Kaiser Family Foundation, August 2, 2013, http://kff.org/medicaid/issue-brief/what-is-medicaids-impact-on-access-to-care-health-outcomes-and-quality-of-care-setting-the-record-straight-on-the-evidence.

474. Coyle, *Roberts Court*, 347–49.

475. Matthew Buettgens, John Holahan and Hannah Recht, "Medicaid Expansion, Health Coverage, and Spending: An Update for the 21 States that Have Not Expanded Eligibility," Kaiser Family Foundation, April 29, 2015, http://kff.org/medicaid/issue-brief/medicaid-expansion-health-coverage-and-spending-an-update-for-the-21-states-that-have-not-expanded-eligibility.

476. Sean Gorman, "Mary Mannix Says about Half of Virginia's Rural Hospitals Run in the Red," Politifact, *Richmond Times-Dispatch*, September 22, 2015, http://www.politifact.com/virginia/statements/2015/sep/22/mary-mannix/mary-mannix-says-about-half-virginias-rural-hospit.

477. Kaiser Health News, "KHN Morning Briefing: With Lawmakers Blocking Medicaid Expansion, Va. Governor Scales Back Plan," September 9, 2014, http://kaiserhealthnews.org/morning-breakout/virginia-scaled-back-plan-after-medicaid-expansion; Council of Economic Advisors, "Missed

Opportunities: The Consequences of State Decisions Not to Expand Medicaid," White House, July 2014, p. 9, https://www.whitehouse.gov/sites/default/files/docs/missed_opportunities_medicaid.pdf.

478. Quentin Kidd, "Virginia Voters Support Medicaid Expansion, but Worry About the Feds Paying Their Share, and Doubt Special Session Will Accomplish Anything," Christopher Newport University, September 17, 2014, http://cnu.edu/cpp/pdf/sept%2017%202014%20report.pdf.

479. George Orwell, *Nineteen Eighty-Four*, ch. 9. Available at https://ebooks.adelaide.edu.au/o/orwell/george/o79n/chapter2.9.html.

480. Rick Mayes and Benjamin Paul, "An Analysis of Political and Legal Debates Concerning Medicaid Expansion in Virginia," *University of Richmond Journal of Law and the Public Interest* (Fall 2014): 26, http://scholarship.richmond.edu/cgi/viewcontent.cgi?article=1061&context=polisci-faculty-publications.

481. Michael Martz, "Three Seek Democratic Nod for Pivotal State Senate Seat," *Richmond Times-Dispatch*, May 16, 2015, http://www.richmond.com/news/virginia/government-politics/article_142ed920-9786-5d6c-887e-9e82cf45a884.html.

482. William Howelland Kirk Cox, "Medicaid Expansion: Promises on Future Costs Don't Ring True," *Richmond Times-Dispatch*, February 2, 2014, http://www.richmond.com/opinion/their-opinion/columnists-blogs/guest-columnists/howell-and-cox-medicaid-expansion-promises-on-future-costs-don/article_0285f36b-9652-5a5a-9524-ae0f914d4afc.html.

483. Jennifer Haberkorn, "7.3 Million in Obamacare Plans, Beats CBO Forecast," Politico, September 18, 2014, http://www.politico.com/story/2014/09/obamacare-enrollment-numbers-111097.html.

484. Rick Mayes and Benjamin Paul, "An Analysis of Political and Legal Debates Concerning Medicaid Expansion in Virginia," *University of Richmond Journal of Law and the Public Interest* (Fall 2014): 26, http://scholarship.richmond.edu/cgi/viewcontent.cgi?article=1061&context=polisci-faculty-publications.

485. Dan Mangan, "Medicaid Expansion Could Cost States Less, Help Uninsured," CNBC, May 9, 2014, http://www.cnbc.com/id/101659823.

486. United States Government Accountability Office, "Medicare and Medicaid Waste, Fraud, and Abuse: Effective Implementation of Recent Laws and Agency Actions Could Help Reduce Improper Payments," March 9, 2011, http://www.gao.gov/assets/130/125646.pdf.

487. Travis Fain, "McAuliffe, Lawmakers in Tiff Over Office Building," *Daily Press*, July 9, 2014, http://articles.dailypress.com/2014-07-09/news/dp-nws-gab-construction-20140709_1_mcauliffe-house-appropriations-chairman-s-house-republicans.

488. Andy Sullivan, "Republican White House Hopefuls Attack Obamacare but Take Money," *Reuters*, April 1, 2015, http://www.reuters.com/article/2015/04/01/us-usa-election-obamacare-idUSKBN0MS38I20150401.

489. Joint Legislative Audit and Review Commission, "Size and Impact of Federal Spending in Virginia," Commonwealth of Virginia, June 2014, pp. 1–2, http://jlarc.virginia.gov/pdfs/reports/Rpt455.pdf.

490. Kaiser Family Foundation, "Federal Medical Assistance Percentage (FMAP) for Medicaid and Multiplier," http://kff.org/medicaid/state-indicator/federal-matching-rate-and-multiplier.

491. Frederick Kunkle, "Cuccinelli Teams with Paul Ryan to Rip New Health-care [*sic*] Law," *Washington Post*, October 23, 2013, http://www.washingtonpost.com/local/virginia-politics/cuccinelli-teams-with-paul-ryan-to-rip-new-health-care-law/2013/10/23/0a164dc6-3b8d-11e3-b6a9-da62c264f40e_story.html.

492. Michael Shapiro, "Cuccinelli Slams President's Health Care Law in Williamsburg," *Daily Press*, October 3, 2013, http://articles.dailypress.com/2013-10-03/news/dp-nws-cuccinelli-obamacare-20131003_1_attorney-general-ken-cuccinelli-health-care-law-medicaid-program; William Howell and Kirk Cox, "Medicaid Expansion: Promises on Future Costs Don't Ring True," *Richmond Times-Dispatch*, February 2, 2014, http://www.richmond.com/opinion/their-opinion/columnists-blogs/guest-columnists/howell-and-cox-medicaid-expansion-promises-on-future-costs-don/article_0285f36b-9652-5a5a-9524-ae0f914d4afc.html; Nancy Madsen, "Boycotting Medicaid Expansion Puts a Small Dent in U.S. Deficits," *Richmond Times-Dispatch* and Politifact, April 29, 2014, http://www.politifact.com/virginia/article/2014/apr/29/boycotting-medicaid-expansion-puts-small-dent-us-d.

493. Massey Whorley and Michael Cassidy, "Medicaid Expansion Would Pay for Itself," Commonwealth Institute, August 2013, http://www.thecommonwealthinstitute.org/wp-content/uploads/2013/08/medex_pays_for_itself.pdf.

494. Sharon Long et al., "Taking Stock: Gains in Health Insurance Coverage Under the ACA as of March 2015," Urban Institute, April 16, 2015, http://hrms.urban.org/briefs/Gains-in-Health-Insurance-Coverage-under-the-ACA-as-of-March-2015.html.

495. Jeremy Diamond, "New Obamacare Numbers: 16.4 Million Covered," CNN, March 17, 2015, http://www.cnn.com/2015/03/16/politics/obamacare-numbers-16-million-insured-rate.

496. Matt O'Brien, "Paul Ryan Has a Trick Up His Sleeve When It Comes to Taxes. It Won't Work," *Washington Post*, October 14, 2014, https://www.washingtonpost.com/news/wonk/wp/2014/10/14/paul-ryan-has-a-trick-up-his-sleeve-when-it-comes-to-taxes-it-wont-work.

497. Michael Martz, "$2.1 Billion Bond Bill Ties New Capital Spending to Completing Capitol Square Project," *Richmond Times-Dispatch*, March 12, 2016, http://www.richmond.com/news/virginia/government-politics/general-assembly/article_9b7a2130-11ed-541b-92b0-13f014a21956.html.

498. Staff, "Hospitals' 'Lobby Day' Meets GOP Opposition," *Richmond Times-Dispatch*, January 21, 2016, http://www.richmond.com/news/virginia/government-politics/article_98b1f86e-bff7-11e5-bf02-479a87198a92.html.

499. Rick Mayes and Benjamin Paul, "An Analysis of Political and Legal Debates Concerning Medicaid Expansion in Virginia," *University of Richmond Journal of Law and the Public Interest* (Fall 2014): 30, http://scholarship.richmond.edu/cgi/viewcontent.cgi?article=1061&context=polisci-faculty-publications.

500. Sean Gorman, "Landes Claim Medicaid Expansion Could Cost $1 Billion a Year Based on Shaky Assumption," Politifact Virginia, January 11, 2016, http://www.politifact.com/virginia/statements/2016/jan/11/steven-landes/landes-says-medicaid-expansion-could-cost-virginia.

501. Michael Martz, "Senate and House Won't Support Medicaid Expansion, Proposed Tax Cuts from Savings," *Richmond Times-Dispatch*, February 17, 2016, http://www.richmond.com/news/virginia/article_9d2c513e-652e-546b-ab50-4c9151b125c9.html.

502. Sara Corbett, "Patients Without Borders," *New York Times Magazine*, November 18, 2007, http://www.nytimes.com/2007/11/18/magazine/18healthcare-t.html?_r=0.

503. *60 Minutes*, "U.S. Health Care Gets Boost from Charity," CBS News, February 28, 2008, http://www.cbsnews.com/news/us-health-care-gets-boost-from-charity.

504. David Cecere, "New Study Finds 45,000 Deaths Annually Linked to Lack of Health Coverage," *Harvard Gazette*, http://news.harvard.edu/gazette/story/2009/09/new-study-finds-45000-deaths-annually-linked-to-lack-of-health-coverage.

505. Scully, *Dominion*, x.

506. Trip Gabriel, "After First Plan Is Blocked, Virginia Governor Terry McAuliffe Reduces Medicaid Expansion Goals," *New York Times*, September 8, 2014, http://www.nytimes.com/2014/09/09/us/after-first-plan-is-blocked-virginia-governor-terry-mcauliffe-reduces-medicaid-expansion-goals.html?_r=0.

507. Potter, *Deadly Spin*, 69.

508. Ibid., 76.

509. Ibid., 77.

510. John Blake, "A Health Care 'Judas' Recounts His Conversion," CNN, June 27, 2012, http://religion.blogs.cnn.com/2012/06/27/a-health-care-judas-recounts-his-conversion.

511. *Richmond Times-Dispatch*, "Top 50 Local Employers in Richmond, VA," http://www.richmond.com/business/local/top-50-employers; Altria Group, Inc., "2014 Annual Report," 2014, https://materials.proxyvote.com/Approved/02209S/20150330/AR_240595.PDF; "About Altria: At-A-Glance," http://www.altria.com/About-Altria/At-A-Glance/Pages/default.aspx.

512. "The High Cost of Compromise: Tobacco Industry Political Influence and Tobacco Control Policy in Virginia, 1977–2009," Center for Tobacco Control Research & Education at the University of California, 2010, 9.

513. Centers for Disease Control, "Smoking & Tobacco Use: Fast Facts," http://www.cdc.gov/tobacco/data_statistics/fact_sheets/fast_facts.

514. "High Cost of Compromise," 1; Federal Reserve Bank of St. Louis, "Total Gross Domestic Product by State for Virginia," June 10, 2015, https://research.stlouisfed.org/fred2/series/VANGSP. For consistency, GDP figure used for 0.5 percent calculation is from 2009. Centers for Disease Control, "Smoking & Tobacco Use: Fast Facts"; Fortune, "Fortune 500: Altria," 2015, http://fortune.com/fortune500/altria-group-inc-161.

515. Greenwald, *With Liberty and Justice for Some*, 222.

516. Jeff Sturgeon, "Western District of Virginia Dominated by Hard Drug Cases," *Roanoke Times*, April 25, 2015, http://www.roanoke.com/news/crime/western-

district-of-virginia-dominated-by-hard-drug-cases/article_fb2ae185-5e8b-56dc-a787-ab1a6d3b2d58.html.

517. Human Rights Watch, "Tobacco's Hidden Children: Hazardous Child Labor in United States Tobacco Farming," May 2014, pp. 38–39, http://www.hrw.org/sites/default/files/reports/us0514_UploadNew.pdf. Names are pseudonymous.

518. Human Rights Watch, "Tobacco's Hidden Children: Hazardous Child Labor in United States Tobacco Farming," May 2014, http://www.hrw.org/sites/default/files/reports/us0514_UploadNew.pdf.

519. Ibid., 37, 22.

520. Ibid., 33.

521. Ibid., 36.

522. Ibid., 35.

523. Ibid., 39.

524. Ibid., 40.

525. Ibid., 41.

526. Ibid., 49.

527. Ibid., 45–46.

528. Ibid., 48.

529. Ibid., 49.

530. Ibid., 54.

531. Ibid.

532. Ibid., 55.

533. Ibid., 56. Bracketed text in original.

534. Ibid., 62. Bracketed text in original.

535. Editorial Board, "Children's Don't Belong in Tobacco Fields," *New York Times*, May 17, 2014, http://www.nytimes.com/2014/05/18/opinion/sunday/children-dont-belong-in-tobacco-fields.html; Tripp Mickle, "Reynolds American, Altria Set New Policies for Young Field Workers," *Wall Street Journal*, December 12, 2014, http://www.wsj.com/articles/reynolds-american-altria-set-new-policies-for-young-field-workers-1418425372; Editorial Board, "Obama Administration Must Do More to Protect Children Harvesting Tobacco," *Washington Post*, May 18, 2014, http://www.washingtonpost.com/opinions/obama-administration-must-do-more-to-protect-children-harvesting-tobacco/2014/05/18/23b8a7c4-dd36-11e3-b745-87d39690c5c0_story.html; Sandra Young, "Kids Deal with Vomiting, Burning Eyes Working on Tobacco Farms," CNN, May 18, 2014, http://www.cnn.com/2014/05/17/health/hrw-children-tobacco-workers-report; Associated Press, "Children as Young as 7 Working Tobacco Farms, Report Says," NBC News, May 14, 2014, http://www.nbcnews.com/business/consumer/children-young-7-working-tobacco-farms-report-says-n105021; Charlie Campbell, "Young Children Are Getting Sick Working on U.S. Tobacco Farms," *Time*, May 14, 2014, http://time.com/98781/us-tobacco-farms-child-labor.

536. Margaret Wurth, "A Move to Protect State's Children," *Richmond Times-Dispatch*, January 19, 2015, http://www.richmond.com/opinion/their-opinion/guest-columnists/article_3c384ee8-14fe-56f6-8088-12d15aad8c31.html.

537. Virginia House Bill 1906, 2015, http://leg1.state.va.us/cgi-bin/legp504. exe?151+ful+HB1906+pdf.

538. Mickle, "Reynolds American."

539. Staff, "VA Lawmakers Defeat Bill to End Use of Child Labor on Tobacco Farms," WVIR-NBC, February 3, 2015, http://www.nbc29.com/story/28016174/va-lawmakers-defeat-bill-to-end-use-of-child-labor-on-tobacco-farms.

540. Zama Coursen-Neff, "Dispatches: No Virginia, Tobacco Fields Are Not a Place for Children," Human Rights Watch, February 5, 2015, http://www.hrw.org/news/2015/02/05/dispatches-no-virginia-tobacco-fields-are-not-place-children.

541. Staff, "VA Lawmakers Defeat Bill."

542. Virginia House Bill 1906, "Children, Employment on Tobacco Farms Prohibited, Exception," http://leg1.state.va.us/cgi-bin/legp504.exe?151+cab+HC10120HB1906+BREF.

543. Kessler, *Question of Intent.*

544. Ibid., 361.

545. National Cancer Institute, "The Role of the Media in Promoting and Reducing Tobacco Use," 2008, pp. 182–83, http://cancercontrol.cancer.gov/Brp/tcrb/monographs/19/m19_complete.pdf.

546. Freudenberg, *Lethal but Legal*, 19–28.

547. Danny Hakim, "U.S. Chamber of Commerce Works Globally to Fight Antismoking Measures," *New York Times*, June 30, 2015, http://www.nytimes.com/2015/07/01/business/international/us-chamber-works-globally-to-fight-antismoking-measures.html.

548. Virginia Department of Agriculture and Consumer Services, "Virginia's Top 20 Farm Commodities," February 24, 2015, http://www.vdacs.virginia.gov/agfacts/top20.shtml.

549. "High Cost of Compromise," 15.

550. Human Rights Watch, "Tobacco's Hidden Children," 25.

551. Ann Boonn, "State Cigarette Excise Tax Rates & Rankings," Campaign for Tobacco-Free Kids, June 30, 2015, https://www.tobaccofreekids.org/research/factsheets/pdf/0097.pdf.

552. Asthma and Allergy Foundation of America, "There's More to Asthma than Meets the Air."

553. Virginia Public Access Project, "Top Donors: All Years," http://www.vpap.org/money/top-donors/?year=all.

554. "High Cost of Compromise," 22.

555. Virginia Public Access Project, "Altria: Campaign Contributions, All Years," http://www.vpap.org/donors/110931-altria/?start_year=all&end_year=all; "High Cost of Compromise," 24.

556. "High Cost of Compromise," 23.

557. Virginia Public Access Project, "Altria: Employer," http://vpap.org/seis/employer/110931-altria/?sei_period=3.

558. Mark Rozell, "Virginia: From Red to Blue?" in Bullock and Rozell, *New Politics of the Old South*, 150.

559. Domhoff, *Who Rules America?*, 30, 116.

560. Alan Finder, "At One University, Tobacco Money Is a Secret," *New York Times*, May 22, 2008, http://www.nytimes.com/2008/05/22/us/22tobacco.html?pagewanted=all.

561. Chris Dovi, "Lung Association Chastises VCU for Tobacco Ties," *Style Weekly*, September 3, 2008, http://www.styleweekly.com/richmond/lung-association-chastises-vcu-for-tobacco-ties/Content?oid=1370965.

562. Ibid., "Patch Job," *Style Weekly*, August 13, 2008, http://www.styleweekly.com/richmond/patch-job/Content?oid=1369402.

563. Virginia Commonwealth University, "Senior Leadership," https://www.vcuhealth.org/?id=12&sid=1.

564. Joint Legislative Audit and Review Commission, "Review of the Tobacco Indemnification and Community Revitalization Commission: Commission Briefing," June 13, 2011, p. 9, http://jlarc.virginia.gov/meetings/June11/TICRbrf.pdf.

565. National Association of Attorneys General, "Payments to Date," Master Settlement Agreement, http://www.naag.org/assets/redesign/files/msa-tobacco/2014-06-25%2BPayments_to_States_Inception_thru_June_24_2014_.pdf; Virginia Tobacco Indemnification and Community Revitalization Commission, "The National Tobacco Settlement," http://www.tic.virginia.gov/mastersettlement.shtml.

566. Richmond Division, "Former Virginia Secretary of Finance Sentenced for Embezzling $4 Million from Tobacco Indemnification Fund," Federal Bureau of Investigation, November 23, 2010, http://www.fbi.gov/richmond/press-releases/2010/ri112310a.htm. The remaining $1 million was distributed for scholarships.

567. Larry O'Dell, "Ex-Va. Finance Chief Gets 10 Years for Wire Fraud," Bloomberg BusinessWeek, November 24, 2010, http://www.businessweek.com/ap/financialnews/D9JMH6FO0.htm.

568. Rosalind Helderman, "Va. Official Is Sentenced to Prison in Fraud Case," *Washington Post*, November 24, 2010, http://www.washingtonpost.com/wp-dyn/content/article/2010/11/23/AR2010112307228.html.

569. Associated Press, "Tobacco Commission Grants Go to Kilgore Family Connections," *Roanoke Times*, September 1, 2014, http://www.roanoke.com/ap/state/tobacco-commission-grants-go-to-kilgore-family-connections/article_400af2de-a58d-568a-ae8c-212994009b1c.html.

570. Michael Martz, "Jonnie Williams to Wrap Up Testimony on Monday," *Richmond Times-Dispatch*, August 2, 2014, http://www.roanoke.com/news/virginia/jonnie-williams-to-wrap-up-testimony-on-monday/article_55a42c25-26eb-50bd-a2ee-3c0f962b9270.html.

571. Jackie Morlock, "McDonnell Trial: Was Star Scientific CEO Jonnie Williams Buying Support or Just a Generous Friend?" WTKR-CBS, August 12, 2014, http://wtkr.com/2014/08/12/mcdonnell-trial-was-star-scientific-ceo-jonnie-williams-buying-support-or-just-a-generous-friend.

572. Frank Green and Jim Nolan, "Williams Touted McDonnells' Support, Jerry Kilgore Says," *Richmond Times-Dispatch*, August 11, 2014, http://www.richmond.com/news/virginia/article_53791c06-2164-11e4-ac58-0017a43b2370.html.

573. Alan Suderman, "Tobacco Commission Grant Above Recommended Amount," *Virginian-Pilot*, November 30, 2014, http://hamptonroads.com/2014/11/tobacco-commission-grant-above-recommended-amount.

574. Peter Galuszka, "Tobacco Corruption in Virginia," *Washington Post*, November 24, 2010, http://voices.washingtonpost.com/local-opinions/2010/11/corruption_at_virginias_tobacc.html.

575. Sean Gorman, "Senate Democrats U-Turn on Power Sharing," *Richmond Times-Dispatch* and Politifact, January 29, 2014, http://www.politifact.com/virginia/statements/2014/jan/29/virginia-senate-democratic-caucus/senate-democrats-u-turn-power-sharing.

576. Jenna Portnoy, "Va. Attorney General Hires Law Expert as Possible Shutdown Looms," *Washington Post*, May 30, 2014, http://www.washingtonpost.com/local/virginia-politics/va-attorney-general-hires-law-expert-as-possible-shutdown-looms/2014/05/30/80a523da-e83b-11e3-8f90-73e071f3d637_story.html.

577. Laura Vozzella, "Virginia Democratic Senator Puckett to Resign, Possibly Dooming Push to Expand Medicaid," *Washington Post*, June 8, 2014, http://www.washingtonpost.com/local/virginia-politics/2014/06/08/901edf8e-ef54-11e3-914c-1fbd0614e2d4_story.html. The Senate was then split 20–19 in favor of Republicans; the lieutenant governor could vote only to break ties.

578. Laura Vozzella and Michael Laris, "Virginia Republicans Snatched Control of the State Senate, Ended Budget-Medicaid Impasse," *Washington Post*, June 9, 2014, http://www.washingtonpost.com/local/virginia-politics/amid-firestorm-of-criticism-virginia-democrats-resignation-becomes-official/2014/06/09/b04d6760-efd3-11e3-914c-1fbd0614e2d4_story.html.

579. Laura Vozzella, "Sen. Warner Discussed Job for Puckett's Daughter, Puckett's Son Says," *Roanoke Times*, October 10, 2014, http://www.roanoke.com/news/virginia/sen-warner-discussed-job-for-puckett-s-daughter-puckett-s/article_fa1b0e54-d87b-5403-83d1-3e92df339c6a.html; Rachel Weiner, "Mark Warner Denies Offering Job to Senator's Daughter," *Washington Post*, October 13, 2014, http://www.washingtonpost.com/local/virginia-politics/mark-warner-denies-offering-job-to-senators-daughter/2014/10/13/7d5fff5a-5303-11e4-809b-8cc0a295c773_story.html.

580. Ibid., "Puckett's Senate Exit Undid McAuliffe's Secret Plan to Pass Medicaid Expansion," *Washington Post*, November 22, 2014, http://www.washingtonpost.com/local/virginia-politics/pucketts-senate-exit-undid-mcauliffes-secret-plan-to-pass-medicaid-expansion/2014/11/22/c5edf09e-59f5-11e4-b812-38518ae74c67_story.html.

581. Alan Suderman and Eric Tucker, "FBI Probes Virginia State Senator Phil Puckett's Resignation," NBC DC, June 19, 2014, http://www.nbcwashington.com/news/local/FBI-Probes-Virginia-State-Senator-Phil-Pucketts-Resignation-263900561.html; Travis Fain, "Subpoenas Show Grand Jury Underway in Former Senator Puckett Case," *Daily Press*, June 25, 2014, http://articles.dailypress.com/2014-06-25/news/dp-nws-tobacco-commission-20140625_1_grand-jury-virginia-senate-state-senator; "Lawyer: No Charges in Puckett Investigation," *Daily Press*, December 12, 2014,

http://www.dailypress.com/news/politics/dp-lawyer-no-charges-in-puckett-investigation-20141212-story.html.

582. Laura Vozzella and Jenna Portnoy, "Judicial Appointment for Puckett's Daughter Clears Va. Legislature," *Washington Post*, January 20, 2015, http://www.washingtonpost.com/local/virginia-politics/judicial-appointment-for-pucketts-daughter-expected-to-move-forward-in-va-capitol/2015/01/20/6bda197a-a0d1-11e4-b146-577832eafcb4_story.html.

583. Anita Kumar, "Legislative Audit Is Critical of Virginia's Tobacco Commission," *Washington Post*, June 13, 2011, http://www.washingtonpost.com/local/dc-politics/legislative-audit-is-critical-of-virginias-tobacco-commission/2011/06/13/AG1YcgTH_story.html.

584. David Toscano, "Big Mess at Tobacco Commission," *Virginian-Pilot*, July 8, 2014, http://hamptonroads.com/2014/07/toscano-big-mess-tobacco-commission.

585. Office of the Governor, "Governor McAuliffe Announces New Executive Director for Virginia Tobacco Commission," May 15, 2015, https://governor.virginia.gov/newsroom/newsarticle?articleId=8426; Virginia House Bill 2330, 2015, https://leg1.state.va.us/cgi-bin/legp504.exe?151+ful+CHAP0399+pdf.

586. Robert McCartney, "Virginia Tobacco Body Under Scrutiny (Again) for Suspiciously Large Gas Project Grant," *Washington Post*, December 10, 2014, http://www.washingtonpost.com/local/virginia-tobacco-body-under-scrutiny-again-for-suspiciously-large-gas-project-grant/2014/12/10/f7e1958c-80b1-11e4-8882-03cf08410beb_story.html.

587. Frank Green, "Man Facing Cigarette-Trafficking Charges Denied Bond," *Richmond Times-Dispatch*, June 1, 2015, http://www.richmond.com/news/article_49686971-1b3a-56da-9fe3-941ab3c09476.html.

588. Ibid., "Alleged Illicit Cigarette Dealer Arraigned in Federal Court," *Richmond Times-Dispatch*, May 26, 2015, http://www.richmond.com/news/article_e093f162-2cd3-5cd7-9c37-efe6be66fafe.html.

589. Ibid., "Cigarette Trafficking Thriving in Richmond Area," *Richmond Times-Dispatch*, May 2, 2015, http://www.richmond.com/news/local/central-virginia/article_c1b62eb1-1c70-5753-826f-89d051340830.html.

590. Ibid., "Cigarette Trafficking Spawning Other Crimes and Possibly Violence," *Richmond Times-Dispatch*, March 28, 2015, http://www.richmond.com/news/local/crime/article_e101477f-1c3d-5117-bcce-f8839f52485c.html.

591. Ibid., "Efforts to Curb Illicit Cigarettes Sold Widely in New York City," *Richmond Times-Dispatch*, March 14, 2015, http://www.richmond.com/news/article_1e46495b-1be8-54d4-b726-b93ad8886ce3.html.

592. Jim Nolan, "Despite Trafficking, Va. Cigarette Tax Appears Unlikely to Rise," *Richmond Times-Dispatch*, April 25, 2015, http://www.richmond.com/news/virginia/government-politics/article_df0aba3b-27a3-5a51-acf3-ce98bab938db.html.

593. Clean Air Task Force, "Mortality Risk: Cities," http://www.catf.us/fossil/problems/power_plants//Existing_Plants_Per_Capita_by_MSA.pdf.

594. Ibid., "Mortality Risk: States," http://www.catf.us/fossil/problems/power_plants//Existing_Plants_by_State_Per_Capita.pdf.

595. Environmental Protection Agency, "Virginia Electric and Power Company (VEPCO) Clean Air Act (CAA) Settlement," April 17, 2003, http://www2.epa.gov/enforcement/virginia-electric-and-power-company-vepco-clean-air-act-caa-settlement; Michael Kilian, "EPA Touts Pollution Settlement," *Chicago Tribune*, April 22, 2003, http://articles.chicagotribune.com/2003-04-22/news/0304220295_1_new-source-review-epa-administrator-christie-whitman-clean-air-act.

596. King, *Dominion's First Century*, 108.

597. Environmental Protection Agency, "Dominion Energy, Inc.," April 1, 2013, http://www2.epa.gov/enforcement/dominion-energy-inc.

598. Associated Press, "NRC Suspects Violations at Dominion Site in Conn.," *Richmond Times-Dispatch*, May 1, 2015, http://www.richmond.com/business/local/article_1c18e37a-f06e-11e4-9175-bbc8623869e9.html.

599. Ibid., "Dominion to Mediate on Conn. Plant Violations," *Richmond Times-Dispatch*, May 13, 2015, http://www.richmond.com/business/local/article_0bf2568e-f95b-11e4-aefb-b79177fb245d.html.

600. Environmental Protection Agency, "Arch Coal Clean Water Act Settlement," March 1, 2011, http://www2.epa.gov/enforcement/arch-coal-clean-water-act-settlement.

601. Ibid., "Alpha Natural Resources Inc. Settlement," March 5, 2014, http://www2.epa.gov/enforcement/alpha-natural-resources-inc-settlement.

602. Nash, *Virginia Climate Fever*, 129.

603. Jeff Inglis, Tony Dutzik and John Rumpler, "Wasting Our Waterways: Toxic Industrial Pollution and Restoring the Promise of the Clean Water Act," Environment America Research and Policy Center, June 2014, http://environmentamericacenter.org/sites/environment/files/reports/US_wastingwaterways_scrn%20061814_0.pdf.

604. Galuszka, *Thunder on the Mountain*, 81–83.

605. Virginia Public Access Project, "Alpha Natural Resources: Donor: All Years," http://vpap.org/donors/110889-alpha-natural-resources/?start_year=all&end_year=all.

606. Adriana Diaz, "Flint Water Crisis: High Lead Levels Could Impact Flint for Years," CBS News, March 4, 2016, http://www.cbsnews.com/news/flint-water-crisis-high-lead-levels-could-impact-city-for-years.

607. Peter Galuszka, "Dominion Gets Approval to Dump Treated Coal Ash Wastewater in James River," *Style Weekly*, January 19, 2016, http://www.styleweekly.com/richmond/dominion-gets-approval-for-coal-ash-waste-dumping-in-james-river/Content?oid=2281180; Ray Daudani and Mike Valerio, "Student Protesters Stage Sit-in at DEQ Offices over Dominion Permit," NBC WWBT-12, March 7, 2016, http://www.nbc12.com/story/31405848/student-protesters-stage-sit-in-at-deq-offices-over-dominion-permit; Occupational Health and Safety Administration, "Hexavalent Chromium," United States Department of Labor, https://www.osha.gov/SLTC/hexavalentchromium.

608. Pamela Faggert, "Dominion Virginia Power: Don't Worry, Trust Us," *Style Weekly*, March 8, 2016, http://www.styleweekly.com/richmond/letter-dominion-virginia-power-dont-worry-trust-us/Content?oid=2298686.

609. Jill Palermo, "Dominion Released Millions of Gallons of Coal-Ash Water," Inside NoVA, February 8, 2016, http://www.insidenova.com/headlines/exclusive-

dominion-released-millions-of-gallons-of-coal-ash-water/article_02a2700e-ce8b-11e5-9370-aff33f0f4afb.html; "Dumfries Calls for Coal Ash Probe," Inside NoVA, March 31, 2016, http://www.insidenova.com/headlines/dumfries-calls-for-coal-ash-probe/article_dc6688ec-f105-11e5-bd58-ef6ddd29a864.html.

610. Patrick Madden, "Has Dominion's Political Power Clouded the Fight over Coal Ash?" WAMU, March 14, 2016, http://wamu.org/news/16/03/14/has_dominions_political_power_clouded_the_fight_over_coal_ash. Bracketed text in original.

611. Pamela Wood, "Maryland Takes Virginia to Court over Coal Ash Plan on the Potomac," *Baltimore Sun*, February 17, 2016, http://www.baltimoresun.com/news/maryland/bs-md-coal-ash-20160216-story.html. The suit was still pending as of March 2016.

612. Palermo, "Dominion Released Millions" and "Dumfries Calls for Coal Ash Probe."

613. Pamela Faggert, "Dominion Virginia Power: Don't Worry, Trust Us," *Style Weekly*, March 8, 2016, http://www.styleweekly.com/richmond/letter-dominion-virginia-power-dont-worry-trust-us/Content?oid=2298686.

614. Kelsey Jo Starr, "Breathing Easy? Thomas Hall Health Debate Revolves Around Coal Plant," *Collegiate Times*, May 1, 2012, http://www.collegiatetimes.com/news/virginia_tech/breathing-easy-thomas-hall-health-debate-revolves-around-coal-plant/article_c47ab228-6185-5737-a8ef-71cb6dfc2b37.html.

615. Allison Sanders, "Campus Power Plant Generates New Controversy," *Collegiate Times*, November 6, 2009, http://www.collegiatetimes.com/news/virginia_tech/campus-power-plant-generates-new-controversy/article_e0142b8f-e2c8-5fd6-91d2-7f49ee44d58a.html.

616. Starr, "Breathing Easy?"

617. Amila Tola, "Tech Should Remove Coal Plant," *Collegiate Times*, October 29, 2014, http://www.collegiatetimes.com/opinion/tech-should-remove-coal-plant/article_bd6018f4-5fc1-11e4-9a9b-001a4bcf6878.html.

618. Jonathan Pillow, "Filtered, but Still Sooty," *Collegiate Times*, February 14, 2006, http://www.collegiatetimes.com/news/filtered-but-still-sooty/article_a8d4102c-4792-5100-811d-e7365d2ad4fe.html.

619. Kelsey Jo Starr, "Clean Coal?" *Collegiate Times*, October 26, 2011, http://www.collegiatetimes.com/news/state/clean-coal/article_3dd48311-142f-523c-8e8d-d405dfe7da17.html.

620. Virginia Tech, "University Facts & Figures, 2013–2014," p. 6, https://www.vt.edu/about/facts-figures-2014.pdf.

621. Jessica Groves, "Club Rallies Against Coal," *Collegiate Times*, April 22, 2013, http://www.collegiatetimes.com/lifestyle/people_and_clubs/club-rallies-against-coal/article_19d79c1b-68d7-5356-a862-b639bd54a487.html.

622. Galuszka, *Thunder on the Mountain*, 3.

623. Patricia Sullivan, "How Two Accidental Virginia Activists Have (Almost) Closed GenOn Coal Plant," *Washington Post*, September 1, 2011, http://www.washingtonpost.com/local/how-two-accidental-virginia-activists-have-almost-closed-genon-coal-plant/2011/09/01/gIQABxA3zJ_story_1.html.

624. Ibid., "GenOn Power Plant in Alexandria Is Set to Close," *Washington Post*, September 29, 2012, http://www.washingtonpost.com/local/genon-power-

plant-in-alexandria-is-set-to-close/2012/09/29/daa355ea-08d7-11e2-858a-5311df86ab04_story.html.

625. Joint Legislative Audit and Review Commission, "Review of the Effectiveness of Virginia Tax Preferences," November 14, 2011, http://jlarc.virginia.gov/meetings/November11/TaxPref.pdf. pp. 67-69.

626. Alicia Petska, "Senate OKs Coal Tax Credit Extension with Veto-Proof Margin," *Roanoke Times*, February 16, 2016, http://www.richmond.com/news/local/city-of-richmond/article_e79df178-0a1e-5662-9a6a-6af6afbc11b1.html; Graham Moomaw, "Senators Claim McAuliffe Veto on Coal Tax Credits Was Retaliation for Supreme Court Vote," *Richmond Times-Dispatch*, March 12, 2016, http://www.richmond.com/news/virginia/government-politics/article_ec4ed915-35a3-5ee3-9f3a-04f6182bb329.html.

627. Virginia's Legislative Information System, "Constitution of Virginia," Article XI Section 3, http://constitution.legis.virginia.gov.

628. Nash, *Virginia Climate Fever*, 36–38.

629. Ibid., 24.

630. Ibid., 69.

631. Ibid., 87.

632. Ibid., 71–86. The three most populous cities in Virginia are Virginia Beach, Norfolk and Chesapeake. Daryl Grove, "10 Most Populous Counties in Virginia," *Virginia Living*, http://www.virginialiving.com/blogs/virginia-living-blog/10-most-populous-counties-in-virginia.

633. Trip Pollard, "Damage Control: Adapting Transportation to a Changing Climate," *William & Mary Law and Policy Review* 39, no. 2 (2015): 365–400; Molly Mitchell, William Stiles and Troy Hartley, "Sea Level Rise: A Relentless Reality that Virginia Must Continue to Plan Carefully for," *Virginia News Letter* 90, no. 6 (August 2014): 1, http://www.coopercenter.org/sites/default/files/publications/Virginia%20News%20Letter%202014%20Vol.%2090%20No%206.pdf. Accessed May 14, 2016.

634. Nash, *Virginia Climate Fever*, 11–12.

635. Ibid., 132.

636. Pollard, "Damage Control," 387.

637. Nash, *Virginia Climate Fever*, 131.

638. Pollard, "Damage Control," 387–88; Mitchell, Stiles and Hartley, "Sea Level Rise," 3–4.

639. Editorial Board, "Science Subpoenaed," *Nature* 465 (May 13, 2010): 135–36; McGarity and Wagner, *Bending Science*, 275–78.

640. Mark Drajem, "NASA's Hansen Arrested Outside White House at Pipeline Protest," Bloomberg, August 29, 2011, http://www.bloomberg.com/news/articles/2011-08-29/nasa-s-hansen-arrested-outside-white-house-at-pipeline-protest; Hamilton, *Requiem for a Species*, xi.

641. Scully, *Dominion*, 250–53; Leonard, *Meat Racket*, 167–68, 240–42.

642. Staff, "Smithfield Is Fined $12.6 Million for Dumping Waste into River," *Wall Street Journal*, August 9, 1997, http://www.wsj.com/articles/SB871121628389896000; Richard Stradling, "Smithfield Fined $12.6

Million," *Daily Press*, August 9, 1997, http://articles.dailypress.com/1997-08-09/news/9708090064_1_smithfield-foods-water-pollution-pagan-river.

643. Jeff Tietz, "Boss Hog," in Imhoff, *CAFO Reader*, 111.

644. Staff, "Smithfield Is Fined $12.6 Million."

645. Ibid.; Stradling, "Smithfield Fined $12.6 Million."

646. Associated Press, "Pigs Subject to Abuse at Virginia Factory Farm, Humane Society of the United States Says," *Los Angeles Times*, December 16, 2010, http://latimesblogs.latimes.com/unleashed/2010/12/pigs-subject-to-abuse-at-virginia-factory-farm-humane-society-of-the-united-states-says.html.

647. Associated Press, "Smithfield Foods Fires Three Workers for Mistreating Pigs," *Cleveland Plain Dealer*, December 21, 2010, http://www.cleveland.com/business/index.ssf/2010/12/smithfield_foods_fires_three_w.html. Video at Humane Society of the United States, "HSUS Exposes Inhumane Treatment of Pigs at Smithfield," December 15, 2010, http://www.humanesociety.org/news/press_releases/2010/12/smithfield_pigs_121510.html.

648. Dana Mattioli, Dana Cimilluca and David Kesmodel, "China Makes Biggest U.S. Play," *Wall Street Journal*, May 30, 2013, http://www.wsj.com/articles/SB10001424127887324412604578512722044165756.

649. David Kesmodel, "Shuanghui to Boost Smithfield Exports as First Priority," *Wall Street Journal*, September 26, 2013, http://www.wsj.com/articles/SB10001424052702304795804579099421443260970.

650. Schlosser, *Fast Food Nation*, 239–52; Tanya Wanchek, "Why We Are Losing the Fight Against Obesity," *Virginia News Letter* 83, no. 2 (December 2007), http://www.coopercenter.org/sites/default/files/autoVANLPubs/Virginia%20News%20Letter%202007%20Vol.%2083%20No.%202.pdf.

651. M. Thorogood, J. Mann, P. Appleby and K. McPherson, "Risk of Death from Cancer and Ischaemic Heart Disease in Meat and Non-Meat Eaters," *British Medical Journal* 308 (June 25, 1994): 1669.

652. American Heart Association, "Vegetarian Diets," http://www.americanheart.org/presenter.jhtml?identifier=4777.

653. Amanda Cross, Michael Leitzmann, Mitchell Gail, Albert Hollenbeck, Arthur Schatzkin and Rashmi Sinha, "A Prospective Study of Red and Processed Meat Intake in Relation to Cancer Risk," *PLoS Medicine* 4, no.12 (December 2007).

654. Alice Lichtenstein et al., "Diet and Lifestyle Recommendations Revision 2006: A Scientific Statement from the American Heart Association Nutrition Committee," *Circulation* 114 (2006): 83–85; American Institute for Cancer Research, "Recommendations for Cancer Prevention," 2010, pp. 18–19, http://preventcancer.aicr.org/site/DocServer/Guidelines_Brochure.pdf?docID=1550&JServSessionIdr00q3q8xo3ga5.app46a.

655. Johns Hopkins Bloomberg School of Public Health, "Health & Environmental Implications of U.S. Meat Consumption and Production," http://www.jhsph.edu/research/centers-and-institutes/johns-hopkins-center-for-a-livable-future/projects/meatless_monday/resources/meat_consumption.html. The researchers cite eighteen separate medical studies (citations not reproduced here).

656. Gina Kolata, "Animal Fat Is Tied to Colon Cancer," *New York Times*, December 13, 1990, http://www.nytimes.com/1990/12/13/us/animal-fat-is-tied-to-colon-cancer.html; Harvard School of Public Health, "Walter Willett," http://www.hsph.harvard.edu/walter-willett.

657. Nestle, *Food Politics*, 31–50.

658. Leonard, *Meat Racket*, 164–66.

659. World Health Organization, "Life Expectancy at Birth, 1990–2013," http://gamapserver.who.int/gho/interactive_charts/mbd/life_expectancy/atlas.html.

660. Richardson, *Built by Blacks*, 113–15; Edwin Slipek, "The Lost Neighborhood," *Style Weekly*, November 8, 2006, http://www.styleweekly.com/richmond/the-lost-neighborhood/Content?oid=1363378.

661. Tammie Smith, "Where You Live Determines How Long You Live," *Richmond Times-Dispatch*, January 27, 2013, http://www.richmond.com/life/health/article_2cc6b9b5-b2cb-5d45-838a-6765c30bc20b.html.

662. Karin Kapsidelis, "Juvenile Wounded by Gunfire During Police Walk in Gilpin Court," *Richmond Times-Dispatch*, April 11, 2015, http://www.richmond.com/news/local/city-of-richmond/article_4b9566e7-d3e8-5c6c-8708-69ec040c6c9c.html.

663. Laura Kebede, "4 Injured in Gilpin Court Shooting," *Richmond Times-Dispatch*, April 19, 2015, http://www.richmond.com/news/local/city-of-richmond/article_d6647e6f-dd0f-5edf-b43b-4c981e8eb9aa.html.

664. Jeremy Lazarus, "Short-Term Fix Restores Power to Fay Towers Residents," *Richmond Free Press*, April 23, 2015, http://richmondfreepress.com/news/2015/apr/23/short-term-fix-restores-power-fay-towers-residents.

665. Ilya Grossman, "Gilpin Court Residents Without Hot Water for Nearly 5 Days," WRIC-ABC, June 3, 3015, http://wric.com/2015/06/03/gilpin-court-residents-without-hot-water-for-nearly-5-days.

666. Michael Paul Williams, "Life Expectancy in Gilpin Court 20 Years Shorter Than Westover Hills," *Richmond Times-Dispatch*, April 30, 2015, http://www.richmond.com/news/local/michael-paul-williams/article_c5c14d95-1cf6-5be3-86ec-6943f30e1f78.html.

667. *Richmond Times-Dispatch*, "Our New Children's Hospital," April 8, 2015, http://www.richmond.com/opinion/their-opinion/guest-columnists/article_c82bf78f-db4b-5c9f-8162-59c97c4c6e5f.html.

668. Karin Kapsidelis, "Juvenile Wounded by Gunfire During Police Walk in Gilpin Court," *Richmond Times-Dispatch*, April 11, 2015, http://www.richmond.com/news/local/city-of-richmond/article_4b9566e7-d3e8-5c6c-8708-69ec040c6c9c.html; Ashley Killough, "Virginia Governor Admitted to Hospital After Fall from Horse in Africa," CNN, January 19, 2015, http://www.cnn.com/2015/01/19/politics/terry-mcauliffe-injury.

669. Tammie Smith, "VCU Medical Center's Trauma Unit Saves Richmond's Most Gravely Injured," *Richmond Times-Dispatch*, April 18, 2015, http://www.richmond.com/life/health/article_22b5d4ad-3e49-5c27-a58a-7d2c5f858f69.html.

670. Quadagno, *One Nation, Uninsured*, 2.

671. A. Barton Hinkle, "Your Prices on Drugs," *Richmond Times-Dispatch*, January 24, 2015, http://www.richmond.com/opinion/our-opinion/bart-hinkle/article_186e840d-baab-5dcc-8677-fbedca4c33b4.html; Dean Baker, "Health Care Budget Deficit Calculator, Version 1," Center for Economic and Policy Research, http://www.cepr.net/calculators/hc/hc-calculator-old.html.

672. Quoted in Farmer, *Infections and Inequalities*, 262.

673. *60 Minutes*, "Affordable Care for Those Still Uninsured," CBS, August 17, 2014, http://www.cbsnews.com/news/affordable-care-for-those-still-uninsured-2. All errors in original.

674. Ress, "Virginia Way, Part 1."

CHAPTER 4

675. Cited in Hannah Arendt, "Thinking and Moral Considerations: A Lecture," *Social Research* 3, no. 3 (Autumn 1971): 440.

676. Asthma and Allergy Foundation of America, "There's More to Asthma than Meets the Air."

677. Paul Spencer, "Richmond Is Now an Asthma Capital and Doctors Say Schools Are Part of the Problem," *Style Weekly*, October 20, 2015, http://www.styleweekly.com/richmond/richmond-is-now-an-asthma-capital-and-doctors-say-schools-are-part-of-the-problem/Content?oid=2251399.

678. Tom Nash, "Caving In," *Style Weekly*, April 8, 2014, http://www.styleweekly.com/richmond/caving-in/Content?oid=2055218.

679. Louis Llovio, "5-Pound Piece of Falling Tile Hits Carver Fifth-Grader, Who's Reported to Be Fine," *Richmond Times-Dispatch*, February 20, 2016, http://www.richmond.com/news/local/city-of-richmond/article_e79df178-0a1e-5662-9a6a-6af6afbc11b1.html.

680. K. Burnell Evans, "School Board Votes to Close Armstrong Due to AC Issues," *Richmond Times-Dispatch*, September 29, 2015, http://www.richmond.com/news/local/city-of-richmond/article_308cfa2c-a794-5b53-8cfb-6e1a66feff6e.html.

681. Louis Llovio, "Richmond School Officials to Consider Closing Armstrong High, Five [*sic*] Elementary Schools," *Richmond Times-Dispatch*, April 5, 2016, http://www.richmond.com/news/local/education/article_7127a4b6-3329-5287-b984-65e265b477fd.html.

682. Nash, "Caving In." Unless otherwise noted, the introductory section to this chapter is based on and quoting from this article.

683. Kelly Avellino, "Richmond Mayor Proposes Tax Cut Amid Needed School Repairs," WWBT-NBC, September 2, 2014, http://www.nbc12.com/story/26429361/richmond-mayor-proposes-tax-cut-amid-needed-school-repairs.

684. K. Burnell Evans and Ned Oliver, "With Budget Talks Looming, Richmond's Limited Debt Capacity Could Hamper Ambitious School Plan," *Richmond Times-Dispatch*, December 13, 2015, http://www.richmond.com/news/local/city-of-richmond/article_fdb5e2b8-efb0-57f6-a29f-db0f446dc6b2.html. Ellipsis in original.

685. Norman Leahy and Paul Goldman, "Richmond Won't Spend Money to Repair Decrepit Schools," *Washington Post*, September 8, 2014, http://www.washingtonpost.

com/blogs/all-opinions-are-local/wp/2014/09/08/richmond-wont-spend-money-to-repair-decrepit-schools; *U.S. News & World Report*, "Did the '47 Percent' Video Sink Romney's Campaign?" September 18, 2012, http://www.usnews.com/debate-club/did-the-47-percent-video-sink-romneys-campaign.

686. Norman Leahy and Paul Goldman, "Richmond Won't Spend Money to Repair Decrepit Schools," *Washington Post*, September 8, 2014, http://www.washingtonpost.com/blogs/all-opinions-are-local/wp/2014/09/08/richmond-wont-spend-money-to-repair-decrepit-schools.

687. *Forbes*, "The World's 50 Most Valuable Sports Teams 2014: #9 Washington Redskins," http://www.forbes.com/pictures/mli45ejlgl/9-washington-redskins.

688. Michael Phillips, "Redskins Defense Enjoys $22,159 Dinner Before Leaving for Bye Week," *Richmond Times-Dispatch*, October 27, 2015, http://www.richmond.com/redskins-xtra/article_5c83e8ac-7ccc-11e5-8666-c7a6220ff4a5.html.

689. Scott Bass, "Redskins to Boost Richmond Economy by 85 Million? Not Really," *Style Weekly*, September 18, 2012, http://www.styleweekly.com/richmond/redskins-to-boost-richmond-economy-by-85-million-not-really/Content?oid=1758975.

690. Noah Frank, "Is Redskins Camp Bringing Promised Boost to Richmond?" WTOP Radio, August 6, 2014, http://wtop.com/news/2014/08/is-redskins-camp-bringing-promised-boost-to-richmond; David Larter, "Bon Secours Makes a Big Play," Richmond BizSense, October 23, 2012, http://www.richmondbizsense.com/2012/10/23/bon-secours-makes-a-big-play.

691. Janet Giampietro, "The Greatest Show on Turf?" *Richmond Magazine*, July 9, 2013, http://richmondmagazine.com/news/the-greatest-show-on-turf-07-09-2013.

692. Warren Fiske and Nancy Madsen, "Mayor Jones Says Redskins Training Camp Deal 'Generated $40 Million in New Private Investment,'" *Richmond Times-Dispatch* and Politifact, March 4, 2014, http://www.politifact.com/virginia/statements/2014/mar/04/dwight-jones/mayor-jones-says-redskins-training-camp-deal-gener; Tom Nash, "Under Contract," *Style Weekly*, August 26, 2014, http://www.styleweekly.com/richmond/under-contract/Content?oid=2110903.

693. Ned Oliver, "Hunting for Gold," *Style Weekly*, October 7, 2014, http://www.styleweekly.com/richmond/hunting-for-gold/Content?oid=2127042.

694. Ned Oliver, "Redskins Camp Goes Over Budget, Council Members Angry," *Style Weekly*, May 14, 2013, http://www.styleweekly.com/richmond/redskins-camp-over-budget-councilmen-angry/Content?oid=1889943.

695. Nathan Cushing, "A Look at the Redskins Summer Training Camp," RVA News, February 11, 2013, http://rvanews.com/sports/mayor-vows-investigation-after-trees-razed-on-redskins-site/61457.

696. Ned Oliver, "Dollars and Sense," *Style Weekly*, March 24, 2015, http://www.styleweekly.com/richmond/dollars-and-sense/Content?oid=2188781; Kelly Avellino, "Trees Mistakenly Tackled on Redskins Training Camp Site," WWBT-NBC, January 24, 2013, http://www.nbc12.com/story/20587218/trees-mistakenly-tackled-on-redskins-training-camp-site.

697. Scott Bass, "Skinned Trees No Mistake," *Style Weekly*, January 15, 2013, http://www.styleweekly.com/richmond/skinned-trees-no-mistake/Content?oid=1810663.

698. Ned Oliver, "Richmond Retail Sales Declines During Redskins Camp," *Style Weekly*, October 10, 2013, http://www.styleweekly.com/richmond/richmond-retail-sales-declined-during-redskins-camp/Content?oid=1966172.

699. Ned Oliver, "Food Truck Fee Will Go to Redskins," *Style Weekly*, June 4, 2014, http://www.styleweekly.com/richmond/food-truck-fee-will-subsidize-redskins/Content?oid=2083228.

700. Ned Oliver, "City Council Waits on Redskins Analysis," *Style Weekly*, December 17, 2013, http://www.styleweekly.com/richmond/city-council-waits-on-redskins-analysis/Content?oid=2005809.

701. Ned Oliver, "Food Trucks Flame Out at Redskins Camp," *Style Weekly*, August 12, 2014, http://www.styleweekly.com/richmond/food-trucks-flame-out-at-redskins-camp/Content?oid=2107287.

702. Ned Oliver, "Redskins 'Ambassadors' Program Walks Fine Line of Labor Laws," *Style Weekly*, July 8, 2014, http://www.styleweekly.com/richmond/redskins-ambassadors-program-walks-fine-line-of-labor-laws/Content?oid=2091810.

703. Fiske and Madsen, "Mayor Jones Says Redskins Training Camp."

704. Ned Oliver, "Hunting for Gold," *Style Weekly*, October 7, 2014, http://www.styleweekly.com/richmond/hunting-for-gold/Content?oid=2127042.

705. Ibid.

706. Ned Oliver, "Richmond Payment to Redskins Climbs to $360K Going into Fourth Year of Training Camp," *Richmond Times-Dispatch*, March 31, 2016, http://www.richmond.com/news/local/city-of-richmond/article_978e7368-34d1-5c58-86d1-d44030bb8229.html.

707. Michael Kranish, "Richmond Split Over Confederate History," *Boston Globe*, July 4, 2015, http://www.bostonglobe.com/news/nation/2015/07/04/capital-old-confederacy-new-fight-about-inequality-how-remember-past/NmoeO0dcJfaU9PqUAwuNuI/story.html.

708. A.O. Carol Wolf, "Kicking the Can," *Style Weekly*, February 11, 2014, http://www.styleweekly.com/richmond/kicking-the-can/Content?oid=2031231.

709. Staff reports, "Local News: Officials Withdraw Plan Involving Redskins Facility," *Richmond Times-Dispatch*, May 17, 2015, http://www.richmond.com/article_b6870c3d-07fb-51e6-9d06-048ffb7d5456.html.

710. Michael Phillips, "Redskins Return amid Renewed Concerns about Economic Performance," *Richmond Times-Dispatch*, July 25, 2015, http://www.richmond.com/sports/article_a31a808d-7b6c-5fca-91b8-3a2fcf648ea4.html.

711. Associated Press, "Washington Redskins Moving Training Camp to Richmond," *USA Today*, June 6, 2012, http://usatoday30.usatoday.com/sports/football/nfl/story/2012-06-06/redskins-training-camp-richmond/55419716/1; A. Barton Hinkle, "The Washington Redskins Are About to Fleece Virginia Taxpayers," *Reason*, June 18, 2012, http://reason.com/archives/2012/06/18/the-washington-redskins-are-about-to-fle.

712. Fiske and Madsen, "Mayor Jones Says Redskins Training Camp"; Tom Nash, "Under Contract," *Style Weekly*, August 26, 2014, http://www.styleweekly.com/richmond/under-contract/Content?oid=2110903.

713. Tom Nash, "City Slow to Collect Money for Schools," *Style Weekly*, February 25, 2014, http://www.styleweekly.com/richmond/city-slow-to-collect-money-for-schools/Content?oid=2036699.

714. Joey Matthews, "School Board Weighs Options to Close Schools," *Richmond Free Press*, April 21, 2015, http://richmondfreepress.com/news/2015/apr/21/school-board-weighs-options-close-schools.

715. Facilities Task Force, "Richmond Public Schools Facilities Needs Report for the Period of FY 2016–FY 2025," *Richmond School Board*, April 13, 2015, p. 18, http://www.croppermap.com/documents/SBPresentationApril132015v3.pdf.

716. Zachary Reid, "Richmond School Board Receives Ambitious Facilities Report," *Richmond Times-Dispatch*, April 13, 2015, http://www.richmond.com/news/local/city-of-richmond/article_23a22a63-d53c-5eb9-a633-35e02eff5281.html.

717. Michael Martz, "House Panel Wants JLARC Oversight of Economic Development Spending," *Richmond Times-Dispatch*, February 2, 2016, http://www.richmond.com/news/virginia/government-politics/general-assembly/article_c251aca6-d917-55eb-8749-ddd2fef599d8.html.

718. Paul Woody, "Stadium Talk Has to Be Backed by Money Talk," *Richmond Times-Dispatch*, July 1, 2015, http://www.richmond.com/sports/flying-squirrels/article_a0ac3379-4ef2-5111-af6f-c8b67ad01fef.html.

719. Joey Matthews, "School Board Weighs Options to Close Schools," *Richmond Free Press*, http://richmondfreepress.com/news/2015/apr/21/school-board-weighs-options-close-schools.

720. Mark Robinson, "Much Talk, Little Action," *Richmond Magazine*, March 14, 2016, http://richmondmagazine.com/news/richmond-news/council-school-board-joint-meeting.

721. Tracy Sears and Jake Burns, "Moving Richmond Public Schools into the 21st Century—What Will It Cost?" WTVR-CBS, April 14, 2015, http://wtvr.com/2015/04/14/moving-richmond-public-schools-into-the-21st-century-what-will-it-cost.

722. Thomas Farrell et al., "Business Leaders Pledge Help to Improve City Schools," *Richmond Times-Dispatch*, August 8, 2007, http://www.richmond.com/news/article_96d5d47c-3b87-51b3-8967-99b545e9d57c.html.

723. Chris Dovi, "Firing Back," *Style Weekly*, August 15, 2007, http://www.styleweekly.com/richmond/firing-back/Content?oid=1367605. Respondents' quotes are in "double" quotes, while the reporter's words are in 'single' quotes.

724. Greg Muzik, "Munford Principal Responds to 26 Business Leaders Who Call for Appointed School Board," *Near West End News*, September 4, 2007, http://nearwestendnews.net/2007/09/04/munford-principal-responds-to-26-business-leaders-who-call-for-appointed-school-board.

725. *Near West End News*, "Gang of 26 Just Won't Go Away," September 12, 2007, http://nearwestendnews.net/2007/09/12/gang-of-26-just-wont-go-away.

726. Don Harrison, "The Gang of 26," *Style Weekly*, August 15, 2007, http://www.styleweekly.com/richmond/the-gang-of-26/Content?oid=1373052.

727. Dovi, "Firing Back."

728. Scott Bass, "The Power List 2008," *Style Weekly*, July 23, 2008, http://www.styleweekly.com/richmond/the-power-list-2008/Content?oid=1369517.

729. Pamela Levy, "What We Know About Dave Brat, the Tea Party Candidate Who Beat Eric Cantor," *Newsweek*, June 11, 2014, http://www.newsweek.com/dave-brat-beat-eric-cantor-and-hes-probably-headed-congress-254551.

730. Teresa Sullivan, "Higher Education as the Engine of the American Economy," *Virginia News Letter* 87, no. 7 (October 2011): 3.

731. C. Kirabo Jackson, Rucker Johnson and Claudia Persico, "The Effects of School Spending on Educational and Economic Outcomes: Evidence from School Finance Reforms," *National Bureau of Economic Research Working Paper* No. 20847 (January 2015), http://www.nber.org/papers/w20847.

732. Kirp, *Sandbox Investment*, 50–58.

733. Finn and Hockett, *Exam Schools*, 149–58.

734. Moriah Balingit, "Principal of Thomas Jefferson High, One of Nation's Top Schools, to Leave for New York," *Washington Post*, March 16, 2016, https://www.washingtonpost.com/news/education/wp/2016/03/15/principal-of-thomas-jefferson-high-one-of-nations-top-schools-to-leave-for-new-york.

735. Jefferson Scholars Foundation, "Scholarship," http://www.jeffersonscholars.org/scholarship.

736. Collegiate School, "Tuition & Payment," http://www.collegiate-va.org/Page/Admission/Tuition--Payment. Disclosure: I attended Collegiate School.

737. Hochschild and Scovronick, *American Dream*, 56.

738. Meg Gruber and Brenda Sheridan, "Are Virginia's Leaders Ready to Put Kids First?" *Richmond Times-Dispatch*, April 13, 2014, http://www.richmond.com/opinion/their-opinion/guest-columnists/article_620881c3-6b99-5409-a8b9-cde329d5f9d8.html.

739. Ryan, *Five Miles Away*, 148–49.

740. Hochschild and Scovronick, *American Dream*, 56.

741. Edwin Slipek, "Up from the Asphalt," *Style Weekly*, August 5, 2014, http://www.styleweekly.com/richmond/up-from-the-asphalt/Content?oid=2105233.

742. David Larter, "Downtown Skyscraper's Biggest Number Might Be Developer's To-Do Items," Richmond BizSense, January 31, 2013, http://www.richmondbizsense.com/2013/01/31/downtown-skyscrapers-biggest-number-might-be-developers-to-do-items.

743. Edwin Slipek, "Isolated Beacon," *Style Weekly*, September 24, 2013, http://www.styleweekly.com/richmond/isolated-beacon/Content?oid=1957395.

744. Michael Schwartz, "Let the Digging Begin," Richmond BizSense, August 26, 2013, http://www.richmondbizsense.com/2013/08/26/let-the-digging-begin.

745. Robert Zullo, "Richmond Financing for Gateway Office Building Advances," *Richmond Times-Dispatch*, June 21, 2013, http://www.richmond.com/news/local/city-of-richmond/article_ca5a22ab-1ae4-585c-82dd-db05be0dc2f9.html.

746. Burl Rolett, "Bill Goodwin's Firm to Get a New Downtown View," *Richmond BizSense*, July 8, 2014, http://www.richmondbizsense.com/2014/07/08/bill-goodwins-firm-to-get-a-new-downtown-view; Virginia Business, "CCA Industries Leases Space in Richmond's New Gateway Plaza," July 10, 2014, http://www.virginiabusiness.com/news/article/cca-industries-leases-space-in-richmonds-new-gateway-plaza.

747. Jim Bacon, "Parking Drove Richmond's Gateway Plaza Participation," Bacon's Rebellion, June 28, 2013, http://www.baconsrebellion.com/2013/06/parking-drove-richmonds-gateway-plaza-participation.html.

748. Gregory Gilligan, "New 15-Story Office Tower Planned for Downtown Richmond," *Daily Progress*, January 30, 2013, http://www.dailyprogress.com/workitcville/news/new--story-office-tower-planned-for-downtown-richmond/article_090cd23c-6aec-11e2-a8ab-0019bb30f31a.html.

749. Tayleigh Davis, "18-Story Office Tower Set for Richmond's Downtown Business District," WSMV-NBC, September 13, 2013, http://www.wsmv.com/story/23457560/developers-break-ground-for-new-downtown-high-rise.

750. Carol Hazard, "SunTrust to Anchor New 21-Story Office Tower; Building Includes 187 Apartments," *Richmond Times-Dispatch*, January 20, 2016, http://www.richmond.com/business/local/article_214de9ae-82aa-54de-9bea-7ec4b8c54779.html.

751. Office of the Press Secretary to the Mayor, "Officials Break Ground on Gateway Plaza in Richmond," City of Richmond, September 17, 2013, http://richmondvaannouncements.blogspot.com/2013/09/officials-break-ground-on-gateway-plaza.html.

752. Robert Zullo, "Richmond Financing for Gateway Office Building Advances," *Richmond Times-Dispatch*, June 21, 2013, http://www.richmond.com/news/local/city-of-richmond/article_ca5a22ab-1ae4-585c-82dd-db05be0dc2f9.html. Ellipsis in original.

753. Jim Bacon, "City Investment of $11.25 Million in Gateway Plaza Seems Justified," Bacon's Rebellion, June 27, 2013, http://www.baconsrebellion.com/2013/06/city-investment-of-11-25-million-in-gateway-plaza-seems-justified.html.

754. Michael Schwartz, "Tower's Tale Gets a Few More Stories," Richmond BizSense, September 17, 2013, http://www.richmondbizsense.com/2013/09/17/towers-tale-gets-a-few-more-stories. Calculations based on Richmond's real estate tax of 1.20 percent. Department of Finance, "Real Estate FAQs," City of Richmond, http://www.richmondgov.com/Finance/documents/faqRealEstateTax.pdf.

755. Burl Rolett, "Office Tower Lenders Brace for Gaping Vacancy," Richmond BizSense, October 27, 2014, http://www.richmondbizsense.com/2014/10/27/office-tower-lenders-brace-for-gaping-vacancy; Carol Hazard, "Loan on James Center Complex Is in Default," *Richmond Times-Dispatch*, February 13, 2016, http://www.richmond.com/business/local/article_d5a3c0a4-52da-543b-be02-8e2901b809b4.html; Katie Demeria, "James Center Headed to Foreclosure," Richmond BizSense, February 23, 2016, http://richmondbizsense.com/2016/02/23/james-center-headed-to-foreclosure.

756. Ned Oliver, "In Advance of Big Bike Race, a Homeless Shuffle at Kanawha Plaza," *Style Weekly*, February 10, 2015, http://www.styleweekly.com/richmond/in-advance-of-big-bike-race-a-homeless-shuffle-at-kanawha-plaza/Content?oid=2173208.

757. Robert Zullo, "Richmond Financing for Gateway Office Building Advances," *Richmond Times-Dispatch*, June 21, 2013, http://www.richmond.com/news/local/city-of-richmond/article_ca5a22ab-1ae4-585c-82dd-db05be0dc2f9.html.

758. WGCL-CBS, "Richmond-Area Shelters May Have Room but Some Are Refusing to Come Indoors," January 7, 2014, http://www.cbs46.com/story/24390367/richmond-area-shelters-may-have-room-but-some-are-refusing-to-come-indoors.

759. Edwin Slipek, "Now Developing: How 11 Richmond Public Spaces Are Being Re-Imagined for Better or for Worse," *Style Weekly*, December 15, 2015, http://www.styleweekly.com/richmond/now-developing-how-11-richmond-public-spaces-are-being-re-imagined-for-better-or-for-worse/Content?oid=2272764.

760. Leah Small, "The Death of a Warmly Remembered Homeless Man Brings a Bleak Reminder to Richmond," *Style Weekly*, February 2, 2016, http://www.styleweekly.com/richmond/the-death-of-a-warmly-remembered-homeless-man-brings-a-bleak-reminder-to-richmond/Content?oid=2288699.

761. Carol Hazard, "Dominion Plans to Build 20-Story Office Tower in Downtown and Possibly a Second One," *Richmond Times-Dispatch*, May 13, 2016, http://www.richmond.com/business/local/article_7c03758c-45d4-528b-a713-387ebbaaa4f5.html.

762. Ned Oliver and K. Burnell Evans, "Jones' Lawyer: No Laws Broken, but Jones May Have Acted Differently in Retrospect," *Richmond Times-Dispatch*, March 20, 2016, http://www.richmond.com/news/local/city-of-richmond/article_b48a036a-d048-53ed-bf52-a2c817252e28.html.

763. Jim Nolan, "Special Report: Poverty's Shadow over Education," *Richmond Times-Dispatch*, October 11, 2015, http://www.richmond.com/news/article_03fedf03-34d5-5233-84d7-fe65adba5b45.html.

764. Graham Moomaw, "Washington Statue at Capitol Square Getting $1.3 Million in Repairs," *Richmond Times-Dispatch*, October 11, 2015, http://www.richmond.com/news/virginia/government-politics/article_f6939ff0-b0fa-5b82-98bd-4a980fb3b403.html.

765. Southern Environmental Law Center, "New U.S. Route 460 in Virginia: A $1.8 Billion Boondoggle," https://www.southernenvironment.org/uploads/cases/_1140x550/casepage-rt-460.jpg.

766. Michael Laris, "How Virginia Paid More than $250 Million for a Road that Never Got Built," *Washington Post*, May 30, 2015, http://www.washingtonpost.com/local/trafficandcommuting/how-virginia-paid-more-than-250-million-for-a-road-that-never-got-built/2015/05/30/39a1a222-062d-11e5-a428-c984eb077d4e_story.html; Jim Bacon, "The Great U.S. 460 Swamp," Bacon's Rebellion, July 9, 2014, http://www.baconsrebellion.com/2014/07/swampland.html; Michael Laris, "Va. Spends $260 Million on Unbuilt Road, Says It Could've Been Worse," *Washington Post*, July 2, 2015, http://www.

washingtonpost.com/local/trafficandcommuting/va-spends-260-million-on-unbuilt-road-but-says-it-could-have-been-worse/2015/07/02/638d9b62-20d2-11e5-aeb9-a411a84c9d55_story.html.

767. Travis Fain, "Va. Taxpayers on the Hook for Private U.S. 460 Investments," *Daily Press*, May 30, 2015, http://www.dailypress.com/news/dp-nws-460-bonds-20150529-story.html.

768. Alan Suderman, "Gov. McAuliffe Announces Settlement on Route 460 Project," Progress-Index, July 3, 2015, http://www.progress-index.com/article/20150703/NEWS/150709890.

769. Peter Galuszka, "Pulp and Circumstance," *Chesterfield Monthly*, April 2015, http://www.chesterfieldmonthly.com/news/pulp-and-circumstance; Michael Martz, "Chesterfield: Big Win on Paper," *Richmond Times-Dispatch*, June 19, 2014, http://www.richmond.com/business/manufacturing/article_90e6d3f4-f7ab-11e3-9e7b-0017a43b2370.html; John Reid Blackwell, "Speed of Paper Company Deal 'Unparalleled,' Economic Development Leader Said," *Richmond Times-Dispatch*, July 9, 2014, http://www.richmond.com/business/article_81d5bb60-fbb4-5ed5-81e7-86c67780e6ff.html.

770. Editorial Board, "Virginia's Pipeline to Jail," *Virginian-Pilot*, May 11, 2015, http://hamptonroads.com/2015/05/virginias-pipeline-jail.

771. Susan Ferriss, "Virginia Tops Nation in Sending Students to Cops, Courts: Where Does Your State Rank?" Center for Public Integrity, April 10, 2015, http://www.publicintegrity.org/2015/04/10/17089/virginia-tops-nation-sending-students-cops-courts-where-does-your-state-rank.

772. Michael Paul Williams, "Schools Should Not Be Pipeline to Prison," *Richmond Times-Dispatch*, April 13, 2015, http://www.richmond.com/news/local/michael-paul-williams/article_4a5866e7-eb00-5a89-b929-c4d32c788622.html.

773. Graham Moomaw, "House Defeats Bill to Limit Criminal Charges for Student Misbehavior," *Richmond Times-Dispatch*, February 16, 2016, http://www.richmond.com/news/virginia/government-politics/article_145d6413-15db-5522-81fe-ec763585641f.html.

774. Jenna Portnoy, "Va. Legislature Passes Bill to Shield Special-Needs Minors from Some Charges," *Washington Post*, March 7, 2016, https://www.washingtonpost.com/local/virginia-politics/va-legislature-passes-bill-to-shield-special-needs-minors-from-some-misdemeanor-charges/2016/03/07/cc78240e-e499-11e5-bc08-3e03a5b41910_story.html.

775. Mark Christie, "Virginia's Education Reform Works," *Virginia News Letter* 77, no. 5 (August 2001), http://www.coopercenter.org/sites/default/files/autoVANLPubs/Virginia%20News%20Letter%202001%20Vol.%2077%20No.%205.pdf.

776. Virginia House Bill 930, 2014, http://lis.virginia.gov/cgi-bin/legp604.exe?141+ful+HB930ER+pdf.

777. Virginia Department of Education, "Accreditation: High Standards for Learning & Achievement," Commonwealth of Virginia, http://www.doe.virginia.gov/statistics_reports/school_report_card/accountability_guide.pdf.

778. Ibid., "The Reform Models," Commonwealth of Virginia, http://www.doe. virginia.gov/support/school_improvement/priority_schools/index.shtml.

779. Ibid., "2014–2015 Priority Schools," Commonwealth of Virginia, September 12, 2014, http://www.doe.virginia.gov/statistics_reports/ accreditation_federal_reports/federal_accountability/reports/2014-15/ priority_schools_2014-15.pdf.

780. Ibid., "Virginia Standards of Learning Assessments: Sample Items for World History I," Commonwealth of Virginia, Fall 2011, http://www.doe.virginia. gov/testing/sol/released_tests/2011/history_sample/wh1_history.pdf.

781. Stephanie van Hover, David Hicks and Jeremy Stoddard, "The Development of Virginia's History and Social Studies Standards of Learning (SOLs), 1995–2010," *Virginia News Letter* (August 5, 2010): 1–3.

782. Virginia Department of Education, "History and Social Science Standards of Learning: Curriculum Framework 2008: World History and Geography: 1500 A.D. to the Present," Commonwealth of Virginia, http://www.doe.virginia.gov/testing/ sol/frameworks/history_socialscience_framewks/2008/2008_final/framewks_ worldhistory_geo1500-present.pdf; "History and Social Science Standards of Learning: Curriculum Framework 2008: United States History: 1865 to the Present," Commonwealth of Virginia, http://www.doe.virginia.gov/testing/sol/frameworks/ history_socialscience_framewks/2008/2008_final/framewks_ushist1865-present.pdf.

783. Ibid., "Virginia Studies," Commonwealth of Virginia, p. 39, http:// www.doe.virginia.gov/testing/sol/frameworks/history_socialscience_ framewks/2008/2008_final/framewks_virginia_studies.pdf.

784. Ibid., "History and Social Science Standards of Learning: Curriculum Framework 2008: United States History: 1865 to the Present," Commonwealth of Virginia, p. 31, http://www.doe.virginia.gov/testing/sol/frameworks/history_ socialscience_framewks/2008/2008_final/framewks_ushist1865-present.pdf. This Kafkaesque pattern was followed with the World History Standards, Virginia Department of Education, "History and Social Science Standards of Learning: Curriculum Framework 2008: World History and Geography: 1500 A.D. to the Present," Commonwealth of Virginia, p. 59, http://www.doe.virginia.gov/ testing/sol/frameworks/history_socialscience_framewks/2008/2008_final/ framewks_worldhistory_geo1500-present.pdf.

785. Editorial Board, "Sadly Obsessed with the SOLs," *Staunton News Leader*, May 9, 2015, http://www.newsleader.com/story/opinion/editorials/2015/05/09/ sadly-obsessed-sols/27062009.

786. Ned Oliver, "Why Is Teacher Turnover on the Rise in Richmond and Chesterfield?" *Richmond Times-Dispatch*, June 28, 2015, http://www.richmond.com/news/local/ chesterfield/article_76d5de73-133f-596a-8124-17e4f92df723.html.

787. Finn and Hockett, *Exam Schools*, 149–58.

788. Van Hover, Hicks and Stoddard, "Development of Virginia's History and Social Studies Standards of Learning," 5.

789. Ravitch, *Reign of Error*, 113.

790. Anne Holton, "Revising—Not Eliminating—Tests to Make Va. Schools Better," *Washington Post*, July 3, 2015, http://www.washingtonpost.com/opinions/revising-

-not-eliminating--tests-to-make-va-schools-better/2015/07/02/18a632c6-1376-11e5-9ddc-e3353542100c_story.html.

791. Jim Nolan, "Senate Panel Scraps Bills Requiring Full-Day Kindergarten, Early Education Programs," *Richmond Times-Dispatch*, February 5, 2016, http://www.richmond.com/news/virginia/government-politics/article_ff8c0051-8407-5b58-b0dc-0dc4a6ec5c4c.html.

792. Elizabeth Harris and Ford Fessenden, "'Opt Out' Becomes Anti-Test Rallying Cry in New York State," *New York Times*, May 20, 2015, http://www.nytimes.com/2015/05/21/nyregion/opt-out-movement-against-common-core-testing-grows-in-new-york-state.html.

793. RVA Opt Out, "Parental Rights," http://www.rvaoptout.com/parental-rights.html.

794. Peter Galuszka, "Richmond Parents Take a Pass on SOL Tests," *Style Weekly*, May 12, 2015, http://www.styleweekly.com/richmond/richmond-parents-take-a-pass-on-sol-tests/Content?oid=2203681.

795. Jennifer Williams, "SOL Opt-Outs Rare on Peninsula, but Are an Option for Parents," *Daily Press*, April 30, 2015, http://www.dailypress.com/news/education/dp-nws-sol-optouts-20150430-story.html.

796. Editorial Board, "Sadly Obsessed with the SOLs," *Staunton News Leader*, May 9, 2015, http://www.newsleader.com/story/opinion/editorials/2015/05/09/sadly-obsessed-sols/27062009.

797. James Scott, "Resistance Without Protest and Without Organization: Peasant Opposition to the Islamic Zakat and the Christian Tithe," *Comparative Studies in Society and History* 29, no. 3 (1987): 421–22, 441; Jennifer Williams, "SOL Opt-Outs Rare on Peninsula, but Are an Option for Parents," *Daily Press*, April 30, 2015, http://www.dailypress.com/news/education/dp-nws-sol-optouts-20150430-story.html.

798. Hochschild and Scovronick, *American Dream*, 9–12.

799. Joint Legislative Audit and Review Commission, "Review of State Economic Development Incentive Grants," Commonwealth of Virginia, November 2012, http://leg2.state.va.us/dls/h&sdocs.nsf/fc86c2b17a1cf388852570f9006f1299/dcb518b6abb5218c8525798e0077e20f/$FILE/SD8.pdf.

800. Meg Gruber and Brenda Sheridan, "Are Virginia's Leaders Ready to Put Kids First?" *Richmond Times-Dispatch*, April 13, 2014, http://www.richmond.com/opinion/their-opinion/guest-columnists/article_620881c3-6b99-5409-a8b9-cde329d5f9d8.html.

801. Green, *Something Must Be Done*, 222.

CHAPTER 5

802. Anita Kumar and Daniel de Vise, "U-Va. Board Ouster of President Teresa Sullivan Sparks Anger," *Washington Post*, June 11, 2012, http://www.washingtonpost.com/local/dc-politics/outrage-mounts-over-u-va-presidents-ouster/2012/06/11/gJQAU4F0VV_story.html; Staff, "Thank You, Leonard," *UVA Magazine*, Fall 2011, http://uvamagazine.org/articles/thank_you_leonard.

803. Larry Gerber et al., "College and University Governance: The University of Virginia Governing Board's Attempt to Remove the President," Investigating Committee of

the American Association of University Professors, March 2013, p. 10, http://www.aaup.org/file/aaupBulletin_UVA_July22final.pdf. Errors in original.

804. Office of the President, "About the President," University of Virginia, http://president.virginia.edu/about.

805. *UVA Magazine*, "Timeline: Teresa Sullivan's Resignation and Reinstatement," http://uvamagazine.org/articles/timeline_teresa_sullivans_resignation_and_reinstatement.

806. Peter Kiernan, "Letters from Darden Foundation Board Chair Peter Kiernan," Letter 1, *Hook*, June 10, 2012, http://www.readthehook.com/letters-darden-foundation-board-chair-peter-kiernan. All errors in original.

807. Ibid., Letter 2, June 14, 2012.

808. Anita Kumar and Daniel de Vise, "Three Members of U-Va. Board Were Kept in Dark About Effort to Oust Sullivan," *Washington Post*, June 14, 2012, http://www.washingtonpost.com/local/education/three-members-of-u-va-board-were-kept-in-dark-about-effort-to-oust-sullivan/2012/06/14/gJQAXsBddV_story.html.

809. Hawes Spencer, "Dragas on Board: The Rector Who Wouldn't Go," *Hook*, August 23, 2012, http://www.readthehook.com/106973/dragas-board-rector-who-wouldnt-go.

810. Staff, "University of Virginia President Teresa Sullivan's Ouster: The Key Players," *Washington Post*, June 19, 2012, http://www.washingtonpost.com/blogs/college-inc/post/university-of-virginia-president-teresa-sullivans-ouster-the-key-players/2012/06/19/gJQAKI4eoV_blog.html.

811. David McNair, "Leadership Fitness: Did Dragas Engage in Plus-Sized Bullying?" *Hook*, June 28, 2012, http://www.readthehook.com/104327/leadership-fitness.

812. Helen Dragas, "Rector Dragas' Remarks to VPs and Deans," University of Virginia, June 10, 2012, http://news.virginia.edu/content/rector-dragas-remarks-vps-and-deans.

813. Gerber et al., "College and University Governance," 13.

814. Hawes Spencer, "Now Nau: Beer Tycoon Pays Dragas' Hill + Knowlton Bills," *Hook*, August 30, 2012, http://www.readthehook.com/107008/now-nau-south-lawn-benefactor-funds-dragas.

815. Daniel de Vise and Anita Kumar, "U-Va. Board Leaders Wanted President Teresa Sullivan to Make Cuts," *Washington Post*, June 17, 2012, https://www.washingtonpost.com/local/education/u-va-board-leaders-wanted-president-teresa-sullivanto-make-cuts/2012/06/17/gJQA4ijrhV_story.html.

816. Andrew Rice, "Anatomy of a Campus Coup," *New York Times Magazine*, September 11, 2012, http://www.nytimes.com/2012/09/16/magazine/teresa-sullivan-uva-ouster.html?_r=0.

817. Kiernan, "Letters from Darden Foundation Board Chair Peter Kiernan."

818. Lisa Provence, "Bad Form? BOV Ignored Own President-Replacing Precedent," *Hook*, June 21, 2012, http://www.readthehook.com/104249/bad-form-bov-ignored-president-replacing-precedent.

819. David McNair, "'Spines Need Stiffening' Casteen Leading Protest Charge," *Hook*, June 21, 2012, http://www.readthehook.com/104256/spines-need-stiffening-casteen-leading-protest-charge.

820. Carl Zeithaml, "Message from Carl Zeithaml Suspending His Interim Presidency," *Hook*, http://www.readthehook.com/message-carl-zeithaml-suspending-his-interim-presidency.

821. Anita Kumar and Daniel de Vise, "U-Va. Board Ouster of President Teresa Sullivan Sparks Anger," *Washington Post*, June 11, 2012, http://www.washingtonpost.com/local/dc-politics/outrage-mounts-over-u-va-presidents-ouster/2012/06/11/gJQAU4F0VV_story.html; Staff, "Thank You, Leonard," *UVA Magazine*, Fall 2011, http://uvamagazine.org/articles/thank_you_leonard.

822. Staff, "University of Virginia President Teresa Sullivan's Ouster: The Key Players," *Washington Post*, June 19, 2012, http://www.washingtonpost.com/blogs/college-inc/post/university-of-virginia-president-teresa-sullivans-ouster-the-key-players/2012/06/19/gJQAKI4eoV_blog.html.

823. Hawes Spencer, "Sullivan Stripped: V-P Simon Hints at Quit if No BOV Change," *Hook*, June 21, 2012, http://www.readthehook.com/104263/sullivan-stripped-v-p-simon-hints-quit-if-bov-doesnt-change.

824. Daniel de Vise and Anita Kumar, "U-Va. Board: President Teresa Sullivan's Removal Came After an 'Extended' Talk over School's Health," *Washington Post*, June 13, 2012, https://www.washingtonpost.com/local/education/u-va-board-president-teresa-sullivans-removal-came-after-an-extended-talk-over-schools-health/2012/06/13/gJQAV1E9aV_story.html.

825. University of Virginia Faculty Senate, "Faculty Declares Lack of Confidence in Rector, Vice Rector, Board," University of Virginia, http://www.virginia.edu/presidentialtransition/120614faculty.html.

826. Daniel de Vise and Anita Kumar, "Teresa Sullivan Ouster: 33 Faculty Leaders Protest Her Dismissal from University of Virginia Presidency," *Washington Post*, June 13, 2012, http://www.washingtonpost.com/blogs/college-inc/post/33-faculty-leaders-oppose-teresa-sullivan-ouster/2012/06/13/gJQAE4CSaV_blog.html.

827. Courteney Stuart, "Resignations Begin: Esteemed Computer Science Prof Pulls Plug," *Hook*, June 28, 2012, http://www.readthehook.com/104300/resignations-begin-esteemed-computer-science-prof-pulls-plug.

828. William Wulf, "Message from Bill Wulf," Materials Relating to the Resignation and Reinstatement of President Teresa Sullivan, University of Virginia, http://sullivan.lib.virginia.edu/items/show/148. See also http://sullivan.lib.virginia.edu/items/browse. All errors in original.

829. Matt Kelly, "Rally for Honor Seeks Reinstatement of U.Va. President Teresa Sullivan," University of Virginia, June 24, 2012, https://news.virginia.edu/content/rally-honor-seeks-re-instatement-uva-president-teresa-sullivan.

830. Andrew Rice, "Anatomy of a Campus Coup," *New York Times Magazine*, September 11, 2012, http://www.nytimes.com/2012/09/16/magazine/teresa-sullivan-uva-ouster.html?_r=0.

831. For a list, see *UVA Magazine*, "Timeline: Teresa Sullivan's Resignation and Reinstatement," http://uvamagazine.org/articles/timeline_teresa_sullivans_resignation_and_reinstatement.

832. Graelyn Brashear and Laura Ingles, "Sullivan, Dragas Call for Unity Following Reinstatement," *C'ville Weekly*, June 26, 2012, http://www.c-ville.com/Sullivan_Dragas_call_for_unity_following_reinstatement/#.VVqi9lVViko.

833. *UVA Magazine*, "Timeline: Teresa Sullivan's Resignation and Reinstatement," http://uvamagazine.org/articles/timeline_teresa_sullivans_resignation_and_reinstatement.

834. Susan Svrluga and Donna St. George, "Helen Dragas: The Leader Who Forced Out U-Va.'s President," *Washington Post*, June 21, 2012, http://www.washingtonpost.com/local/education/helen-dragas-the-leader-who-forced-out-u-vas-president/2012/06/21/gJQA4ds5sV_story.html.

835. Hawes Spencer, "Transparency Now: Protestors Call for Dragas' Resignation," *Hook*, November 15, 2012, http://www.readthehook.com/108739/transparency-now-protestors-call-dragas-resignation.

836. Ibid.

837. Jeff Schapiro, "Sullivan's Ouster a Coup d'état at UVA," *Richmond Times-Dispatch*, June 13, 2012, http://www.richmond.com/archive/article_376502f6-09b6-59b3-8f0d-c8888076905b.html.

838. David McNair, "Thanks for Donating! McDonnell Appoints Check Writers to UVA BOV," *Hook*, July 8, 2010, http://www.readthehook.com/67183/thanks-donating-mcdonnell-appoints-check-writers-uva-bov.

839. Liana Bayne, Nate Delesline III, K. Burnell Evans, J. Reynolds Hutchins, Bryan McKenzie and Aaron Richardson, "UVa Board of Visitors Lead the Way in State Political Giving," *Daily Progress*, September 28, 2013, http://www.dailyprogress.com/news/uva-board-of-visitors-lead-the-way-in-state-political/article_6e02daec-28b5-11e3-ae2b-0019bb30f31a.html.

840. Hawes Spencer, "McDonnell's BOV: Who Gets Their Donations?" *Hook*, September 27, 2012, http://www.readthehook.com/107453/bov-who-gets-their-donations.

841. Bayne et al., "UVa Board of Visitors."

842. University of Virginia, "2013–2014 Budget Summary All Divisions," May 21, 2013, http://www.virginia.edu/budget/Docs/2013-14%20Budget%20Summary.All%20Divisions.pdf.

843. Rebecca Arrington, "U.Va. Community Invited to Honor Sandridge at April 4, Luncheon," University of Virginia, March 18, 2011, http://news.virginia.edu/content/uva-community-invited-honor-sandridge-april-4-luncheon.

844. Staff, "Thank You, Leonard," *UVA Magazine*, Fall 2011, http://uvamagazine.org/articles/thank_you_leonard.

845. Scott Bass, "The Power List 2008: 2. William H. Goodwin Jr.," *Style Weekly*, July 23, 2008, http://www.styleweekly.com/richmond/the-power-list-2008/Content?oid=1369517.

846. Peter Galuszka, Tina Griego, Ned Oliver, Jason Roop and Melissa Scott Sinclair, "The 2013 Power List," *Style Weekly*, August 13, 2013, http://www.styleweekly.com/richmond/2-william-h-goodwin-jr/Content?oid=1934873.

847. Jeff Burke Thomas, "Our New Children's Hospital," *Richmond Times-Dispatch*, April 9, 2015, http://www.richmond.com/opinion/their-opinion/guest-columnists/article_c82bf78f-db4b-5c9f-8162-59c97c4c6e5f.html.

848. Alberta Lindsey, "Some Episcopalians Cut Back Donations," *Richmond Times-Dispatch*, January 17, 2004, http://listserv.virtueonline.org/pipermail/virtueonline_listserv.virtueonline.org/2004-January/006493.html.

849. Matt Zapotosky and Rosalind Helderman, "McDonnell Prosecutors Allege Undisclosed Gifts from People Other than Williams," *Washington Post*, June 23, 2014, http://www.washingtonpost.com/local/crime/mcdonnell-prosecutors-allege-undisclosed-gifts-from-people-other-than-williams/2014/06/23/b4b43736-fae4-11e3-b1f4-8e77c632c07b_story.html.

850. *Richmond Times-Dispatch*, "Prosecution Witness List Filed in the McDonnell Case," July 28, 2014, http://www.richmond.com/news/virginia/government-politics/article_9aa1cbc4-1669-11e4-914d-0017a43b2370.html.

851. Virginia Public Access Project, "Bob McDonnell: Gift Recipient: Disclosed by Candidate: All Years," http://vpap.org/gifts/recipient/5666-bob-mcdonnell/disclosed_by_candidate/?start_year=all&end_year=all; Virginia Public Access Project, "Bob McDonnell: Gift Recipient: Disclosed by Lobbyists: All Years," http://vpap.org/gifts/recipient/5666-bob-mcdonnell/disclosed_by_lobbyists/?start_year=all&end_year=all; "William H Goodwin Jr: Gift Giver: All Years," http://vpap.org/gifts/gifter/5595-william-h-goodwin-jr/disclosed_by_candidate/?start_year=all&end_year=all.

852. Hawes Spencer, "Dragas on Board: The Rector Who Wouldn't Go," *Hook*, August 23, 2012, http://www.readthehook.com/106973/dragas-board-rector-who-wouldnt-go.

853. Larry Gerber et al., "College and University Governance: The University of Virginia Governing Board's Attempt to Remove the President," Investigating Committee of the American Association of University Professors, March 2013, p. 10, http://www.aaup.org/file/aaupBulletin_UVA_July22final.pdf. Errors in original.

854. Hawes Spencer, "Presidential Gag: UVA Board Still Trying to Silence Sullivan," *Hook*, September 20, 2012, http://www.readthehook.com/107351/presidential-gag-uva-board-still-trying-silence-sullivan.

855. Hawes, "Dragas on Board."

856. Jenna Johnson, "At U-Va., Tensions Between Sullivan and Dragas Hit a New Boiling Point," *Washington Post*, March 1, 2013, http://www.washingtonpost.com/local/education/at-u-va-tensions-between-sullivan-and-dragas-hit-a-new-boiling-point/2013/03/01/6cf65212-810a-11e2-8074-b26a871b165a_story.html.

857. Office of the Secretary of Administration, "Governor McAuliffe Announces Appointments to the Virginia Commission on Higher Education Board Appointments," Commonwealth of Virginia, February 7, 2014, https://administration.virginia.gov/news/newsarticle?articleId=3238.

858. Unless otherwise cited, this narrative is from Rector and Visitors of the University of Virginia, "Board Meeting Minutes," August 2–3, 2013, http://www.virginia.edu/bov/meetings/13aug%20Retreat/'13%20AUG%20BOV%20RETREAT%20MINS.pdf.

859. Joseph Liss, "BOV Requires All New AccessUVA Recipients to Take Loans," *Cavalier Daily*, August 5, 2013, http://www.cavalierdaily.com/article/2013/08/bov-requires-all-new-accessuva-recipients-take-loans.

860. Helen Dragas, "Giving the Public a Say at U.Va.," *Richmond Times-Dispatch*, April 7, 2015, http://www.richmond.com/opinion/their-opinion/guest-columnists/article_51555561-e8be-53fe-bb4a-133fc056afe1.html.

861. McGregor McCance, "Board of Visitors Reauthorizes Acclaimed AccessUVA Financial Aid Program," University of Virginia Office of University Communications, August 5, 2013, https://news.virginia.edu/content/board-visitors-reauthorizes-acclaimed-accessuva-financial-aid-program.

862. Ibid.

863. Jenna Johnson, "U-Va. to Scale Back Financial Aid Program for Low- and Middle-Income Students," *Washington Post*, August 6, 2013, http://www.washingtonpost.com/local/education/u-va-to-scale-back-financial-aid-program-for-low--and-middle-income-students/2013/08/06/33c424f8-fec6-11e2-9711-3708310f6f4d_story.html.

864. Ry Rivard, "Killing Off a Success," *Inside Higher Ed*, January 27, 2014, https://www.insidehighered.com/news/2014/01/27/uva-backs-away-loan-free-offer-its-poorest-students.

865. Stiglitz, *Price of Inequality*, 195–96.

866. Sarah Pritchett, "Student Council Passes All-Grant Aid Resolution," *Cavalier Daily*, November 12, 2013, http://www.cavalierdaily.com/article/2013/11/student-council-passes-all-grant-aid-resolution.

867. Managing Board, "Accumulating Interest," *Cavalier Daily*, http://www.cavalierdaily.com/article/2013/11/accumulating-interest.

868. Jenna Dickerson, "Students Protest AccessUVA Cuts at BOV Meeting," *Cavalier Daily*, November 17, 2013, http://www.cavalierdaily.com/article/2013/11/students-protest-accessuva-cuts-at-bov-meeting.

869. Staff, "UVa's Strategic Plan Estimated to Cost $564 Million," *Daily Progress*, December 7, 2013, http://www.dailyprogress.com/news/uva-s-strategic-plan-estimated-to-cost-million/article_e6ab6a2e-5fae-11e3-86fc-0019bb30f31a.html.

870. Carman Joyce, "Foundation Announces 36-Member Jefferson Scholars Class of 2018," University of Virginia, May 6, 2014, https://news.virginia.edu/content/foundation-announces-36-member-jefferson-scholars-class-2018.

871. Jefferson Scholars Foundation, "Enrichment," http://www.jeffersonscholars.org/enrichment.

872. Ibid., "Scholarship," http://www.jeffersonscholars.org/scholarship.

873. Richard Vedder and Christopher Denhart, "22 Richest Schools in America," *Forbes*, July 30, 2014, http://www.forbes.com/sites/ccap/2014/07/30/22-richest-schools-in-america; University of Virginia, "Facts at a Glance: Finance & Endowment," http://www.virginia.edu/Facts/Glance_FinanceEndowment.html.

874. Nick Anderson, "Top College Endowments Per Student in 2013," *Washington Post*, January 28, 2014, http://www.washingtonpost.com/local/education/top-college-endowments-per-student-in-2013/2014/01/28/ed582efe-881f-11e3-a5bd-844629433ba3_story.html.

875. Zack O'Malley Greenburg, "The Fastest-Growing University Endowments," *Forbes*, February 23, 2012.

876. Michael McDonald and Lauren Streib, "New Breed of Endowment Managers Beat Harvard at Its Own Game," Bloomberg Business, May 15, 2015, http://www.bloomberg.com/news/articles/2015-05-15/new-breed-of-endowment-managers-beats-harvard-at-its-own-game.

877. University of Virginia, "Facts at a Glance: Finance & Endowment," http://www.virginia.edu/Facts/Glance_FinanceEndowment.html.

878. Virginia Commonwealth University, "Quest for Distinction," May 20, 2011, p. 49, http://www.quest.vcu.edu/media/quest/pdf/theplan_full.pdf.

879. Institutional Assessment & Studies, "High School Class Rank of First-Year Undergraduate Matriculants," University of Virginia, http://avillage.web.virginia.edu/iaas/instreports/studat/dd/adm_rank.htm.

880. Collegiate School, "Tuition & Payment," http://www.collegiate-va.org/Page/Admission/Tuition--Payment.

881. I attended Collegiate for twelve years.

882. Golden, *Price of Admission*.

883. Ibid., 6.

884. Peter Wallenstein, "Desegregation in Higher Education," *Encyclopedia of Virginia*, April 7, 2011, http://www.encyclopediavirginia.org/Desegregation_in_Higher_Education#its2.

885. Richard Kahlenberg, "10 Myths About Legacy Preferences in College Admissions," *Chronicle of Higher Education*, September 22, 2010, http://chronicle.com/article/10-Myths-About-Legacy/124561.

886. Kennedy, *For Discrimination*, 78–146.

887. Golden, *Price of Admission*, 146.

888. University of Virginia, "Scholarships," http://giving.virginia.edu/scholarships.

889. Rector and Visitors of the University of Virginia, "Board Meeting Minutes," August 2–3, 2013, p. 9179, http://www.virginia.edu/bov/meetings/13aug%20Retreat/'13%20AUG%20BOV%20RETREAT%20MINS.pdf. "WHEREAS, the University is committed to need-blind admissions for undergraduate applicants…"

890. Kim Clark, "Chart: Generous Colleges that Claim to Admit Only on Merit," *U.S. News & World Report*, March 22, 2010, http://www.usnews.com/education/articles/2010/03/22/chart-generous-colleges-that-claim-to-admit-only-on-merit.

891. Golden, *Price of Admission*, 247–49.

892. Ibid., 154–55.

893. Ibid., 152.

894. Ibid., 247–49.

895. Steve Berkowitz, Christopher Schnaars et al., "NCAA: Finances," USA Today and Indiana University National Sports Journalism Center, http://sports.usatoday.com/ncaa/finances. Only Texas, Ohio State, Louisiana State, Oklahoma, Penn State, Nebraska and Purdue athletics made net profits.

896. Will Hobson and Steven Rich, "Why Students Foot the Bill for College Sports, and How Some Are Fighting Back," *Washington Post*, November 30, 2015, https://www.washingtonpost.com/sports/why-students-foot-the-bill-for-college-sports-and-how-some-are-fighting-back/2015/11/30/7ca47476-8d3e-11e5-ae1f-af46b7df8483_story.html?hpid=hp_rhp-top-table-main_ncaa-fees-

315pm%3Ahomepage%2Fstory. The second-highest charge was $406 per year at the University of Maryland.

897. Golden, *Price of Admission*, 158–59.

898. Rosalind Helderman, "Virginia Governor's Wife Was Paid $36,000 as Consultant to Coal Philanthropy," *Washington Post*, June 2, 2013, http://www.washingtonpost.com/local/va-politics/virginia-governors-wife-was-paid-36000-as-consultant-to-coal-philanthropy/2013/06/02/c8d6ff50-c868-11e2-9245-773c0123c027_story.html; Nanette Byrnes, "Does the President Really Make Just $400,000 a Year?" *Bloomberg BusinessWeek*, February 11, 2009, http://www.businessweek.com/careers/managementiq/archives/2009/02/does_the_president_really_make_just_400000_a_year.html.

899. *Richmond Times-Dispatch*, "Data Center: 2013 Salaries of Virginia State Employees," September 21, 2014, http://www.richmond.com/data-center/salaries-virginia-state-employees-2013.

900. FlightAware, "Activity Log: N800VA: University of Virginia Foundation," http://flightaware.com/live/flight/N800VA.

901. David Ramadan, "Outrageous Actions on Tuition by U.Va. Board," *Richmond Times-Dispatch*, March 31, 2015, http://www.richmond.com/opinion/their-opinion/guest-columnists/article_0f8df424-0cdd-5fdc-8e64-982bcbac0f44.html; What2Fly, "Aircraft Operating Cost: Cessna Citation II," http://www.what2fly.com/operating_cost/cessna/citation_ii.php.

902. Associated Press, "Jefferson's Iconic U.Va. Rotunda amid $58 Million Facelift," *Richmond Times-Dispatch*, July 3, 2015, http://www.richmond.com/news/virginia/ap/article_1088a2bf-055c-5ff3-a2a7-71b0a09ef665.html; Hawes Spencer, "UVA Spending $450K to Give Rotunda that '70s Look," *C'ville Weekly*, June 16, 2015, http://www.c-ville.com/uva-spending-450k-give-rotunda-70s-look/#.VZxR58ZVikq.

903. Anita Kumar, "McDonnell Reappoints Dragas to U-Va. Board," *Washington Post*, June 29, 2012, http://www.washingtonpost.com/local/dc-politics/mcdonnell-re-appoints-dragas-to-u-va-board/2012/06/29/gJQAD6u6BW_story.html.

904. Liana Bayne, Nate Delesline III, K. Burnell Evans, J. Reynolds Hutchins, Bryan McKenzie and Aaron Richardson, "UVa Board of Visitors Lead the Way in State Political Giving," *Daily Progress*, September 28, 2013, http://www.dailyprogress.com/news/uva-board-of-visitors-lead-the-way-in-state-political/article_6e02daec-28b5-11e3-ae2b-0019bb30f31a.html.

905. Larry Gerber et al., "College and University Governance: The University of Virginia Governing Board's Attempt to Remove the President," Investigating Committee of the American Association of University Professors, March 2013, pp. 20–21, http://www.aaup.org/file/aaupBulletin_UVA_July22final.pdf.

906. Thomas Friedman, "Come the Revolution," *New York Times*, May 16, 2012, http://www.nytimes.com/2012/05/16/opinion/friedman-come-the-revolution.html.

907. Ravitch, *Reign of Error*, 187.

908. Ibid., 189.

909. Spencer, "Dragas on Board."

910. Ted Strong, "UVa's Massive Open Online Courses Sees High Enrollment," *Daily Progress*, October 13, 2012, http://www.dailyprogress.com/news/uva-s-

massive-open-online-courses-sees-high-enrollment/article_1e79e67b-e8f3-5cf0-9749-147de2273d43.html.

911. Coursera, "University of Virginia," https://www.coursera.org/uva.

912. Bob McDonnell, "Statement by Governor McDonnell Regarding Appointments to the Board of Visitors to the University of Virginia," University Messages Following President Sullivan's Reinstatement, *UVA Magazine*, June 29, 2012, http://uvamagazine.org/articles/university_messages_following_president_sullivans_reinstatement.

913. Karin Kapsidelis, "Tuition Increase Averages 6% at Virginia Colleges," *Richmond Times-Dispatch*, August 4, 2015, http://www.richmond.com/news/article_a5028c6d-4f01-5724-912a-903615f552c5.html.

914. Derek Quizon, "UVa's New Tuition Plan, How It Passed Draw Criticism," *Daily Progress*, April 4, 2015, http://www.dailyprogress.com/news/local/uva/uva-s-new-tuition-plan-how-it-passed-draw-criticism/article_64face1c-db26-11e4-981b-73f6bcb312cc.html.

915. Peter Norton, "UVa Board Flouted Guidelines During Vote on Tuition Increase," *Daily Progress*, May 10, 2015, http://www.dailyprogress.com/opinion/opinion-column-uva-board-flouted-guidelines-during-vote-on-tuition/article_14b691c2-f5aa-11e4-b5c3-6f4b4a9364bf.html.

916. Unless otherwise cited, this list is based on Courteney Stuart, "'Important Alum': Donor Jones Had Role in Sullivan Ouster," *Hook*, June 21, 2012, http://www.readthehook.com/104250/important-alums-did-they-topple-presidency.

917. Donna St. George, "U-Va.: A Donor in the Crisis," *Washington Post*, August 4, 2012, http://www.washingtonpost.com/local/education/u-va-a-donor-in-the-crisis/2012/08/04/b9e0e146-ce86-11e1-aa14-708bac2c7ee9_story.html.

918. Virginia Public Access Project, "Paul T Jones, II," http://www.vpap.org/donors/85986-paul-t-jones-ii/?start_year=all&end_year=all&contrib_type=all.

919. Paul Tudor Jones II, "Aspiring to Achieve Greatness," *Daily Progress*, June 17, 2012, http://www.dailyprogress.com/news/op-ed-aspiring-to-achieve-greatness/article_be382c81-3059-56a2-81c5-3eb85627c978.html.

920. Jenna Johnson, "Wealthy U-Va. Alumni Pushing for Major Change to Board of Visitors," *Washington Post*, September 19, 2013, http://www.washingtonpost.com/local/education/wealthy-u-va-alumni-pushing-for-major-change-to-board-of-visitors/2013/09/19/27967056-2139-11e3-a358-1144dee636dd_story.html.

921. Jenna Johnson, "U-Va. Alum Discussed University Issues with Terry McAuliffe—and Donated $50,000," *Washington Post*, September 24, 2013, http://www.washingtonpost.com/local/education/u-va-alum-discussed-university-issues-with-terry-mcauliffe--and-donated-50000/2013/09/24/fc8eeb38-2537-11e3-b3e9-d97fb087acd6_story.html.

922. Laura Vozzella, "Donor Who Pressed McAuliffe on U-Va. Issues Wins Spot on University Board," *Washington Post*, June 2, 2015, http://www.washingtonpost.com/local/virginia-politics/donor-who-pressed-mcauliffe-on-u-va-issues-wins-spot-on-university-board/2015/06/02/ea6786d4-0962-11e5-9e39-0db921c47b93_story.html?hpid=z4.

923. Hawes Spencer, "Dragas to Simon: 'Quite an Unhelpful Comment,'" *Hook*, July 5, 2012, http://www.readthehook.com/104458/dragas-simon-quite-unhelpful-comment.

924. Maria Everett, "AO-9-08: Reply to Heather M. Harvey," Virginia Freedom of Information Advisory Council, October 16, 2008, http://foiacouncil.dls. virginia.gov/ops/08/AO_09_08.htm; Editorial Board, "Seize This Opportunity to Improve Transparency in Virginia," *Daily Press*, June 28, 2015, http://www. dailypress.com/news/opinion/editorials/dp-edt-foia-council-review-editorial-20150628-20150628-4-story.html.

925. Jeff Schapiro, "Imagining a Call on the McDonnell, Farrell Party Line," *Richmond Times-Dispatch*, July 4, 2012, http://www.richmond.com/archive/article_35a541c7-b492-577c-845a-8efd6db29655.html.

926. University of Virginia, "Thomas F. Farrell II to Become U.Va.'s 38th Rector; He Succeeds Gordon F. Rainey Jr.," http://www.virginia.edu/topnews/releases2005/bov-june-10-2005.html; Karin Kapsidelis, "U.Va. Leaders Protest Sullivan Firing," *Richmond Times-Dispatch*, June 14, 2012, http://www.richmond. com/archive/article_75caa8fb-3942-51b3-ab27-405f74a03261.html; Lisa Provence, "Connections: Who Are the BOV's Kington and Craig?" *Hook*, June 21, 2012, http://www.readthehook.com/104276/connections-executive-bovs-kington-and-craig.

927. Virginia Business Higher Education Council, http://growbydegrees.org/who_ we_are/about-the-virginia-business-higher-education-council-vbhec.

928. Karin Kapsidelis, "U.Va. Leaders Protest Sullivan Firing," *Richmond Times-Dispatch*, June 14, 2012, http://www.richmond.com/archive/article_75caa8fb-3942-51b3-ab27-405f74a03261.html; Virginia Public Access Project, "Thomas F. Farrell II," http://www.vpap.org/donors/6856-thomas-f-farrell-ii/?start_year=all&end_year=all&contrib_type=all. Amounts for McDonnell for Governor: Bob, $71,960; Opportunity Virginia PAC, $50,000; McDonnell for Attorney General: Bob, $14,789.

929. Thomas Farrell, "The Future of Higher Education in Virginia," Virginia State Council of Higher Education, October 17, 2011, http://www.schev. edu/bov/2011/10.17.11%20TFF%20BOV%20training%20presentation-FINAL.pdf.

930. Ibid., 14–17; Daniel de Vise, "A Glimpse at the Players in Va. Higher Education," *Washington Post*, July 10, 2012, http://www.washingtonpost.com/blogs/college-inc/post/are-va-college-trustees-groomed-for-activism/2012/07/10/gJQA37miaW_blog.html.

931. Jeff Schapiro, "Sullivan's Ouster a Coup d'état at U.Va.," *Richmond Times-Dispatch*, June 13, 2012, http://www.richmond.com/archive/article_376502f6-09b6-59b3-8f0d-c8888076905b.html; Hawes Spencer, "Prospective Presidents: How They Might Appeal to the BOV," *Hook*, September 27, 2012, http://www. readthehook.com/107414/prospective-presidents-how-they-might-appeal-mcdonnells-bov.

932. Peter Galuszka, "Study Hall," *Style Weekly*, June 26, 2012, http://www. styleweekly.com/richmond/study-hall/Content?oid=1726835.

933. Billy Hunt, "Billion with a 'B': UVA Sets Groundbreaking Fund Goal," *Hook*, October 5, 2006, http://www.readthehook.com/80004/photophile-billion-b-uva-sets-groundbreaking-fund-goal.

934. Andrew Rice, "Anatomy of a Campus Coup," *New York Times Magazine*, September 11, 2012, http://www.nytimes.com/2012/09/16/magazine/teresa-sullivan-uva-ouster.html?_r=0.

935. Hawes Spencer, "Dragas to Kington: 'Why We Can't Afford to Wait.'" *Hook*, July 5, 2012, http://www.readthehook.com/104310/dragas-kington-why-we-cant-afford-wait.

936. University of Virginia, "The University in a New Century," December 17, 2002, http://www.virginia.edu/newcentury/commonthemes.html.

937. Kirp, *Shakespeare, Einstein*, 130–45. This section is based on this source unless otherwise noted.

938. Rector and Visitors of the University of Virginia, "Approval of the Five Foundational Principles of the 'Cornerstone' Strategic Plan," November 2013, http://www.virginia.edu/bov/meetings/13nov/AMENDED-APPROVAL-OF-THE-FIVE-FOUNDATIONAL-PILLARS-RESOLUTION.pdf.

939. Public University Working Group, "A Defining and Differentiated Vision for UVA as a Unique and Preeminent Public Institution," Presidential Working Papers: University of Virginia Strategic Planning Initiative, April 7, 2013, http://s3.documentcloud.org/documents/785804/university-of-virginia-planning-group-report.pdf.

940. Darden School of Business, "Executive MBA Tuition & Fees," University of Virginia, http://www.darden.virginia.edu/emba/financial-aid/tuition.

941. Ibid., "Inn at Darden," University of Virginia, http://www.innatdarden.com.

942. David Schutte, "Building and Grounds Committee Discusses Facilities, Renames South Lawn Commons," *Cavalier Daily*, February 22, 2016, http://www.cavalierdaily.com/article/2016/02/building-and-grounds-committee-meets-to-discuss-future-plans.

943. Pelfrey, *Entrepreneurial President*.

944. Newfield, *Unmaking the Public University*, 11.

945. University of Virginia, "Board of Visitors," http://www.virginia.edu/bov.

946. Larry Gerber et al., "College and University Governance: The University of Virginia Governing Board's Attempt to Remove the President," Investigating Committee of the American Association of University Professors, March 2013, p. 13, http://www.aaup.org/file/aaupBulletin_UVA_July22final.pdf; Honor Committee, "Honor Case Flow Chart," University of Virginia, http://www.virginia.edu/honor/wp-content/uploads/2015/07/Honor-Case-Flow-Chart.pdf.

947. Richard Pérez-Peña, "University of Virginia's Crisis Reflects Wider Conflict," *New York Times*, March 15, 2013, http://www.nytimes.com/2013/03/16/education/university-of-virginia-crisis-reflects-wider-fight.html; Jenna Johnson, "University of Virginia Accreditation Warning Lifted," *Washington Post*, December 10, 2013, http://www.washingtonpost.com/local/education/university-of-virginia-accreditation-warning-lifted/2013/12/10/40c64a68-61d2-11e3-94ad-004fefa61ee6_story.html.

948. Hawes Spencer, "Dragas on Board: The Rector Who Wouldn't Go," *Hook*, August 23, 2012, http://www.readthehook.com/106973/dragas-board-rector-who-wouldnt-go.

949. Jenna Johnson, "Helen Dragas Points to Positive Outcomes of U-Va. Leadership Crisis," *Washington Post*, July 6, 2013, http://www.washingtonpost.com/local/education/helen-dragas-points-to-positive-outcomes-of-u-va-leadership-crisis/2013/07/06/3e0cd422-e31a-11e2-aef3-339619eab080_story.html.

950. Kirp, *Shakespeare, Einstein*, 144.

951. Carolyn Chappell, "The Virginia Commission on Higher Education Board Appointments: The Impact of Legislative Reform on Public University Governance," unpublished dissertation, George Mason University, Summer 2013, 148, 151, http://digilib.gmu.edu/jspui/bitstream/handle/1920/8350/Chappell_gmu_0883E_10415.pdf;jsessionid=84B4F49125E634D93D0EBDA4 5FB1BCB7?sequence=1.

952. Susan Svrluga and Donna St. George, "Helen Dragas: The Leader Who Forced Out U-Va.'s President," *Washington Post*, June 21, 2012, http://www.washingtonpost.com/local/education/helen-dragas-the-leader-who-forced-out-u-vas-president/2012/06/21/gJQA4ds5sV_story.html.

953. Nick Anderson, "Medical Executive Quits U-Va. Governing Board, Blasts Administration on Way Out," *Washington Post*, April 13, 2015, http://www.washingtonpost.com/news/grade-point/wp/2015/04/13/medical-executive-quits-u-va-governing-board-blasts-administration-on-way-out.

954. Derek Quizon, "UVa Board Member Speaks About Stepping Down Early," *Daily Progress*, April 12, 2015, http://www.dailyprogress.com/news/local/uva-board-member-speaks-about-stepping-down-early/article_b39aa4b4-e0b4-11e4-b8d2-d3514dd21a3b.html.

955. Kirp, *Shakespeare, Einstein*, 144–45.

956. Newfield, *Unmaking the Public University*.

957. Teles, *Rise of the Conservative Legal Movement*.

958. Mayer, *Dark Money*, 73, 76.

959. Freudenberg, *Lethal but Legal*, 71–72.

960. Sierra Bellows, Carianne King and Emma Rathbone, "Women at the University of Virginia," *UVA Magazine*, Spring 2011, http://uvamagazine.org/articles/women_at_the_university_of_virginia; Peter Wallenstein, "Desegregation in Higher Education," *Encyclopedia of Virginia*, April 7, 2011, http://www.encyclopediavirginia.org/Desegregation_in_Higher_Education#its2; Lara Couturier, "Checks and Balances at Work: The Restructuring of Virginia's Public Higher Education System," National Center for Public Policy and Higher Education, June 2006, http://www.highereducation.org/reports/checks_balances/virginia.pdf.

961. Andrew Rice, "Anatomy of a Campus Coup," *New York Times Magazine*, September 11, 2012, http://www.nytimes.com/2012/09/16/magazine/teresa-sullivan-uva-ouster.html?_r=0.

Conclusion

962. Dewey and Boydston, *Later Works of John Dewey*, 163.

963. Laura Vozzella, "In a Virginia Lately Used to Legislative Fireworks, a Bewildering Calm Prevails," *Washington Post*, February 14, 2015, https://

www.washingtonpost.com/local/virginia-politics/in-a-virginia-lately-used-to-legislative-fireworks-a-bewildering-calm-prevails/2015/02/14/77e1f278-b144-11e4-886b-c22184f27c35_story.html.

964. An abbreviated version of this section appeared in a commentary I wrote: "'The Virginia Way' Is a Euphemism for Corruption," *Roanoke Times*, August 23, 2015, http://www.roanoke.com/opinion/commentary/thomas-the-virginia-way-is-a-euphemism-for-corruption/article_dae6cdf1-e606-559c-b338-30ad20ebb86e.html.

965. Portnoy, "VA Senate Leaders Spar."

966. Martz, "$2.1 Billion Bond Bill."

967. Dominion was the sixth-largest employer in the Richmond region, behind Capital One, Virginia Commonwealth University Health System, HCA, Bon Secours and Walmart. Altria was the ninth largest, behind SunTrust and Food Lion. If business and politics were the same, these larger employers, of which health care (#2, #3, #4) was by far the largest industry, should have dominated discussion in Richmond. And those numbers are just for Richmond. The Virginia company with the highest ranking on the Fortune 500 was Freddie Mac (#32), followed by Northrop Grumman (#99), General Dynamics (#122) and Capital One (#124). Altria was #161, and Dominion Power was #212. See *Richmond Times-Dispatch*, "Top 50 Local Employers in Richmond, VA," http://www.richmond.com/business/local/top-50-employers; *Fortune*, "Fortune 500," http://fortune.com/fortune500.

968. Virginia Public Access Project, "Top Donors: All Years," http://www.vpap.org/money/top-donors/?year=all.

969. Jeff Schapiro, "Unforeseen Consequences of Dominion 'Power' Politics," *Richmond Times-Dispatch*, February 3, 2015, http://www.richmond.com/news/virginia/government-politics/jeff-schapiro/article_2660e707-afcb-5908-bed3-202626acc532.html; Jeff Schapiro, "Name from the Past in Fight for the Future," *Richmond Times-Dispatch*, January 27, 2015, http://www.richmond.com/news/virginia/government-politics/jeff-schapiro/article_6b0c5d18-ea8b-5e31-87ef-39339897993c.html.

970. Fairfax County, "Dillon Rule in Virginia," http://www.fairfaxcounty.gov/government/about/dillon-rule.htm; Neal Menkes, "A Review of the State-Local Fiscal Relationship in Virginia: Not So Good Now, and It Could Get Worse," *Virginia News Letter* 86, no. 6 (November 2010): 2.

971. Tarter, *Grandees of Government*, 388.

972. Shapiro, *Yale Book of Quotations*, 101.

973. Joseph Stiglitz, "Of the 1%, By the 1%, For the 1%," *Vanity Fair*, May 2011, http://www.vanityfair.com/news/2011/05/top-one-percent-201110.

974. Dave Ress, "Virginia Legislators Don't Always Report Their Lobbyist Freebies," *Daily Press*, February 7, 2015, http://www.dailypress.com/news/politics/dp-nws-ga-disclosure-20150207-story.html-page=1.

975. Laura Vozzella, "In VA, $100,000 Will Get You a Sit-Down with 'Policy Experts,' Governor's New PAC Says," *Washington Post*, March 18, 2014, http://www.washingtonpost.com/local/virginia-politics/in-va-100000-will-get-you-a-

sit-down-with-policy-experts-governors-new-pac-says/2014/03/18/af3ab0e0-aeb4-11e3-9627-c65021d6d572_story.html.

976. Full text of letter available at http://origin.library.constantcontact.com/download/get/file/1103923423545-124/213088818-McAuliffe-PAC-Announcement-for-High-Dollar-Donors.pdf.

977. Vozzella, "In VA, $100,000 Will Get You a Sit-Down." The invitation was recalled after media scrutiny.

978. Mich Wilkinson, "Funding Virginia Services: A Decade of Contention," *Virginia News Letter* 80, no. 4 (September 2004), http://www.coopercenter.org/sites/default/files/autoVANLPubs/Virginia_News_Letter_2004_Vol._80_No._4.pdf.

979. Virginia Department of Taxation, "Individual Income Tax," http://www.tax.virginia.gov/income-tax-calculator.

980. Virginia Public Access Project, "Donor: William H Goodwin, Jr.: All Years," http://vpap.org/donors/5595-william-h-goodwin-jr/?start_year=all&end_year=all.

981. Ress, "Virginia Way, Part 8."

982. State Integrity Investigation, "Virginia: Corruption Risk Report Card," http://www.stateintegrity.org/virginia.

983. Laura Harmon, Charles Posner, Michele Jawando and Matt Dhaiti, "The Health of State Democracies," Center for American Progress Action Fund, July 2015, https://cdn.americanprogressaction.org/wp-content/uploads/2015/07/HSD-report-FINAL.pdf.

984. Cynthia Terrell, "In VA Politics, the Glass Ceiling Has Few Cracks," *Washington Post*, November 29, 2013, http://www.washingtonpost.com/opinions/in-va-politics-the-glass-ceiling-has-few-cracks/2013/11/29/6baf0bd2-561c-11e3-ba82-16ed03681809_story.html.

985. Laura Goren, "Virginia Is Exceptionally Unequal," Commonwealth Institute for Fiscal Analysis, February 23, 2016.

986. Tarter, *Grandees of Government*, 392.

987. Elliott Robinson, "Quioccasin Selected as New Name for Byrd Middle School," *Richmond Times-Dispatch*, April 29, 2016, http://www.richmond.com/news/local/education/henrico/article_bc859e10-312f-55a1-91d7-e5febecdd1.html.

988. Caro, *Passage of Power*, 67–68.

989. Key, *Southern Politics in State and Nation*, 19.

990. John Chichester, "The Virginia Way," in Morgan and Giesen, *Governing Virginia*, 233.

991. Caro, *Passage of Power*, xiv; italics in original.

992. Potterfield, *Nonesuch Place*, 21.

993. Peter Bacqué, "Chesterfield Power Station Emits Greatest Amount of Carbon Emissions in the State," *Richmond Times-Dispatch*, September 11, 2013, http://www.richmond.com/news/local/city-of-richmond/article_56b67d22-a3af-5218-87e1-99adccae0ea1.html.

994. Paul Spencer, "Richmond Is Now an Asthma Capital and Doctors Say Schools Are Part of the Problem," *Style Weekly*, October 20, 2015, http://www.styleweekly.com/richmond/richmond-is-now-an-asthma-capital-and-doctors-say-schools-are-part-of-the-problem/Content?oid=2251399.

METHODOLOGY AND LITERATURE REVIEW

995. Skocpol and Williamson, *Tea Party*, 13.

996. At the Library of Virginia, for example, "Governors—Virginia—History—21st Century"; "Richmond (VA)—Politics and Government—21st Century; Virginia—Economic Conditions—21st Century"; "Democratic Party (VA)—History—21st Century." Virginia Capitol Correspondents Association, "VCCA Members," http://www.vapress.org/Vcca_Members.htm. The rankings are: *Washington Post, Virginian-Pilot, Richmond Times-Dispatch, Roanoke Times, Loudon Times-Mirror, Arlington Catholic Herald* and *Daily Press. MondoTimes*, "Highest Circulation Virginia Newspapers," http://www.mondotimes.com/newspapers/usa/virginia-newspaper-circulation.html; Infoplease, "Top 100 Newspapers in the United States," http://www.infoplease.com/ipea/A0004420.html.

997. Dinan, *Virginia State Constitution*.

998. Kidd, *Government and Politics in Virginia*.

999. Morris and Sabato, *Virginia Government and Politics*.

1000. Atkinson, *Virginia in the Vanguard*.

1001. Jeff Schapiro, "Holiday Goodies for Politicos, Naughty and Nice," *Richmond Times-Dispatch*, December 1, 2013, http://www.richmond.com/news/virginia/government-politics/article_13298711-d04b-537d-89da-62cd08b8e2e0.html; Rosalind Helderman and Matt Zapotosky, "How the Federal Corruption Case Against the McDonnells Came Together," *Washington Post*, September 6, 2014, http://www.washingtonpost.com/local/virginia-politics/how-the-federal-corruption-case-against-the-mcdonnells-came-together/2014/09/06/16e15b92-3559-11e4-a723-fa3895a25d02_story.html; Peter Galuszka, "What About Bob?" Bacon's Rebellion, June 27, 2011, http://www.baconsrebellion.com/2011/06/what-about-bob.html; McGuireWoods Consulting, "Our People: Frank Atkinson," http://www.mwcllc.com/our-people/a/frank-b-atkinson.aspx.

1002. Atkinson, *Virginia in the Vanguard*, xxviii.

1003. Morgan and Giesen, *Governing Virginia*; Swartz and Peaslee, *Virginia Government*.

1004. Wallenstein, *Cradle of America*, 432–34. Disclosure: Wallenstein taught me in a seminar on the civil rights movement at Virginia Tech in 2009. Mark Rozell, "Virginia: From Red to Blue?" in Bullock and Rozell, *New Politics of the Old South*, 137–55.

1005. Tarter, *Grandees of Government*.

1006. Feld and Wilcox, *Netroots Rising*.

1007. Winter, Robisheaux and Robinson, *Swing County*.

1008. Rozell and Wilcox, *Second Coming*.

1009. Yancey, *When Hell Froze Over*.

1010. Edds, *Claiming the Dream*; Jeffries, *Virginia's Native Son*.

1011. Epps, *Shad Treatment*.

1012. Payne, *Mark Warner the Dealmaker*.

1013. Lynch, *Starting Over*; Holton, *Opportunity Time*.

1014. Wilder, *Son of Virginia*.

1015. Campbell, *Richmond's Unhealed History*.

1016. Potterfield, *Nonesuch Place*; Richardson, *Built by Blacks*.

1017. Randolph, *Rights for a Season*.

1018. Ryan, *Five Miles Away*.

1019. Galuszka, *Thunder on the Mountain*.

1020. Nash, *Virginia Climate Fever*.

1021. Green, *Something Must Be Done*.

1022. Golden, *Price of Admission*; Goldfield, *Still Fighting the Civil War*.

1023. Macy, *Factory Man*.

1024. Jack Shafer, "Who Said It First?" *Slate*, August 30, 2010, http://www.slate.com/articles/news_and_politics/press_box/2010/08/who_said_it_first.html.

1025. Peter Galuszka, "Run to Cover," *Chesterfield Monthly*, October 2014, http://www.chesterfieldmonthly.com/index.php/news/run-to-cover.

BIBLIOGRAPHY

BOOKS

Atkinson, Frank. *Virginia in the Vanguard: Political Leadership in the 400-Year-Old Cradle of American Democracy*. Lanham, MD: Rowman & Littlefield Publishers, 2006.

Bullock, Charles, and Mark Rozell, eds. *The New Politics of the Old South: An Introduction to Southern Politics*. 5th ed. Lanham, MD: Rowman & Littlefield, 2014.

Campbell, Benjamin. *Richmond's Unhealed History*. Richmond, VA: Brandylane Publishers, 2011.

Caro, Robert. *The Passage of Power: The Years of Lyndon Johnson*. New York: Knopf, 2012.

Chemerinsky, Erwin. *Constitutional Law: Principles and Policies*. 4th ed. New York: Wolters Kluwer Law & Business, 2011.

Coburn, Tom, and John Hart. *Breach of Trust: How Washington Turns Outsiders into Insiders*. Nashville, TN: Thomas Nelson, 2013.

Coyle, Marcia. *The Roberts Court: The Struggle for the Constitution*. New York: Simon & Schuster, 2013.

Dewey, John, and Jo Ann Boydston, eds. *The Later Works of John Dewey*. Vol. 6, *1925–1953: 1931–1932, Essays, Reviews, and Miscellany*. Carbondale: Southern Illinois University Press, 2008.

Dinan, John. *The Virginia State Constitution*. Oxford Commentaries on the State Constitutions of the United States. 2nd ed. New York: Oxford University Press, 2014.

Domhoff, William. *Who Rules America? Power, Politics, and Social Change*. 5th ed. Boston: McGraw-Hill, 2006.

Edds, Margaret. *Claiming the Dream: The Victorious Campaign of Douglas Wilder of Virginia*. Chapel Hill, NC: Algonquin Books, 1990.

Epps, Garrett. *The Shad Treatment*. New York: Putnam, 1977.

Farmer, Paul. *Infections and Inequalities: The Modern Plagues*. Updated ed. Berkeley: University of California Press, 2001.

Feld, Lowell, and Nate Wilcox. *Netroots Rising: How a Citizen Army of Bloggers and Online Activists Is Changing American Politics*. Westport, CT: Praeger Press, 2008.

Finn, Chester, and Jessica Hockett. *Exam Schools: Inside America's Most Selective Public High Schools*. Princeton, NJ: Princeton University Press, 2012.

Freire, Paulo. *Pedagogy of the Oppressed*. 30th Anniversary ed. New York: Bloomsbury Academic Press, 2000.

Freudenberg, Nicholas. *Lethal but Legal: Corporations, Consumption, and Protecting Public Health*. New York: Oxford University Press, 2014.

Galuszka, Peter. *Thunder on the Mountain: Death at Massey and the Dirty Secrets Behind Big Coal*. New York: St. Martin's Press, 2012.

Golden, Daniel. *The Price of Admission: How America's Ruling Class Buys Its Way into Elite Colleges—And Who Gets Left Outside the Gates*. New York: Broadway Books, 2007.

Goldfield, David. *Still Fighting the Civil War: The American South and Southern History*. 2nd ed. Baton Rouge: Louisiana State University Press, 2013.

Green, Kristen. *Something Must Be Done About Prince Edward County*. New York: HarperCollins Publishers, 2015.

Greenwald, Glenn. *With Liberty and Justice for Some: How the Law Is Used to Destroy Equality and Protect the Powerful*. New York: Metropolitan Books, 2011.

Guerrero, Andrea. *Silence at Boalt Hall: The Dismantling of Affirmative Action*. Berkeley: University of California Press, 2002.

Hacker, Jacob, and Paul Pierson. *Winner-Take-All Politics: How Washington Made the Rich Richer—and Turned Its Back on the Middle Class*. New York: Simon & Schuster, 2010.

Hamilton, Clive. *Requiem for a Species: Why We Resist the Truth about Climate Change*. Washington, D.C.: EarthScan, 2010.

Hedges, Chris, and Joe Sacco. *Days of Destruction, Days of Revolt*. New York: Nation Books, 2012.

Hochschild, Jennifer, and Nathan Scovronick. *The American Dream and the Public Schools*. New York: Oxford University Press, 2003.

Holton, Linwood. *Opportunity Time*. Charlottesville: University of Virginia Press, 2008.

Imhoff, Daniel, ed. *The CAFO Reader: The Tragedy of Industrial Animal Factories*. Healdsburg, CA: Watershed Media, 2010.

Jeffries, J.L. *Virginia's Native Son: The Election and Administration of Governor L. Douglas Wilder*. West Lafayette, IN: Purdue University Press, 2000.

Kennedy, Randall. *For Discrimination: Race, Affirmative Action, and the Law*. New York: Random House, Pantheon Books, 2013.

Kessler, David. *A Question of Intent: A Great American Battle with a Deadly Industry*. New York: PublicAffairs, 2001.

Key, Valdimer Orlando. *Southern Politics in State and Nation*. New York: Alfred A. Knopf, 1949.

Kidd, Quentin, ed. *Government and Politics in Virginia: The Old Dominion at the 21st Century*. New York: Simon & Schuster, 1999.

Kirp, David. *The Sandbox Investment: The Preschool Movement and Kids-First Politics*. Cambridge, MA: Harvard University Press, 2007.

————. *Shakespeare, Einstein, and the Bottom Line: The Marketing of Higher Education.* Cambridge, MA: Harvard University Press, 2003.

Leonard, Christopher. *The Meat Racket: The Secret Takeover of America's Food Business.* New York: Simon & Schuster, 2014.

Lynch, Edward. *Starting Over: A Political Biography of George Allen.* Lanham, MD: Hamilton Books, 2010.

Macy, Beth. *Factory Man: How One Furniture Maker Battled Offshoring, Stayed Local—and Helped Save an American Town.* New York: Little, Brown and Company, 2014.

Mayer, Jane. *Dark Money: The Hidden History of the Billionaires Behind the Rise of the Radical Right.* New York: Doubleday, 2016.

McGarity, Thomas, and Wendy Wagner. *Bending Science: How Special Interests Corrupt Public Health Research.* Cambridge, MA: Harvard University Press, 2010.

Mendell, David. *Obama: From Promise to Power.* New York: Amistad, 2008.

Morgan, Anne Marie, and A.R. Pete Giesen, eds. *Governing Virginia.* N.p.: Pearson Learning Solutions, 2011.

Morris, Thomas, and Larry Sabato. *Virginia Government and Politics: Readings and Comments.* 3rd ed. Charlottesville: University of Virginia Weldon Cooper Center, 1990.

Moser, Bob. *Blue Dixie: Awakening the South's Democratic Majority.* New York: Times Books, 2008.

Nash, Stephen. *Virginia Climate Fever: How Global Warming Will Transform Our Cities, Shorelines, and Forests.* Charlottesvile: University of Virginia Press, 2014.

Nestle, Marion. *Food Politics: How the Food Industry Influences Nutrition and Health.* Revised and expanded ed. Berkeley: University of California Press, 2007.

Newfield, Christopher. *Unmaking the Public University: The Forty-Year Assault on the Middle Class.* Cambridge, MA: Harvard University Press, 2011.

Nichols, John, and Robert McChesney. *Dollarocracy: How the Money and Media Complex Is Destroying America.* New York: Nation Books, 2013.

Orwell, George. *Nineteen Eighty-four.* Free e-book, https://ebooks.adelaide.edu.au.

Payne, Will. *Mark Warner the Dealmaker: From Business Success to the Business of Governing.* Charleston, SC: The History Press, 2015.

Pelfrey, Patricia. *Entrepreneurial President: Richard Atkinson and the University of California, 1995–2003.* Berkeley: University of California Press, 2012.

Perkinson, Robert. *Texas Tough: The Rise of America's Prison Empire.* New York: Metropolitan Books, 2010.

Potter, Wendell. *Deadly Spin: An Insurance Company Insider Speaks Out on How Corporate PR Is Killing Health Care and Deceiving Americans.* New York: Bloomsbury Press, 2010.

Potterfield, T. Tyler. *Nonesuch Place: A History of the Richmond Landscape.* Charleston, SC: The History Press, 2009.

Quadagno, Jill. *One Nation, Uninsured: Why the U.S. Has No National Health Insurance.* New York: Oxford University Press, 2006.

Randolph, Lewis. *Rights for a Season: The Politics of Race, Class, and Gender in Richmond, Virginia.* Knoxville: University of Tennessee Press, 2003.

Ravitch, Diane. *Reign of Error: The Hoax of the Privatization Movement and the Danger to America's Public Schools.* New York: Alfred A. Knopf Press, 2013.

Richardson, Selden. *Built by Blacks: African American Architecture and Neighborhoods in Richmond.* Charleston, SC: The History Press, 2008.

Rozell, Mark, and Clyde Wilcox. *Second Coming: The New Christian Right in Virginia Politics.* Baltimore, MD: Johns Hopkins University Press, 1996.

Ryan, James. *Five Miles Away, a World Apart: One City, Two Schools, and the Story of Educational Opportunity in Modern America.* New York: Oxford University Press, 2011.

Schlosser, Eric. *Fast Food Nation: The Dark Side of the All-American Meal.* New York: HarperCollins, 2002.

Scully, Matthew. *Dominion: The Power of Man, the Suffering of Animals, and the Call to Mercy.* New York: St. Martin's Press, 2002.

Shapiro, Fred, ed. *The Yale Book of Quotations.* New Haven, CT: Yale University Press, 2006.

Skocpol, Theda, and Vanessa Williamson. *The Tea Party and the Remaking of Republican Conservatism.* New York: Oxford University Press, 2012.

Starr, Paul. *Remedy and Reaction: The Peculiar American Struggle over Health Care Reform.* New Haven, CT: Yale University Press, 2011.

Stiglitz, Joseph. *Freefall: America, Free Markets, and the Sinking of the World Economy.* New York: W.W. Norton, 2010.

————. *The Price of Inequality: How Today's Divided Society Endangers Our Future.* New York: W.W. Norton, 2012.

Swartz, Nicholas, and Liliokanio Peaslee. *Virginia Government: Institutions and Policy.* Washington, D.C.: CQ Press, 2013.

Tarter, Brent. *The Grandees of Government: The Origins and Persistence of Undemocratic Politics in Virginia.* Charlottesville: University of Virginia Press, 2014.

Teles, Steven. *The Rise of the Conservative Legal Movement: The Battle for Control of the Law.* Princeton, NJ: Princeton University Press, 2010.

Toobin, Jeffrey. *The Oath: The Obama White House and the Supreme Court.* New York: Random House, Anchor Books, 2013.

Wallenstein, Peter. *Cradle of America: A History of Virginia.* 2nd ed. Lawrence: University Press of Kansas, 2014.

Wilder, L. Douglas. *Son of Virginia: A Life in America's Political Arena.* Guilford, CT: Lyons Press, 2015.

Winter, Rollie, Ed Robisheaux and S. Ann Robinson. *Swing County.* N.p.: CreateSpace Independent Publishing Platform, 2012.

Wolin, Sheldon. *Managed Democracy and the Specter of Inverted Totalitarianism.* Princeton, NJ: Princeton University Press, 2008.

Yancey, Dwayne. *When Hell Froze Over: The Untold Story of Doug Wilder: A Black Politician's Rise to Power in the South.* Dallas, TX: Taylor Publishing, 1989.

GOVERNMENT DOCUMENTS AND RESOURCES

Centers for Disease Control, City of Richmond, Code of Virginia, Division of Capitol Police (VA), Encyclopedia Virginia, Energy Information Administration, Environmental Protection Agency, Fairfax County, Federal Bureau of Investigation,

Federal Election Commission, Federal Reserve, Government Accountability Office, Joint Legislative Audit and Review Commission, McAuliffe PAC, McDonnell indictments, National Bureau of Economic Research, National Cancer Institute, National Park Service, Office of the Attorney General (VA), Office of the Governor (VA), Office of the Secretary of the Commonwealth (VA), Office of United States Senator Mark Warner, Richmond Public Schools, State Council of Higher Education for Virginia, United States Census, United States Court of Appeals for the Fourth Circuit, Virginia Board of Elections, Virginia Constitution, Virginia Department of Agriculture and Consumer Services, Virginia Department of Education, Virginia Department of Elections, Virginia Department of Taxation, Virginia Freedom of Information Advisory Council, Virginia General Assembly, Virginia House of Delegates, Virginia Tobacco Indemnification and Community Revitalization Commission, Virginia State Senate, Washington Public Utility Districts Association, White House Council of Economic Advisors, World Health Organization.

JOURNALS

Brigham Young University Education and Law Journal, British Medical Journal, Circulation, Comparative Studies in Society and History, Harvard Business Review, Nature, New England Journal of Medicine, Perspectives on Politics, PLoS Medicine, PS: Political Science and Politics, Social Research, University of Richmond Journal of Law and the Public Interest, University of Richmond Law Review, Virginia News Letter, William & Mary Environmental Law & Policy Review.

NEWSPAPERS AND NEW SERVICES

Associated Press, Bloomberg, Boston Globe, Bristol Herald-Courier, Capital News Service, Cavalier Daily, CBS DC, CBS News, Central Virginian, Chicago Tribune, Christian Science Monitor, Chronicle of Higher Education, Cleveland Plain Dealer, CNBC, CNN, Collegiate Times, Daily Press, Daily Progress, Danville Register & Bee, Fox News, Fredericksburg Free Lance-Star, Harrisonburg Daily News-Record, Harvard Gazette, The Hill, Hollywood Reporter, Inside Higher Ed, Kaiser Health News, Los Angeles Times, Loudon Times-Mirror, Lynchburg News & Advance, Martinsville Bulletin, National Review, National Public Radio, NBC DC, NBC News, New York Times, Newsmax, Northern Virginia Daily, Petersburg Progress-Index, Politico, Reuters, Richmond BizSense, Richmond Free Press, Richmond Times-Dispatch, Roanoke Times, RVA News, Slate, Staunton News Leader, Southwest Times, Suffolk News-Herald, Tampa Bay Times, USA Today, Virginia Public Radio, Virginian-Pilot, Wall Street Journal, Washington Post, WAVY-NBC, Waynesboro News Virginian, WGCL-CBS, WRIC-ABC, WSMV-NBC, WTKR-CBS, WTOP Radio, WTVR-CBS, WVIR-NBC, WVTF Radio, WWBT-NBC.

BIBLIOGRAPHY

NEWSMAGAZINES

Bloomberg BusinessWeek, *Chesterfield Monthly*, *C'ville Weekly* (formerly *Hook*), *Forbes*, *Fortune*, *Governing*, *New York Times Magazine*, *New Yorker*, *Newsweek*, *Politico Magazine*, *Reason*, *Richmond Magazine*, *Style Weekly*, *Time*, *US News & World Report*, *UVA Magazine*, *Vanity Fair*, *Virginia Living*.

NONGOVERNMENTAL ORGANIZATIONS AND REPORTS

American Council for an Energy-Efficient Economy, American Heart Association, American Institute for Cancer Research, American Legislative Exchange Council, Asthma and Allergy Foundation of America, Brookings Institution, Campaign for Tobacco-Free Kids, Center for American Progress, Center for Public Integrity, Center for Tobacco Control Research & Education at the University of California, CERES, Clean Air Task Force, Commonwealth Institute, Cook Political Report, Economic Policy Institute, Fels Institute of Government, Harvard School of Public Health, Human Rights Watch, Humane Society of the United States, Johns Hopkins School of Public Health, Kaiser Family Foundation, National Association of Attorneys General, National Center for Public Policy and Higher Education, National Collegiate Athletic Association, National Conference of State Legislatures, National Sports Journalism Center, Our Campaigns, ProPublica, Rockefeller Institute of State Government, The Sentencing Project, Southern Environmental Law Center, State Integrity Investigation, Sunlight Foundation, Transparency Virginia, Urban Institute, Virginia Business Higher Education Council, World Top Incomes Database.

TREATISES

James Madison, John Milton, Pope Francis.

WEBSITES

Altria, American Civil War Museum, Bacon's Rebellion, Ballotopedia, Bearing Drift, Blue Virginia, The Bull Elephant, Center for Responsive Politics, Christopher Newport University, Collegiate School, Dominion Power, Equilar, FlightAware, Google Earth, GovTrack, Indiegogo, Inn at Darden, Internet Movie Database, Jefferson Scholars Foundation, McGuireWoods, Near West End News, RealRadio804, RVA Opt Out, TheStreet, University of Virginia, University of Virginia Athletics, University of Virginia Board of Visitors, University of Virginia Center for Politics, University of Virginia Honor Committee, Virginia Business, Virginia Commonwealth University, The Virginia Conservative, Virginia Public Access Project, Virginia Tech, What2Fly, William & Mary Election Law Society.

INDEX

A

Adams, John (the Martin Agency) 120
Akomolafe, Olusoji 28
Alexander, Kenny 55, 66
Alexandria, Virginia 102
Allen, George 31, 52, 129, 177, 178
Allen, Ray 53
Alpha Natural Resources 100
Altria 57, 87, 88, 91, 92, 93, 94, 95,
      99, 100, 168
  and Dominion Resources 94
  campaign contributions 93
  legislators with stakes in 94
Amazon, Inc. 75
American Association of University
      Professors 135, 159
American Legislative Exchange
      Council 29
Anatabloc 17, 18, 19
Arch Coal 100
Armstrong High School, Richmond 113
Asthma and Allergy Foundation of
      America 79
Atkinson, Frank 31, 177
Atlantic Coast Pipeline. *See* pipelines

B

Bacon, James 36, 181
Baker, Dean 70
Bedden, Dana 113
Blackburn, John 155
Boehner, John 53, 54
Bolling, Bill 46
Bon Secours 111, 115, 117
Botkins, David 55, 65, 74, 101
Bowles, Mark 31, 165
Brandeis, Louis 169
Brat, Dave 25, 52, 54, 121
  comments on public education 121
Brink, Bob 31
Bristol, Virginia 99, 100, 125
Bruner, Bob 134
Bush, Jeb 13, 184
Byrd, Harry, Sr. 172, 173

C

Cantor, Eric 25, 52, 53, 54
capitalism 78, 169
Capitol Square. *See* Virginia State
      Capitol
Caro, Robert 11, 172

Carver Elementary School, Richmond 111
Casey, Dan 28
Casteen, John 136
CCA Industries 122, 127
Charlottesville, Virginia 155
Chesapeake Bay 74, 100, 103
Chesterfield, Virginia 60, 126, 130, 174
Chichester, John 11, 174
Christopher Newport University 53, 80
cigarettes 16, 38, 57, 87, 88, 90, 92, 93, 94, 95, 98, 99, 106, 107, 113, 168. *See also* tobacco smuggling 99
CIGNA 86, 87
Clean Air Act 60, 75, 77, 99, 105
clean energy 71. *See* also solar energy
Clean Water Act 100, 105
climate change 103, 104, 105
Clinton, Hillary 13
coal 59, 60, 70, 75, 99, 100, 101, 103
  and health hazards at Virginia Tech 102
  coal ash 100, 101, 102
  coal country mortality 99
  divestment 70
  pollution 100, 101, 103
  tax credits 103
Coburn, Tom 44
Cody, John Donald 29
Cohen, George 144
Cole, Mark 28, 40
Collegiate School, Richmond 121, 148, 151, 182
Common Core 132. *See* also Standards of Learning tests
Commonwealth Institute 83
Comstock, Barbara 43
Connaughton, Sean 126
corruption 11, 14, 15, 21, 22, 23, 24, 29, 65, 92, 124, 139, 142, 143, 164, 167, 171, 174
Coursera. *See* University of Virginia, Online education
Cox, Kirk 27, 81

Craig, Hunter 134
Cuccinelli, Ken 28, 29, 72, 82, 105
Culbertson, Todd 181
Cullen, Richard 13, 26, 31, 66, 122, 123, 125

D

Dabney, Virginius 172
Daily Press 37, 41, 47, 64, 175
Davies, Gordon 165
Democratic National Committee 14
Dillon's Rule 105, 169
Dinan, John 177
Dominion Resources 14, 26, 34, 55, 56, 57, 58, 59, 60, 61, 62, 63, 65, 66, 68, 69, 70, 71, 72, 73, 74, 75, 76, 77, 78, 81, 92, 93, 94, 95, 96, 97, 99, 100, 101, 103, 105, 117, 120, 122, 127, 161, 168, 174, 176
  and Altria 94
  Clean Air Act violations 99
  coal 59
  effective tax rate 76
  guaranteed rate of return 68
  negotiations with Terry McAuliffe 62
  nuclear infractions 100
  official corporate history 59, 71, 99
  peer comparisons 71
  pitch to investors 69
  rate-hike bill 59
  reliability 71
  Richmond explosions, 2015 70
  stock performance 70
Douglas Southall Freeman High School, Richmond 179
Dovi, Chris 119
Dragas, Helen 134, 135, 136, 138, 145, 157, 158, 159, 160, 161, 162, 164

E

Elkhardt Middle School, Richmond 118
eminent domain 72, 73

Environmental Protection Agency 59, 60, 61, 75, 77, 99, 100
ethics
   2015 ethics bill 63

F

Faggert, Pam 74
Fain, Travis 47, 181
Fairfield Court Elementary School, Richmond 118
Farrell, Peter 25, 26, 33, 35, 41, 52, 54
   election of 25
   Field of Lost Shoes 36
   political donations 26
Farrell, Thomas 26, 34, 35, 60, 62, 69, 70, 72, 76, 120, 122, 161, 162, 169
   Field of Lost Shoes 35
   performance and salary 69
Federal Bureau of Investigation 19, 20, 21, 66, 96, 98, 125
Feld, Lowell 47, 52, 181
Field of Lost Shoes 34, 35, 36
   public subsidies for 34
Fifth Amendment 73
Filler-Corn, Eileen 32
First Amendment 13
First Baptist Church, Richmond 124
Food and Drug Administration 92
Forbes, John 96
Forbes, Randy 45
Fort Monroe Authority 31
Fourteenth Amendment 45
Fourth Circuit Court of Appeals 24, 123
fracking (hydraulic fracturing) 73
Freedom of Information Act (FOIA) 26, 40, 41, 144, 145, 160
Freeman, Douglas Southall 172
Friberg, Elizabeth 138

G

Galuszka, Peter 59, 97, 102, 161, 181
Garrett, Tom 58

General Assembly. *See* Virginia legislature
Genest, Dan 60
gerrymandering 15, 26, 42, 44, 45, 46, 47, 49
Gilbert, C. Todd 63
Gillespie, Ed 12, 14, 44
Gilmore, Jim 14, 31, 111
Gilpin Court, Richmond 107
Golden, Daniel 149, 152
Goldman, Paul 114, 178
Goodwin, William 30, 122, 133, 143, 144, 146, 161, 162, 163, 169, 171
Government Accountability Office 81
Gray, Elmon 26
Gray, Garland 26
Gray, Kim 113
Graziano, Kathy 118
Green, Kristin 131

H

Halsey, Brenton 169
Hamlin, Thomas 69
Hampton Roads, Virginia 103
health care 19, 79, 80, 111, 220, 259, 260
Helderman, Rosalind 19, 179, 181
Henrico County, Virginia 103
Herring, Mark 12, 62, 69
Hinkle, A. Barton 73, 181
Hogan, Larry 101
Hook (newspaper) 135, 139, 160, 161, 181
Horton, Willie 44
Howell, Algie 31
Howell, Henry 76
Howell, William 29, 47, 55, 67, 81, 84, 109
Hugo, Tim 32
Hulcher, Sarah 131
Humane Society of the United States 105
Human Rights Watch 88, 89, 91, 181
Hunton and Williams 31, 123

J

James River 100
Jankowski, Chris 44
Jefferson Hotel, Richmond 13, 17, 28, 34
Jefferson, Thomas 121, 130, 143,
    169, 172
Joannou, Johnny 91
John Birch Society 166
Johnson, Lyndon 12, 52
Jones, Chris 28, 37, 48, 126
Jones, Dwight 113, 114, 115, 116, 118,
    120, 123, 125, 127
  FBI investigation of 124
Jones, Maurice 64
Jones, Paul Tudor 160, 161, 162

K

K12, Inc. 158
Kaine, Tim 14, 52, 104
Kanawha Plaza, Richmond 124
Kenney, Shaun 23
Kessler, David 92
Ketron, Martha Puckett 98
Key, V.O. 173
Kidd, Quentin 53, 177
Kiernan, Peter 134, 135, 160
Kilberg, Bobbie 144
Kilgore, Jerry 96
Kilgore, John, Jr. 96
Kilgore, John, Sr. 96
Kilgore, Terry 96, 98
Kington, Mark 134, 159, 160, 161, 162
Kinloch Golf Club 18

L

Landes, Steven 84
Larson, Kristin 112, 113
Lazarus, Jeremy 181
Leahy, Norman 114, 181
Lincoln (film) 33
lobbyists 28, 58, 64, 65, 66, 67, 75, 96,
    103, 130, 166, 167, 170
Loupassi, Manoli 64

M

Madison, James 15, 172
Marsden, David 27
Marshall, Bob 79
Marshall, Byron 41
Marshall, Daniel 91
Marsh, Henry 30, 46
Martin, George Keith 123
Martin, Jeanine 181
Maryland 74, 101, 147
Mary Munford Elementary School,
    Richmond 120
Massey Energy 100, 179
Master Settlement Agreement (tobacco)
    92, 95, 96
Mayer, Jane 166
May, Joe 28
McAuliffe, Terry 13, 14, 31, 32, 35, 37,
    51, 60, 62, 64, 73, 86, 97, 98,
    101, 103, 104, 108, 126, 144,
    160, 165, 170, 176
McCance, McGregor 145
McClellan, Jennifer 32
McDonnell, Bob 11, 14, 16, 17, 18,
    19, 20, 21, 22, 23, 24, 30, 31,
    32, 33, 35, 36, 41, 51, 64, 75,
    81, 97, 104, 117, 126, 133, 138,
    139, 142, 143, 144, 156, 157,
    158, 159, 160, 161, 162, 164,
    167, 168, 170, 174, 176, 177,
    179
  film subsidies 33
McDonnell, Bob and Maureen 19
  charges against 21
  criminal defense 22
  elite opinion of 24
  indictment 20
  public opinion of 24
  sentence 22
  verdicts 22
McDonnell, Maureen (First Lady) 16,
    17, 18, 19, 20, 21, 22
McDowell, Lola 131
McEachin, Donald 14

McGuireWoods 26, 31, 32, 122, 123, 127, 177
  public subsidies 125
Meola, Olympia 181
Miller, Edward 165
Mook, Robby 13
Moomaw, Graham 181
Moore, Glenda 108, 109
Morrissey, Joe 67, 68, 167
Mountain Valley Pipeline. *See* pipelines
Mustafa, Maher 98
Muzik, Greg 120

N

Nestle, Marion 107
Newfield, Christopher 163
Newport News 77
Newport News, Virginia 103, 128
Nixon, Richard 64, 166
Norfolk State University 28
Norfolk, Virginia 73, 74, 103, 128, 131
Norment, Tommy 28, 48, 55, 58, 59, 64, 66, 67
  affair with lobbyist 66
Northam, Ralph 97
North Carolina 73, 89, 127, 152
Nuclear Regulatory Commission 100

O

Obama, Barack 12, 14, 33, 44, 46, 59, 65, 114, 178
O'Bannon, John 99
Obenshain, Mark 32
Oder, Glenn 31
Oliver, Ned 181
O'Neil, Robert 136
Owczarski, Mark 102

P

Pagan River 105
Philip Morris. *See* Altria
Pinkney-Eppes, Tichi 119
pipelines 60, 73, 74, 96, 97
political power. *See* Caro, Robert

Politifact 82, 84, 116
pollution 59, 61, 74, 75, 99, 100, 174
Pope Francis 78
Portnoy, Jenna 179, 181
Potomac River 101
Potter, Wendell 86, 87
poverty 80, 86, 88, 89, 107, 116, 121, 122, 128, 158, 179
Powell, Lewis 166
Prince Edward County 131, 179
public schools 33, 77, 86, 114, 118, 119, 120, 121, 122, 128, 131, 147, 158, 159, 180
  funding 121
  Kings Dominion Law 130
public utilities 78
Puckett, Phil 31, 98

R

Radtke, Jamie 53
Ramadan, David 30, 155
Randolph-Macon College 78, 121
Ransone, Margaret 36
Ravitch, Diane 130, 158
Rawlings, Hunter 136
Reagan, Paul 32
redistricting 26, 38, 41, 43, 44, 45
REDMAP 44
Redskins. *See* Washington Redskins
Reich, Gabriel 131
Reisler, Mark 163
Remote Area Medical 85
Republican National Committee 12, 14
Ress, Dave 26, 49, 181
Rettig, Terry 105
Richmond City Council 117, 118, 161
Richmond City Hall 111
Richmond County, Virginia 103
Richmond Public Schools 111, 117, 119, 120, 121
  juvenile arrests 127
  letter from Richmond CEOs 119
Richmond School Board 112, 113, 117, 119, 120, 132, 161

Richmond Times-Dispatch 36, 42, 48, 57, 59, 91, 127, 175
Richmond, Virginia 13, 17, 18, 28, 30, 31, 35, 57, 60, 61, 64, 68, 70, 77, 78, 79, 81, 87, 93, 94, 100, 101, 107, 108, 111, 113, 114, 115, 117, 118, 119, 120, 121, 122, 123, 124, 125, 126, 128, 130, 131, 132, 139, 143, 148, 161, 162, 165, 166, 168, 171, 174, 179, 180, 181
  life expectancy 107
Roanoke Times 28, 48, 175
Robb, Chuck 52
Romney, Mitt 114
Rove, Karl 12, 43
Ryan, James 122
Ryan, Paul 82

S

Sabato, Larry 177
Sandridge, Leonard 133, 136, 143, 144
Saslaw, Dick 33, 37, 47, 58, 168
Schapiro, Jeff 61, 181
Schmidt, Markus 181
Sentencing Project 50
Shandong Tranlin Paper Co. 126
Simon, John 136, 164
Simon, Marcus 28
60 Minutes 85, 108
Slipek, Edwin 181
Smithfield Foods 105, 106, 107
  animal care 106
  environmental record 105
  human health consequences 106
Smith, Ralph 49
Smith, Tammie 181
socialism 78
solar energy 60, 63, 71, 75
South Carolina 32, 103
Standards of Learning tests 128, 129, 130, 131, 132
  effects on teachers and students 130
  opt-out movement 131

penalties 128
  sample questions 129
Stanley, William 30, 167
Star Scientific 16, 17, 18, 19, 93
State Corporation Commission 32, 56, 61, 63, 68, 69, 76
State Route 460 Project 125, 126, 127
Stiglitz, Joseph 78
Strauss, Jerome 95
Suderman, Alan 28, 34, 181
Suetterlein, David 49
  election of 49
Sullivan, Teresa 41, 133, 134, 135, 136, 137, 138, 139, 144, 145, 147, 157, 158, 159, 160, 161, 162, 166, 176
Surovell, Scott 36, 65

T

Tarter, Brent 172
tax credits 28, 33, 34, 35, 36, 103
tax cuts 83
Tea Party 33, 51, 52, 53, 175, 180
Tenth Amendment 169
Thomas Jefferson High School for Science and Technology, Alexandria 121, 130
Thomas Jefferson High School, Richmond 179
Thomas, Steve 25, 26
Thompson Middle School, Richmond 112
tobacco 16, 17, 18, 22, 79, 87, 88, 89, 90, 91, 92, 93, 94, 95, 96, 97, 98, 99, 120, 127, 166, 168, 181. *See also* cigarettes
  child labor 92
  green nicotine sickness 89
Tobacco Indemnification and Community Revitalization Commission 96, 97, 98
Toscano, David 47, 58
Transparency Virginia 39
Troy, Anthony 23

U

UBS 61, 74
United States Chamber of Commerce 92, 166
United States House of Representatives 36, 42, 43, 44, 54
United States Supreme Court 13, 22, 74, 80, 166, 169, 179
  Citizens United 13
  McCutcheon v. FEC 22
University of Mary Washington 70
University of North Carolina–Chapel Hill 152
University of Richmond 176, 261
University of Virginia 15, 41, 85, 105, 121, 123, 133, 136, 137, 138, 139, 142, 143, 144, 145, 146, 147, 148, 149, 150, 151, 152, 153, 154, 155, 158, 159, 160, 161, 162, 163, 164, 165, 166, 176, 177, 179
  AccessUVA financial aid program 144, 145, 147, 163
  admissions standards 148, 152
  affirmative action 148, 149, 150, 151
  and Freedom of Information Act 144
  appointments made by Bob McDonnell 139
  athletics subsidies 154
  Board of Visitors 123, 133, 134, 135, 136, 137, 138, 139, 143, 144, 145, 146, 147, 151, 156, 157, 158, 159, 160, 162, 163, 164, 165, 166, 176
  bond rating 148
  budget 142
  Darden (Business) School 134, 136, 160, 161, 162, 163
  endowment 147, 165
  faculty retention 158
  Faculty Senate 137, 144
  financial aid 145
  honor system 164
  Inn at Darden 163
  Jefferson Scholars 121, 146, 147
  online education 158
  Pell Grants 148, 151, 152
  police presence at 139
  political donations 139
  private jet 155
  Rally for Honor 138
  rector 123, 133, 134, 137, 138, 144, 161, 162, 163
  salaries 155
  Seven Society 161
  transparency 159
Upper Big Branch Mine Explosion 100

V

Virginia Beach 41, 50, 79, 103
Virginia Commonwealth University 95, 107, 108, 131, 180
  and Tobacco research 95
  Medical Center 108
Virginia Constitution 48, 63, 72, 103, 177
  amendments to 49, 51
Virginia Department of Environmental Quality 104
Virginia Electric and Power Company. *See* Dominion Resources
Virginia House of Delegates 25, 29, 42, 47, 48, 61
  56th district 25
Virginia Military Institute 35
Virginian-Pilot 62, 64, 66, 175
Virginia Public Access Project 30
Virginia State Capitol 27, 35, 37, 58, 78, 83, 108, 111, 123, 125, 169, 172, 174
  George Washington equestrian statue 125
Virginia Supreme Court 41, 123
Virginia Tech 101, 102, 103, 154, 182
  health hazards from coal plant 102
Virginia War Memorial 38
Virginia Way, the 11, 14, 15, 16, 22, 24, 25, 26, 30, 51, 65, 96, 167, 169, 170, 171, 173, 174, 177, 193
  populist backlash 51

Vogel, Jill 32
voting rights 45, 50
Vozzella, Laura 19, 179, 181

W

Wagner, Frank 56, 57, 59, 65, 72
Walker, Jeffrey 160
Wall Street 66, 69, 78, 87, 91, 149
Ward, Irving "Peanut" 124
Ware, Onzlee 31
Warner, Mark 14, 44, 98, 178
Washington and Lee 176
Washington Post 19, 33, 63, 91, 156,
        158, 175
Washington Redskins 52, 64, 66, 114,
        115, 116, 117, 127
  public subsidies 117
Watkins, John 58, 76, 77
Webb, Jim 14, 52, 178
West Virginia 73, 100
White, Tom 53
Wilder, Doug 23, 31, 120, 129, 178, 179
Will, George 22
William and Mary 176
Williams, Jonnie 16, 18, 19, 20, 30, 93,
        96, 142, 168
Williams, Michael Paul 127, 181
Williams Mullen 31, 123
Wintergreen Resort 73
Wise County, Virginia 85, 86, 87, 108
Wohlfarth, Thomas 74
Wolf, Carol 120
Wolf, Frank 43
Wolin, Sheldon 78
Wright, Tommy 97
Wulf, William 137

Y

Yancey, Dwayne 181

Z

Zapotosky, Matt 179, 181
Zeithaml, Carl 136, 162, 164

ABOUT THE AUTHOR

M r. Thomas was born and raised in Richmond, Virginia, and attended home, parochial and private schools. He attended college at the Duke University School of Engineering and graduate school at the Tulane University School of Public Health and Virginia Tech School of Public and International Affairs.

After college, he worked as a public school teacher through the Harvard Center for International Development's World Teach program. After graduate school, he worked in health policy for national nonprofits in Washington, D.C. He currently lives in Richmond.

This is his first project with The History Press; all of his royalties are being donated to Richmond's public schools.